HIROSHIGE

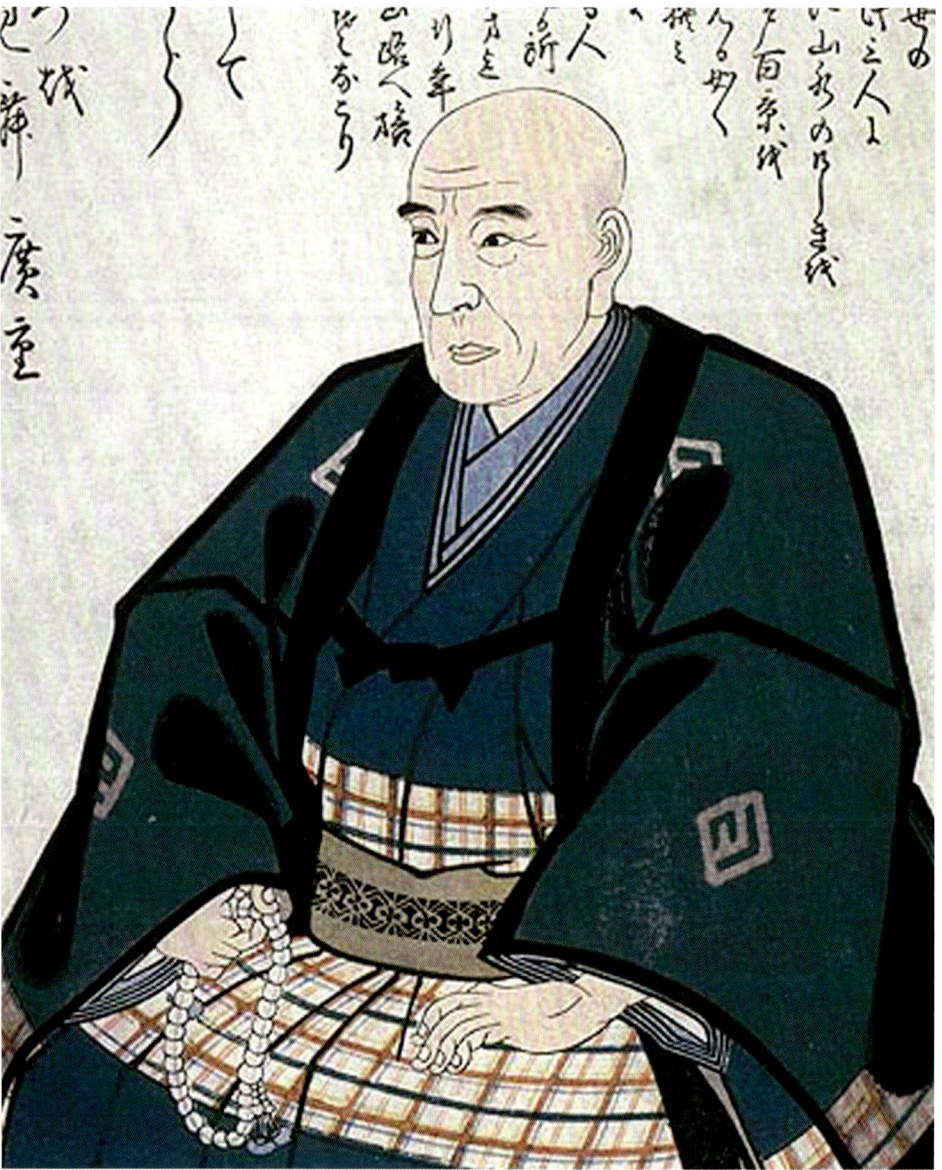

HIROSHIGE

JANINA NENTWIG

p. 2

Kunisada III

Memorial Portrait of Hiroshige (detail)

Portrait posthume d'Hiroshige (détail)

Gedächtnisporträt von Hiroshige (Detail)

Retrato en memoria de Hiroshige (detalle)

Ritratto in memoria di Hiroshige (particolare)

Herdenkingsportret van Hiroshige (uitsnede)

1859/60, Colour woodcut/Gravure sur bois en couleurs, 35,5 × 21,9 cm

KÖNEMANN

© 2016 koenemann.com GmbH
www.koenemann.com

ÉDITIONS
PLACE DES
VICTOIRES

© Éditions Place des Victoires
6, rue du Mail – 75002 Paris
www.victoires.com
ISBN: 978-2-8099-1369-9
Dépôt legal: 4e trimestre 2016

Concept, Project Management: koenemann.com GmbH
Text: Dr. Janina Nentwig
Editing: Petra Böttcher

Translation into French: Denis-Armand Canal

Translations into English, Spanish, Italian and Dutch:
TEXTCASE Translation Agency
info@textcase.nl
textcase.de   textcase.eu

Layout: Guido Behet – vitolution
Picture credits:
akg-images gmbh
except: 10, 12, 143 Bridgeman Images

ISBN: 978-3-7419-1829-2 (international)

Printed in China by Shenzhen Hua Xin Colour-printing & Platemaking Co., Ltd.

Contents   Sommaire   Inhalt   Índice   Indice   Inhoud

À propos

Hiroshige is considered one of the most important artists of the Japanese woodblock print. His landscapes, often combined with serene scenes of everyday life, are especially famous. The *ukiyo-e* ("pictures of the floating world") captivate their audiences with their refined structures and finely tuned colour schemes, allowing a chance to immerse oneself into the Japanese world of the 19th century. They continue to fascinate viewers to this day. The simple aesthetics of the woodblock prints with their spatial compositions and bold perspectives also inspired European artists, particularly the French Impressionists and Post-Impressionists. They found inspiration in Hiroshige's work on how to break away from a naturalistic depiction of the world.

Hiroshige est considéré comme l'un des créateurs les plus importants dans l'art de l'estampe japonaise. Ses paysages surtout sont renommés – souvent mêlés à des scènes tranquilles de la vie quotidienne. Ces « images du monde flottant » *(ukiyo-e)* frappent par leur caractère raffiné et la finesse du choix de leurs couleurs. Elles plongent le spectateur dans la vie japonaise du xixᵉ siècle et exercent depuis leur création une fascination qui ne se dément pas de nos jours. L'esthétique très épurée des estampes, avec leurs compositions en aplats et leurs perspectives audacieuses, enthousiasma aussi les artistes européens – surtout les impressionnistes et post-impressionnistes français, qui trouvèrent dans l'œuvre d'Hiroshige des incitations importantes à se libérer d'un rendu « naturaliste » du monde.

Hiroshige gilt als einer der bedeutendsten Künstler des japanischen Holzschnitts. Berühmt sind vor allem seine Landschaften, die sich oft mit heiteren Alltagsszenen verbinden. Die „Bilder der fließenden Welt" *(ukiyo-e)* bestechen durch ihren raffinierten Aufbau und die fein abgestimmte Farbigkeit. Sie lassen den Betrachter in die japanische Lebenswelt des 19. Jahrhunderts eintauchen und üben bis heute eine große Faszination aus. Die stark vereinfachte Ästhetik der Farbholzschnitte mit ihren flächigen Kompositionen und kühnen Perspektiven begeisterte auch europäische Künstler, allen voran die französischen Impressionisten und Post-Impressionisten. Sie fanden in Hiroshiges Werk wichtige Anregungen, um sich von einer naturalistischen Wiedergabe der Welt zu lösen.

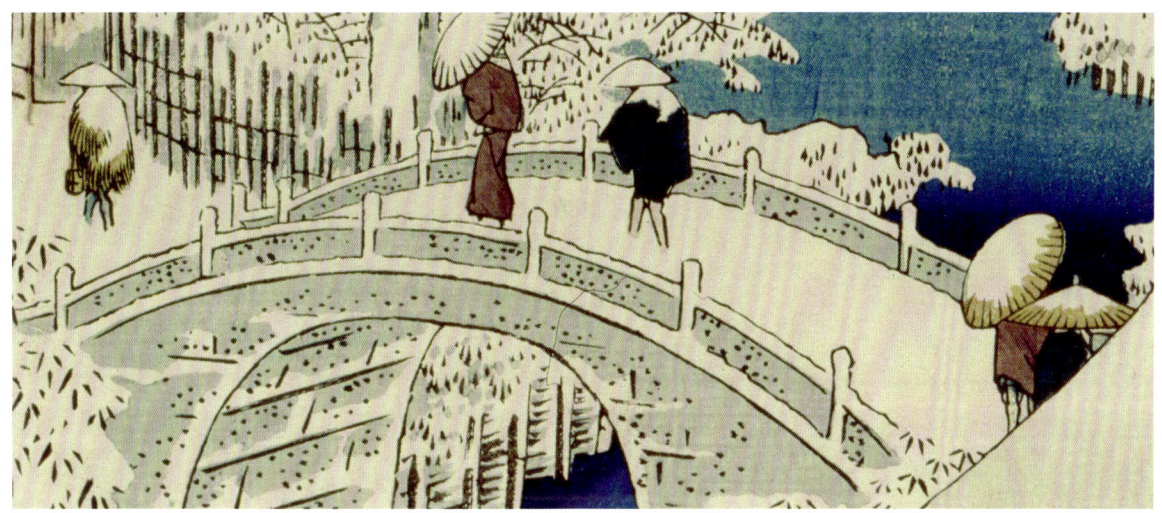

Hiroshige es considerado uno de los artistas más importantes de la xilografía japonesa (también conocida como grabado en madera), siendo especialmente famosos sus paisajes, que a menudo representan joviales escenas cotidianas. Las "imágenes del mundo flotante" *(ukiyo-e)* cautivan gracias a su cuidadoso diseño y la refinada precisión de su coloración. Permiten al espectador sumergirse en el Japón del sigo XIX ejerciendo, todavía hoy, una profunda fascinación. La estética marcadamente simplificada de las xilografías, con sus composiciones planas y audaces perspectivas, apasionaba también a los artistas europeos, sobre todo los impresionistas y postimpresionistas franceses. Estos encontraron en el trabajo de Hiroshige un impulso importante para alejarse de una reproducción naturalista del mundo.

Hiroshige è uno degli artisti più significativi della xilografia giapponese. Sono famosi soprattutto i suoi paesaggi, spesso legati a scene felici della vita quotidiana. Le "immagini del mondo fluttuante" *(ukiyo-e)* risultano particolarmente affascinanti grazie alla raffinata composizione e alla scelta dei colori finemente armonizzata. L'osservatore può così immergersi nel mondo della vita giapponese del XIX secolo e subirne ancora oggi il grande fascino. L'estetica fortemente semplificata delle xilografie a colori, con le composizioni piatte e le prospettive audaci, entusiasmò anche gli artisti europei, in particolare gli impressionisti e i post-impressionisti francesi. Essi trovarono nell'opera di Hiroshige stimoli importanti per distaccarsi da una riproduzione naturalistica del mondo.

Hiroshige wordt gezien als een van de belangrijkste vertegenwoordigers van de Japanse houtsnijkunst. Beroemd zijn vooral zijn landschappen, vaak met kleurrijke taferelen uit het dagelijks leven. Deze "prenten van de vlietende wereld" *(ukiyo-e)* bekoren door hun geraffineerde mis-en-scène en de fijnzinnig op elkaar afgestemde kleuren. Ze geven de beschouwer een zeer fascinerend kijkje achter de schermen van het Japanse leven in de negentiende eeuw. De sterk vereenvoudigde esthetiek van deze houtsneden, met hun compositie van vlakken en gedurfde perspectieven, maakte ook grote indruk op Europese kunstenaars, bovenal op de Franse impressionisten en postimpressionisten, die in het werk van Hiroshige veel aansporingen vonden om zich van een strikt naturalistische weergave van de wereld los te maken.

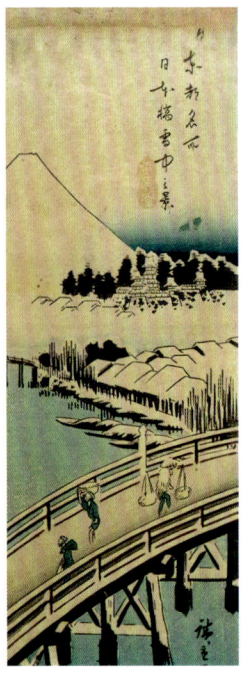

View of Nihonbashi Bridge in the snow, from the series **Famous Views of the Eastern Capital**

Le Pont Nihonbashi sous la neige, de la série **Vues célèbres de la capitale de l'Est**

Ansicht der Nihonbashi-Brücke im Schnee, aus der Serie **Berühmte Ansichten der Östlichen Hauptstadt**

Vista del punte Nihonbashi bajo la nieve, de la serie **Vistas famosas de la Capital del Este**

Veduta del ponte Nihonbashi nella neve, della serie **Vedute famose della capitale orientale**

Gezicht op de Nihonbashi-brug in de sneeuw, uit de serie **Beroemde gezichten op de Oostelijke Hoofdstad**

c. 1837/38, Colour woodcut/Gravure sur bois en couleurs, 37,2 × 12,3 cm, Universität, Trier

The Shinto Tenjin Shrine in Kameido, from the series **Famous Views of Edo**

Le Sanctuaire shinto de Tenjin à Kameido, de la série **Vues célèbres d'Edo**

Der shintoistische Tenjin-Schrein in Kameido, aus der Serie **Berühmte Ansichten von Edo**

El santuario sintoísta Tenjin en Kameido, de la serie **Vistas famosas de Edo**

Il santuario shintoista di Tenjin a Kameido, della serie **Vedute famose di Edo**

De shintoïstische Tenjin-schrijn in Kameido, uit de serie **Beroemde gezichten op Edo**

1840, Colour woodcut/Gravure sur bois en couleurs, 25,6 × 37,5 cm, Universität, Trier

From fire inspector to master of the landscape

Very few facts are known about Hiroshige's life. The autobiography he is said to have written was lost in a fire in 1876, eighteen years after his death. His path to becoming an in-demand woodcut illustrator is best illustrated in his work, which he published as series in several editions. What is clear that this profession was not the original destiny for Hiroshige, born Andō Tokutarō, most likely in 1797. His father was a low-ranking samurai and supervised a fire station in the centre of Edo, modern-day Tokyo. Shortly before his death, Hiroshige's father passed on

De l'inspecteur d'incendie au maître du paysage

On connaît peu de chose sur la vie d'Hiroshige. Une autobiographie prétendument de sa main a été détruite dans un incendie en 1876, dix-huit ans après sa mort. Sa popularité comme créateur d'estampes à succès est avant tout perceptible dans ses œuvres, parues sous forme de séries à tirages multiples. Andō Tokutarō – son véritable nom d'état-civil – n'était pas destiné à cette profession dès le berceau. Il serait né en 1797, dans une classe inférieure de la caste des samouraïs. Son père était officier de brigade dans la caserne de pompiers d'un quartier central d'Edo

Vom Brandinspektor zum Meister der Landschaft

Aus Hiroshiges Leben sind nur wenige Daten und Fakten bekannt. Eine Autobiografie, die er geschrieben haben soll, verbrennt 1876, 18 Jahre nach seinem Tod. Sein Aufstieg zum gefragten Holzschnittzeichner lässt sich vor allem an seinen Werken ablesen, die als Serien in mehreren Auflagen erscheinen. Dabei ist Andō Tokutarō, wie sein erster, bürgerlicher Name lautet, dieser Beruf keineswegs in die Wiege gelegt. Aller Wahrscheinlichkeit nach wird er im Jahr 1797 geboren. Der Vater gehört dem niedrigen Samuraistand an und führt die Aufsicht über eine Feuerwehrwache im

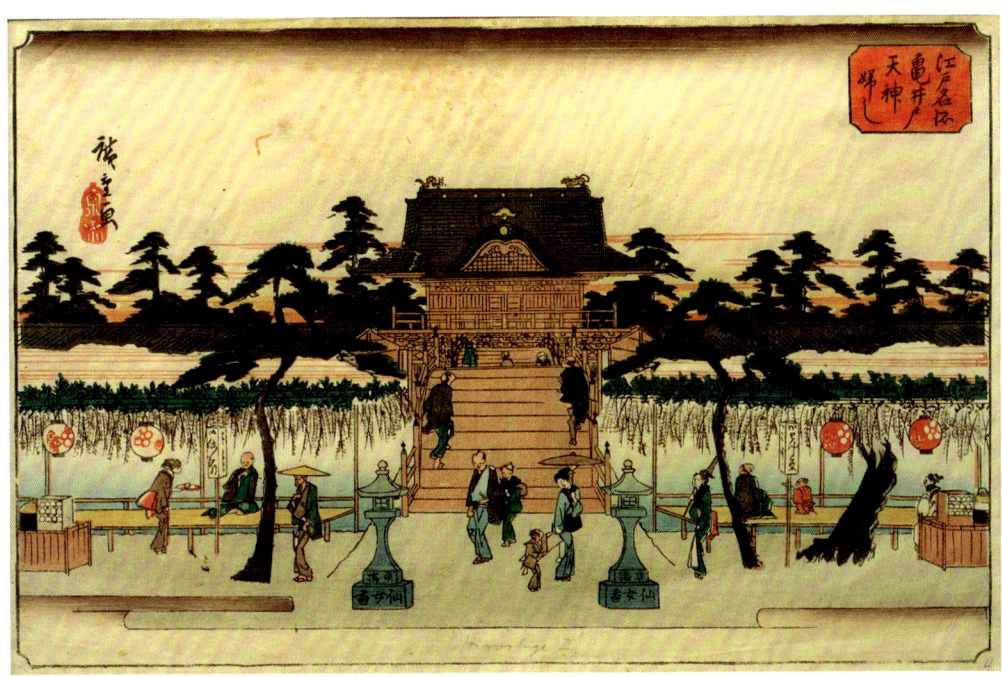

De inspector de incendios a maestro del paisajismo

Solo conocemos un puñado de hechos y datos de la vida de Hiroshige. En 1876, 18 años después de su muerte, se quemó una autobiografía que habría escrito él mismo. Su ascenso hasta convertirse en un solicitado grabador puede reconstruirse sobre todo en base a sus obras, que aparecían como series en diversas ediciones. Como veremos la vida de Andō Tokutarō, su nombre original, en ningún modo parecía encaminada a este oficio. Nació, con toda probabilidad, en 1797. Su padre pertenecía al nivel bajo de la casta samurái y era supervisor de una

Da funzionario per la difesa dagli incendi a maestro del paesaggio

Della vita di Hiroshige si conoscono soltanto poche date ed episodi. Si dice che abbia scritto un'autobiografia che fu bruciata nel 1876, 18 anni dopo la sua morte. Il suo ruolo di xilografo di successo si deduce soprattutto dalle opere, che appaiono in serie in diverse edizioni. Per Andō Tokutarō, il suo primo nome borghese, questo mestiere non è stato affatto ereditato. Con tutta probabilità egli nacque nel 1797. Il padre apparteneva all'umile stato di samurai ed era funzionario di una stazione dei pompieri nel centro di Edo, l'odierna Tokyo. Poco prima della

Van brandwacht tot meester van het landschap

Over Hiroshige's levensloop zijn weinig exacte gegevens bekend. Een autobiografie die hij zelf zou hebben geschreven, ging in 1876 bij een brand verloren, achttien jaar na zijn dood. Zijn loopbaan als veelgevraagd prentkunstenaar is vooral uit zijn werk af te lezen, dat in de vorm van series in meerdere oplagen verscheen. En dat terwijl Andō Tokutarō, zoals zijn eerste burgerlijke naam luidde, helemaal niet in de wieg was gelegd voor deze loopbaan. Zeer waarschijnlijk wordt Hiroshige in 1797 geboren. Zijn vader behoort tot de lagere samoerai-stand en is hoofd van

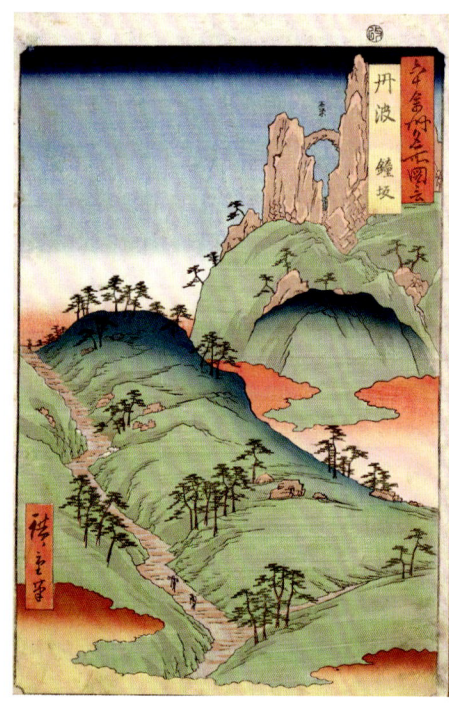
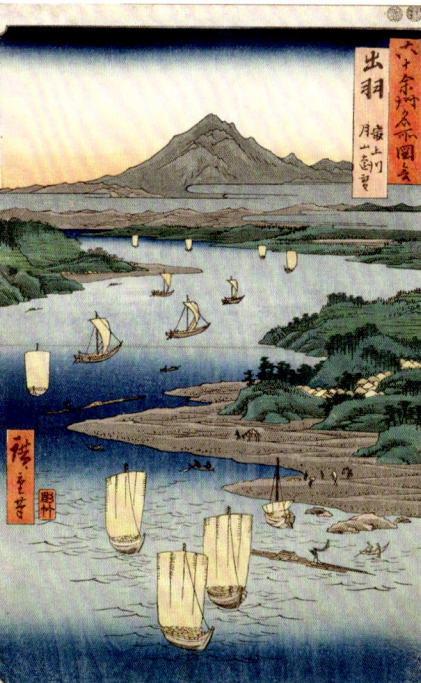

Two views from the series *Famous Views of the 60-odd Provinces*

Deux vues de la série *Vues des sites célèbres des 60 et quelques provinces*

Zwei Ansichten aus der Serie *Berühmte Gegenden der mehr als 60 Provinzen*

Dos ejemplos de la serie *Famosas vistas de las más de 60 provincias*

Due vedute della serie *Luoghi famosi delle oltre 60 province*

Twee gezichten uit de serie *Beroemde streken van de meer dan 60 provincies*

1853, Colour woodcut/ Gravure sur bois en couleurs, Private collection

this office to his son, who became head of the family at the young age of twelve. The rather modest salary forced young Tokutarō, like many of his colleagues, to take on additional work, so he enrolled as an apprentice in the studio of *ukiyo-e* painter Utagawa Toyohiro in 1811. Soon the apprentice had earned his right to assume the name of the Utagawa School, so he signed his early works with Hiroshige. The *hiro* character was based on his teacher's name and the *shige* character, another interpretation of the character *jū*, reflects his later given name Jūemon. So with his new name Utagawa Hiroshige, the

(l'actuel Tokyo). Peu avant sa mort, le père transmet cette charge à son fils qui devient – à douze ans – chef de famille. La solde correspondante, assurément plutôt modeste, force toutefois Tokutarō, comme un bon nombre de ses collègues, à prendre un deuxième travail.

En 1811, il entre comme élève dans l'atelier d'Utagawa Toyohiro, peintre d'*ukiyo-e*. L'apprenti acquiert rapidement le droit d'utiliser le nom de l'école Utagawa et il signe ses premiers travaux « Hiroshige » : le signe *hiro* est tiré du nom de son maître, complété par *shige*, autre lecture du signe *jū* tiré de son autre prénom : Jūemon. Avec ce nom d'Utagawa

Zentrum von Edo, dem heutigen Tokyo. Kurz vor seinem Tod überträgt der Vater dieses Amt auf den Sohn, der mit zwölf Jahren zum Familienoberhaupt wird. Die wohl eher bescheidene Besoldung zwingt Tokutarō jedoch, wie viele seiner Kollegen, einen Nebenberuf zu ergreifen.

1811 tritt er als Schüler in das Atelier des *Ukiyo-e*-Malers Utawaga Toyohiro ein. Schon bald darf der Lehrling den Namen der Utawaga-Schule führen und signiert seine frühen Arbeiten mit Hiroshige, wobei er das Zeichen *hiro* aus dem Namen seines Lehrers entlehnt und mit *shige*, einer anderen Lesart des Zeichens *jū* aus einem seiner späteren

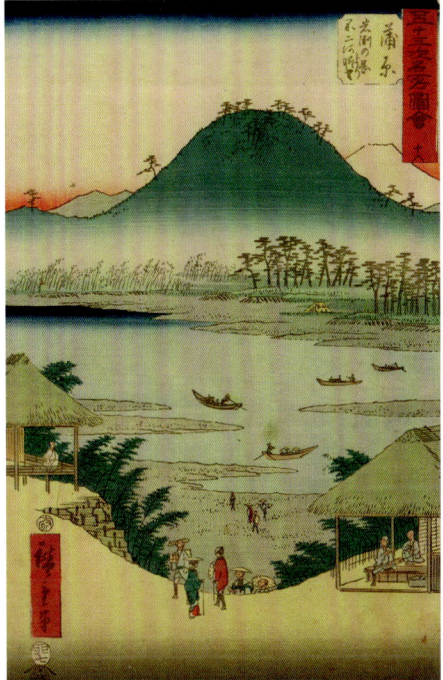

Night view of Kanbara, from the series *53 Stations of Tōkaidō*
Vue nocturne de Kanbara, de la série *53 relais de la route de la mer de l'Est*
Nachtansicht von Kanbara, aus der Serie *53 Stationen der Ostmeerstraße*
Vista nocturna de Kanbara, de la serie *53 estaciones de la ruta Tōkaidō*
Veduta notturna di Kanbara, della serie *Le 53 stazioni della Tokaido*
Kanbara bij nacht, uit de serie *53 halteplaatsen aan de Tōkaidō (Oostelijke Zeeweg)*
1855, Colour woodcut/Gravure sur bois en couleurs, 36,7×24,7 cm, Universität, Trier

estación de bomberos en el centro de Edo, el actual Tokio. Poco antes de morir el padre transmitió este cargo a su hijo, que se convirtió en el cabeza de familia con doce años. La retribución más bien modesta obligó sin embargo a Tokutarō, como a muchos de sus colegas, a adoptar un segundo oficio.

En 1811 entra a formar parte del taller del pintor *Ukiyo-e* Utagawa Toyohiro, como estudiante. Poco después se le permite adoptar el nombre de la escuela Utagawa y firma sus trabajos más tempranos como Hiroshige, combinando el carácter *hiro* (sacado del nombre de su profesor) con *shige*, otra forma de leer

sua morte tramandò questa carica al figlio, che divenne capofamiglia a soli dodici anni. Lo stipendio piuttosto modesto costrinse tuttavia Tokutarō a trovare un secondo impiego, come molti altri suoi colleghi.

Nel 1811 entrò come allievo nello studio del pittore di *Ukiyo-e* Utagawa Toyohiro. Ben presto l'apprendista ebbe il permesso di portare il nome della scuola di Utagawa e firmò i suoi primi lavori come Hiroshige, prendendo in prestito la sigla *hiro* dal nome del suo insegnante e combinandola con *shige*, un'altra variante della sigla *ju* da uno dei suoi

een brandwacht in het centrum van Edo, het huidige Tokio. Kort voor zijn dood draagt hij dit ambt over op zijn zoon, die op 12-jarige leeftijd de heer des huizes wordt. Maar door het vermoedelijk zeer bescheiden salaris is de jonge Tokutarō gedwongen om nog een ander beroep uit te oefenen.

In 1811 wordt hij als leerling in het atelier van de *ukiyo-e*-schilder Utagawa Toyohiro aangenomen. Al snel mag hij de naam van de Utagawa-school als titel dragen en signeert hij zijn vroege werk met "Hiroshige", waarbij hij het Japanse teken *hiro* aan de naam van zijn leermeester ontleent en met *shige* een

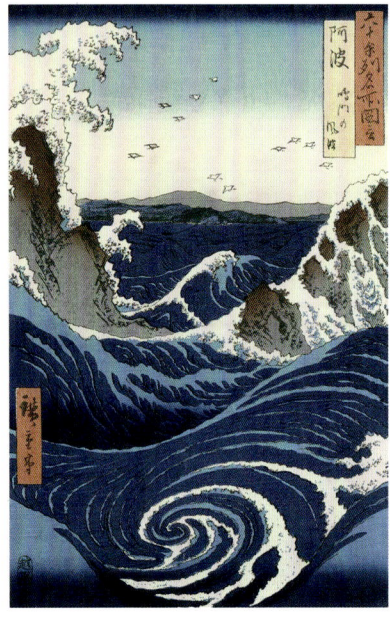

Rough Sea at Naruto in Awa Province, Famous Views of the 60-odd Provinces
Le Tourbillon à Awa, de la série *Vues des sites célèbres des 60 et quelques provinces*
Die Strudel von Awa, aus der Serie *Berühmte Gegenden der mehr als 60 Provinzen*
Los remolinos de Awa, de la serie *Famosas vistas de las más de 60 provincias*
I vortici di Awa, della serie *Luoghi famosi delle oltre 60 province*
De draaikolk van Awa, uit de serie *Beroemde streken van de meer dan 60 provincies*
Colour woodcut/Gravure sur bois en couleurs, 37,7 × 22,1 cm, Musée Claude Monet, Giverny

Porters on the Nihonbashi Bridge, Famous Views of Edo
Porteurs sur le pont Nihonbashi, de la série *Vues célèbres d'Edo*
Lastträger auf der Nihonbashi-Brücke, aus der Serie *Berühmte Ansichten von Edo*
Los portadores en el puente Nihonbashi, de la serie *famosas vistas de Edo*
Trasportatori sul ponte Nihonbashi, della serie *vedute famose di Edo*
Dragers op de Nihonbashi-brug, uit de serie: *Fameuse gezichten op Edo*
Colour woodcut/Gravure sur bois en couleurs

young artist shows his respect for his teacher and positions himself within that artistic tradition. As it turns out, Hiroshige will repeatedly change or add to his name, but always carried the name of his teacher.

Hiroshige's first templates for woodblock prints are entirely in the style of the Utagawa School. His drawings of beautiful women, Kabuki-players, and famous warriors do not yet reveal the talent for which he later became famous. Hiroshige was only able to devote himself entirely to his art from 1832 when his son was finally old enough to take over as fire inspector. It was first significant success that probably encouraged him to give up the family business:

Hiroshige, le jeune artiste paye à son maître le tribut du respect obligatoire dans l'enseignement japonais, tout en se plaçant dans sa tradition artistique. Selon l'usage des artistes, Hiroshige changera encore souvent de nom ou apportera des compléments au sien – mais le nom de son maître y restera toujours associé.

Les premières productions de Hiroshige en matière d'estampes sont totalement dans le style d'Utagawa. Ses portraits de jolies femmes, de joueurs de kabuki et de guerriers célèbres ne révèlent aucun talent particulièrement exceptionnel. Toutefois, il ne peut se consacrer totalement à son art qu'à partir de 1832, lorsque son fils est assez âgé pour reprendre sa charge à la caserne des pompiers. Son premier succès

Vornamen Jūemon, kombiniert. Mit dem neuen Namen Utawaga Hiroshige zollt er seinem Lehrer den für Japan typischen Respekt und stellt sich in dessen künstlerische Tradition. Hiroshige wird noch mehrmals seinen Namen verändern oder ergänzen, führt aber stets den Namen seines Lehrers fort.

Hiroshiges erste Vorlagen für Farbholzschnitte folgen ganz dem Stil der Utawaga-Schule. Seine Entwürfe von schönen Frauen, Kabuki-Spielern und berühmten Kriegern beweisen keine sonderlich herausragende Begabung. Allerdings kann sich Hiroshige erst ab 1832 ganz auf die Kunst konzentrieren, als sein Sohn alt genug ist, das Feuerwehramt zu übernehmen. Auch sein erster nennenswerter Erfolg wird

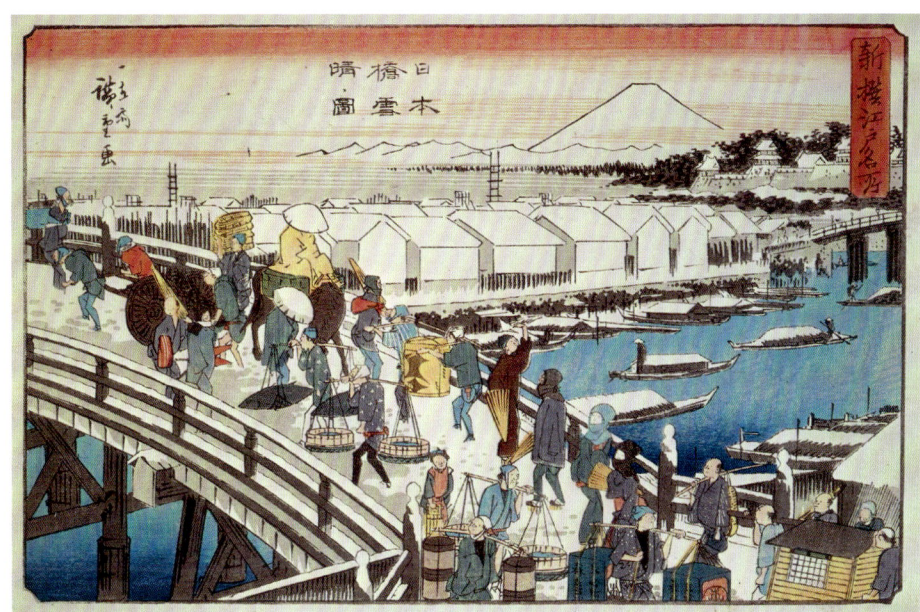

el carácter *jū* (presente en su nombre Jūemon). Con este nuevo nombre Utagawa Hiroshige presenta los respetos típicos a su maestro, integrándose en su tradición artística. Hiroshige cambiará o complementará su nombre en varias ocasiones pero siempre manteniendo el nombre de su maestro.

Los primeros sellos de madera para grabados de Hiroshige siguen el estilo de la escuela de Utagawa. Sus bocetos de bellas mujeres, actores de Kabuki y guerreros famosos no delatan un talento especialmente sobresaliente. Solo a partir de 1832 Hiroshige puede dedicarse por completo al arte, una vez que su hijo es suficientemente mayor para hacerse cargo del puesto como inspector de incendios. Su primer éxito reseñable

altri nomi di battesimo Jūemon. Con il nuovo nome Utagawa Hiroshige diede tributo a quel rispetto per l'insegnante tipico del Giappone, collocandosi nella sua tradizione artistica. Hiroshige cambiò o completò ancora varie volte il suo nome, ma mantenne sempre quello del suo insegnante.

I primi progetti di xilografie a colori di Hiroshige seguono interamente lo stile della scuola di Utagawa. I suoi schizzi di belle donne, attori di kabuki e famosi guerrieri non manifestano un talento particolarmente eccezionale. Tuttavia, solo dal 1832 Hiroshige poté concentrarsi a pieno sull'arte, quando suo figlio fu abbastanza grande per assumere la carica di funzionario nella stazione dei pompieri. Anche il

andere leeswijze van het *jū*-teken kiest, naar een van zijn latere voornamen, Jūemon. Met zijn nieuwe naam, Utagawa Hiroshige, toont hij zijn leermeester het in Japan gebruikelijke respect en plaatst zich in diens artistieke traditie. Hiroshige zal zijn naam later nog vaker veranderen of aanvullen, maar die van zijn leermeester blijft hij tot aan zijn dood voeren.

Zijn eerste ontwerpen voor kleurenhoutsneden creëert Hiroshige volledig in de stijl van de Utagawa-school. Zijn tekeningen van mooie vrouwen, kabukispelers en beroemde krijgers verraden nog niet zijn uitzonderlijke talent. Pas vanaf 1832 kan Hiroshige zich geheel en al op zijn kunst concentreren, wanneer zijn zoon oud genoeg is om het ambt van brandwacht van hem

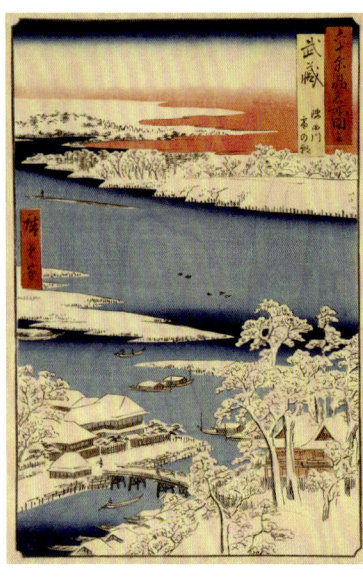

In 1831, the ten-part series *Famous Views of the Eastern Capital* was well received by the public and went through multiple print runs. Hiroshige was then commissioned to do the series *53 Stations of the Tōkaidō*. Here he focuses even more on representing the landscape and helps to create a breakthrough for landscape illustration in the Japanese woodcut. Hiroshige soon became one of the most popular woodcut artists, overtaking the famous Hokusai, almost forty years his senior.

It was in the years that followed that his impressive body of work was created. According to conservative estimates, the artist created some 4500 works, not counting the illustrations he did for approximately 120 books.

In 1856, Hiroshige became a Buddhist monk, a common practise at the time in

digne de ce nom va l'encourager à se retirer complètement de cette fonction. En 1831 est en effet parue une série de dix estampes, *Vues célèbres de la capitale de l'Est,* qui rencontre un accueil très favorable auprès du public et qui connaîtra plusieurs tirages. Il obtient alors la commande de la série des *Cinquante-trois relais de la route de la mer de l'Est,* ou *Cinquante-trois relais du Tōkaidō* : il s'y focalise encore davantage sur la représentation des paysages, en établissant du même coup le sujet comme un incontournable de l'estampe japonaise. Hiroshige devient l'un des créateurs les plus appréciés dans ce genre artistique et surpasse même bientôt l'illustre Hokusai – de quarante ans son aîné.

Les années qui suivent voient ainsi naître un corpus d'œuvres graphiques

ihn ermutigt haben, sich komplett aus dem ererbten Beruf zurückzuziehen: Um 1831 erscheint die zehnteilige Serie *Berühmte Ansichten der Östlichen Hauptstadt*, die großen Anklang beim Publikum findet und in mehreren Auflagen gedruckt wird. Daraufhin erhält Hiroshige den Auftrag zu der Serie *53 Stationen der Ostmeerstraße*. In diesen Blättern konzentriert er sich noch stärker auf die Landschaftsdarstellung und verhilft dem Sujet zum endgültigen Durchbruch im japanischen Holzschnitt. Hiroshige steigt nun zu einem der beliebtesten Holzschnittzeichner auf und übertrumpft bald den berühmten, knapp vierzig Jahre älteren Hokusai.

In den folgenden Jahren entsteht ein beeindruckendes Gesamtwerk. Vorsichtigen Schätzungen zufolge dürfte der Künstler bis zu seinem

Mount Haruna in the Snow, Famous Views of the 60-odd Provinces
Le Mont Haruna sous la neige, de la série *Vues des sites célèbres des 60 et quelques provinces*
Haruna Berg im Schnee, aus der Serie *Berühmte Gegenden der mehr als 60 Provinzen*
La montaña Haruna bajo la nieve, de la serie *Famosas vistas de las más de 60 provincias*
Il monte Haruna sotto la neve, della serie *Luoghi famosi delle oltre 60 province*
De berg Haruna in de sneeuw, uit de serie *Beroemde streken van de meer dan 60 provincies*

1853, Colour woodcut/Gravure sur bois en couleurs

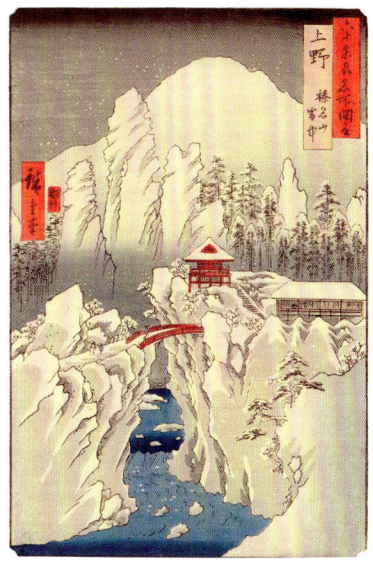

también le habrá animado a abandonar por completo el oficio recibido de su padre: en 1831 se publica la serie *Famosas vistas de la capital oriental*, que obtiene una resonancia pública importante y de la que se imprimen varias ediciones. Seguidamente Hiroshige recibe el encargo para su serie *Cincuenta y tres estaciones de la ruta Tōkaidō*. En estas estampas se concentra todavía más en la representación de los paisajes, impulsando el tema hacia su instauración definitiva en la xilografía japonesa. Hiroshige se convierte entonces en uno de los xilógrafos más reconocidos, sobrepasando poco después al famoso Hokusai, aproximadamente cuarenta años mayor.

Los siguientes años verán surgir una producción impresionante. Según estimaciones conservadoras

suo primo successo significativo lo incoraggiò a ritirarsi del tutto dalla professione ereditata. Intorno al 1831, infatti, apparve la serie in dieci pezzi *Vedute famose della capitale orientale*, che incontrò grande favore tra il pubblico e fu stampata in diverse edizioni. Questo permise a Hiroshige di ricevere l'incarico per la serie *Le 53 stazioni della Tokaido*. In queste stampe l'artista si concentrò ancora di più sulla rappresentazione del paesaggio, aprendo la strada a questo soggetto nella xilografia giapponese. Hiroshige divenne uno degli xilografi più popolari, superando presto il famoso Hokusai, che all'epoca aveva quasi quarant'anni.

Negli anni seguenti nacque un'opera omnia impressionante. Secondo alcune stime piuttosto caute, l'artista deve

over te nemen. Ook zal zijn eerste noemenswaardige succes hem hebben aangemoedigd zich volledig uit het overerfde ambt terug te trekken. Rond 1831 verschijnt Hiroshige's tiendelige serie *Beroemde gezichten op de Oostelijke Hoofdstad* die bij het publiek zeer in de smaak valt en in meerdere oplagen wordt gedrukt. Daarop ontvangt Hiroshige de opdracht voor de serie *53 halteplaatsen van de Oostelijke Zeeweg*. In deze houtsneden richt hij zich nog meer op de uitbeelding van het landschap en zorgt daarmee voor de definitieve doorbraak van dit genre in de Japanse houtsnijkunst. Hiroshige groeit nu uit tot een van de populairste prentkunstenaars van Japan en streeft al snel de beroemde, bijna veertig jaar oudere Hokusai voorbij.

In de jaren daarna bouwt Hiroshige een indrukwekkend oeuvre op. Volgens

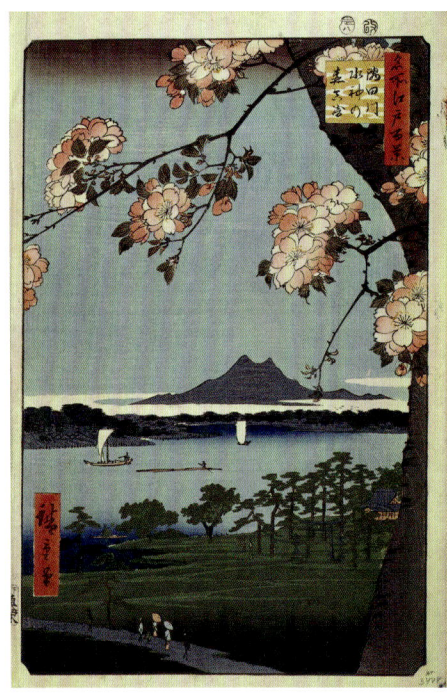

Suijin Shrine and Massaki on the Sumida River, 100 Famous Views of Edo

Le Sanctuaire de Suijin et Massaki près de la fleuve Sumida, de la série *Cent vues d'Edo*

Suijin-Schrein und Massaki am Fluss Sumida, aus der Serie *100 berühmte Ansichten von Edo*

El santuario Suijin y Massaki en el río Sumida, de la serie *100 famosas vistas de Edo*

Santuario di Suijin e Massaki sul fiume Sumida, della serie *100 vedute famose di Edo*

Suijin-schrijn en Masaki aan de rivier de Sumida, uit de serie *100 beroemde gezichten op Edo*

1856–1858, Colour woodcut/Gravure sur bois en couleurs, 39×26 cm, State Hermitage, St. Petersburg

preparation for one's impending death. In the last two years of his life, he draws the designs for the series *100 Famous Views of Edo*, which was the culmination of his life's work. Hiroshige died in 1858 at the age of 62, probably during a cholera epidemic.

impressionnant. Selon des estimations prudentes, l'artiste aurait créé quelque 4500 estampes, sans compter les illustrations d'environ 120 livres.

En 1856, Hiroshige devient moine bouddhiste, préparation spirituelle alors très courante quand on sent approcher la fin de la vie. Dans les deux dernières années de sa vie, il crée les premières feuilles pour la série *Cent vues d'Edo,* qui constitue à la fois l'apogée et la conclusion de son œuvre – mais qu'il n'aura pas le temps d'achever. Hiroshige meurt en 1858 à 62 ans, probablement pendant une épidémie de choléra.

Tod etwa 4500 Arbeiten geschaffen haben, zuzüglich der Illustrationen für ungefähr 120 Bücher.

1856 tritt Hiroshige in den Stand eines buddhistischen Mönches ein, eine nach damaligem Brauch durchaus übliche Vorbereitung auf den näherrückenden Tod. In den letzten beiden Jahren seines Lebens zeichnet er die Entwürfe für die Serie *100 berühmte Ansichten von Edo*, die den Höhepunkt und zugleich den Abschluss seines Schaffens bildet. Hiroshige stirbt 1858 im Alter von 62 Jahren vermutlich während einer Choleraepidemie.

View of Bish Nagoya

Vue de Nagoya, Bishu

Ansicht von Bish Nagoya

Vista de Bish Nagoya

Veduta di Bish Nagoya

Bish Nagoya

Gezicht vanaf de Nagoya-burcht

1858, Colour woodcut/Gravure sur bois en couleurs

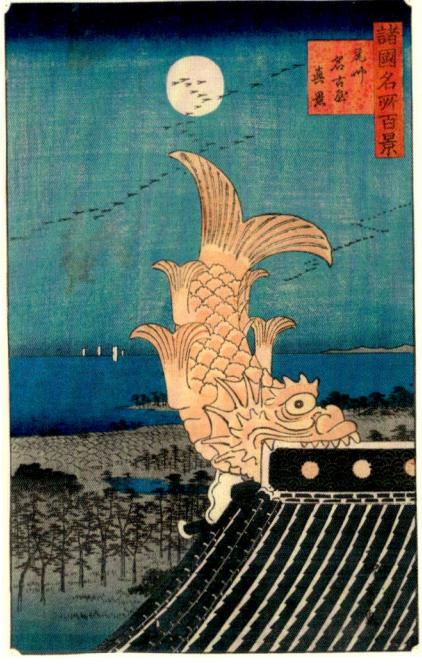

el artista podría haber creado hasta aproximadamente 4500 obras, además de las ilustraciones para unos 120 libros.

En 1856 Hiroshige se convirtió en monje budista, una preparación común para una muerte próxima según las costumbres del momento. En sus últimos dos años pinta los bocetos para la serie *Cien famosas vistas de Edo*, que constituyen a la vez la cumbre y la finalización de su trabajo. Hiroshige murió en 1858 a la edad de 62 años, probablemente durante una epidemia de cólera.

aver creato circa 4500 opere fino alla sua morte, oltre alle illustrazioni per circa 120 libri.

Nel 1856 Hiroshige assunse lo status di monaco buddista, all'epoca normale in preparazione alla morte prossima. Negli ultimi due anni di vita disegnò gli schizzi per la serie *Le cento vedute famose di Edo*, che rappresenta allo stesso tempo l'apice e la fine del suo lavoro. Hiroshige morì nel 1858 all'età di 62 anni, probabilmente durante un'epidemia di colera.

voorzichtige schattingen zou hij tot aan zijn dood ongeveer 4500 werken hebben gecreëerd, en daarnaast de illustraties voor circa 120 boeken.

In 1856 treedt Hiroshige toe tot de stand van boeddhistische monnik, destijds een zeer gebruikelijke voorbereiding op de naderende dood. In de laatste twee jaar van zijn leven tekent hij de ontwerpen voor de serie *100 beroemde gezichten op Edo*, tegelijkertijd het hoogtepunt en de afsluiting van zijn levenswerk. Hiroshige overlijdt in 1858 op 62-jarige leeftijd, vermoedelijk tijdens een cholera-epidemie.

Posthumous Memorial Portrait of Hiroshige

Portrait posthume de Hiroshige

This image is the only known portrait of Hiroshige. Kunisada III (Toyokuni) drew it in 1858 in memory of his dead friend. In the upper part is the memorial poem by Tenmei Rōjin entitled "When we think of him, our tears flow".

Cette image est le seul portrait connu de Hiroshige. Kunisada III (Toyokuni) l'a réalisé en 1858, en mémoire de son ami mort. Dans la partie supérieure de l'estampe figure l'oraison funèbre du poète Tenmei Rōjin, intitulée : « Quand nous pensons à lui, alors coulent nos larmes. »

Posthumes Gedächtnisporträt Hiroshiges

Retrato póstumo a la memoria de Hiroshige

Dieses Bild ist das einzige bekannte Porträt von Hiroshige. Kunisada III (Toyokuni) schuf es 1858 zum Gedenken an den toten Freund. Im oberen Teil steht der Nachruf des Dichters Tenmei Rōjin mit dem Titel „Wenn wir an ihn denken, fließen unsere Tränen".

Esta imagen es el único retrato conocido de Hiroshige. Kunisada III (Toyokuni)lo realizó en 1858, a la memoria de su amigo muerto. En la parte superior encontramos el elogio póstumo del poeta Tenmei Rōjin con el título "Cuando pensamos en él se nos saltan las lágrimas".

Kunisada III:

Ritratto postumo in memoria di Hiroshige

Postuum herdenkingsportret van Hiroshige

1859/60, Colour woodcut/Gravure sur bois en couleurs, 35,5×21,9 cm

Questo quadro è l'unico ritratto conosciuto di Hiroshige. Fu dipinto nel 1858 da Kunisada III (Toyokuni) in memoria dell'amico deceduto. Nella parte superiore si trova il necrologio del poeta Tenmei Rōjin dal titolo "Quando pensiamo a lui, scorrono le lacrime".

Dit werk is het enige bekende portret van Hiroshige. Kunisada III (Toyokuni) creëerde het in 1858 ter nagedachtenis aan zijn overleden vriend. Boven het portret staat Hiroshige's necrologie, van de hand van de dichter Tenmei Rōjin, met de titel "Wanneer wij aan hem denken, vloeien onze tranen".

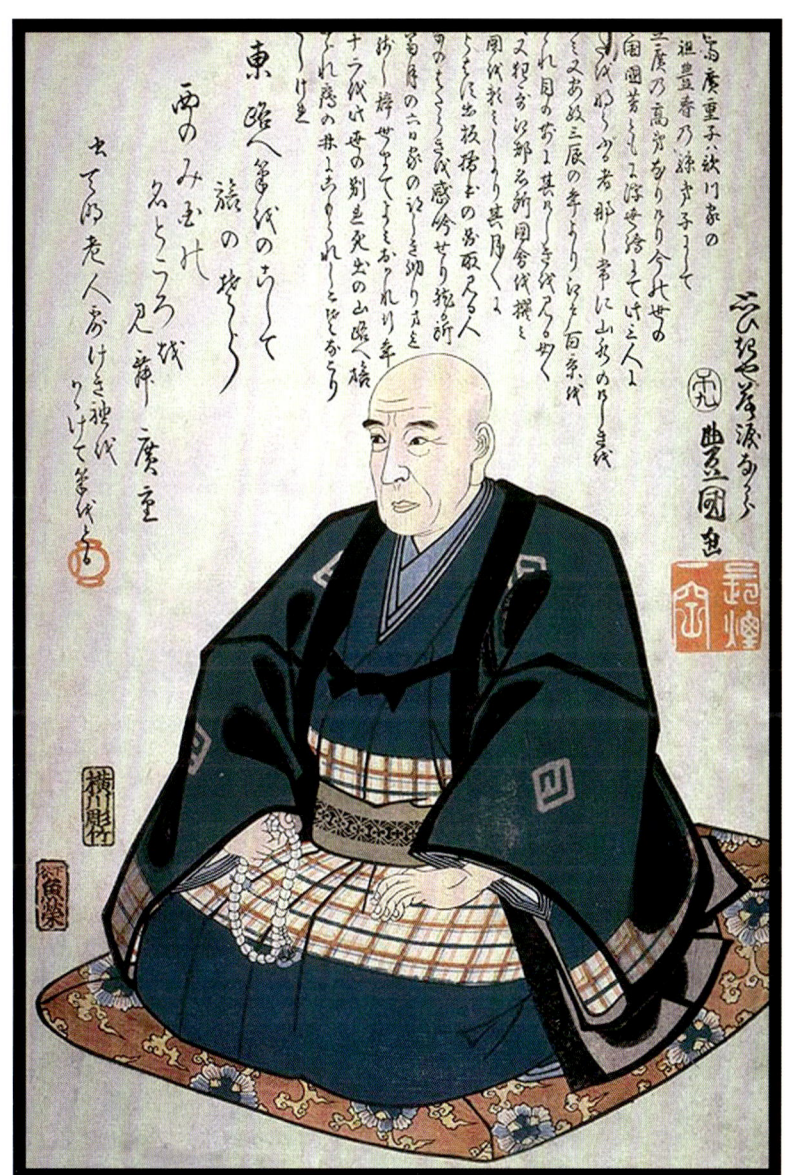

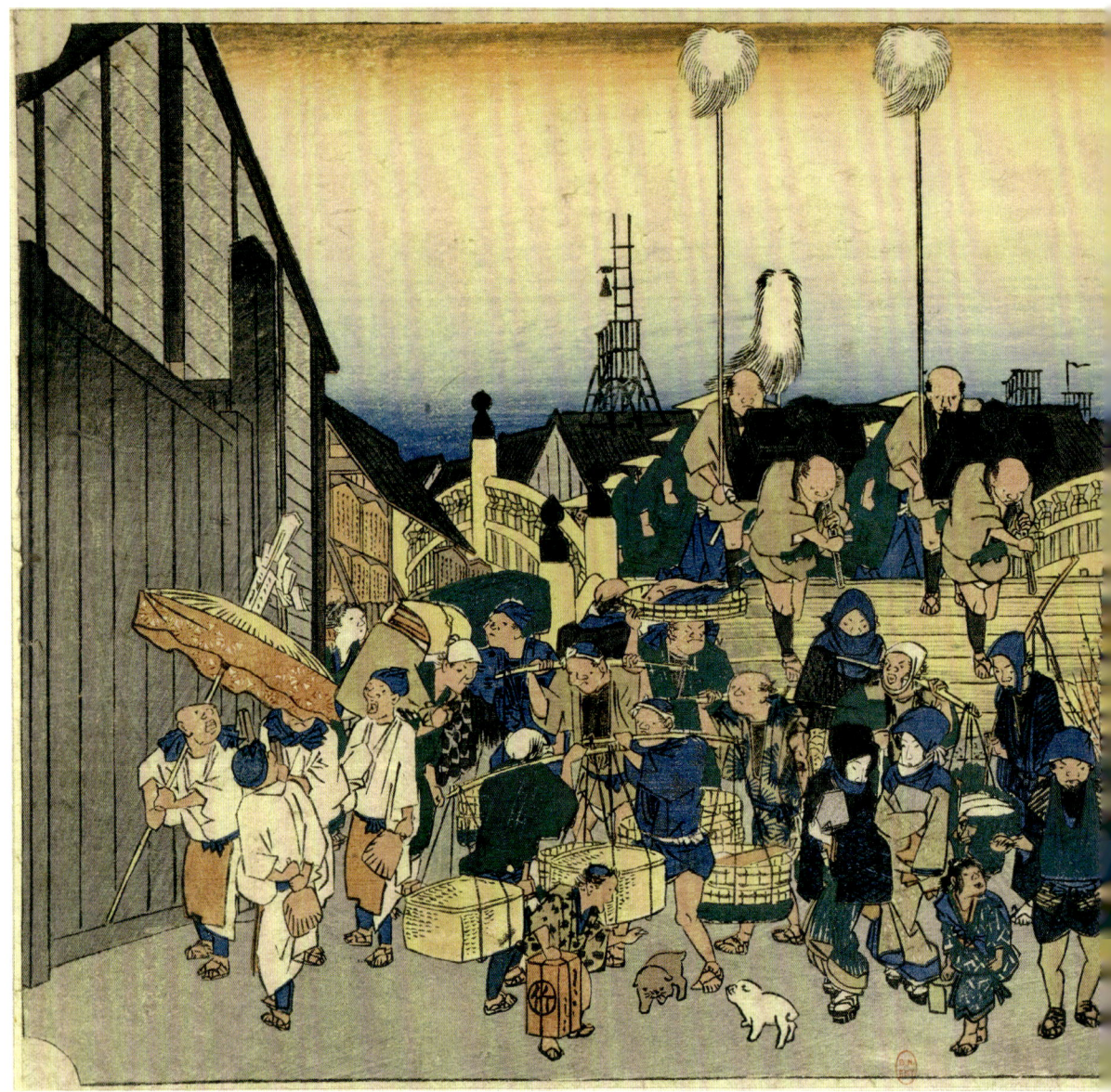

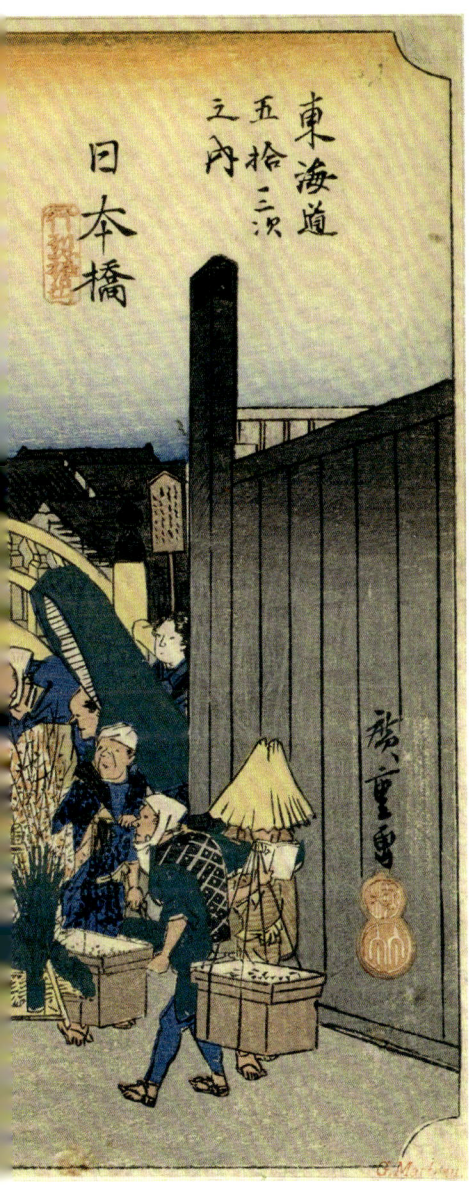

Dawn in Edo. Frontispiece of the series **53 stations of Tōkaidō**

Départ d'Edo. Frontispice de la série **53 relais de la route de la mer de l'Est**

Aufbruch in Edo. Frontispiz der Serie **53 Stationen der Ostmeerstraße**

Abandonando Edo. Frontispicio de la serie **53 estaciones de la ruta Tōkaidō**

Partenza da Edo. Frontespizio della serie **Le 53 stazioni della Tokaido**

Vertrek in Edo. Frontispice van de serie **53 halteplaatsen aan de Tōkaidō (Oostelijke Zeeweg)**

1833/34, Colour woodcut/Gravure sur bois en couleurs, 22,2 × 34,4 cm,
Bibliothèque Nationale, Paris

On the Nihonbashi Bridge, which marks the beginning of the Tōkaidō, already bustling with activity in the early morning. The spatial composition of the print shows the influence of Western representation of perspective. The shading of the gate shows Hiroshige's familiarity with European engravings.

Sur le pont de Nihonbashi, point de départ de la route du Tōkaidō, le trafic est dense dès le petit matin. La composition spatiale de la feuille révèle l'influence de la représentation perspective occidentale. Les dégradés sur la grande porte attestent également la connaissance des gravures sur cuivre.

Auf der Nihonbashi-Brücke, die den Beginn der Reise auf der Ostmeerstraße markiert, ist am frühen Morgen schon reger Betrieb. Die räumliche Komposition des Blattes zeigt den Einfluss der westlichen Perspektivdarstellung. Die Schattierung des Tores belegt Hiroshiges Auseinandersetzung mit europäischen Kupferstichen.

En el puente Nihonbashi, que marca el inicio del viaje por el Camino del Mar del Este, ya hay actividad intensa temprano por la mañana. La composición espacial de la estampa muestra la influencia de la representación en perspectiva occidental. El sombreado de la puerta delata el conocimiento de Hiroshige de las calcografías occidentales.

Sul ponte Nihonbashi, che rappresenta l'inizio del viaggio sulla strada del mare dell'Est, al mattino presto vi è già un'attività frenetica. La composizione spaziale della stampa mostra l'influsso della visione prospettica occidentale. L'ombreggiatura della porta dimostra il contrasto di Hiroshige con le incisioni su rame europee.

Op de Nihonbashi-brug, die het begin van de Oostelijke Zeeweg markeert, is het 's ochtends vroeg een drukte van belang. De ruimtelijke compositie van het blad verraadt de invloed van het westerse perspectief. Uit de schaduwwerking van de poort blijkt dat Hiroshige bekend was met Europese kopergravures.

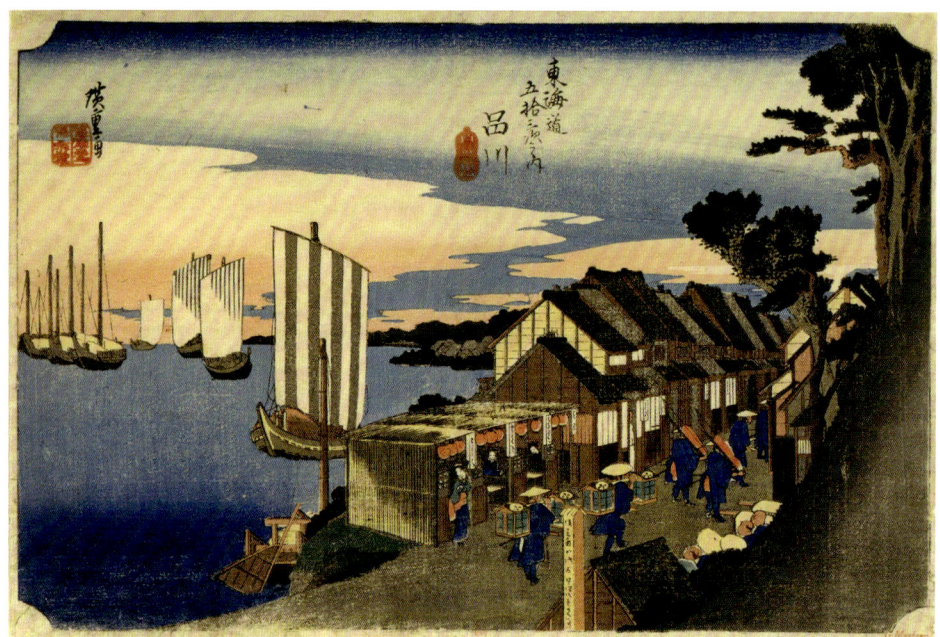

Travelling the roads of life

The east coast highway (Tōkaidō) along the Pacific coast was one of Japan's major thoroughfares in Hiroshige's time. It combines the capital Edo with Kyoto, the old imperial city in the west. Hiroshige's series of the official 53 postal stations and checkpoints along this route were published as a collection. The prints appeared sequentially, probably for the first time between 1832 and 1834. Hiroshige consolidated his reputation as an outstanding woodcut artist with this series, which was reprinted many times, with the quality of the prints varying greatly. It is possible that Hiroshige was

En route sur les grandes voies de communication

La route de la mer de l'Est (Tōkaidō), le long de la côte Pacifique, est à l'époque de Hiroshige une des voies de circulation les plus importantes du Japon, longue d'environ 500 kilomètres. Elle relie la capitale d'alors, Edo, à l'ancienne ville impériale de Kyoto, à l'ouest. La série de Hiroshige, consacrée aux cinquante-trois relais et postes de contrôle qui jalonnent cette route, est éditée en collection d'estampes, dont les feuilles paraissent l'une après l'autre, et vraisemblablement pour la première fois entre 1832 et 1834. Cette série à succès – qui consacre définitivement la renommée de son créateur – fait

Unterwegs auf den großen Verkehrswegen

Die Ostmeerstraße (tōkaidō) entlang der Pazifikküste ist zu Hiroshiges Zeit eine der wichtigsten Verkehrsadern Japans. Sie verbindet die damalige Hauptstadt Edo mit Kyoto, der alten Kaiserstadt im Westen. Hiroshiges Serie der offiziellen 53 Poststationen und Kontrollposten auf dieser Route wird als Bildersammlung verlegt. Die Blätter erscheinen also nacheinander, wahrscheinlich erstmals zwischen 1832 und 1834. Die erfolgreiche Serie, mit der Hiroshige seinen Ruf als herausragender Holzschnittzeichner festigt, wird mehrfach nachgedruckt, wobei die Qualität der Auflagen stark schwankt. Möglicherweise

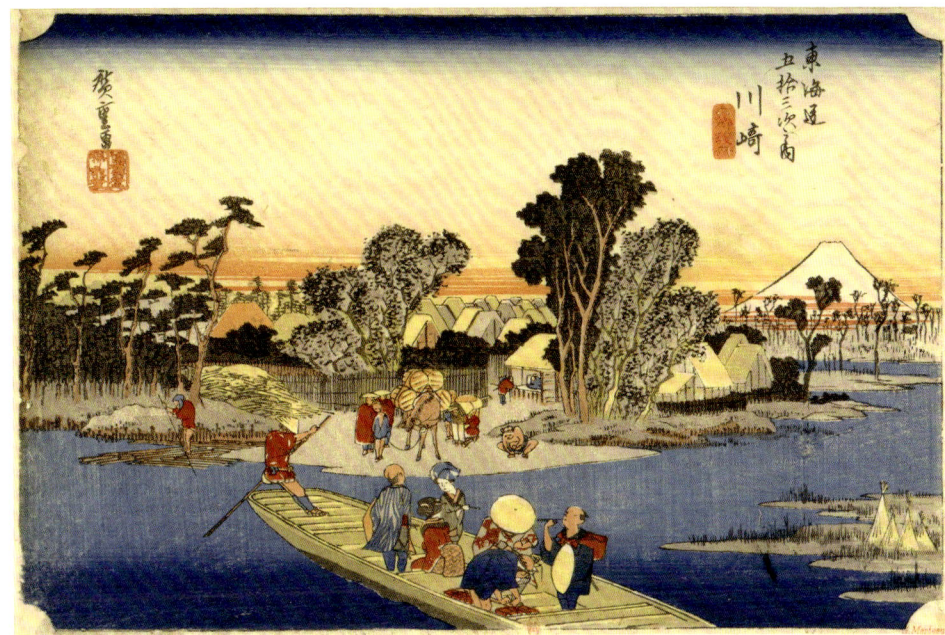

De camino por las grandes rutas

El Camino del Mar del Este (Tōkaidō) a lo lardo de la costa del Pacífico es una de las arterias fundamentales de Japón durante los tiempos de Hiroshige. Comunica la entonces capital Edo con Kyoto, la antigua ciudad imperial del Oeste. La serie de Hiroshige de las 53 estaciones y puestos de control oficiales en esta ruta se publican como una colección de imágenes. Las diferentes estampas aparecen por tanto de manera consecutiva probablemente por primera vez entre 1832 y 1834. La famosa serie, mediante la cual Hiroshige cimenta su fama de extraordinario grabador, se imprime múltiples veces, si bien la calidad de las ediciones varía

In viaggio sulle grandi rotte

La via del mare dell'Est (tōkaidō) lungo la costa del Pacifico, ai tempi di Hiroshige era una delle arterie più importanti del Giappone. Collegava la capitale dell'epoca Edo con Kyoto, l'antica città imperiale dell'Ovest. La serie di Hiroshige delle 53 stazioni di sosta e posti di blocco ufficiali su questa via fu pubblicata come raccolta di immagini. Le stampe apparvero una dopo l'altra, probabilmente per la prima volta tra il 1832 e il 1834. La serie ebbe particolare successo, permettendo a Hiroshige di consolidare la sua fama di eccezionale xilografo, e fu ristampata più volte, anche se la qualità delle edizioni era soggetta a forti oscillazioni. È probabile

Onderweg langs de Japanse hoofdwegen

De Oostelijke Zeeweg of Tōkaidō, langs de Pacifische kust, was in de tijd van Hiroshige een van de belangrijkste verkeersaders van Japan. De route verbond de toenmalige hoofdstad Edo met Kyoto, de oude keizerstad in het westen van het land. Hiroshige's serie over de officiële 53 halteplaatsen en controlestations langs de weg wordt als een reeks losse prenten uitgegeven. De bladen verschijnen dus na elkaar, waarschijnlijk tussen 1832 en 1834. De succesvolle serie, waarmee Hiroshige naam maakt als toonaangevend houtsnijkunstenaar, wordt meerdere malen herdrukt, waarbij de kwaliteit

23

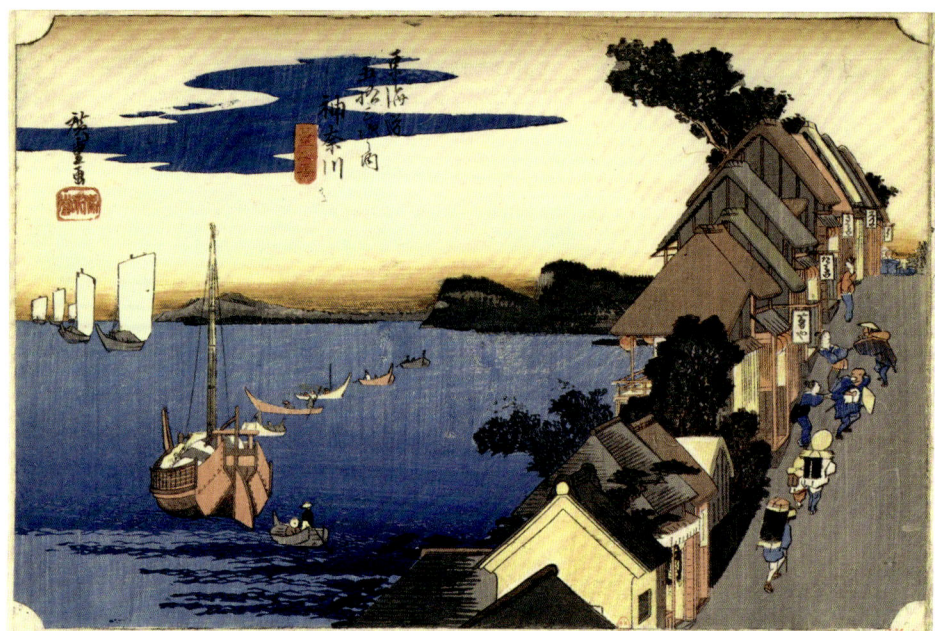

recording his impressions of a journey
that he might have taken with an
official delegation of the shogunate,
although whether this trip actually
occurred remains uncertain. It is
clear that Hiroshige took suggestions
from the illustrated travel literature
of the period.

In the *53 Stations of the Tōkaidō*,
Hiroshige shows an amazing variety
of compositions and image ideas.
He not only shows different times
of the day, but also the different
seasons. The special popularity of
Hiroshige's work is to no small extent
rooted in the popular conception of
his motifs. He took the established
subject of *meisho* ("famous views")

l'objet de nombreuses réimpressions,
d'où la baisse de qualité progressive
des tirages. Il se peut que Hiroshige
ait travaillé d'après des impressions et
des notes prises au cours d'un voyage
fait en accompagnant une mission
diplomatique officielle du régime
shogunal, mais on n'a aucune certitude
à ce sujet. Il est certain en revanche qu'il
s'est inspiré de la littérature de voyage
illustrée préexistante.

La série des *Cinquante-trois relais de
la route de la mer de l'Est* déploie une
gamme étonnante de compositions
et d'inventions iconographiques.
Hiroshige s'intéresse à divers moments
de la journée, mais aussi des saisons.
La faveur dont jouissent ses travaux

verarbeitet Hiroshige Eindrücke
einer Reise, zu der er in Begleitung
einer offiziellen Gesandtschaft der
Shogunatsregierung aufgebrochen
sein soll. Es ist jedoch ungewiss, ob
diese Reise wirklich stattgefunden hat.
Gesichert ist hingegen, dass Hiroshige
Anregungen aus der illustrierten
Reiseliteratur übernahm.

In den *53 Stationen der Ostmeerstraße*
zeigt Hiroshige eine erstaunliche
Bandbreite an Kompositionen und
Bildideen. Er nimmt dabei nicht nur
verschiedene Tages-, sondern auch
Jahreszeiten in den Blick. Die besondere
Beliebtheit von Hiroshiges Arbeiten
begründet sich außerdem nicht zuletzt
in der populären Auffassung seiner

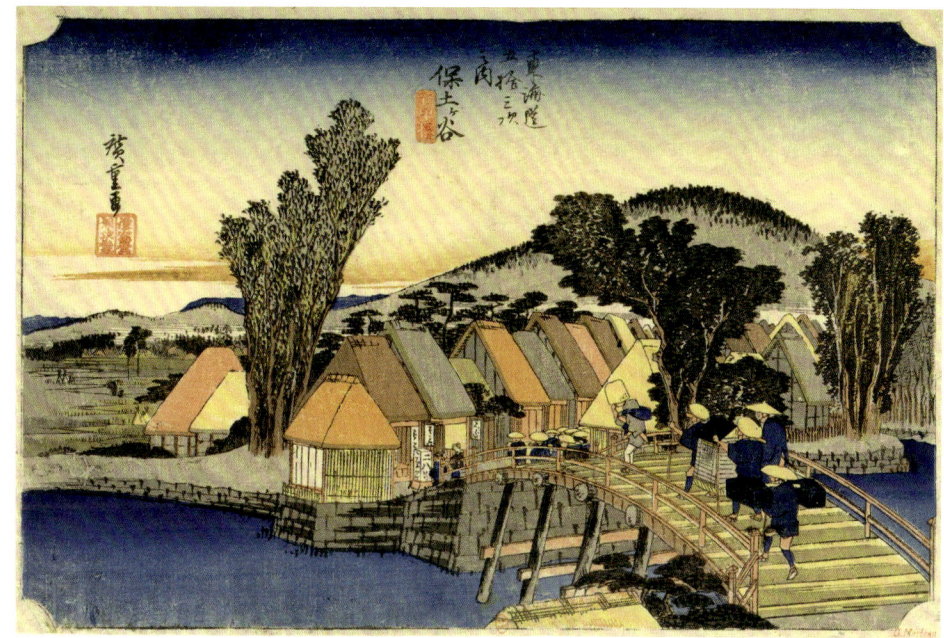

de manera acusada. Probablemente Hiroshige esté aquí trabajando con las impresiones que habría recopilado en un viaje acompañando a una delegación oficial del Shogunato. No es sin embargo seguro que se produjera tal viaje. Lo que sí que es seguro es que Hiroshige habría encontrado un estímulo en las guías ilustradas de viajes de la época.

En las *Cincuenta y tres estaciones de la ruta de Tōkaidō* Hiroshige muestra una increíble variedad de ideas pictóricas y composiciones. Recurre para ello no solo a diferentes momentos del día, sino también diferentes estaciones. La especial popularidad con la que cuentan los trabajos de Hiroshige se fundamenta además en su presentación de los

che Hiroshige abbia elaborato delle impressioni di un viaggio, che avrebbe dovuto intraprendere come accompagnatore di una delegazione ufficiale del governo Shogun. Tuttavia non è sicuro che questo viaggio sia avvenuto realmente. È invece sicuro che Hiroshige abbia trovato degli stimoli nella letteratura di viaggio illustrata.

Ne *Le 53 stazioni della Tokaido*, Hiroshige mostra una sorprendente gamma di composizioni e idee visive. Egli prende in considerazione non solo diverse ore del giorno, ma anche stagioni differenti. La particolare popolarità delle opere di Hiroshige si fonda inoltre, e non per ultimo, nella visione popolare dei suoi motivi. Egli traduce il soggetto

van de oplagen sterk uiteenloopt. Mogelijk heeft Hiroshige in deze serie zijn eigen indrukken verwerkt, namelijk van een reis die hij in het gevolg van een officiële gezant van het shogunaat zou hebben ondernomen. Onduidelijk is of de reis daadwerkelijk heeft plaatsgevonden, maar zeker is wel dat Hiroshige motieven ontleent aan de geïllustreerde reisliteratuur.

In zijn *53 halteplaatsen van de Oostelijke Zeeweg* ontvouwt Hiroshige een verbluffende variëteit aan composities en picturale ideeën, waarbij hij verschillende seizoenen en momenten van de dag uitbeeldt. Maar het grote succes van Hiroshige's werken berust zeker ook op zijn keuze

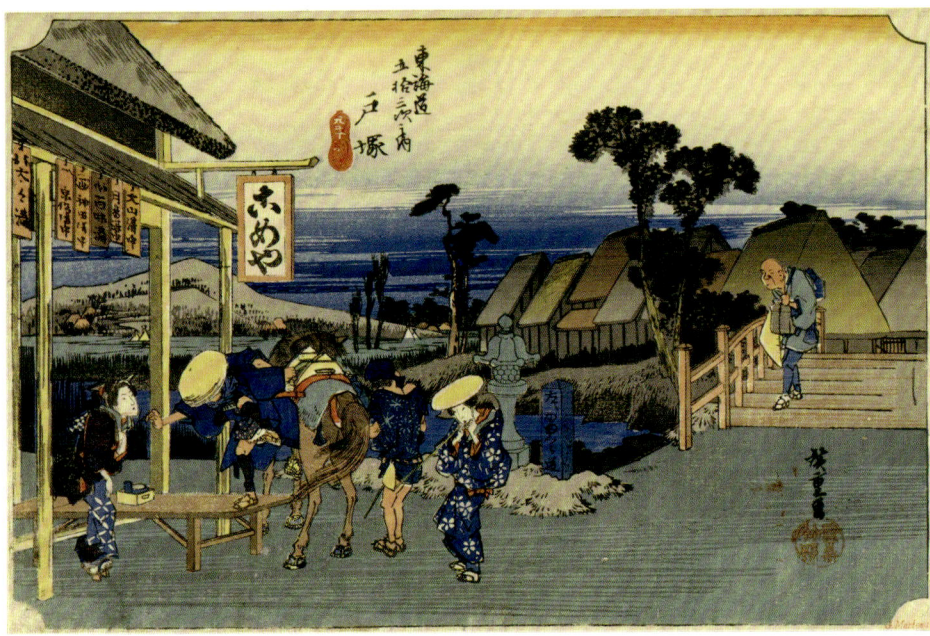

of pilgrimage sites and spectacular
natural phenomena, offered in an
idealized fashion by the traditional
painting schools for the upper class,
and brought it to the medium of
printmaking. His pictures show an
undisguised, realistic view of the
landscape and people. The sometimes
humorous scenes that he adds to
the landscapes allow Hiroshige's
middle class buyers a chance to find
themselves and their daily lives.

Hiroshige also illustrated the
second main highways of the
island nation, the Kisokaidō. This
series appeared between 1837 and
1842 The first prints were done by
Keisai Eisen, but then Hiroshige

repose également sur la version
« populaire » qu'il donne de ses
motifs. Il transpose en effet le thème
traditionnel des « vues célèbres »
(meisho-e) de lieux de pèlerinage et
de phénomènes naturels particuliers
– tels que les écoles de peinture
classiques les représentaient de façon
idéalisée et coûteuse à destination des
élites – grâce au support plus abordable
de la gravure. Ses images traduisent
ainsi un regard neutre et plus réaliste
sur le paysage comme sur les hommes.
Dans les scènes – partiellement
humoristiques – qui se déroulent au
sein des paysages, les amateurs de la
bourgeoisie peuvent se retrouver dans
leur vécu quotidien.

Motive. Er übersetzt das etablierte
Sujet der „berühmten Ansichten"
(meisho) von Pilgerstätten und
besonderen Naturphänomenen, wie
sie von den klassischen Malschulen in
idealisierender Weise für die Oberschicht
angeboten wurden, in das Medium
der Druckgrafik. Seine Bilder zeigen
einen unverstellten, realistischeren
Blick auf Landschaft und Menschen. In
den zum Teil humorvollen Szenen, die
sich in die Landschaftsdarstellungen
einfügen, können die Käufer aus der
bürgerlichen Schicht sich selbst und
ihren Alltag wiederfinden.

Auch die zweite Hauptstraße
des Landes, die Kisokaidō-Route,
setzt Hiroshige in einer Serie um.

Fujisawa (Yugyōji temple), Station 6

Fujisawa (Le Temple Yugyōji), relais 6

Fujisawa (Tempel Yugyōji), Station 6

Fujisawa (Templo Yugyōji), Station 6

Fujisawa (tempio di Yugyōji), stazione 6

Fujisawa (Yugyōji-tempel), halteplaats 6

Colour woodcut/ Gravure sur bois en couleurs, 22,2×34,4 cm Bibliothèque Nationale, Paris

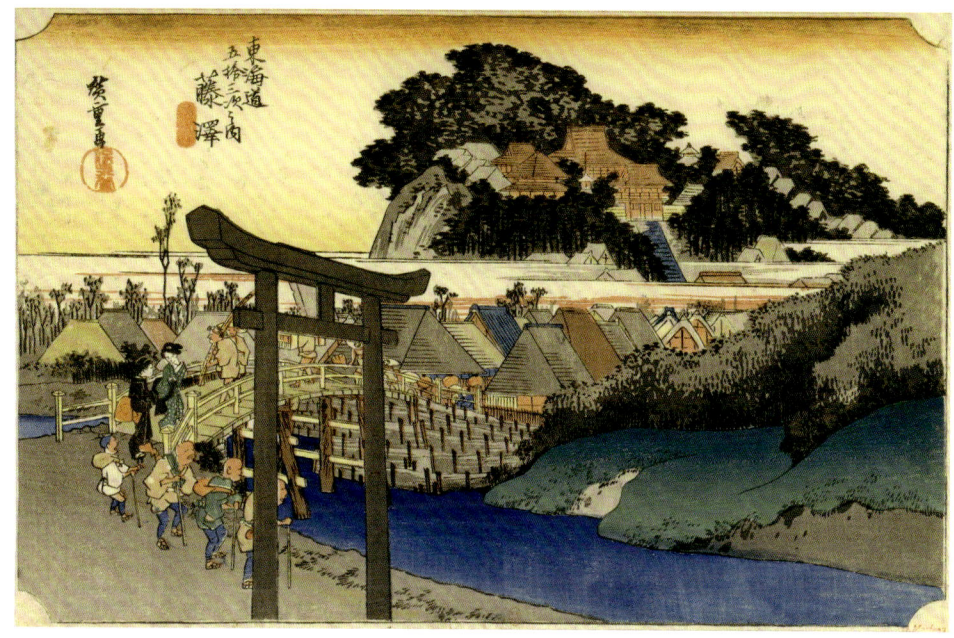

motivos. Traduce el motivo establecido de las "vistas famosas" *(meisho)* de lugares de peregrinación y fenómenos naturales extraordinarios, tal y como se ofrecía a las clases altas de manera idealizada en las escuelas de dibujo, al medio del grabado. Sus imágenes muestran una visión pura y realista del paisaje y la gente. En las escenas, a veces cómicas, que se introducen en las representaciones de paisajes los compradores de la clase burguesa pueden verse representados a sí mismos y su mundo cotidiano.

Hiroshige también muestra la segunda vía principal del país, la ruta Kisokaidō, en otra serie publicada entre 1837 y 1842. Keisai Eisen diseña las

stabilito delle "vedute famose" *(meisho)* di luoghi di pellegrinaggio e fenomeni naturali particolari, come proposti dalle scuole di pittura classiche e idealizzate per il ceto elevato, mediante l'incisione. I suoi quadri mostrano una visione libera e realistica del paesaggio e degli uomini. Nelle scene, in parte spiritose, che si inseriscono nelle rappresentazioni del paesaggio, gli acquirenti della classe media possono ritrovare sé stessi e la loro vita quotidiana.

Anche per la seconda via principale del paese, la strada di Kisokaidō, Hiroshige realizzò una serie, che fu pubblicata tra il 1837 e il 1842. Le prime stampe furono create da Keisai Eisen, in seguito Hiroshige continuò

voor zeer populaire onderwerpen. Daarbij vertaalt hij het traditionele motief van 'beroemde gezichten' *(meishō)* op bedevaartsoorden en bijzondere natuurverschijnselen – die in de klassieke schilderscholen op geïdealiseerde wijze worden verbeeld ten behoeve van de bovenklasse – naar het medium van de prentkunst. Zijn werken tonen een ongekunstelde en realistische blik op het landschap en op mensen. In de vaak humoristische taferelen die in het landschap zijn opgenomen, kunnen de gegoede burgers die zijn werk kopen zichzelf en hun dagelijks leven herkennen.

Ook de tweede hoofdweg van het land, de Centrale Bergweg of

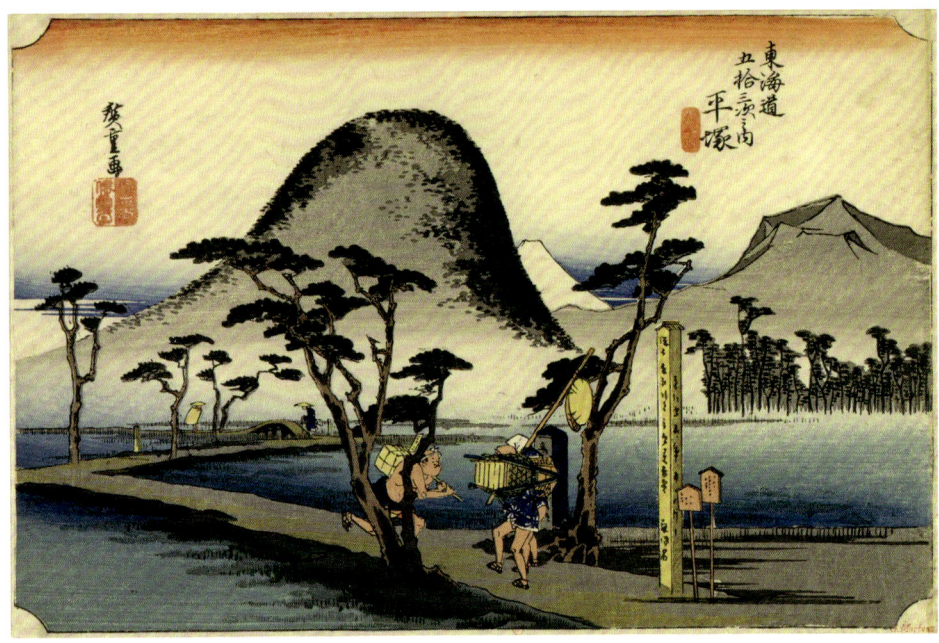

Hiratsuka (Nawate road), Station 7

Hiratsuka (Route de Nawate), relais 7

Hiratsuka (Straße von Nawate), Station 7

Hiratsuka (Camino de Nawate), Estación 7

Hiratsuka (strada di Nawate), stazione 7

Hiratsuka (Nawate-weg), halteplaats 7

Colour woodcut/ Gravure sur bois en couleurs, 22,2×34,4 cm Bibliothèque Nationale, Paris

completed the rest of the 69 stations. This road also leads from Edo to Kyoto, but runs inland. As with the Tōkaidō series, what is particularly striking here are Hiroshige's various strategies for giving his representations spatial depth. This was an innovation compared with traditional Japanese art which tended to emphasise a flatter landscape and was owed to European influence, in particular Western engravings, which came to Japan despite strong trade restrictions. These inspired Hiroshige's use of cross-hatching, light and shadow effects, and alignment of the image along a central perspective. This new view

La deuxième des cinq grandes routes (Gokaidō) du Japon impérial – celle du Kisokaidō ou Nakasendō – fait l'objet d'une autre série, les *Soixante-neuf relais du Kisokaidō,* parue entre 1837 et 1842. Les vingt-quatre premières feuilles sont l'œuvre de Keisai Einen, Hiroshige prenant ensuite le relais pour achever la série. À l'instar du Tokaidō, le Kisokaidō reliait Edo (capitale shogunale) à Kyoto (capitale impériale), mais en passant par l'intérieur des terres. Comme déjà dans la série précédente, on est particulièrement frappé par les différentes stratégies que développe Hiroshige pour donner de la profondeur spatiale à ses représentations. Cette nouveauté, face à la tradition artistique

Sie erscheint zwischen 1837 und 1842. Die ersten Blätter gestaltet Keisai Eisen, dann übernimmt Hiroshige die übrigen der insgesamt 69 Stationen. Diese Straße führt ebenfalls von Edo nach Kyoto, verläuft jedoch im Landesinneren. Besonders auffällig sind, wie schon bei den Ansichten der Ostmeerstraße, Hiroshiges verschiedene Strategien, um seinen Darstellungen räumliche Tiefe zu verleihen. Diese Neuerung gegenüber der japanischen Kunsttradition, in der die Fläche stark betont wird, verdankt sich europäischen Einflüssen. Insbesondere westliche Kupferstiche, die trotz starker Handelseinschränkungen nach Japan gelangten, werden Hiroshige zu seinem

Oiso (Rain of the Tora), Station 8

Oiso (Pluie de Tora), relais 8

Oiso (Regen der Tora), Station 8

Oiso (Lluvia sobre un pueblo de la costa), Estación 8

Oiso (la pioggia di Tora), stazione 8

Ōiso (Tora's regen), halteplaats 8

Colour woodcut/ Gravure sur bois en couleurs, 22,2×34,4 cm Bibliothèque Nationale, Paris

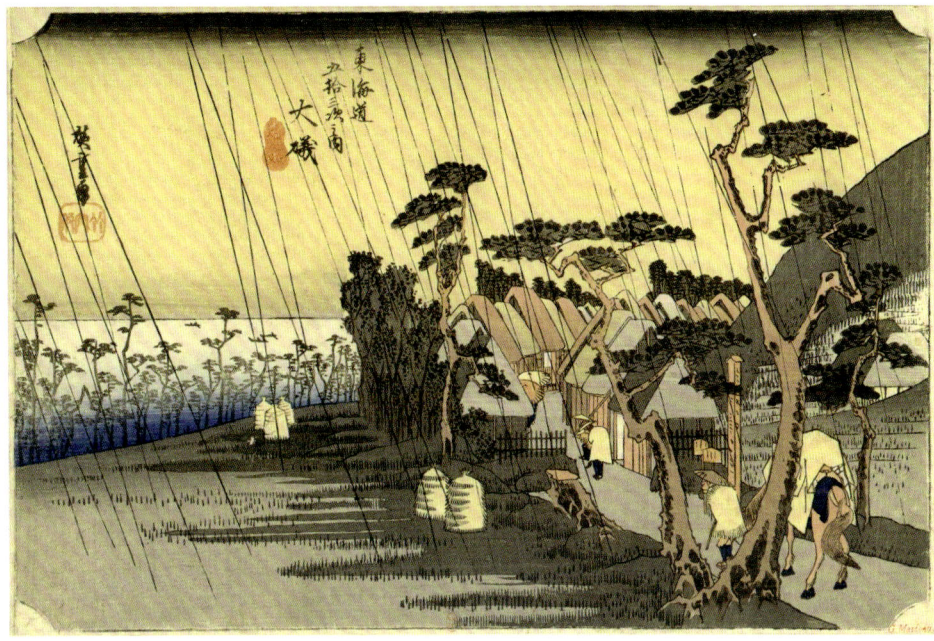

primeras estampas e Hiroshige se ocupa después de las restantes estaciones hasta el total de 69. Esta ruta también comunica Edo con Kyoto, si bien lo hace esta vez por el interior. Como ya se vio en las Vistas del Camino del Este, son especialmente reseñables las diversas estrategias de Hiroshige para dotar a sus representaciones de una profundidad espacial. Esta innovación frente a la tradición japonesa que tiende a acentuar lo plano se debe a influencias europeas. En concreto las calcografías occidentales, que llegaban a Japón a pesar de las marcadas limitaciones comerciales, habrían inspirado a Hiroshige por su trabajo con el rayado, sus efectos de luz/oscuridad

il resto delle 69 stazioni totali. Questa strada conduce da Edo a Kyoto, procedendo però verso l'interno del paese. Come già nel caso delle vedute della Tokaido, sono particolarmente sorprendenti le diverse strategie attuate da Hiroshige per conferire alle sue immagini profondità spaziale. Questa innovazione della tradizione artistica giapponese, in cui la superficie è fortemente evidenziata, è dovuta ad influenze europee. In particolare, le incisioni su rame occidentali che arrivavano in Giappone nonostante le forti restrizioni commerciali, devono aver stimolato Hiroshige nel suo rapporto con i tratteggi, i giochi di luce e ombra e le fughe dal modello della

Nakasendō, verbeeldt Hiroshige in een serie, die tussen 1837 en 1842 verschijnt. De eerste bladen worden getekend door Keisai Eisen, waarna Hiroshige de rest van de in totaal 69 halteplaatsen uitbeeldt. Ook de Nakasendō loopt van Edo naar Kyoto, maar dan door het binnenland. Net als in zijn gezichten op de Oostelijke Zeeweg gebruikt Hiroshige zeer verschillende en opmerkelijke strategieën om zijn taferelen ruimtelijke diepte te geven. Deze vernieuwing binnen de Japanse kunsttraditie, waarin het vlak sterk wordt benadrukt, is te danken aan Europese invloeden. Vooral westerse kopergravures – die ondanks de strikte handelsbeperkingen het land binnenkomen – zouden Hiroshige

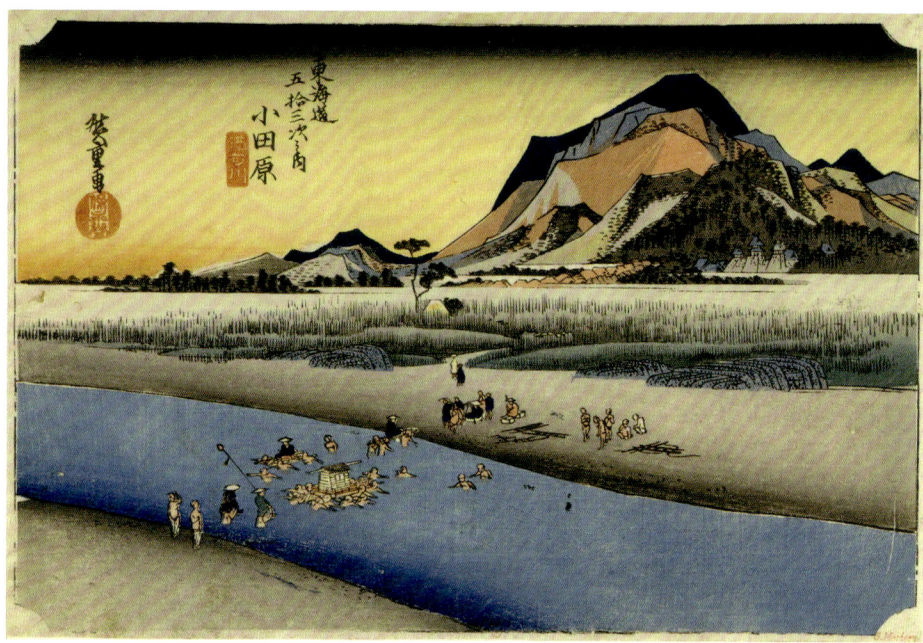

of the countryside was another important factor in Hiroshige's success, and it is significant that it was a woodcut artist and not a member of the traditional Japanese painting schools that was first to implement this innovation.

japonaise qui privilégie et accentue la surface, est due à des influences occidentales. Les gravures occidentales sur cuivre, en particulier, parvenues au Japon malgré des restrictions douanières drastiques, auront inspiré Hiroshige pour son traitement des hachures, des effets d'ombre et de lumière et des lignes de fuite, d'après le modèle de la perspective centrale. Ce regard nouveau sur le paysage est un autre facteur important pour le succès de Hiroshige et il est significatif que ce soient les artistes graveurs et non les membres des écoles traditionnelles de peinture japonaise qui aient mis en œuvre les premiers cette innovation.

Umgang mit Schraffuren, Licht- und Schatteneffekten sowie Fluchten nach Vorbild der Zentralperspektive angeregt haben. Diese neue Sicht auf die Landschaft ist ein weiterer wichtiger Faktor für Hiroshiges Erfolg, und es ist bezeichnend, dass es die Holzschnittkünstler und nicht die Mitglieder der traditionellen japanischen Malschulen sind, die diese Innovation als erste umsetzen.

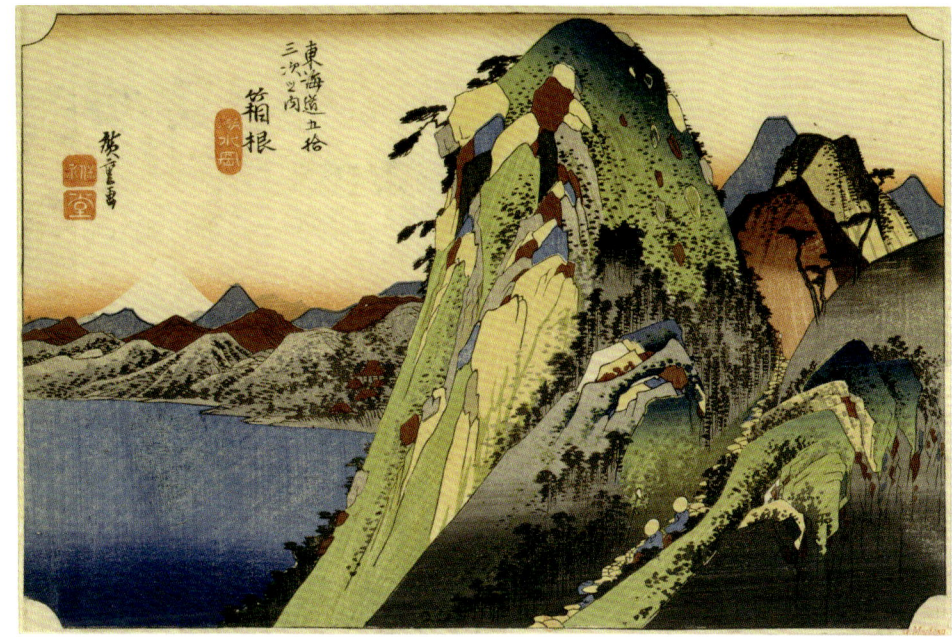

así como sus líneas de fuga siguiendo el ejemplo de la perspectiva frontal. Esta nueva visión del paisaje es otro factor importante en el éxito de Hiroshige, y es significativo que sean los xilógrafos, y no los miembros de las escuelas de dibujo tradicional, los primeros en adueñarse de esta innovación.

prospettiva centrale. Questa nuova visione del paesaggio è un ulteriore fattore di importanza per il successo di Hiroshige, ed è significativo che siano gli artisti xilografi e non i rappresentanti delle scuole di pittura giapponesi tradizionali a realizzare per primi questa tecnica innovativa.

hebben beïnvloed in zijn gebruik van arceringen, licht-donkereffecten en belijningen op basis van het eenpuntsperspectief. Deze nieuwe kijk op het landschap is een andere belangrijke reden voor Hiroshige's succes. Veelzeggend is ook dat het de prentkunstenaars zijn, niet de vertegenwoordigers van de traditionele Japanse schilderscholen, die deze vernieuwing als eersten toepassen.

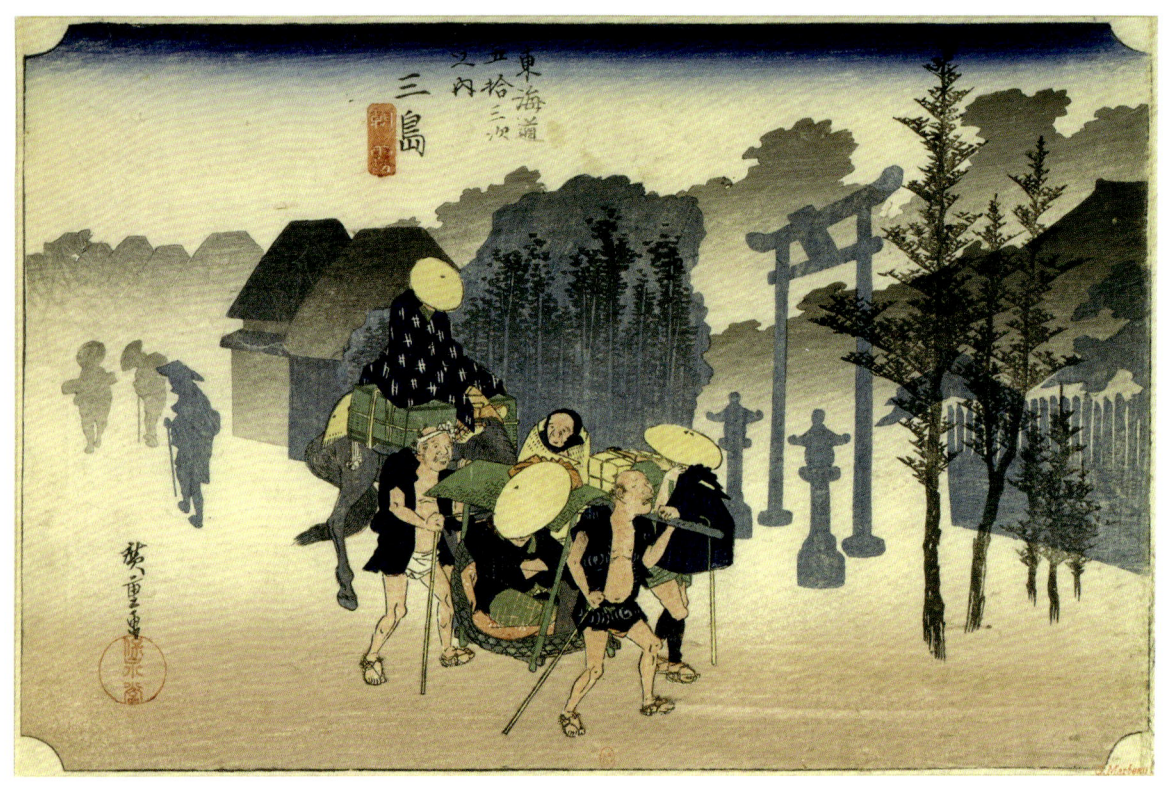

Mishima (early morning fog), Station 11

Brume matinale à Mishima, relais 11

Mishima (Der Frühnebel), Station 11

Mishima (La niebla de mañana), Estación 11

Mishima (nebbia mattutina), stazione 11

Mishima (Ochtendnevel), halteplaats 11

Colour woodcut/Gravure sur bois en couleurs, 22,2 × 34,4 cm, Bibliothèque Nationale, Paris

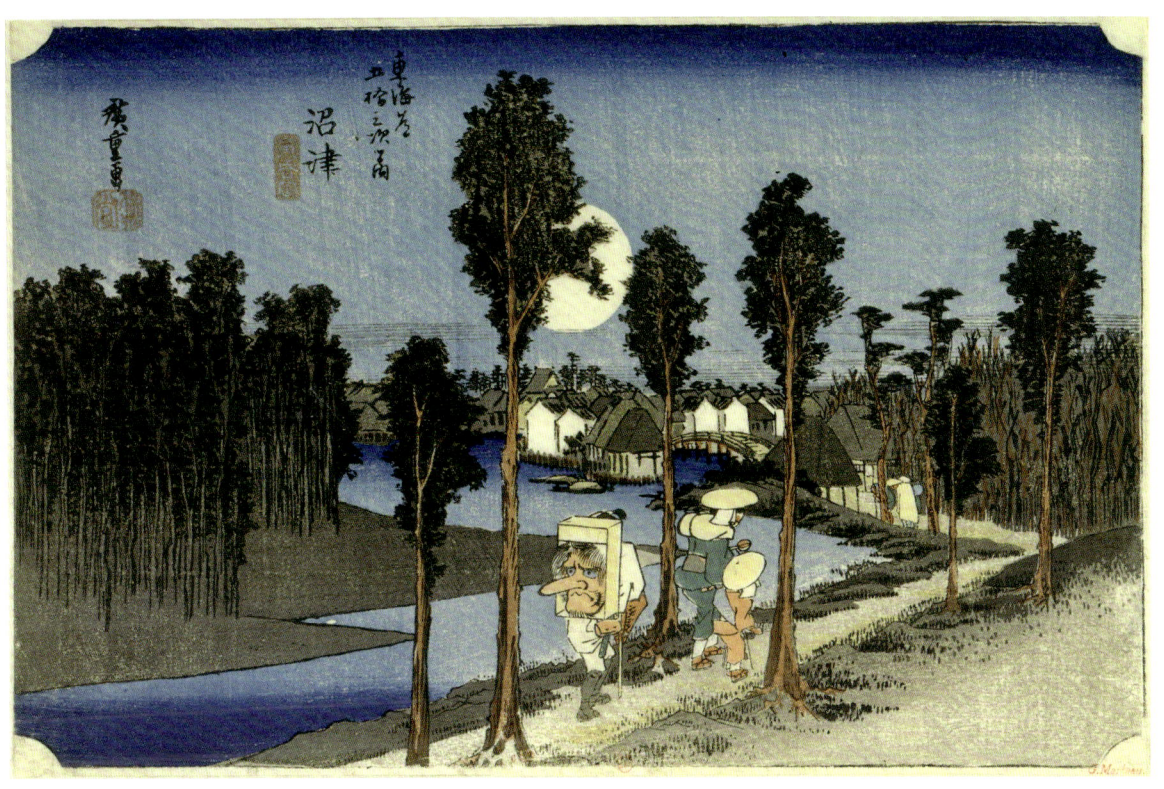

Numazu (at dusk), Station 12

Numazu (Le Crépuscule), relais 12

Numazu (Bei Dämmerung), Station 12

Numazu (Crepúsculo), Estación 12

Numazu (al crepuscolo), stazione 12

Numazu (In de schemering), halteplaats 12

Colour woodcut/Gravure sur bois en couleurs, 22,2×34,4 cm, Bibliothèque Nationale, Paris

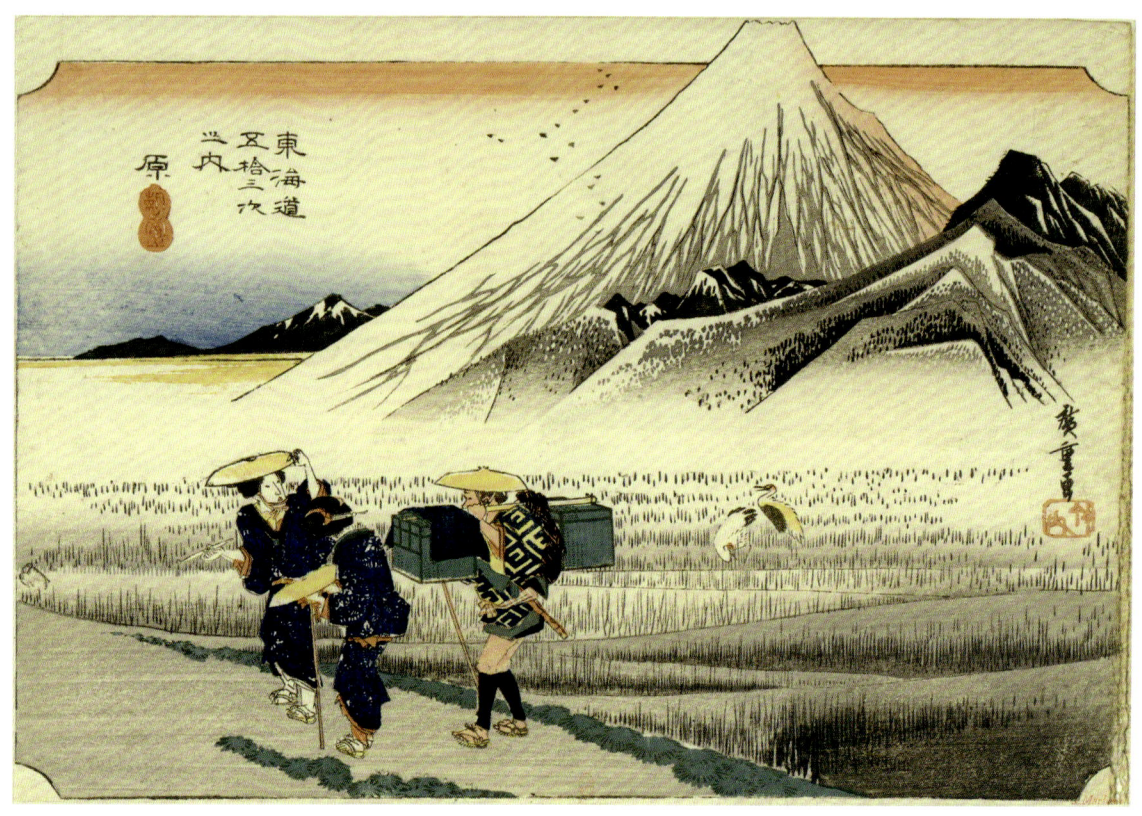

Hara (Mount Fuji in the morning), Station 13

Hara (Le Fuji le matin), relais 13

Hara (Der Fuji am Morgen), Station 13

Hara (El Fuji por la mañana),Estación 13

Hara (il Fuji al mattino), stazione 13

Hara (De Fuji in de ochtend), halteplaats 13

Colour woodcut/Gravure sur bois en couleurs, 22,2×34,4 cm, Bibliothèque Nationale, Paris

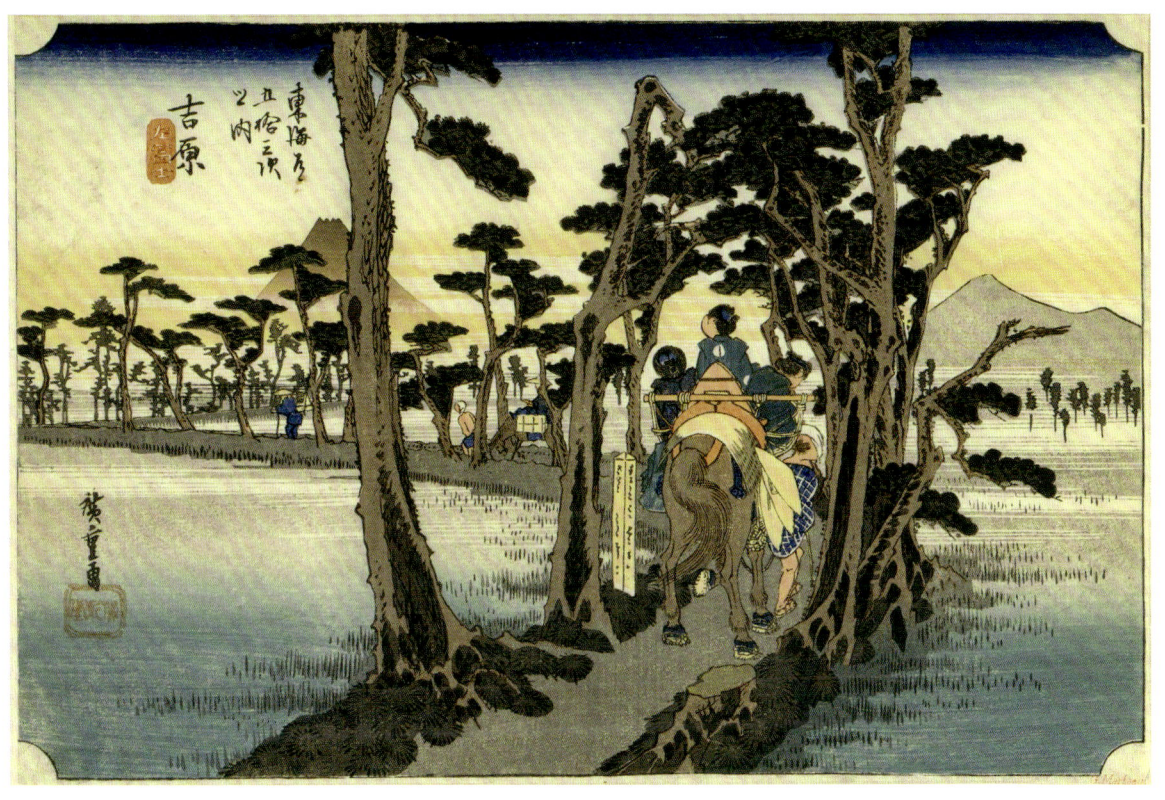

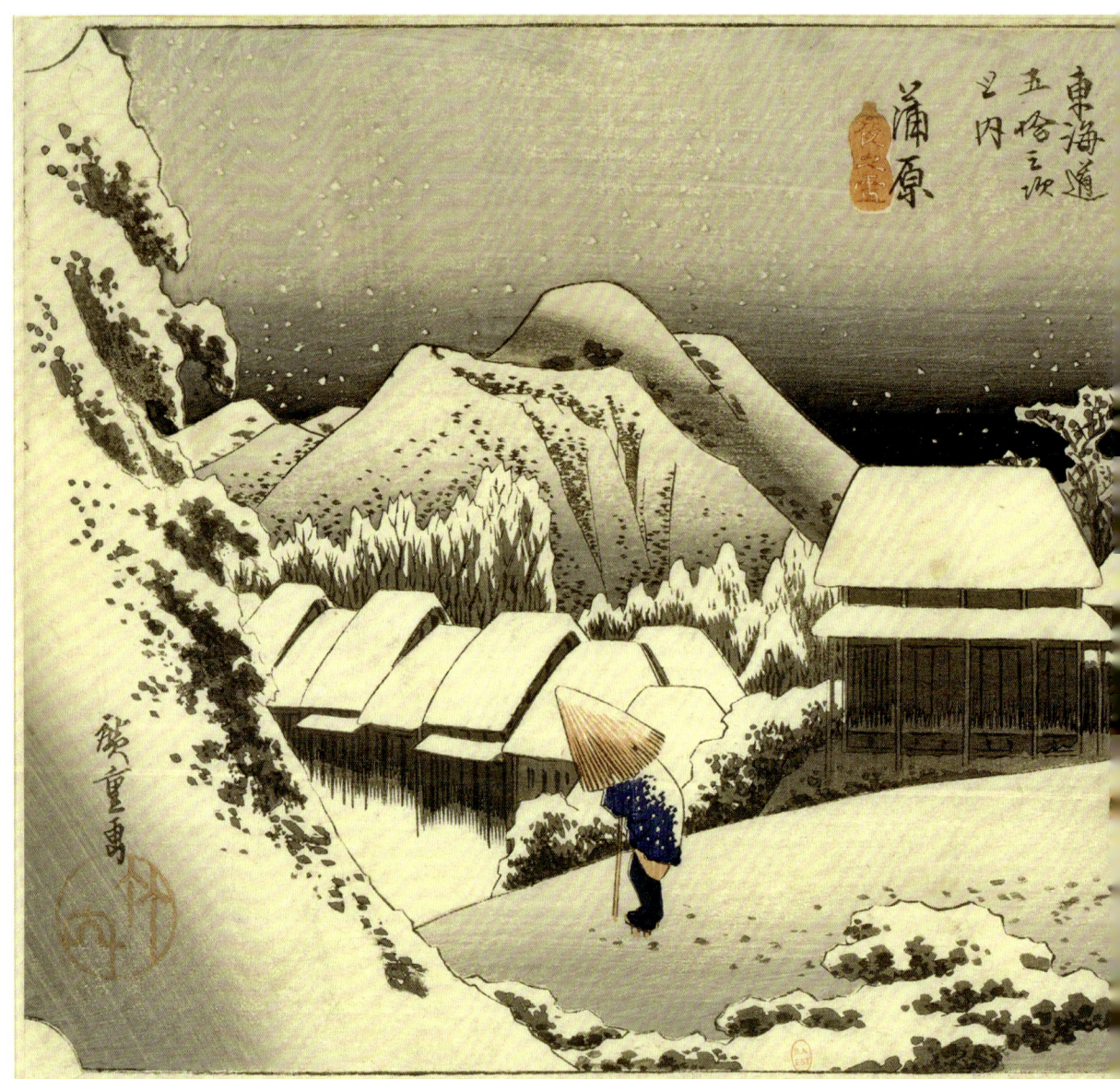

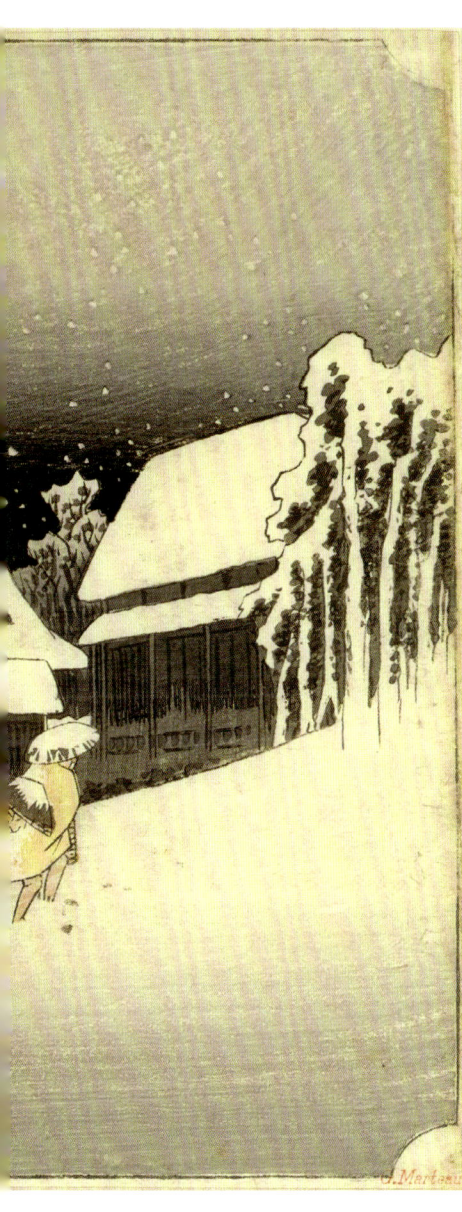

Kambara (snow at night), Station 15

Kambara (Neige de nuit), relais 15

Kambara (Schnee in der Nacht), Station 15

Kambara (Nieve por la noche), Estación 15

Kambara (neve nella notte), stazione 15

Kambara (Sneeuw in de nacht), halteplaats 15

Colour woodcut/Gravure sur bois en couleurs, 22,2×34,4 cm, Bibliothèque Nationale, Paris

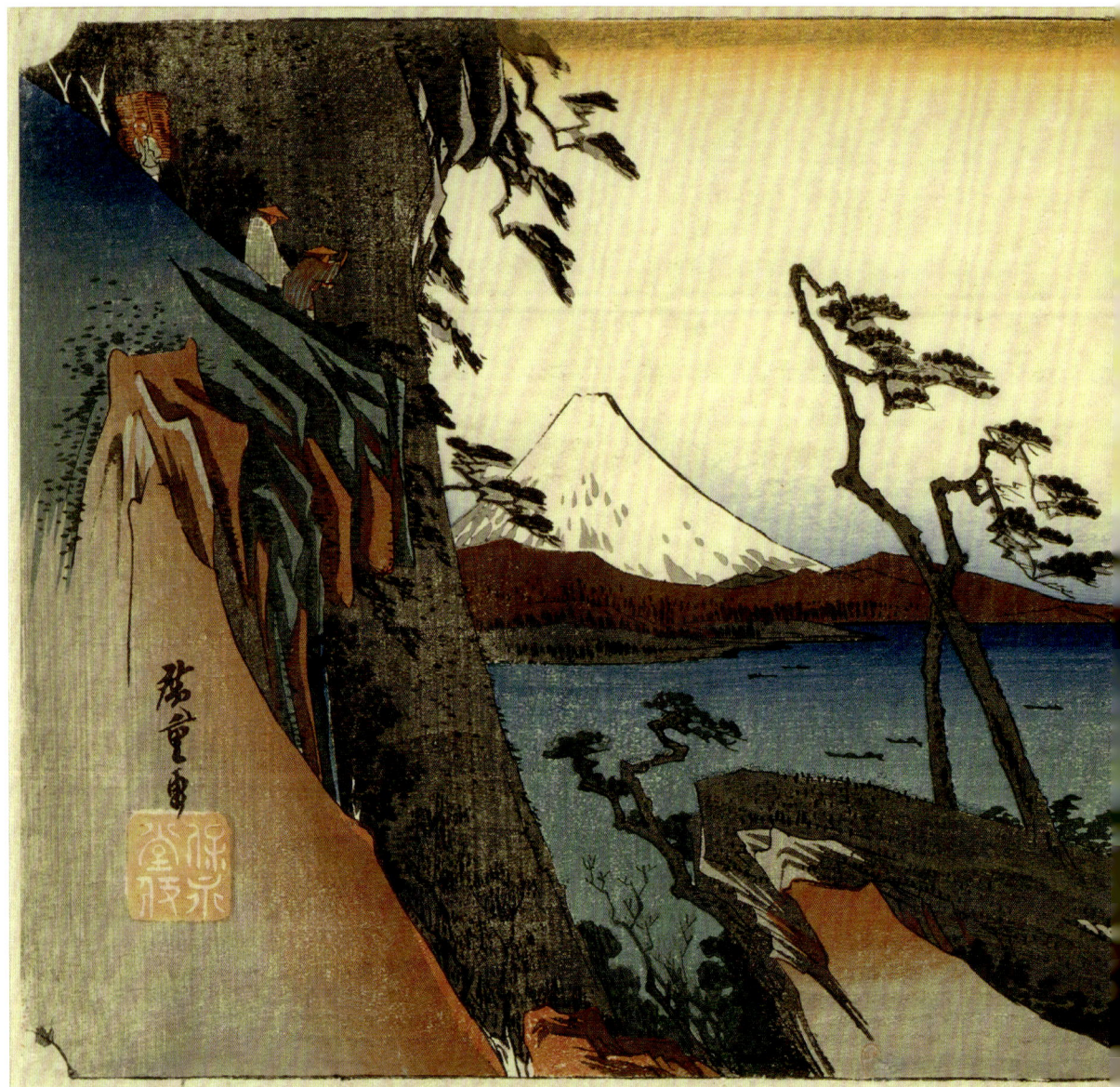

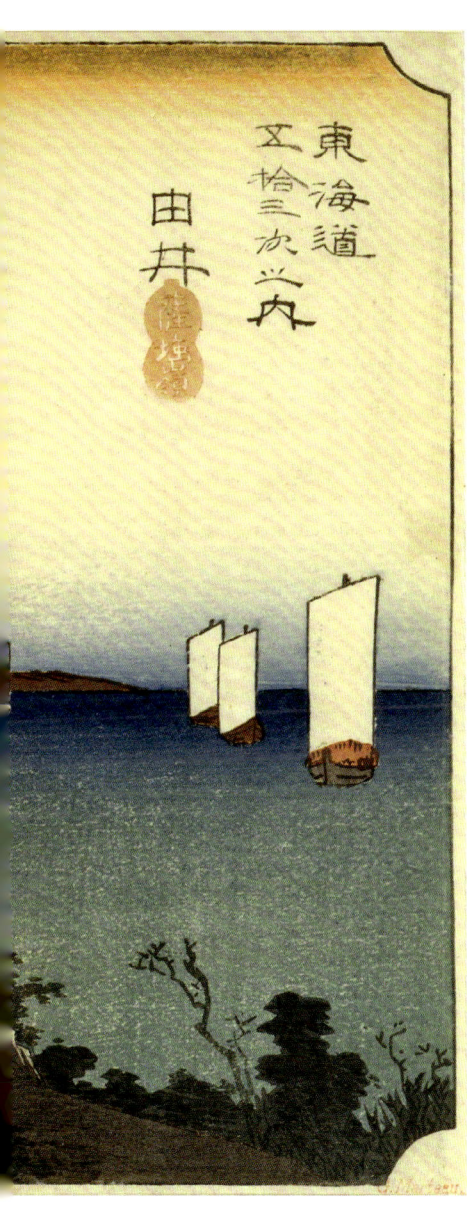

Yui (the Satta ridge), Station 16

Yui (Les Crêtes de Satta), relais 16

Yui (Der Bergkamm von Satta), Station 16

Yui (El pico del Satta), Estación 16

Yui (il passaggio di Satta), stazione 16

Yui (De Satta-bergkam), halteplaats 16

Colour woodcut/Gravure sur bois en couleurs, 22,2×34,4 cm, Bibliothèque Nationale, Paris

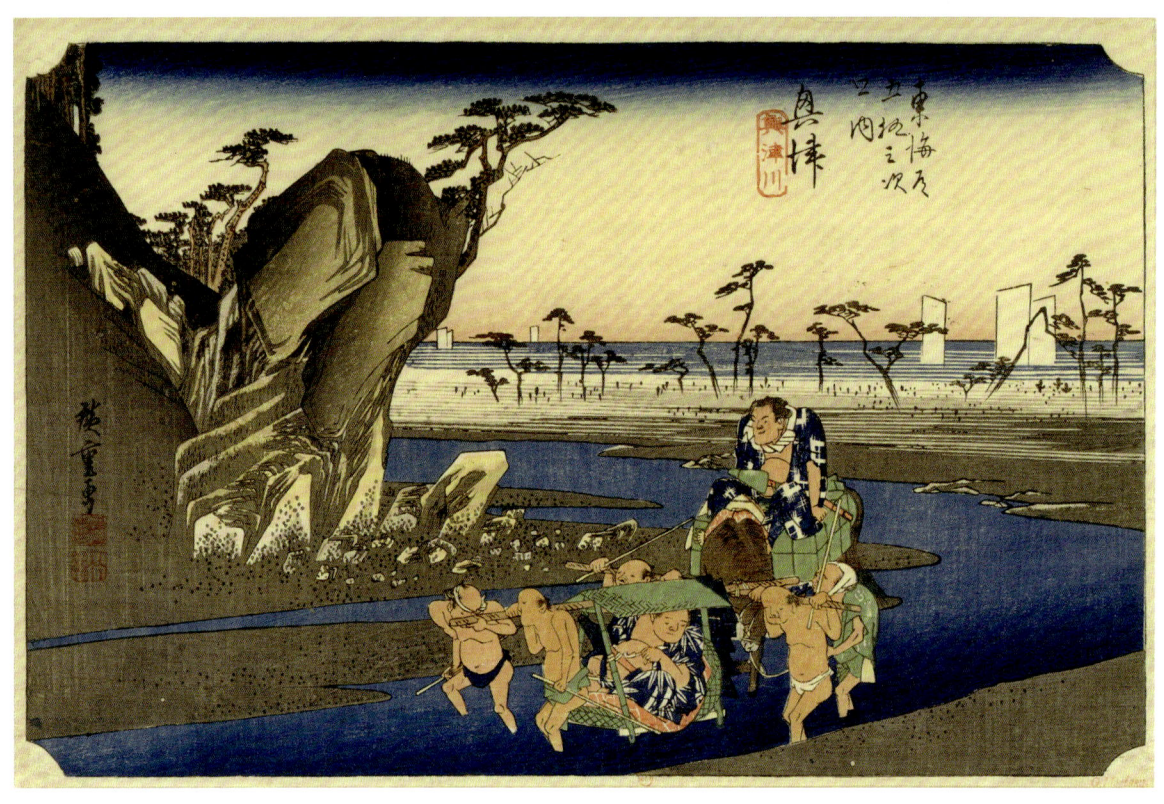

Okitsu (the river Okitsu), Station 17

Okitsu (Le Fleuve Okitsu), relais 17

Okitsu (Der Fluss Okitsu), Station 17

Okitsu (El río Okitsu), Estación 17

Okitsu (il fiume Okitsu), stazione 17

Okitsu (De rivier de Okitsu), halteplaats 17

Colour woodcut/Gravure sur bois en couleurs, 22,2×34,4 cm, Bibliothèque Nationale, Paris

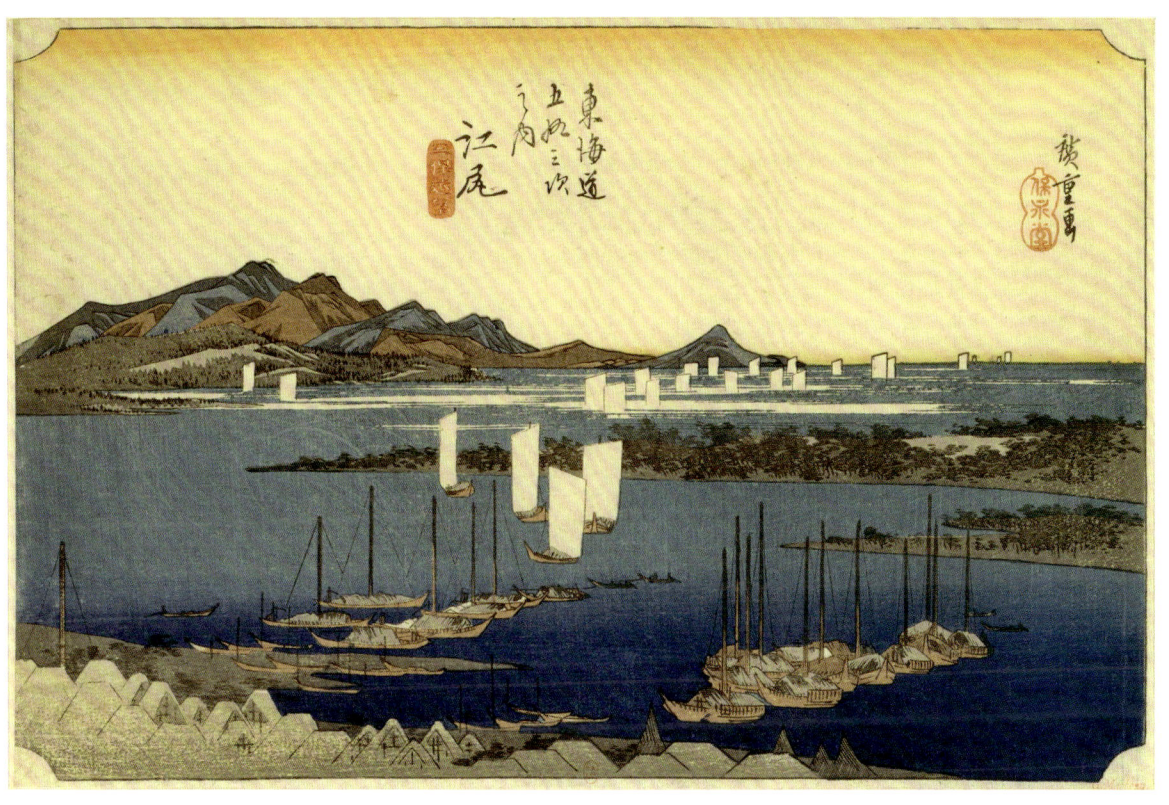

Ejiri (views of the pine forest of Miho), Station 18

Ejiri (Vue lointaine de Miho), relais 18

Ejiri (Ausblick auf den Kiefernwald von Miho), Station 18

Ejiri (Vista del bosque de pinos de Miho), Estación 18

Ejiri (vista sulla pineta di Miho), stazione 18

Ejiri (Uitzicht op het dennenbos van Miho), halteplaats 18

Colour woodcut/Gravure sur bois en couleurs, 22,2×34,4 cm, Bibliothèque Nationale, Paris

41

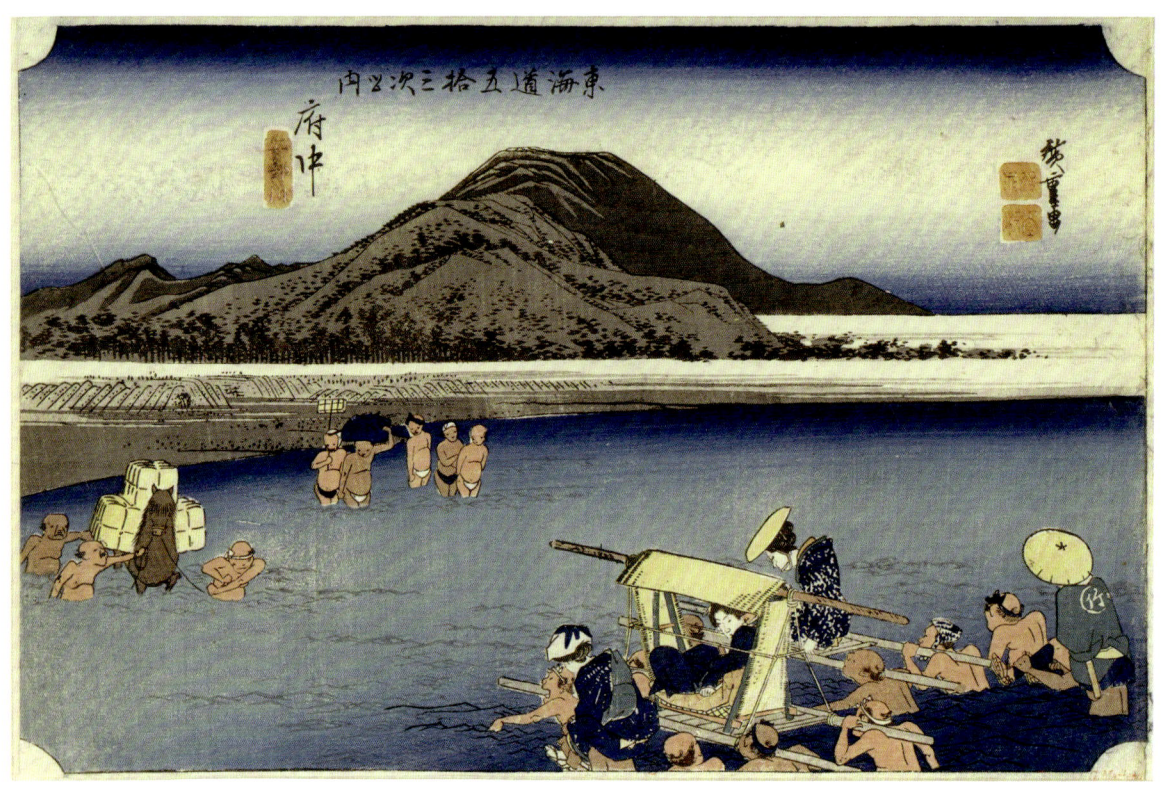

Fuchū (the river Abe), Station 19

Fuchū (Le Fleuve Abe), relais 19

Fuchū (Der Fluss Abe), Station 19

Fuchū (El río Abe), Estación 19

Fuchū (il fiume Abe), stazione 19

Fuchū (De rivier de Abe), Station 19

Colour woodcut/Gravure sur bois en couleurs, 22,2×34,4 cm, Bibliothèque Nationale, Paris

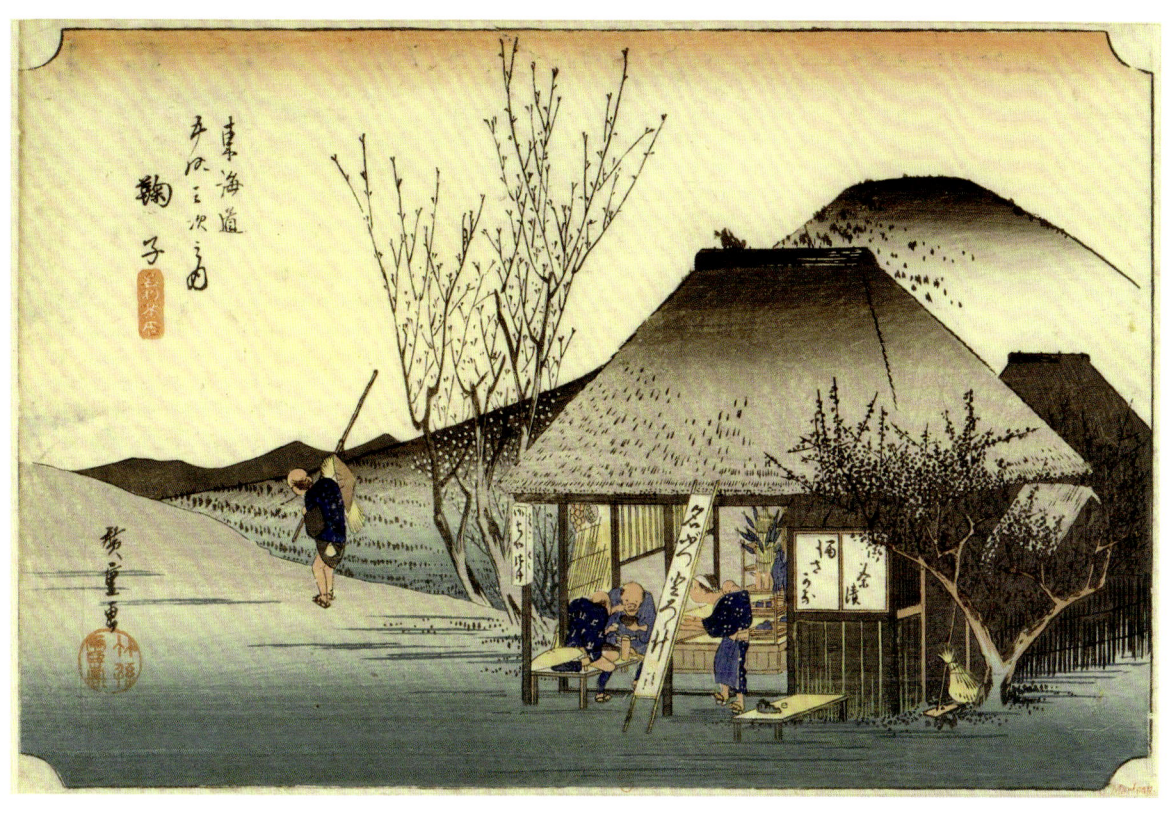

Mariko (tea house famous for its specialities), Station 20

Mariko (La Maison de thé aux spécialités célèbres), relais 20

Mariko (Teehaus der berühmten Spezialitäten), Station 20

Mariko (La tetería de las especialidades típicas), Estación 20

Mariko (casa da tè di famose specialità), stazione 20

Mariko (Theehuis van de beroemde specialiteiten), halteplaats 20

Colour woodcut/Gravure sur bois en couleurs, 22,2×34,4 cm, Bibliothèque Nationale, Paris

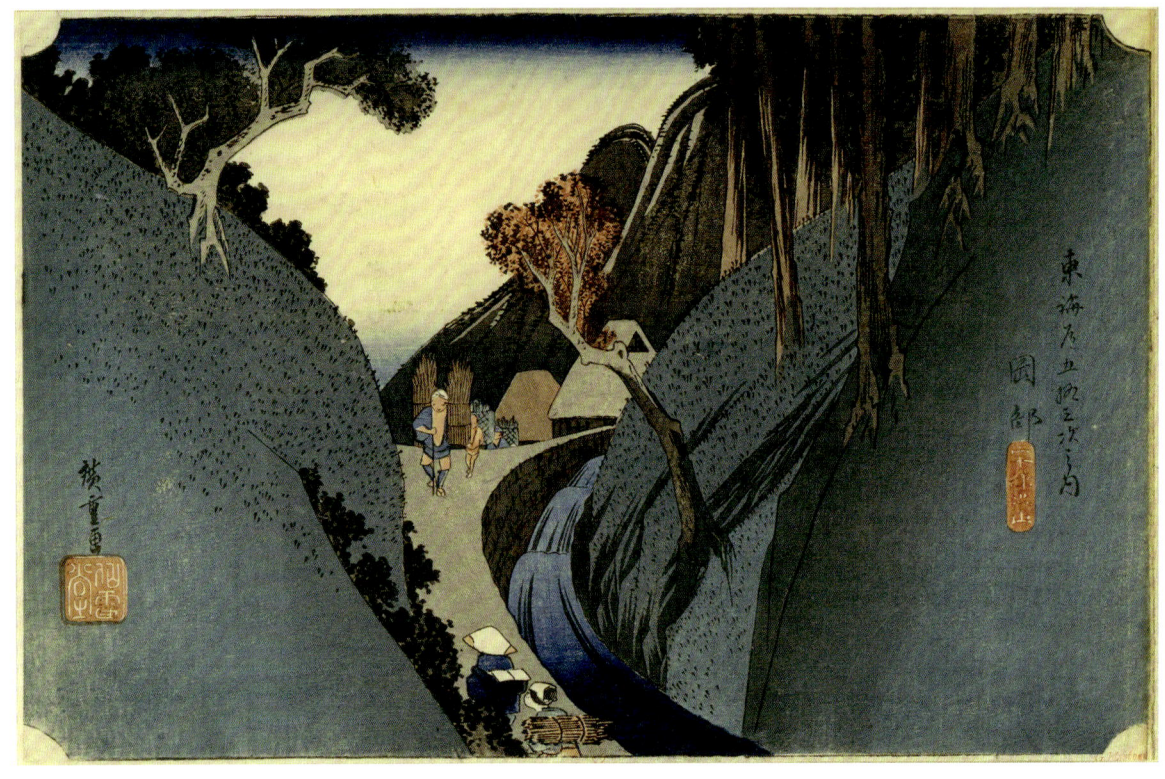

Okabe (Mount Utsu), Station 21

Okabe (Le Mont Utsu), relais 21

Okabe (Der Berg Utsu), Station 21

Okabe (El monte Utsu), Estación 21

Okabe (il monte Utsu), stazione 21

Okabe (De berg Utsu), halteplaats 21

Colour woodcut/Gravure sur bois en couleurs, 22,2×34,4 cm, Bibliothèque Nationale, Paris

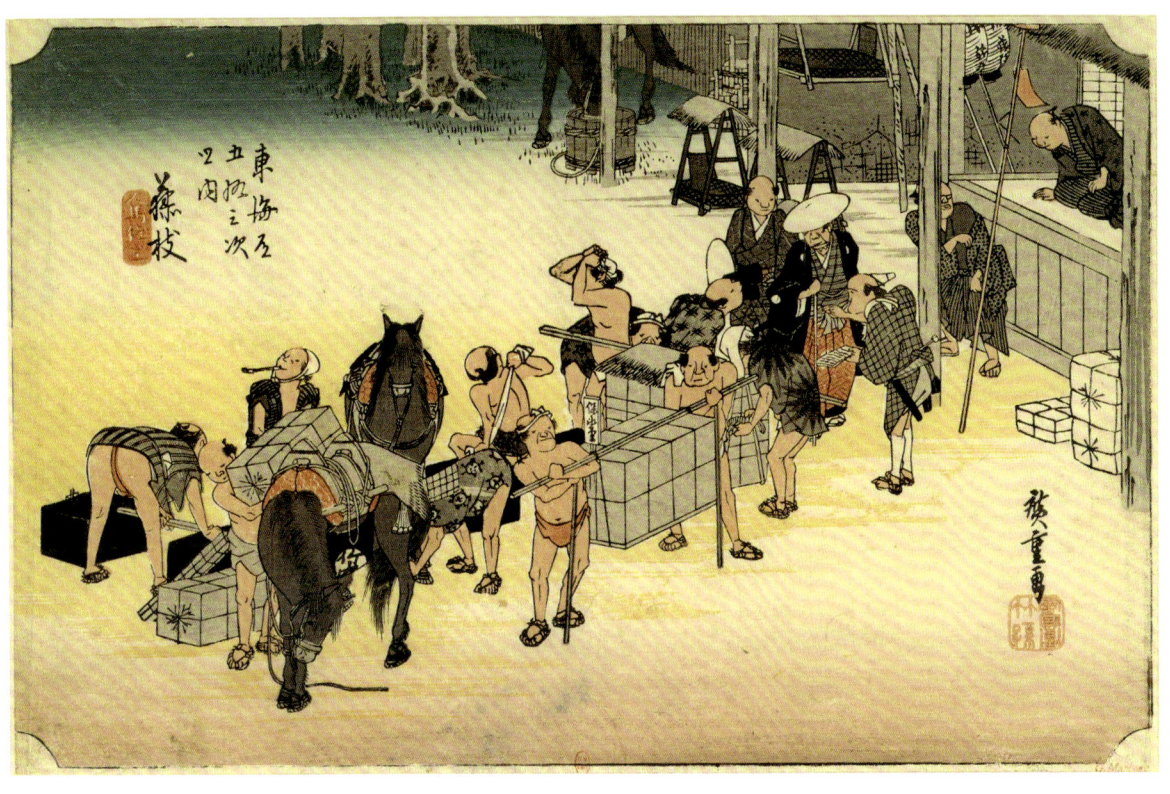

Fujieda (resting place for people and horses), Station 22

Fujieda (Relais de porteurs et de chevaux), relais 22

Fujieda (Rastplatz für Menschen und Pferde), Station 22

Fujieda (Lugar de descanso para caballos y hombres), Estación 22

Fujieda (luogo di sosta per uomini e cavalli), stazione 22

Fujieda (Rustplaats voor mensen en paarden), halteplaats 22

Colour woodcut/Gravure sur bois en couleurs, 22,2×34,4 cm, Bibliothèque Nationale, Paris

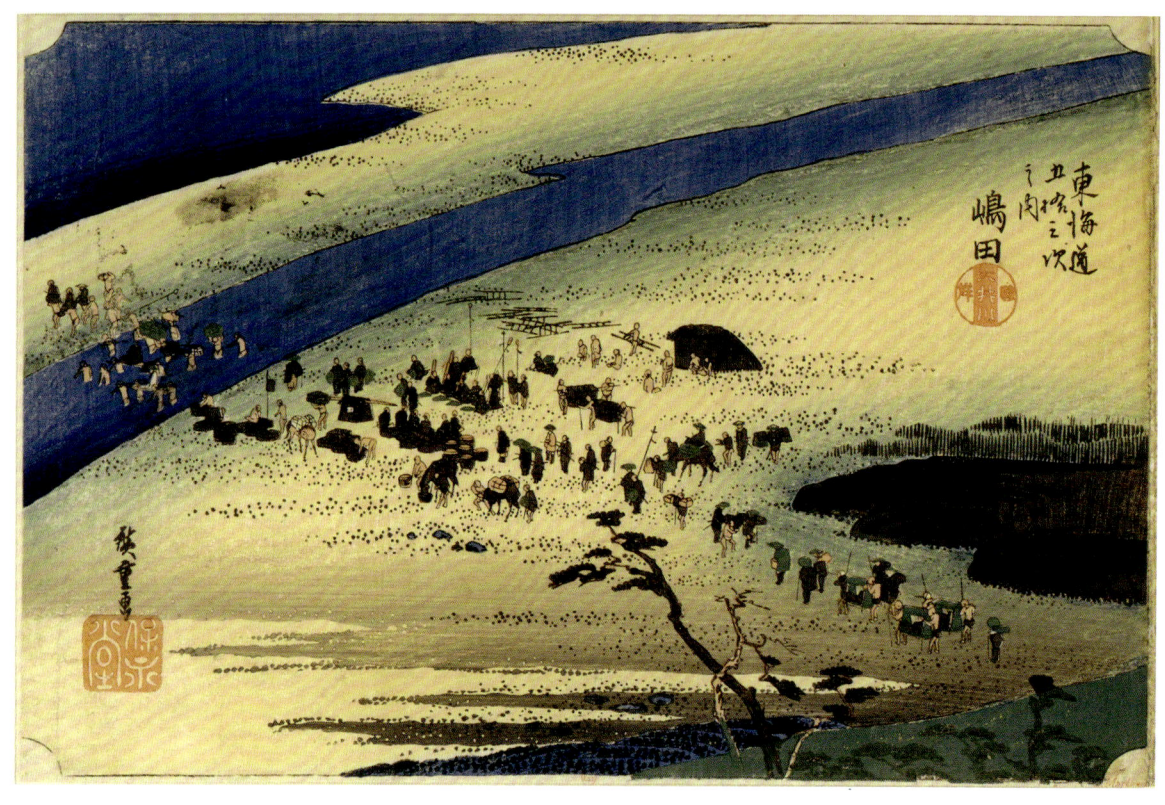

Shimada (the river Oi and the riverbank at Suruga), Station 23

Shimada (Le Fleuve Oi et les berges à Suruga), relais 23

Shimada (Der Fluss Oi und das Flussufer bei Suruga), Station 23

Shimada (El río Oi y la rivera del Suruga), Estación 23

Shimada (il fiume Oi e la riva del fiume a Suruga), stazione 23

Shimada (De rivier de Oi en de rivieroever bij Suruga), halteplaats 23

Colour woodcut/Gravure sur bois en couleurs, 22,2 × 34,4 cm, Bibliothèque Nationale, Paris

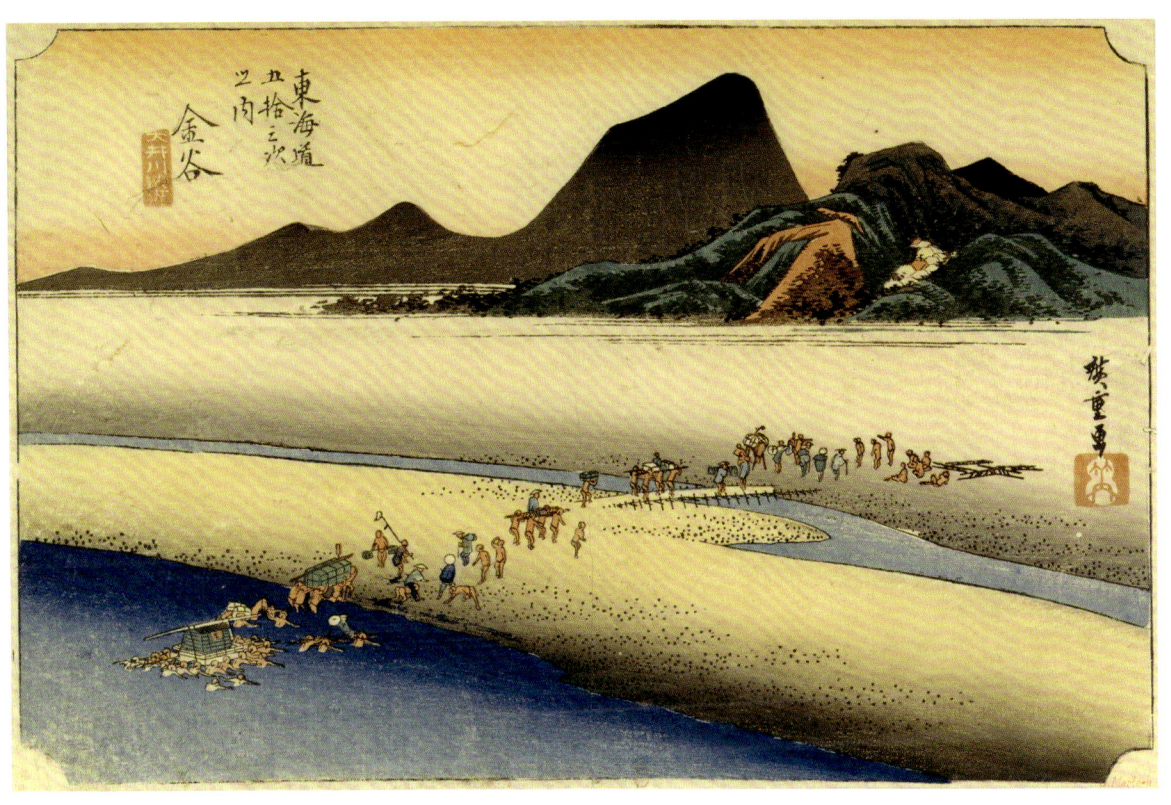

Kanaya (the other bank of the river Oi), Station 24
Kanaya (Rive lointaine du fleuve Oi), relais 24
Kanaya (Das andere Ufer des Flusses Oi), Station 24
Kanaya (La otra orilla del río Oi), Estación 24
Kanaya (l'altra riva del fiume Oi), stazione 24
Kanaya (De andere oever van de rivier de Oi), halteplaats 24
Colour woodcut/Gravure sur bois en couleurs, 22,2×34,4 cm, Bibliothèque Nationale, Paris

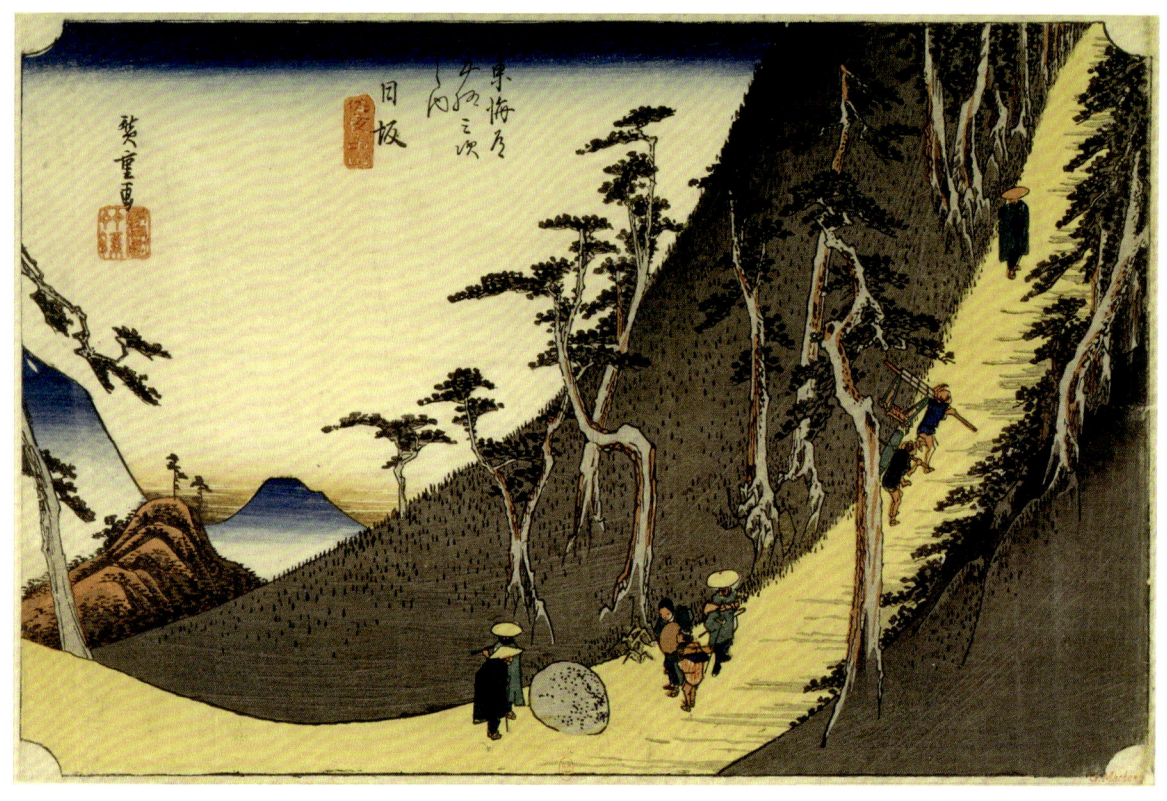

Nissaka (Mount Sayo), Station 25

Nissaka (La montagne de Sayo), relais 25

Nissaka (Der Berg Sayo), Station 25

Nissaka (El monte Sayo), Estación 25

Nissaka (il monte Sayo), stazione 25

Nissaka (De berg Sayo), halteplaats 25

Colour woodcut/Gravure sur bois en couleurs, 22,2×34,4 cm, Bibliothèque Nationale, Paris

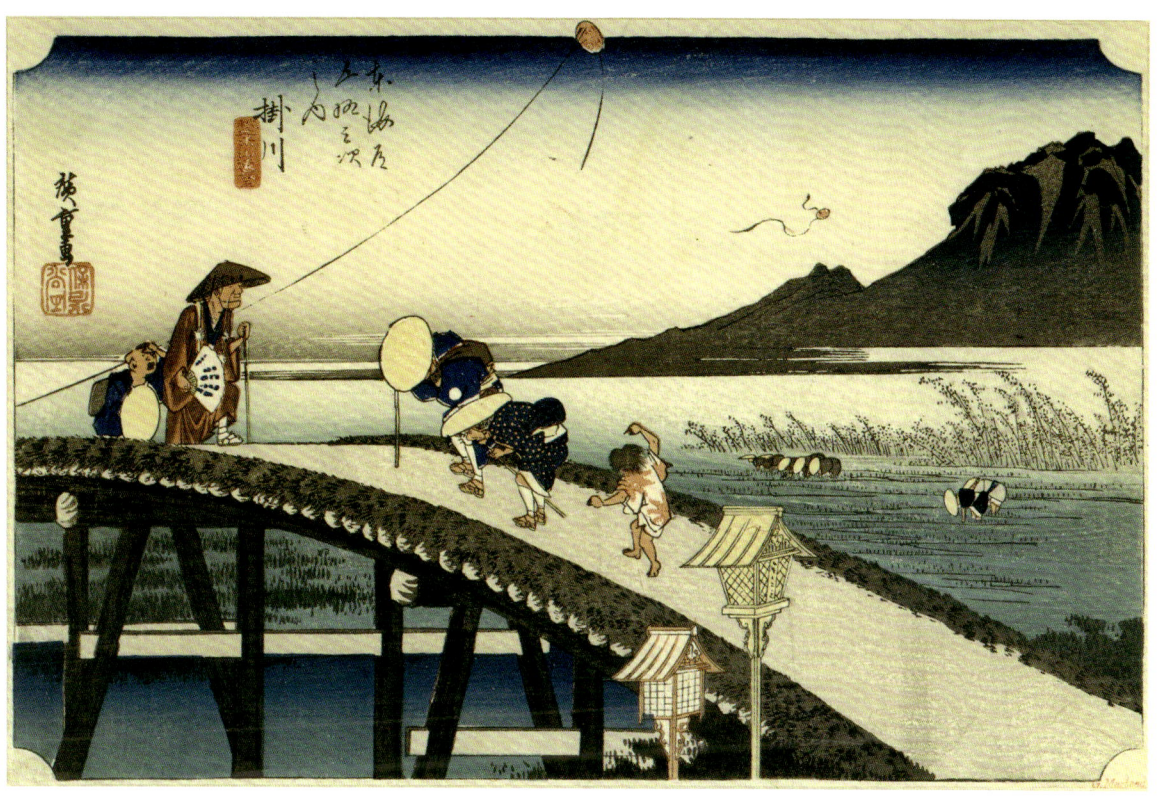

Kagegawa (Mount Akiba in the distance), Station 26
Kagegawa (Vue lointaine du mont Akiba), relais 26
Kagegawa (In der Ferne der Berg Akiba), Station 26
Kagegawa (El monte Akiba en la lejanía), Estación 26
Kagegawa (il monte Akiba in lontananza), stazione 26
Kagegawa (met in de verte de berg Akiba), halteplaats 26
Colour woodcut/Gravure sur bois en couleurs, 22,2×34,4 cm, Bibliothèque Nationale, Paris

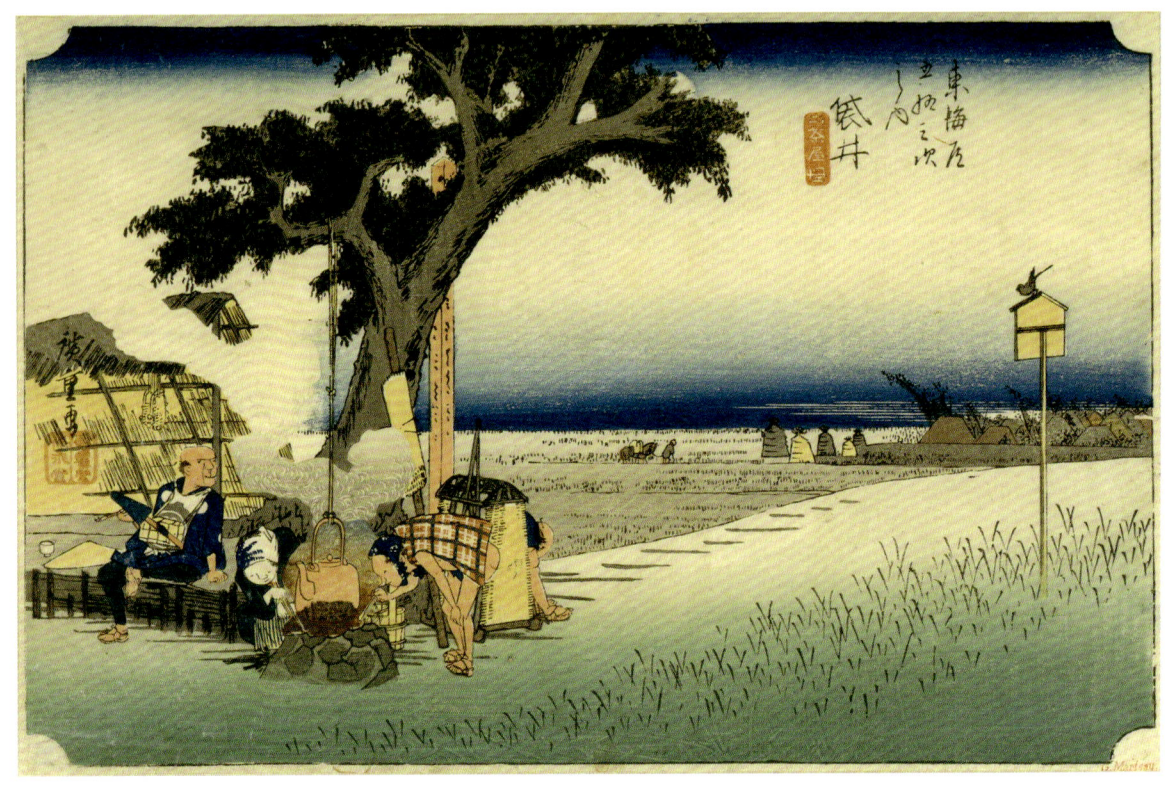

Fukuroi (outdoor tea house), Station 27

Fukuroi (La Maison de thé en plein air), relais 27

Fukuroi (Das Teehaus unter freiem Himmel), Station 27

Fukuroi (La tetería al aire libre), Estación 27

Fukuroi (la casa da tè all'aperto), stazione 27

Fukuroi (Theehuis in de openlucht), halteplaats 27

Colour woodcut/Gravure sur bois en couleurs, 22,2×34,4 cm, Bibliothèque Nationale, Paris

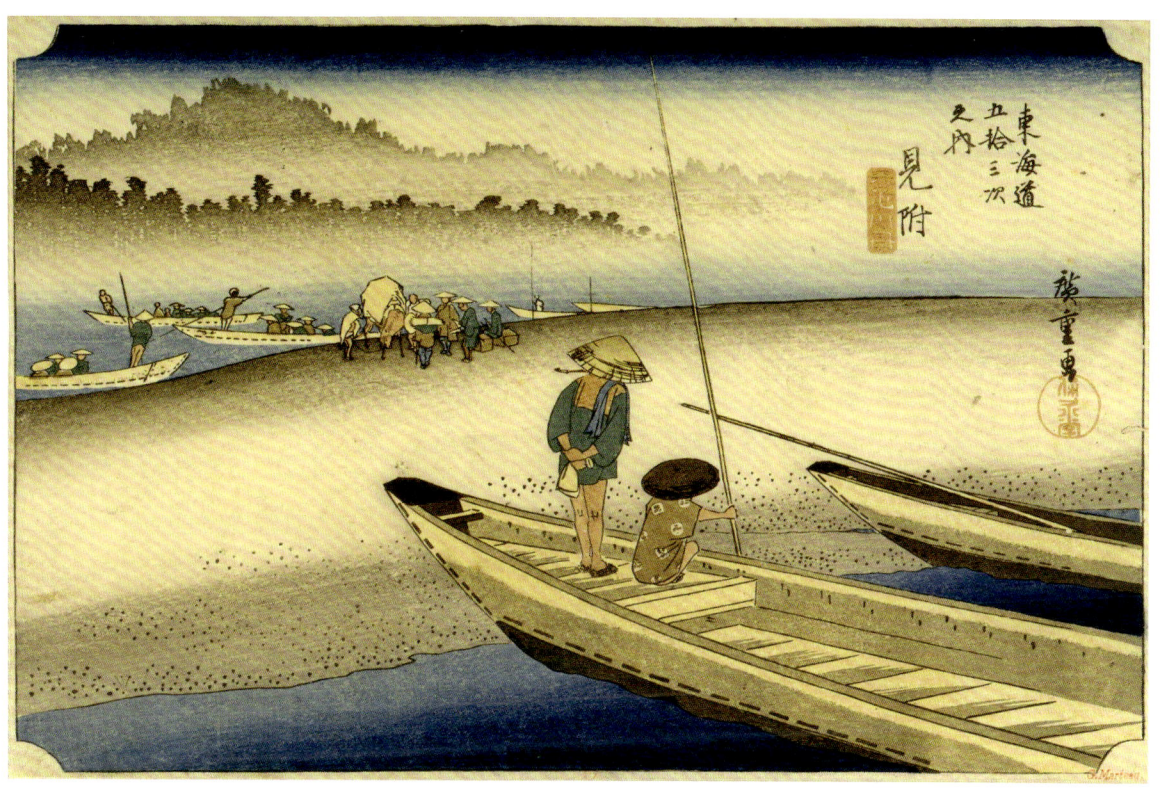

Mitsuke (the river Tenryū), Station 28

Mitsuke (Vue du fleuve Tenryū), relais 28

Mitsuke (Der Fluss Tenryū), Station 28

Mitsuke (El río Tenryū), Estación 28

Mitsuke (il fiume Tenryū), stazione 28

Mitsuke (De rivier de Tenryū), halteplaats 28

Colour woodcut/Gravure sur bois en couleurs, 22,2×34,4 cm, Bibliothèque Nationale, Paris

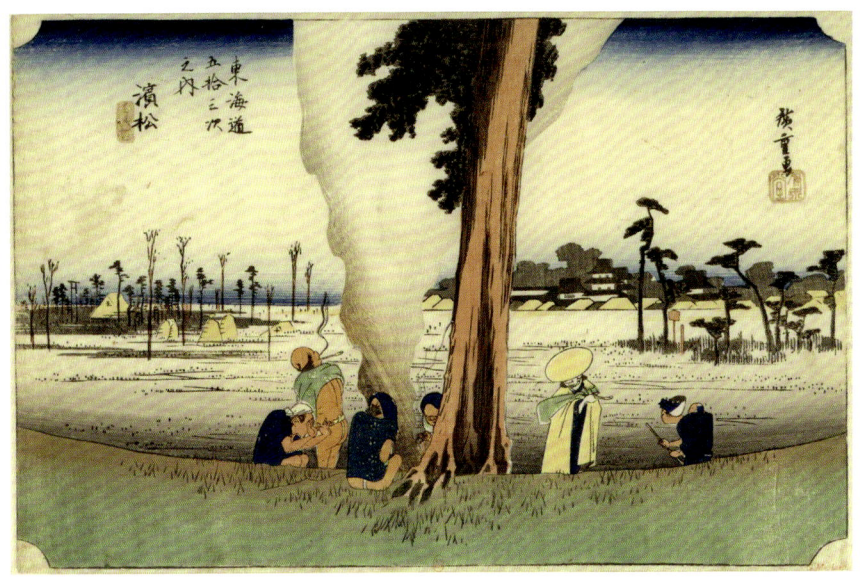

Hamamatsu in dreary winter, Station 29

Hamamatsu, la désolation de l'hiver, relais 29

Hamamatsu im trostlosen Winter, Station 29

Hamamatsu en el sombrío invierno, Estación 29

Hamamatsu nell'inverno desolato, stazione 29

Hamamatsu in een troosteloze winter, halteplaats 29

Colour woodcut/Gravure sur bois en couleurs, 22,2×34,4 cm, Bibliothèque Nationale, Paris

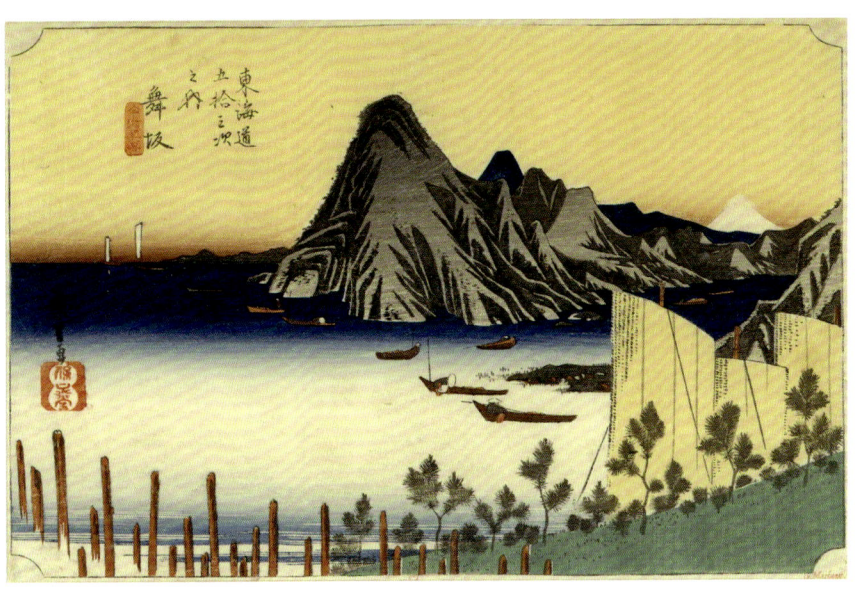

Maisaka (the cliffs of Imagiri), Station 30

Maisaka (Paysage caractéristique d'Imagiri), relais 30

Maisaka (Die Steilküste von Imagiri), Station 30

Maisaka (Los acantilados de Imagiri), Estación 30

Maisaka (la costa ripida di Imagiri), stazione 30

Maisaka (De rotskust van Imagiri), halteplaats 30

Colour woodcut/Gravure sur bois en couleurs, 22,2×34,4 cm, Bibliothèque Nationale, Paris

Arai (ferry), Station 31

Arai (Les Bacs), relais 31

Arai (Die Fähre), Station 31

Arai (Los barcos), Estación 31

Arai (il traghetto), stazione 31

Arai (Veerpont), halteplaats 31

Colour woodcut/Gravure sur
bois en couleurs, 22,2×34,4 cm,
Bibliothèque Nationale, Paris

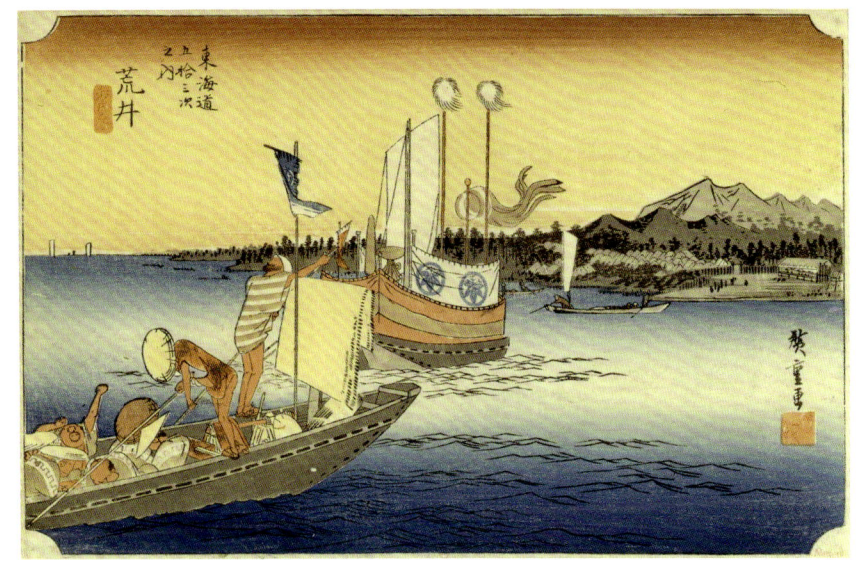

Landscape at Shirasuga, Station 32

Paysage près de Shirasuga, relais 32

*Landschaft bei Shirasuga,
Station 32*

Paisaje en Shirasuga, Estación 32

Paesaggio a Shirasuga, stazione 32

*Landschap bij Shirasuga,
halteplaats 32*

Colour woodcut/Gravure sur
bois en couleurs, 22,2×34,4 cm,
Bibliothèque Nationale, Paris

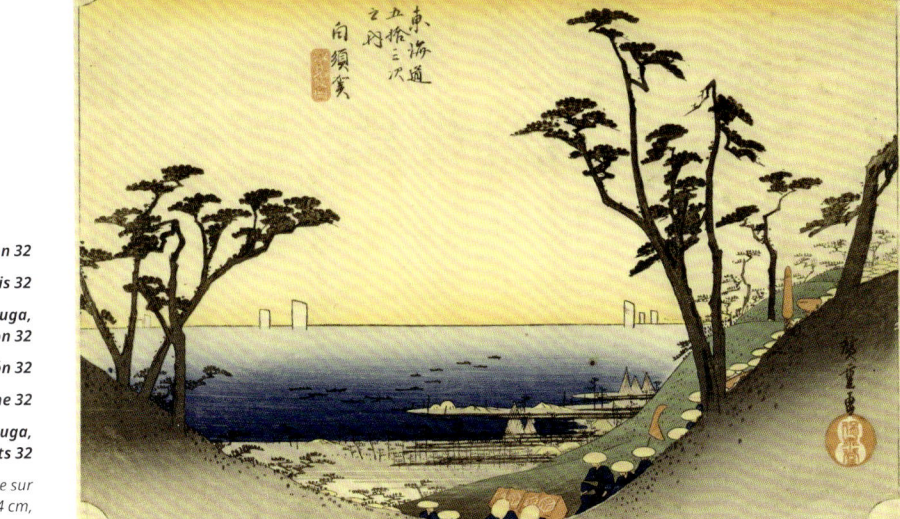

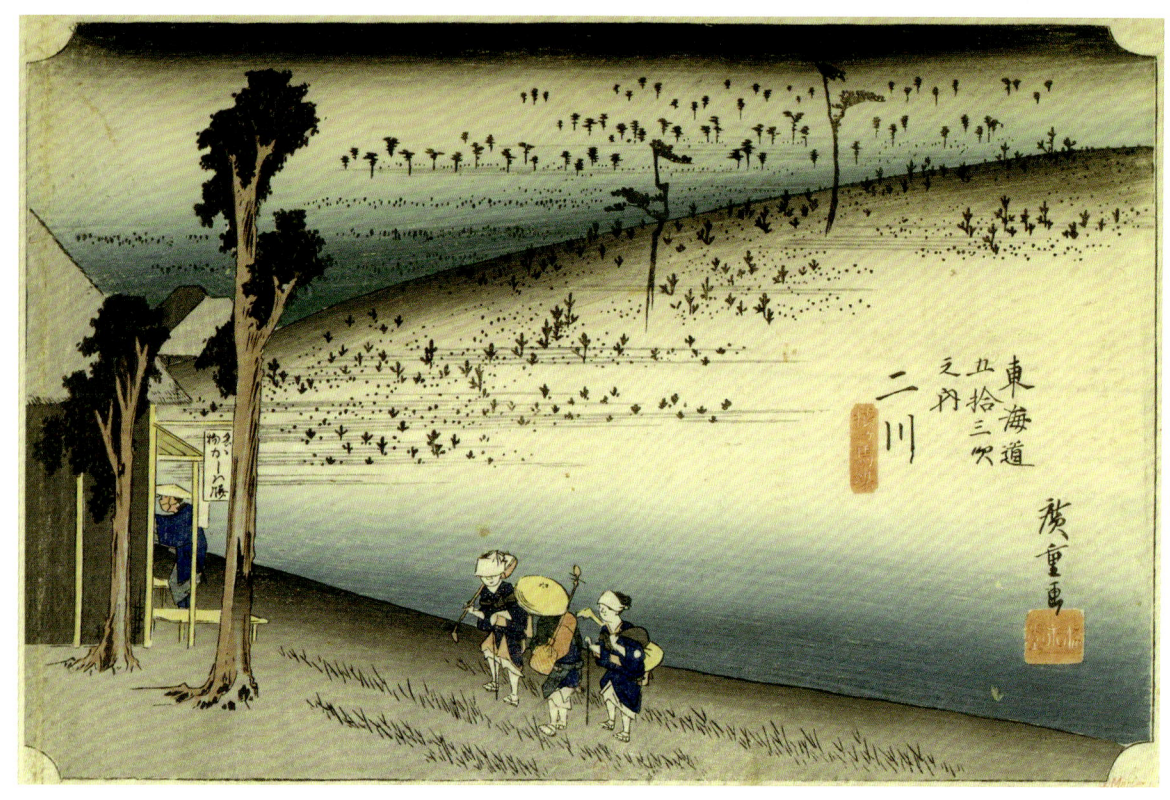

Futagawa (the rest station of the monkeys), Station 33

Futakawa (Le Relais des singes), relais 33

Futagawa (Die Raststation der Affen), Station 33

Futagawa (La llanura de los monos), Estación 33

Futagawa (stazione di sosta delle scimmie), stazione 33

Futagawa (Het apenplateau), halteplaats 33

Colour woodcut/Gravure sur bois en couleurs, 22,2×34,4 cm, Bibliothèque Nationale, Paris

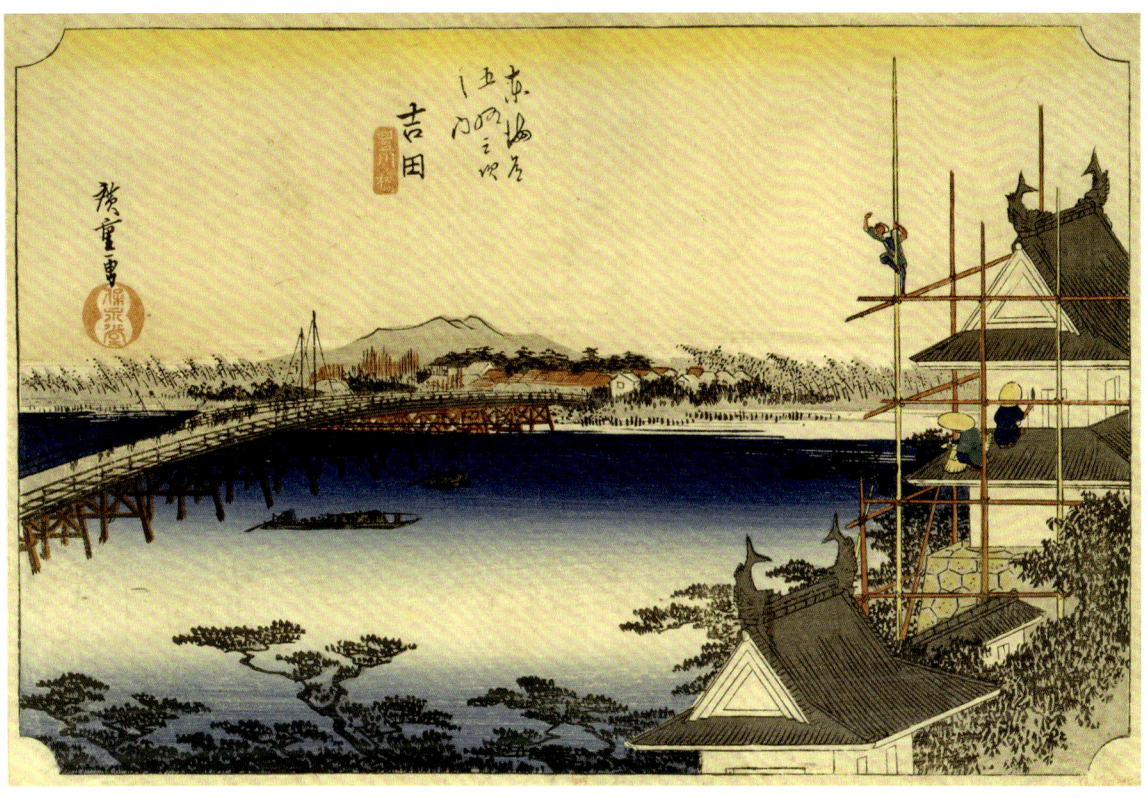

Yoshida (the bridge over the river Toyo), Station 34
Yoshida (Le Pont sur le fleuve Toyo), relais 34
Yoshida (Die Brücke über den Fluss Toyo), Station 34
Yoshida (El puente sobre el río Toyo), Estación 34
Yoshida (il ponte sul fiume Toyo), stazione 34
Yoshida (De brug over de rivier de Toyo), halteplaats 34
Colour woodcut/Gravure sur bois en couleurs, 22,2×34,4 cm, Bibliothèque Nationale, Paris

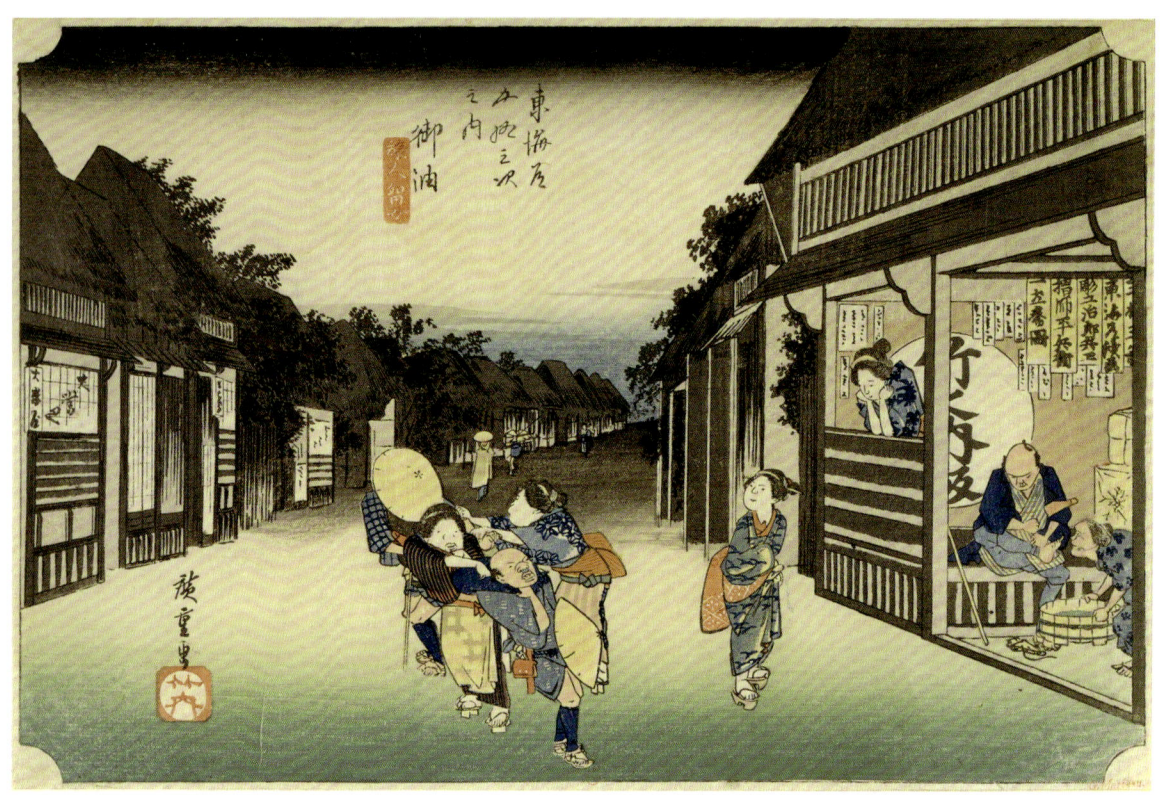

Goyu (women who waylays the traveller), Station 35

Goyu (Les servantes qui racolent les voyageurs), relais 35

Goyu (Die Frauen, die die Reisenden festhalten), Station 35

Goyu (Las mujeres reteniendo a los viajeros), Estación 35

Goyu (Le donne che trattengono i viaggiatori), stazione 35

Goyu (Vrouwen die de reizigers aanklampen), halteplaats 35

Colour woodcut/Gravure sur bois en couleurs, 22,2×34,4 cm, Bibliothèque Nationale, Paris

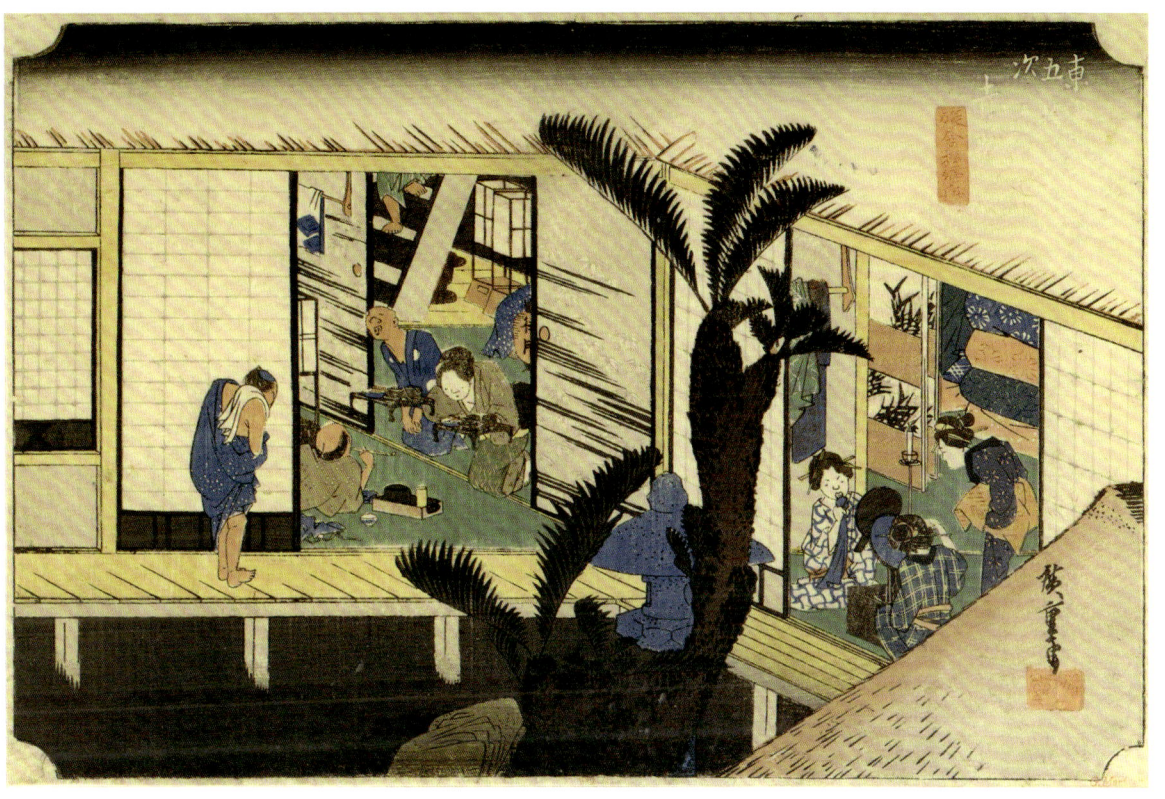

Akasaka (hostesses at the inn), Station 36

Akasaka (Les Hôtesses de l'auberge), relais 36

Akasaka (Die Gastgeberinnen in der Herberge), Station 36

Akasaka (La anfitriona en el albergue), Estación 36

Akasaka (le osti nella locanda), stazione 36

Akasaka (Gastvrouwen in de herberg), halteplaats 36

Colour woodcut/Gravure sur bois en couleurs, 22,2×34,4 cm, Bibliothèque Nationale, Paris

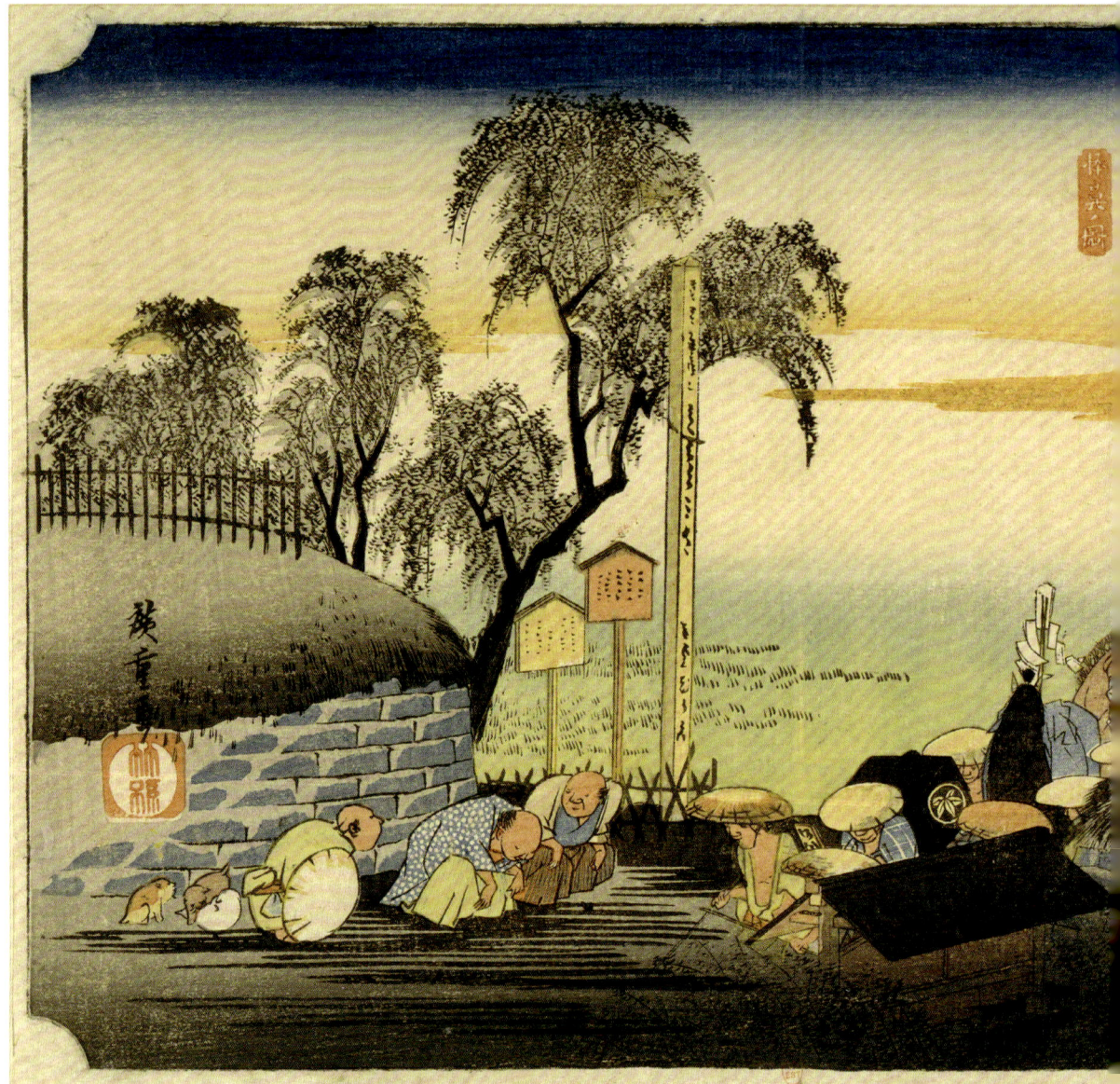

58

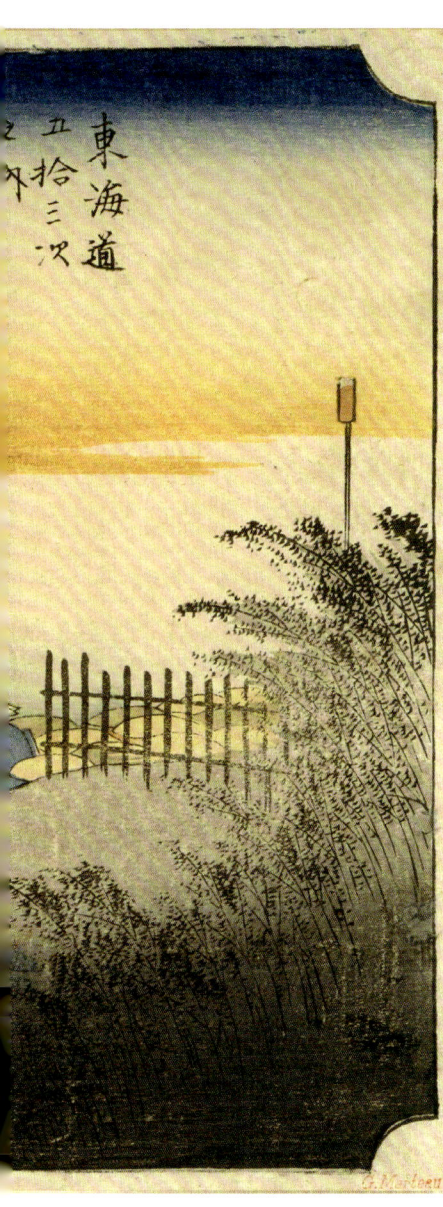

Fujikawa (head of a daimyo's procession), Station 37

Fujikawa (Tête de cortège), relais 37

Fujikawa (Die Spitze eines Fürstengefolges), Station 37

Fujikawa (cabeza del séquito de un príncipe), Estación 37

Fujikawa (la testa di un seguito di un principe), stazione 37

Fujikawa (Aan het hoofd van het gevolg van een vorst), halteplaats 37

Colour woodcut/Gravure sur bois en couleurs, 22,2×34,4 cm, Bibliothèque Nationale, Paris

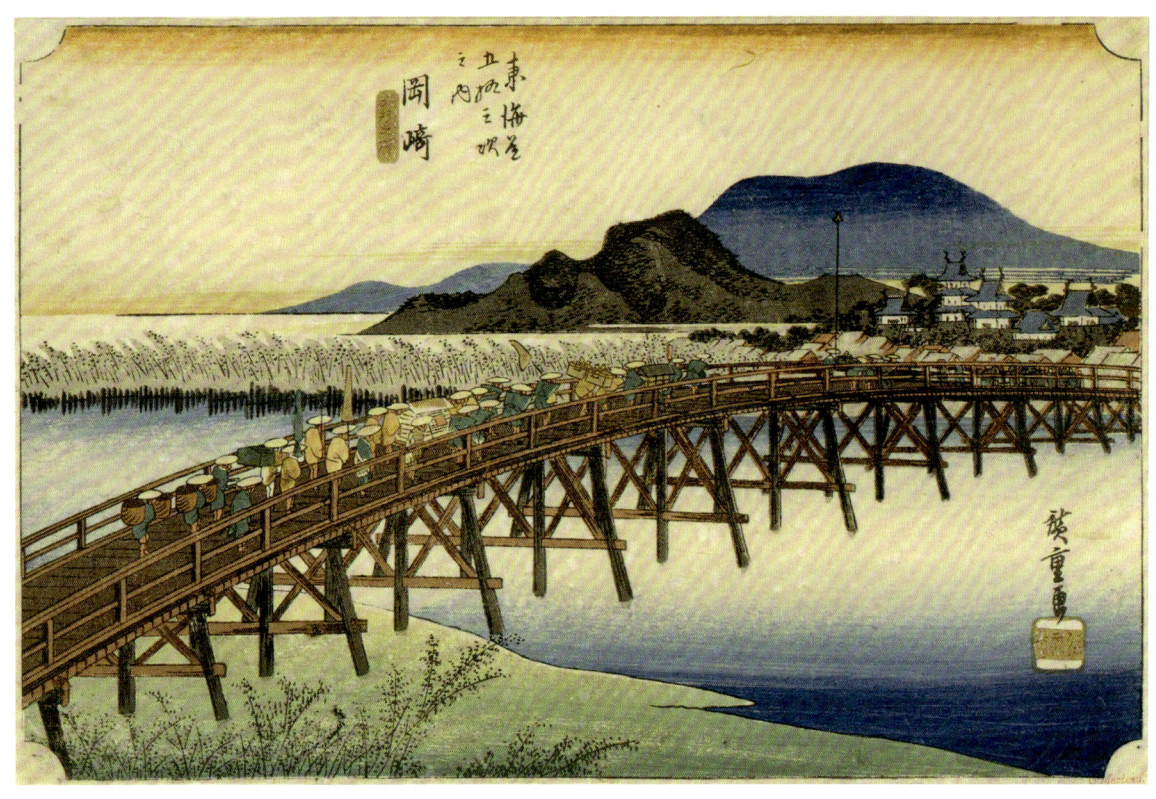

Okazaki (Yahagi bridge), Station 38

Okazaki (Le Pont Yahagi), relais 38

Okazaki (Die Brücke Yahagi), Station 38

Okazaki (El puente Yahagi), Estación 38

Okazaki (il ponte Yahagi), stazione 38

Okazaki (De Yahagi-brug), halteplaats 38

Colour woodcut/Gravure sur bois en couleurs, 22,2 × 34,4 cm, Bibliothèque Nationale, Paris

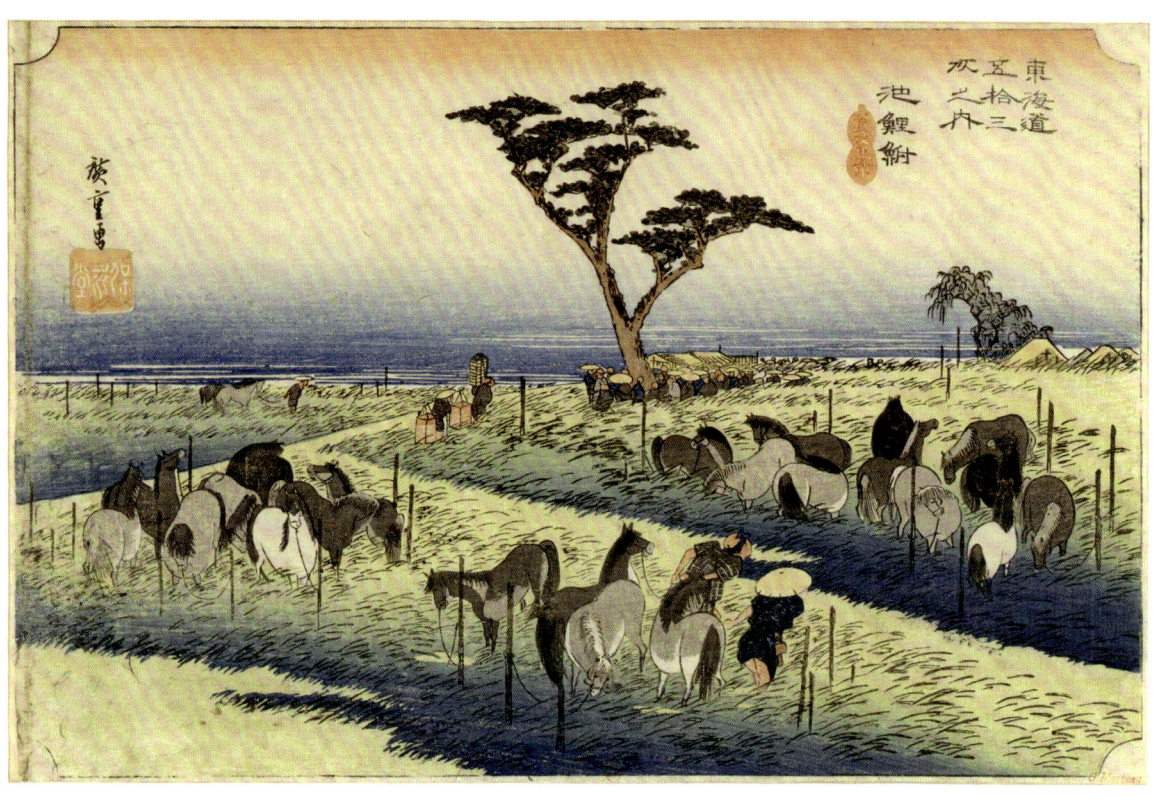

東
海
道
五
拾
三
之
内

池
鯉
鮒

Chiryu (horse market at the beginning of summer), Station 39

Chiryu (La Foire aux chevaux au début de l'été), relais 39

Chiryu (Der Pferdemarkt zu Sommeranfang), Station 39

Chiryu (El mercado de caballos al inicio del verano), Estación 39

Chiryu (il mercato dei cavalli all'inizio dell'estate) stazione 39

Chiryu (Paardenmarkt aan het begin van de zomer), halteplaats 39

Colour woodcut/Gravure sur bois en couleurs, 22,2×34,4 cm, Bibliothèque Nationale, Paris

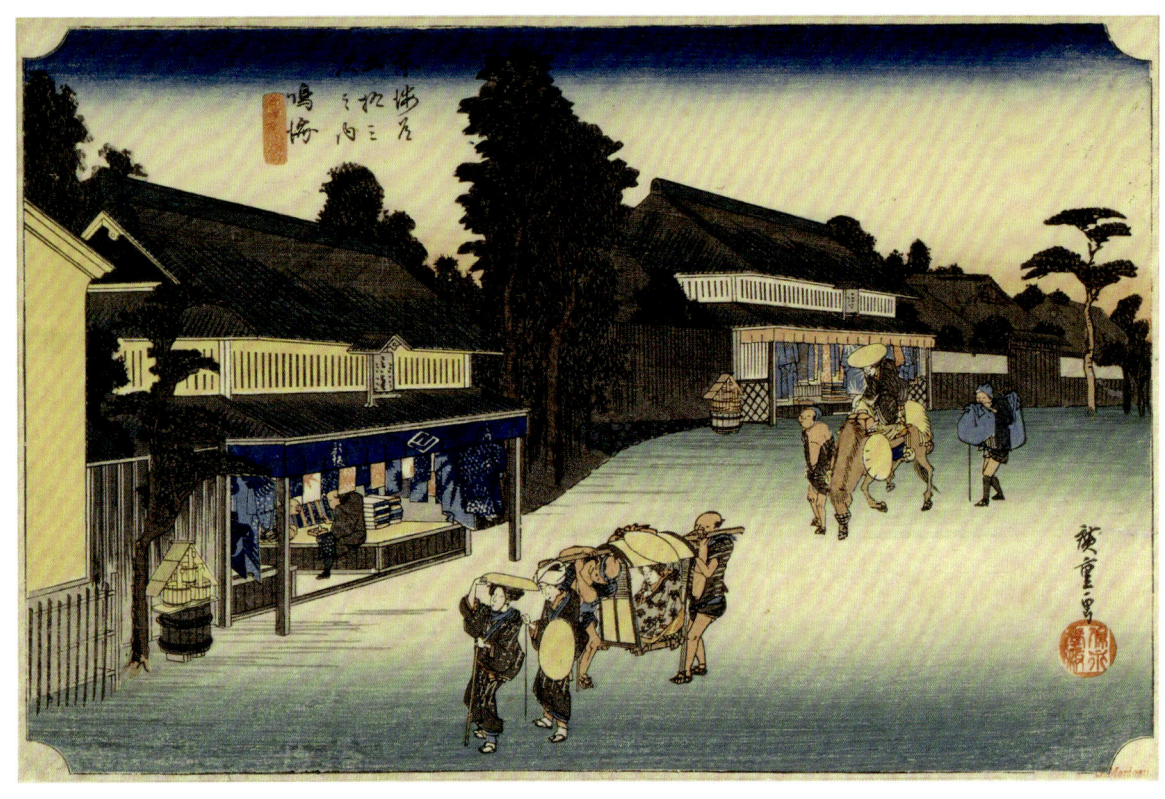

Narumi (speciality of Arimatsu-shibori), Station 40

Narumi (Spécialité d'Arimatsu-shibori), relais 40

Narumi (Spezialität von Arimatsu-shibori), Station 40

Narumi (Especialidad de Arimatsu-shibori), Estación 40

Narumi (specialità di Arimatsu-shibori), stazione 40

Narumi (De specialiteit van Arimatsu-shibori), halteplaats 40

Colour woodcut/Gravure sur bois en couleurs, 22,2×34,4 cm, Bibliothèque Nationale, Paris

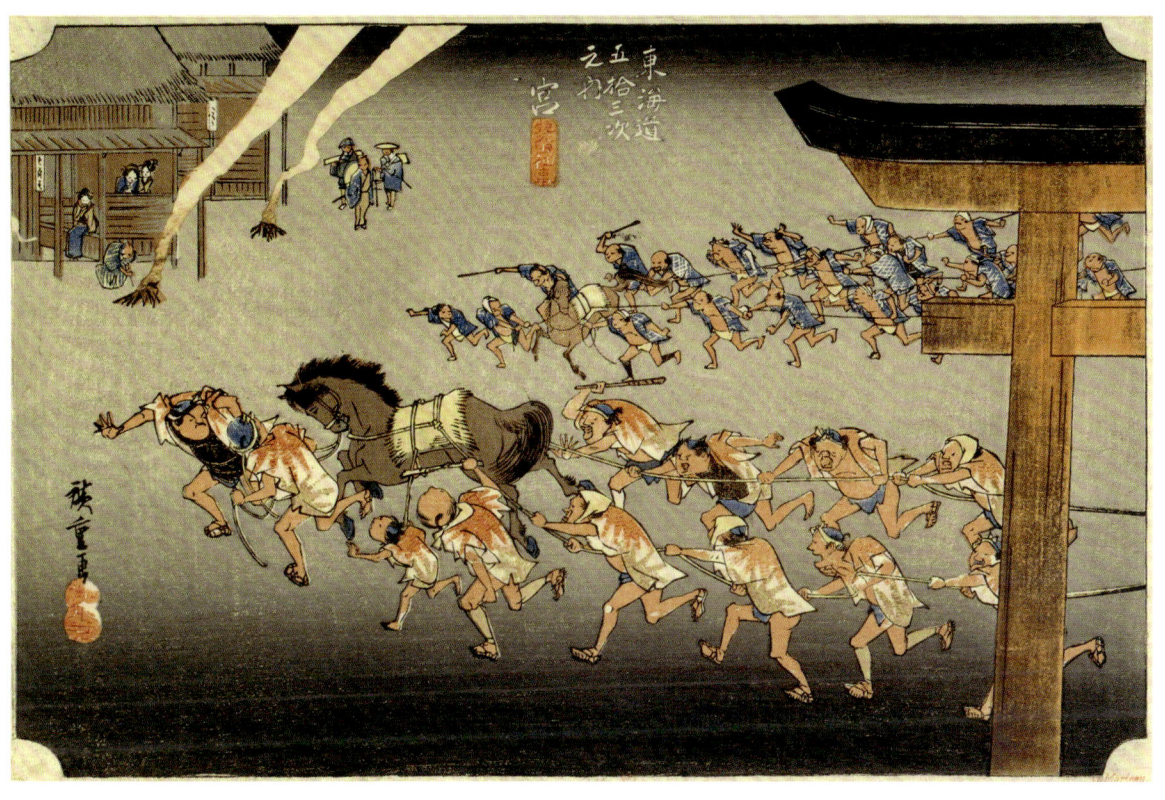

Miya (the Atsuta shrine festival), Station 41

Miya (La Fête d'Atsuta), relais 41

Miya (Das Atsuta-Schrein-Fest), Station 41

Miya (La fiesta del santuario Atsuta), Estación 41

Miya (la festa del santuario di Atsuta), stazione 41

Miya (Het feest van de Atsuta-schrijn), halteplaats 41

Colour woodcut/Gravure sur bois en couleurs, 22,2×34,4 cm, Bibliothèque Nationale, Paris

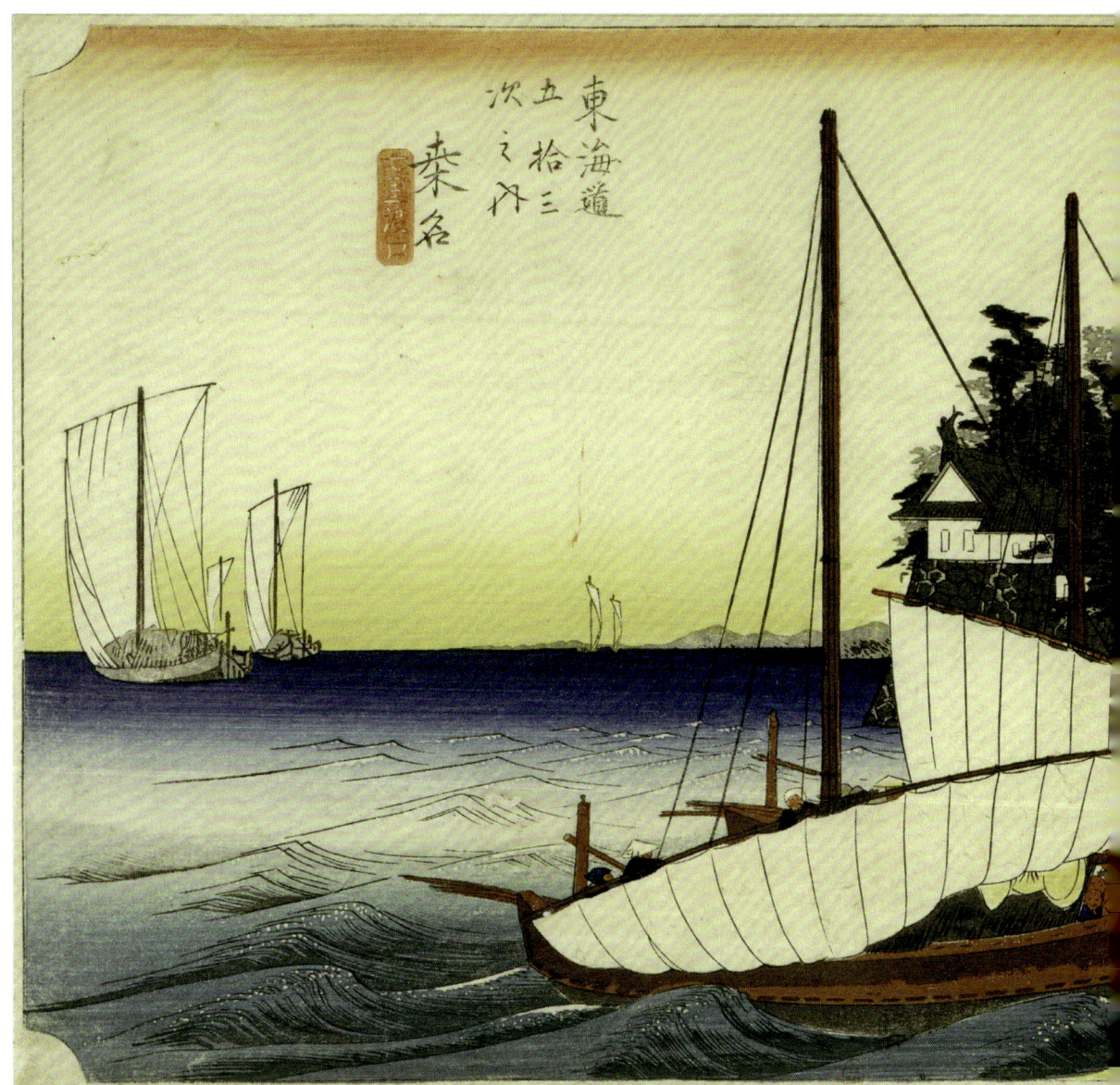

東海道
五拾三
次之内
桑名

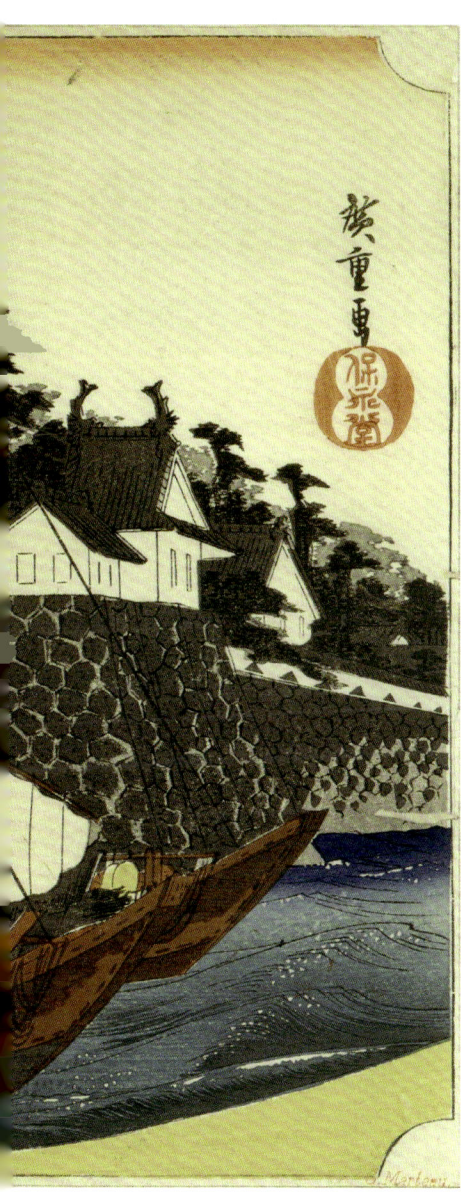

Kuwana (after sailing seven miles along the coast), Station 42

Kuwana (Vers la traversée de sept lieues), relais 42

Kuwana (Nach der Bootsfahrt von sieben Meilen entlang der Küste), Station 42

Kuwana (Tras la travesía de siete millas por la costa), Estación 42

Kuwana (dopo il viaggio in barca di sette miglia lungo la costa), stazione 42

Kuwana (Na de boottocht van zeven mijlen langs de kust), halteplaats 42

Colour woodcut/Gravure sur bois en couleurs, 22,2×34,4 cm, Bibliothèque Nationale, Paris

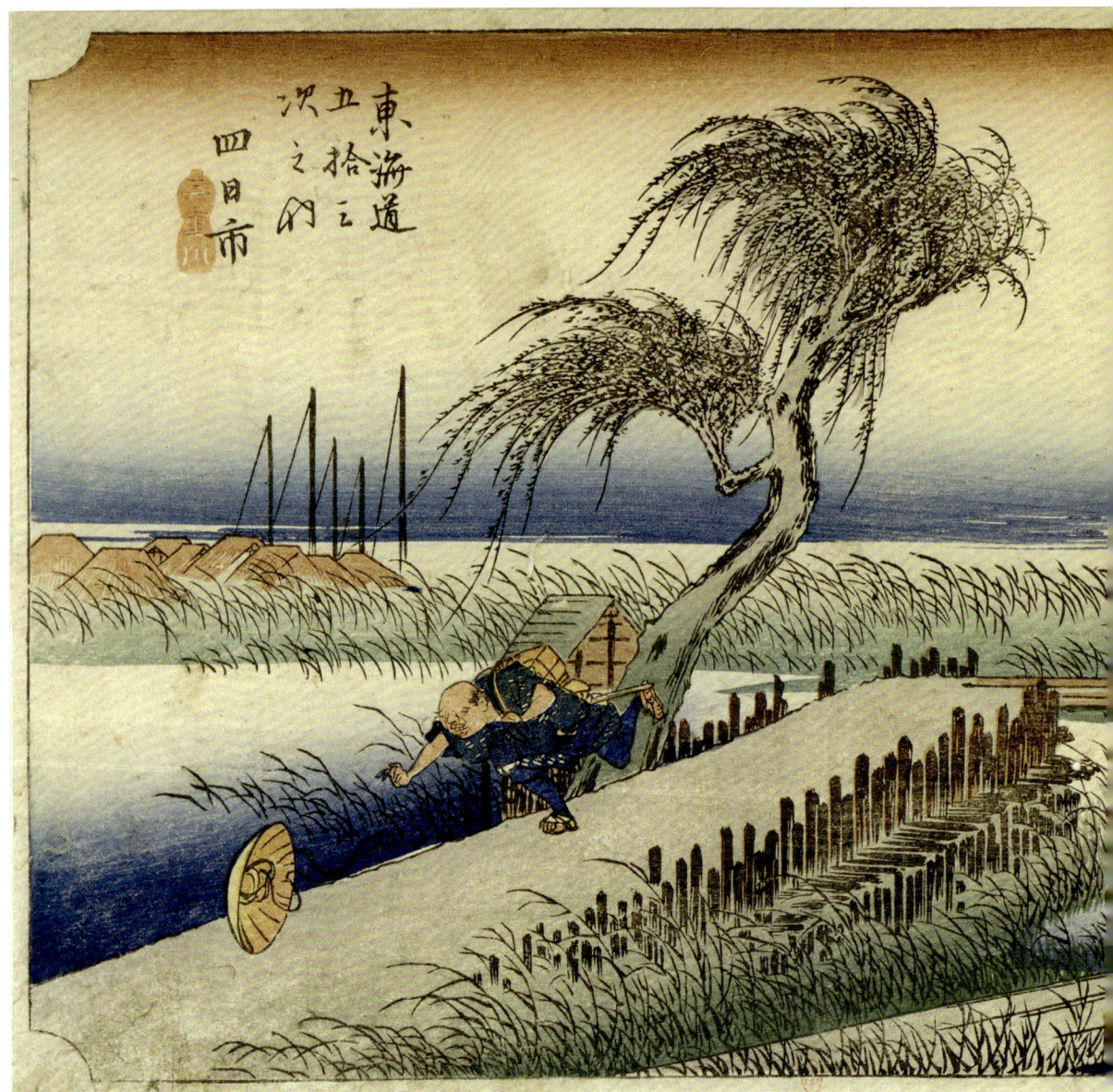

東海道五拾三次之内
四日市

66

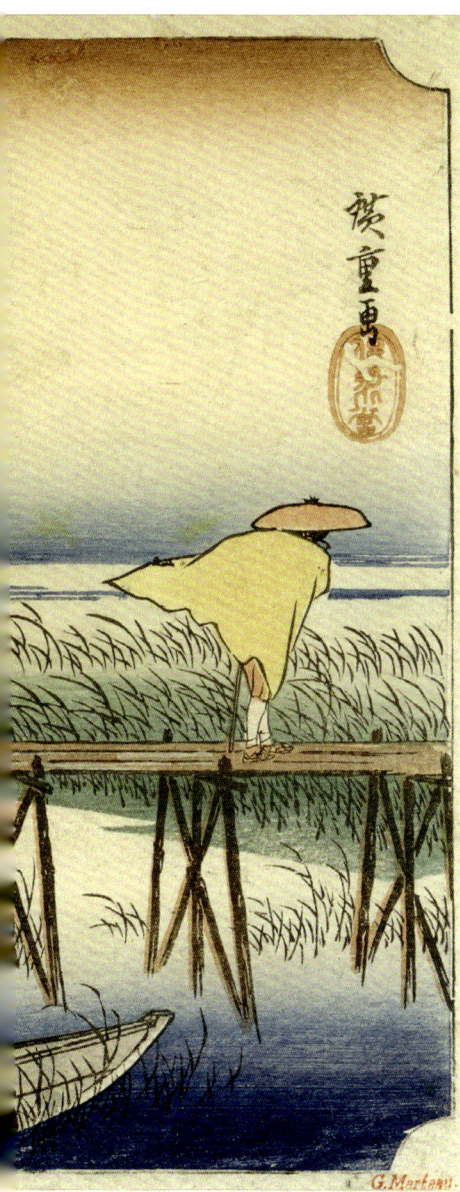

Yokkaichi (the river Mie), Station 43

Le Fleuve Mie à Yokkaichi, relais 43

Yokkaichi (Der Fluss Mie), Station 43

Yokkaichi (El río Mie), Estación 43

Yokkaichi (il fiume Mie), stazione 43

Yokkaichi (De rivier de Mie), halteplaats 43

Colour woodcut/Gravure sur bois en couleurs, 22,2 × 34,4 cm, Bibliothèque Nationale, Paris

Hiroshige often involuntarily portrays comical situations in his 53 Stations of Tōkaidō. Here, the travellers are braving inhospitable weather or groaning under their heavy burdens. A man can be seen chasing after his hat blown off his head by a strong blast of wind.

Dans la série des Cinquante-trois relais du Tōkaidō, *Hiroshige représente fréquemment des situations involontairement comiques. Des voyageurs bravent les intempéries ; d'autres ahanent sous le poids de leur fardeau. Ici, un homme court après son chapeau qu'un violent coup de vent vient de lui arracher.*

Oft schildert Hiroshige in der Serie der 53 Stationen der Ostmeerstraße *unfreiwillig komische Situationen. Die Reisenden trotzen unwirtlichem Wetter oder stöhnen unter ihrem schweren Gepäck. Hier jagt ein Mann seinem Hut hinterher, den ihm ein heftiger Wind vom Kopf gerissen hat.*

En el puente Nihonbashi, que marca el inicio del viaje por el Camino del Mar del Este, ya hay actividad intensa temprano por la mañana. La composición espacial de la estampa muestra la influencia de la representación en perspectiva occidental. El sombreado de la puerta delata el conocimiento de Hiroshige de las calcografías occidentales.

En las 53 estaciones de la ruta Tōkaidō *Hiroshige presenta situaciones involuntariamente cómicas. Los viajeros tienen que capear climas inhóspitos o arrastran, quejumbrosos, sus pesados equipajes. En este ejemplo un hombre persigue su sombrero, que una ráfaga de viento le ha arrancado de la cabeza.*

In zijn serie 53 halteplaatsen aan de Oostelijke Zeeweg *neemt Hiroshige vaak komische situaties op. In gure weersomstandigheden zuchtten reizigers onder de last van hun bagage. Hier holt een man achter zijn hoed aan, die door de harde wind van zijn hoofd is gewaaid.*

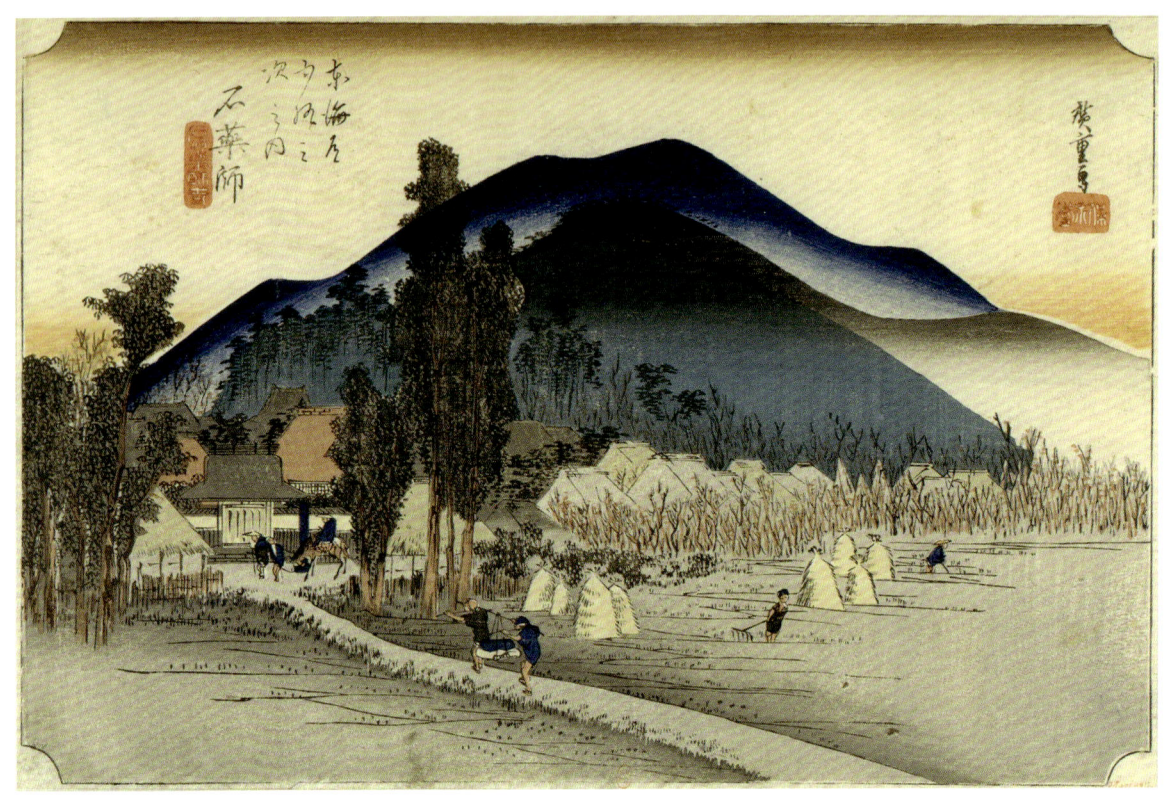

Ishiyakushi (temple with the stone statue of Buddha Yakushi), Station 44

Ishiyakushi (Le Temple de Yakushi), relais 44

Ishiyakushi (Tempel mit der Steinfigur des Buddha Yakushi), Station 44

Ishiyakushi (Templo con la estatua de piedra del Buddha Yakushi), Estación 44

Ishiyakushi (tempio con la statua in pietra del Buddha Yakushi), stazione 44

Ishiyakushi (Tempel met het standbeeld van de Yakushi-boeddha), halteplaats 44

Colour woodcut/Gravure sur bois en couleurs, 22,2 × 34,4 cm, Bibliothèque Nationale, Paris

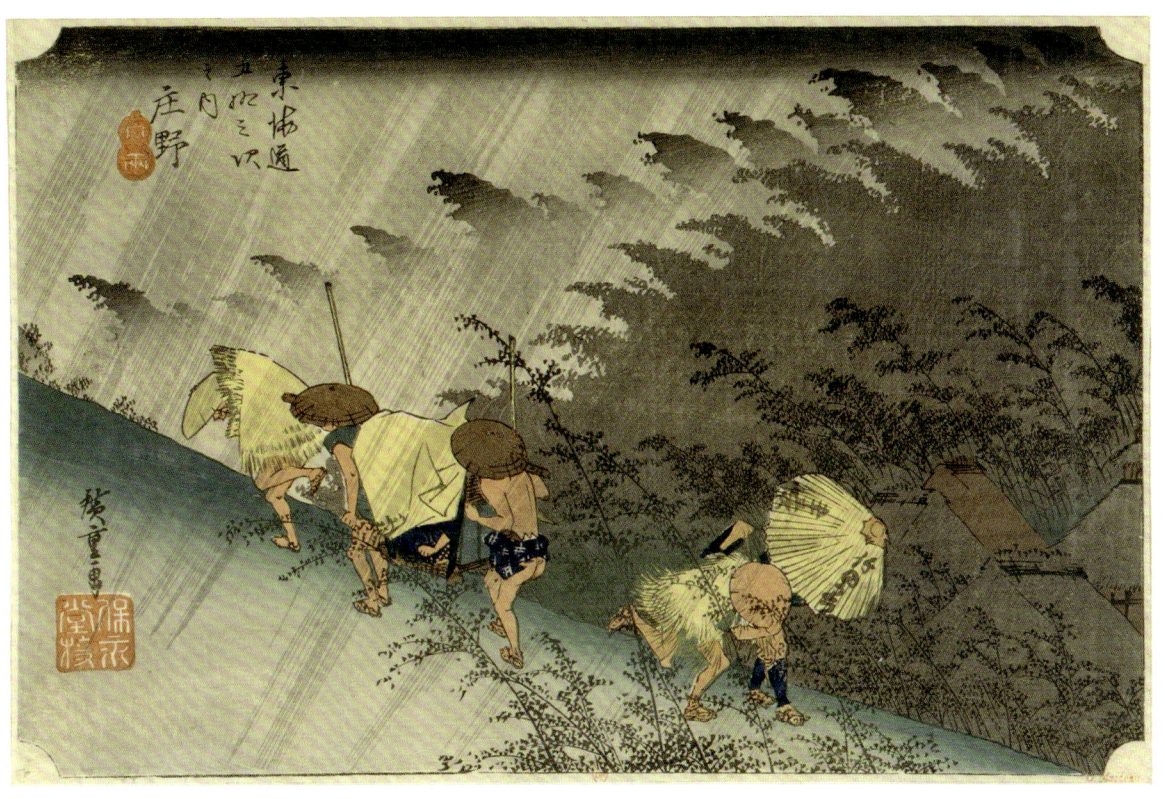

Shōno (deluge), Station 45
L'Averse à Shōno, relais 45
Shōno (Der Platzregen), Station 45
Shōno (El aguacero), Estación 45
Shōno (l'acquazzone), stazione 45
Shōno (De stortregen), halteplaats 45
Colour woodcut/Gravure sur bois en couleurs, 22,2 × 34,4 cm, Bibliothèque Nationale, Paris

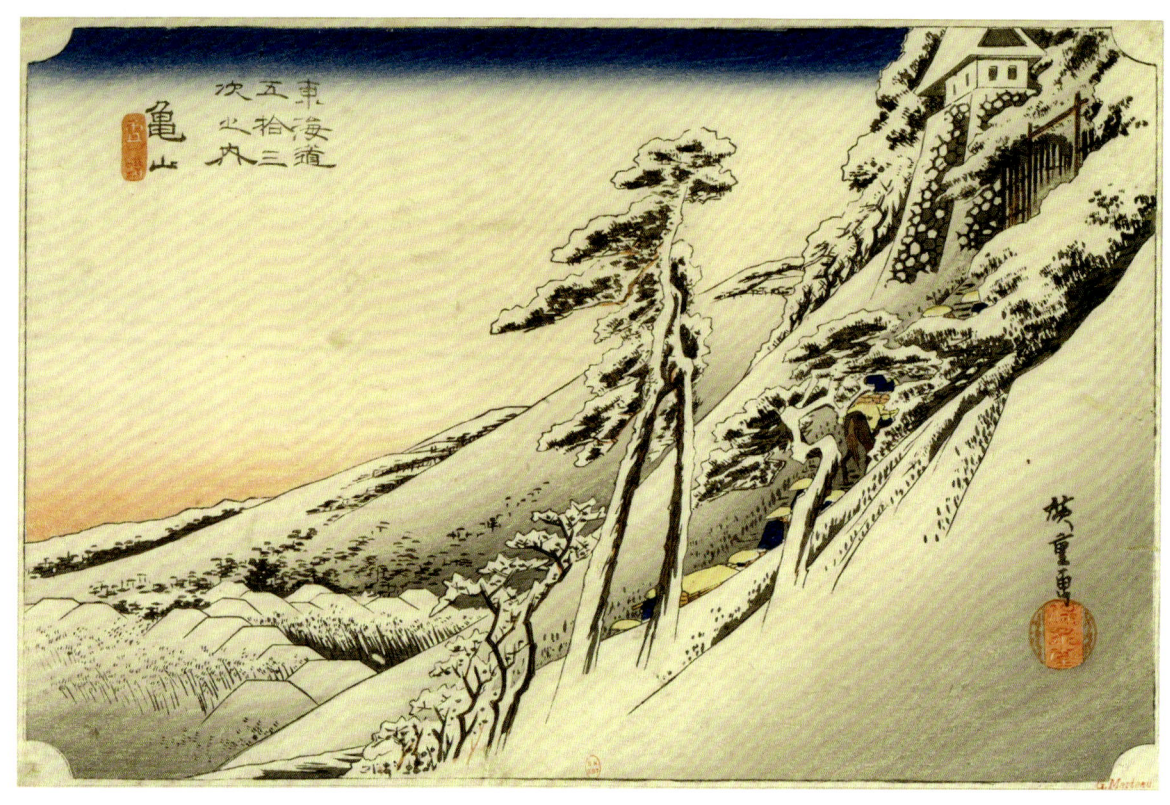

Kameyama (clearing up after the snowfall), Station 46

Matin clair d'hiver à Kameyama, relais 46

Kameyama (Das Aufklaren nach dem Schneefall), Station 46

Kameyama (La claridad tras la nevada), Estación 46

Kameyama (la schiarita dopo la nevicata), stazione 46

Kameyama (Het opklaren na de sneeuwval), halteplaats 46

Colour woodcut/Gravure sur bois en couleurs, 22,2×34,4 cm, Bibliothèque Nationale, Paris

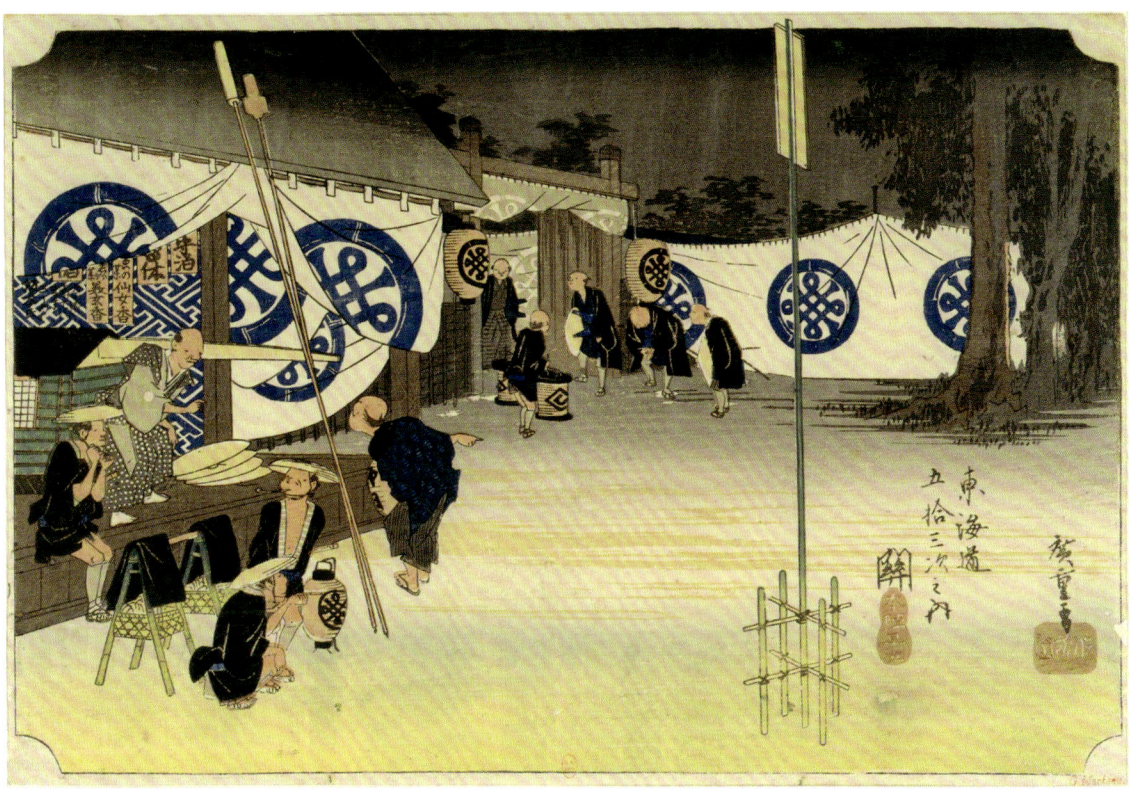

Seki (departure of the prince in the early morning), Station 47
Seki (Départ matinal du daimyō), relais 47
Seki (Der Aufbruch des Fürsten am frühen Morgen), Station 47
Seki (La partida del príncipe muy de mañana), EStación 47
Seki (la partenza del principe al mattino presto), stazione 47
Seki (Vertrek van de vorst in de vroege ochtend), halteplaats 47
Colour woodcut/Gravure sur bois en couleurs, 22,2×34,4 cm, Bibliothèque Nationale, Paris

71

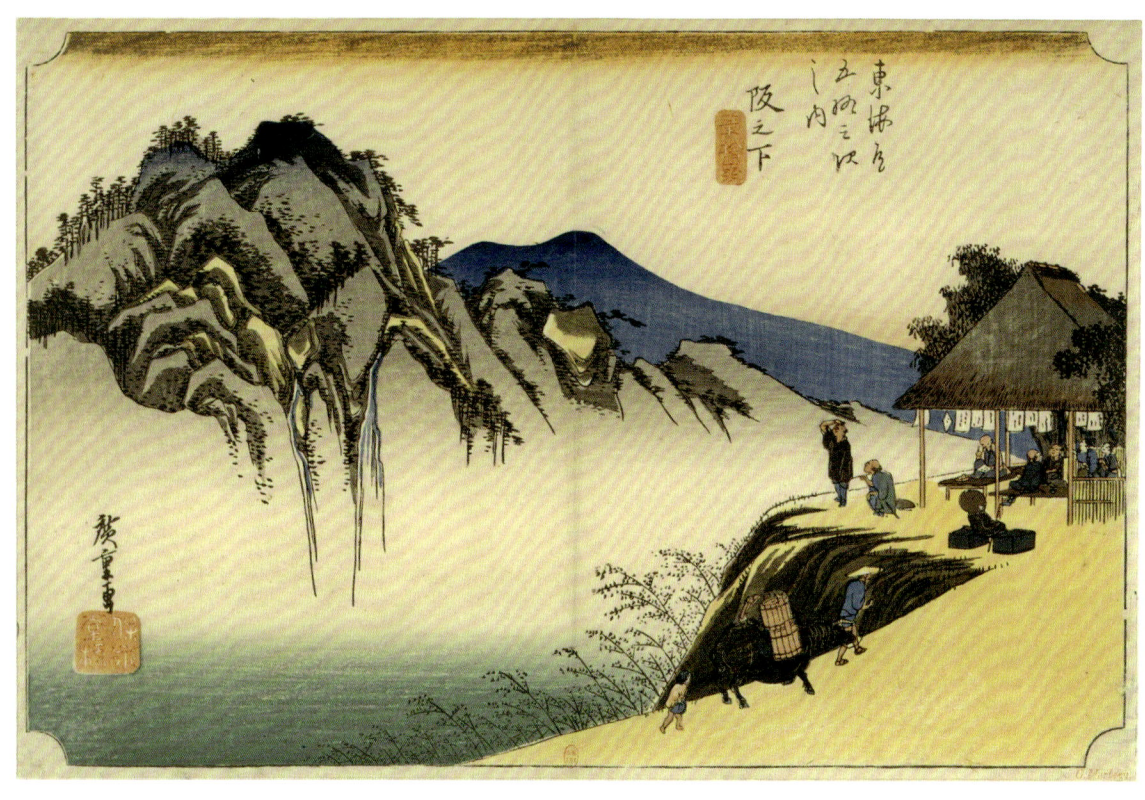

Sakanoshita (the summit from which one throws away his brush), Station 48

Sakanoshita (Le Sommet d'où l'on jette son pinceau), relais 48

Sakanoshita (Der Gipfel, von dem man seinen Pinsel wegwirft), Station 48

Sakanoshita (La cumbre, desde la que se tira el pincel), Estación 48

Sakanoshita (la cima dalla quale si getta via il pennello), stazione 48

Sakanoshita (De bergtop waar het penseel wordt weggegooid), halteplaats 48

Colour woodcut/Gravure sur bois en couleurs, 22,2×34,4 cm, Bibliothèque Nationale, Paris

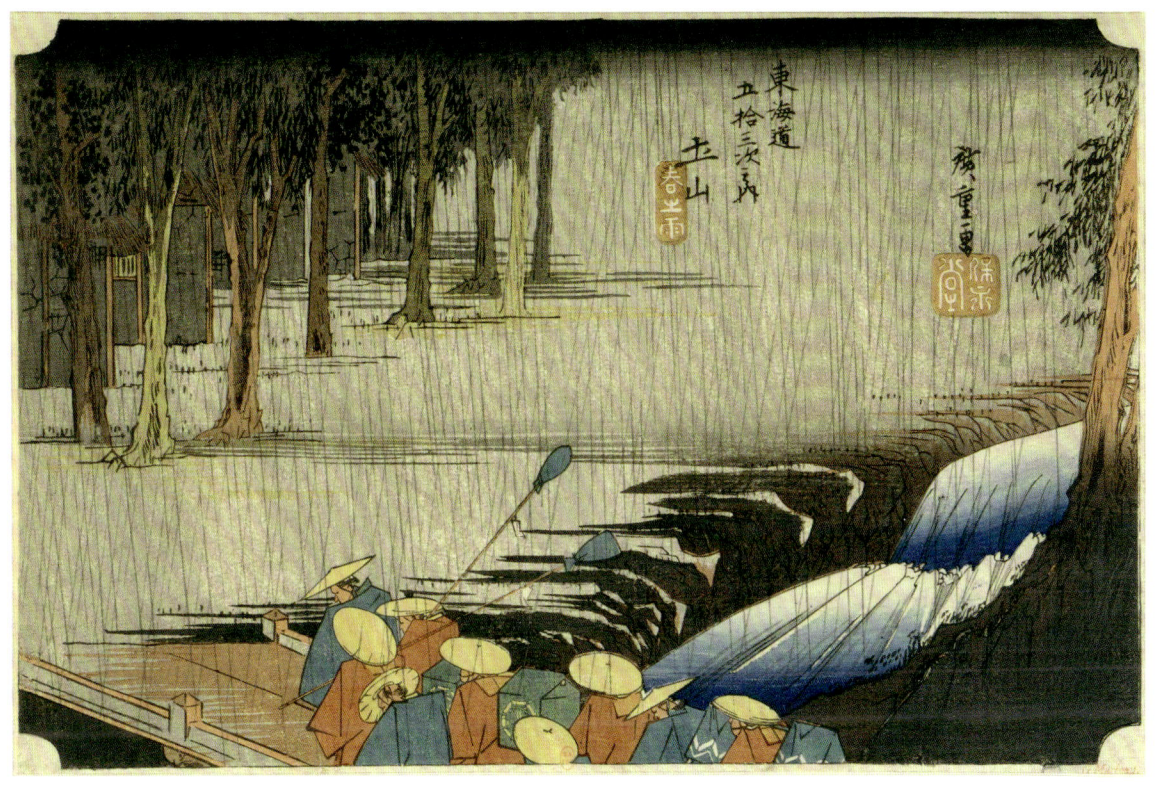

Tsuchiyama (spring rain), Station 49
Tsuchiyama (Pluie printanière), relais 49
Tsuchiyama (Frühlingsregen), Station 49
Tsuchiyama (Lluvia de primavera), Estación 49
Tsuchiyama (pioggia di primavera), stazione 49
Tsuchiyama (Voorjaarsregen), halteplaats 49
Colour woodcut/Gravure sur bois en couleurs, 22,2×34,4 cm, Bibliothèque Nationale, Paris

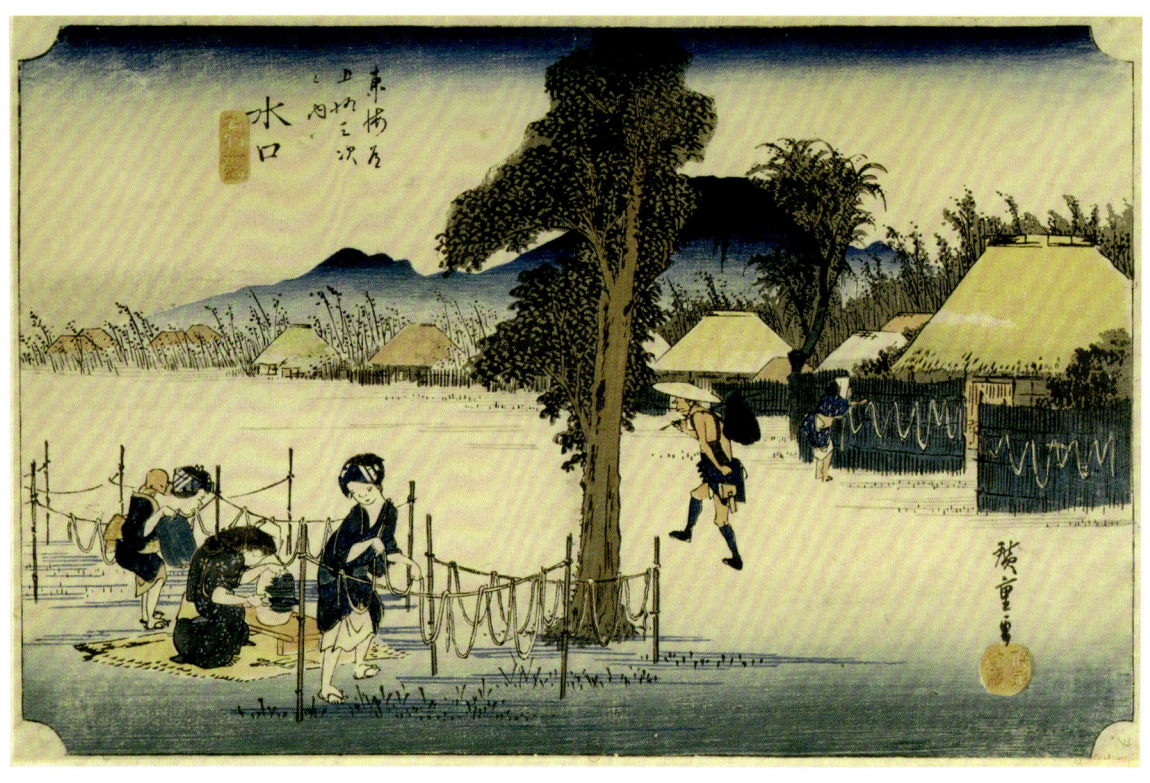

Minakuchi (specialities made from dried gourds), Station 50

Minakuchi (Spécialités de calebasses séchées), relais 50

Minakuchi (Spezialitäten aus getrockneten Kürbissen), Station 50

Minakuchi (Especialidades de calabaza seca), Estación 50

Minakuchi (specialità di zucche essiccate), stazione 50

Minakuchi (Specialiteiten van gedroogde komkommer), halteplaats 50

Colour woodcut/Gravure sur bois en couleurs, 22,2×34,4 cm, Bibliothèque Nationale, Paris

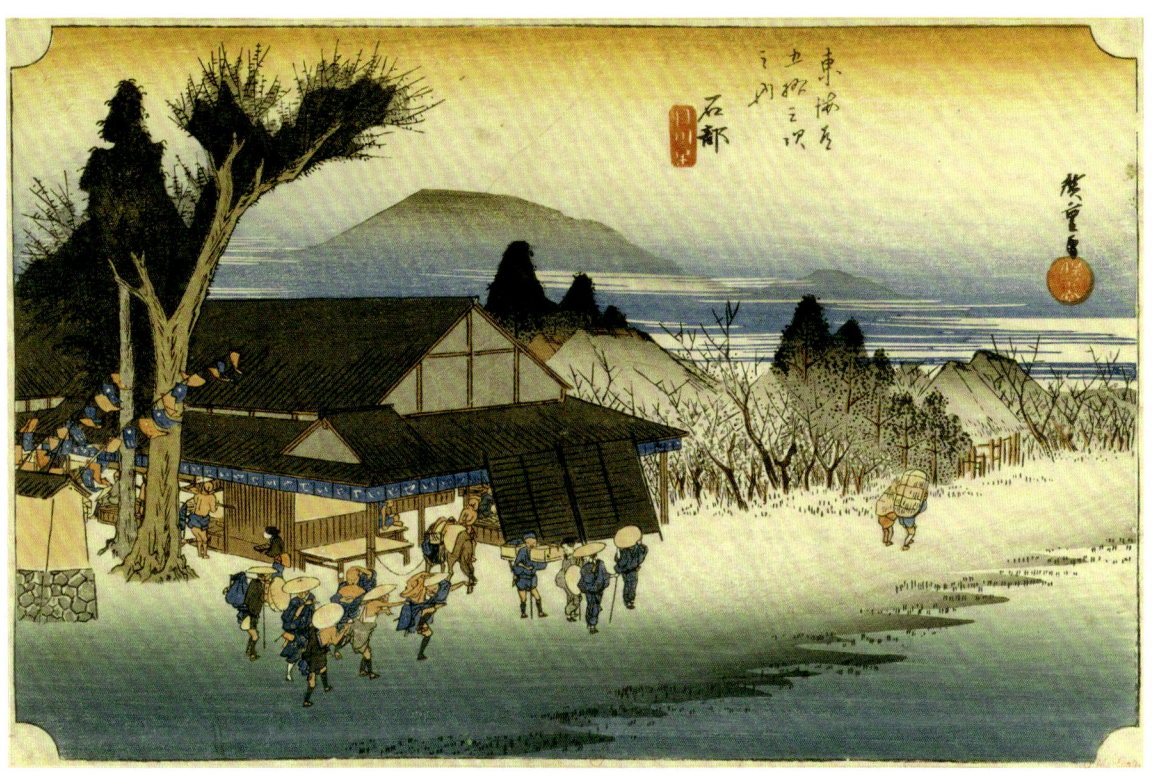

東海道五拾三次之内 石部 目川ノ里

Ishibe (Mekawa village), Station 51

Ishibe (Le Village de Makawa), relais 51

Ishibe (Dorf Mekawa), Station 51

Ishibe (El pueblo de Mekawa), Estación 51

Ishibe (villaggio di Mekawa), stazione 51

Ishibe (Het dorp Mekawa), halteplaats 51

Colour woodcut/Gravure sur bois en couleurs, 22,2×34,4 cm, Bibliothèque Nationale, Paris

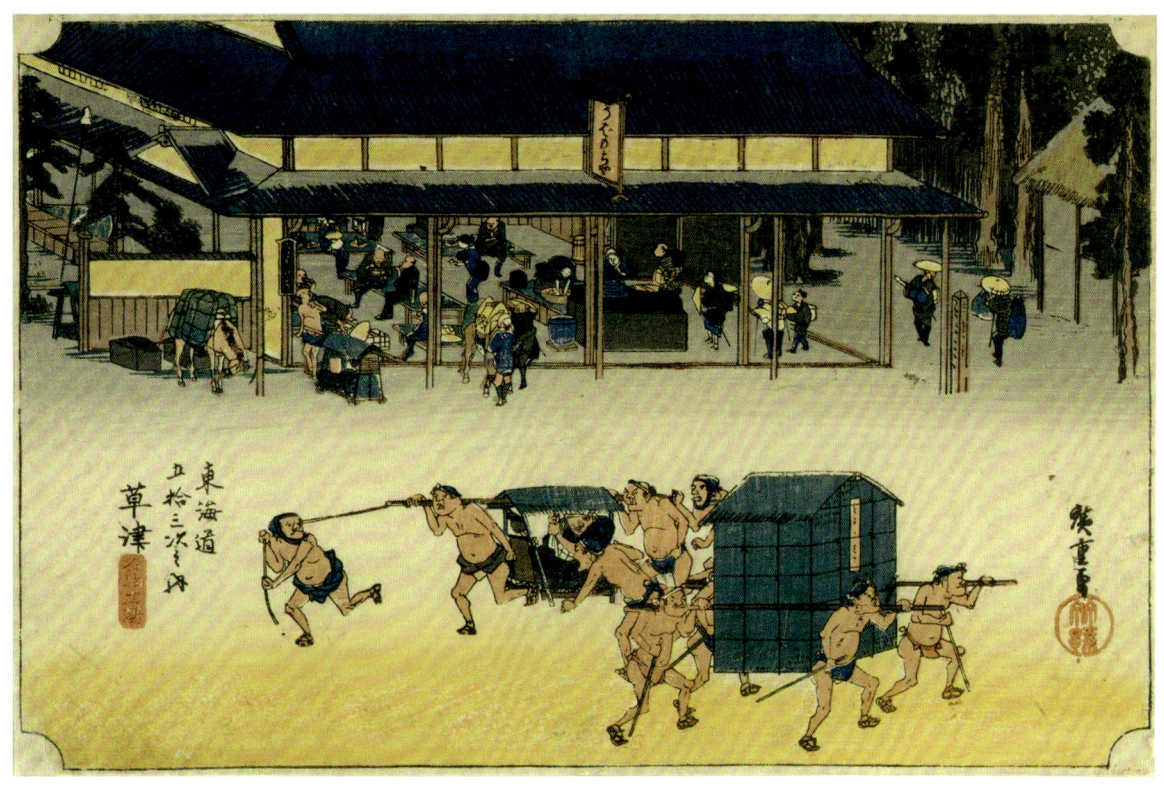

Kusatsu (rest stop for local specialities), Station 52

Kusatsu (Spécialité : le tateba), relais 52

Kusatsu (Raststätte für lokale Spezialitäten), Station 52

Kusatsu (Zona de descanso con especialidades típicas), Estación 52

Kusatsu (luoghi di sosta per specialità locali), stazione 52

Kusatsu (Rustplaats met plaatselijke specialiteiten), halteplaats 52

Colour woodcut/Gravure sur bois en couleurs, 22,2×34,4 cm, Bibliothèque Nationale, Paris

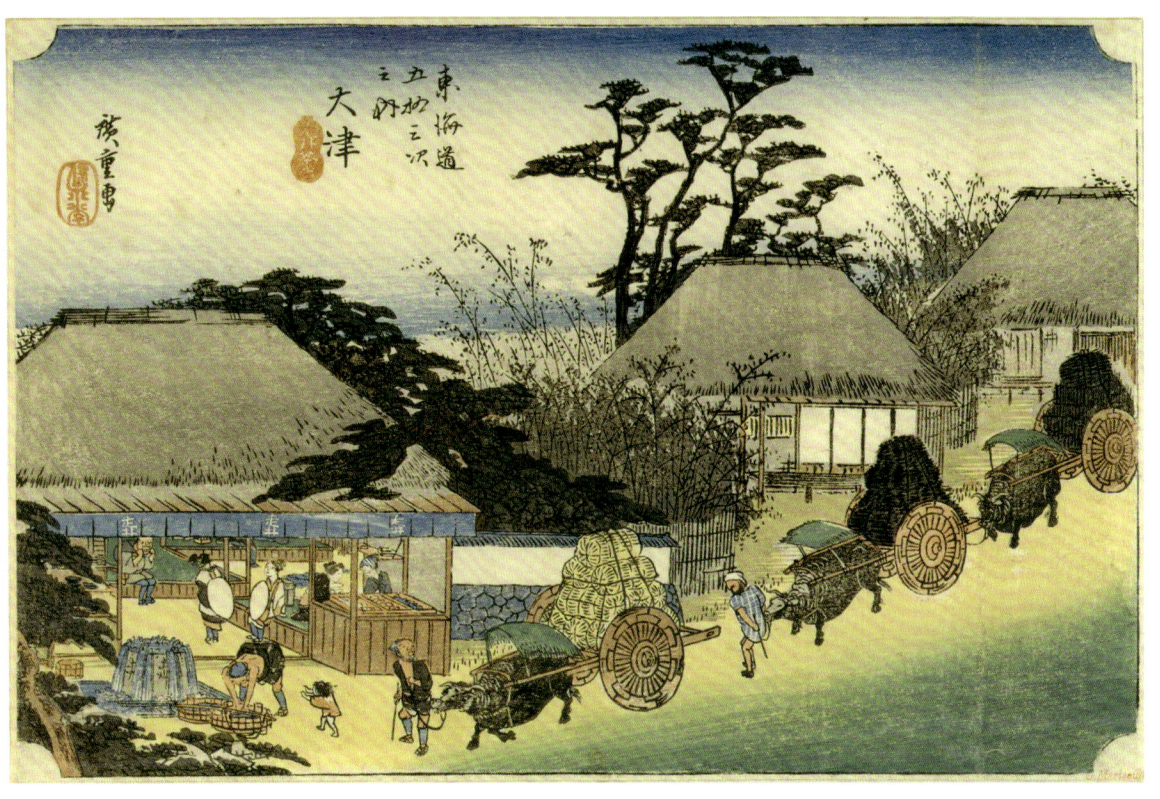

東海道五拾三次 大津

Otsu (tea house at the spring), Station 53

Otsu (La Maison de thé près de la source), relais 53

Otsu (Teehaus an der Quelle), Station 53

Otsu (La tetería en la fuente), Estación 53

Otsu (casa da tè alla fonte), stazione 53

Otsu (Theehuis aan de bron), halteplaats 53

Colour woodcut/Gravure sur bois en couleurs, 22,2 × 34,4 cm, Bibliothèque Nationale, Paris

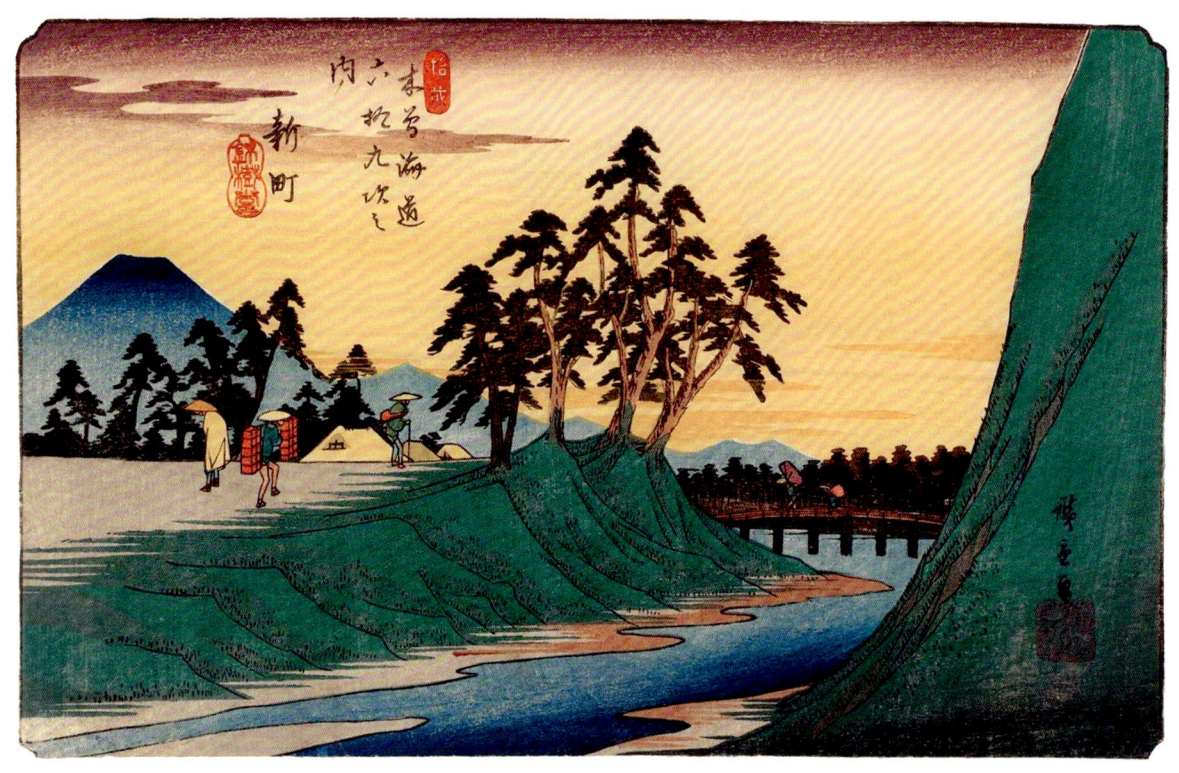

Shinmachi, Station 12 of the series *69 Stations of Kisokaidō*

Shinmachi, relais 12 de la série *69 relais du Kisokaidō*

Shinmachi, Station 12 der Serie *69 Stationen des Kisokaidō*

Shinmachi, Estación 12 de la serie *69 Estaciones de la ruta Kisokaidō*

Shinmachi, stazione 12 della serie *Le 69 stazioni della Kisokaidō*

Shinmachi, halteplaats 12 uit de serie *69 halteplaatsen van de Kisokaidō ('Centrale Bergweg')*

Colour woodcut/Gravure sur bois en couleurs

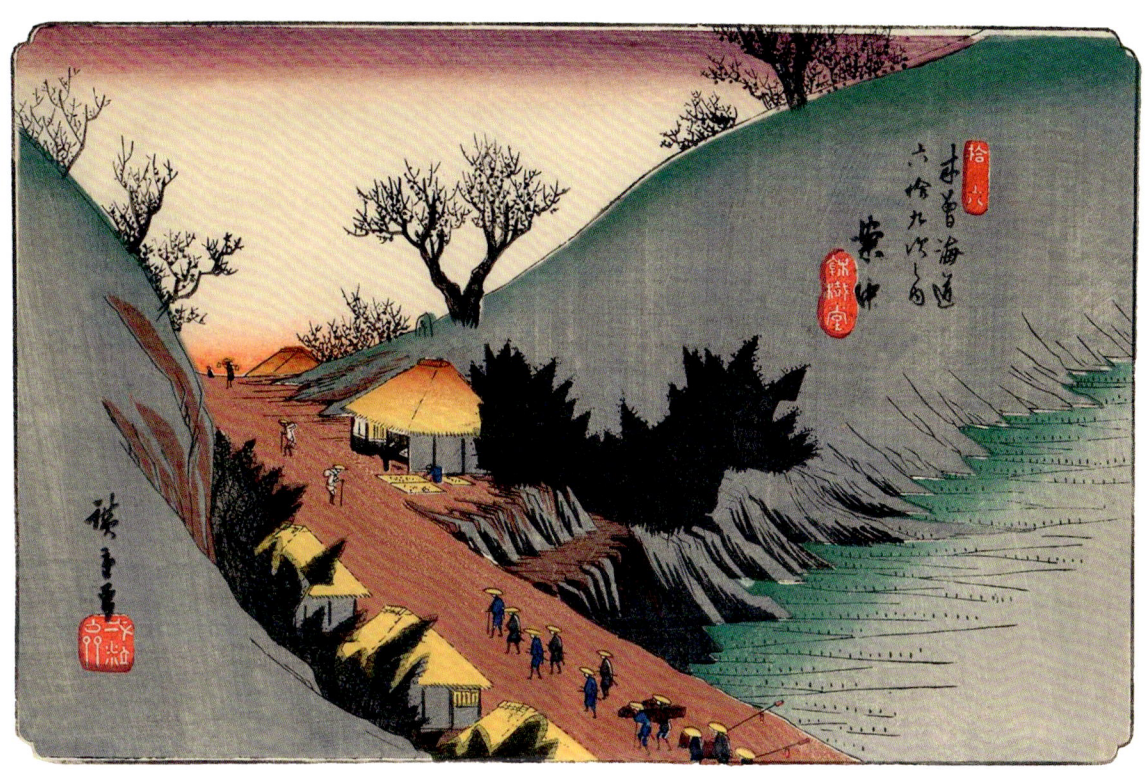

Annaka, Station 16

Annaka, relais 16

Annaka, Station 16

Annaka, Estación 16

Annaka, stazione 16

Annaka, halteplaats 16

Colour woodcut/Gravure sur bois en couleurs

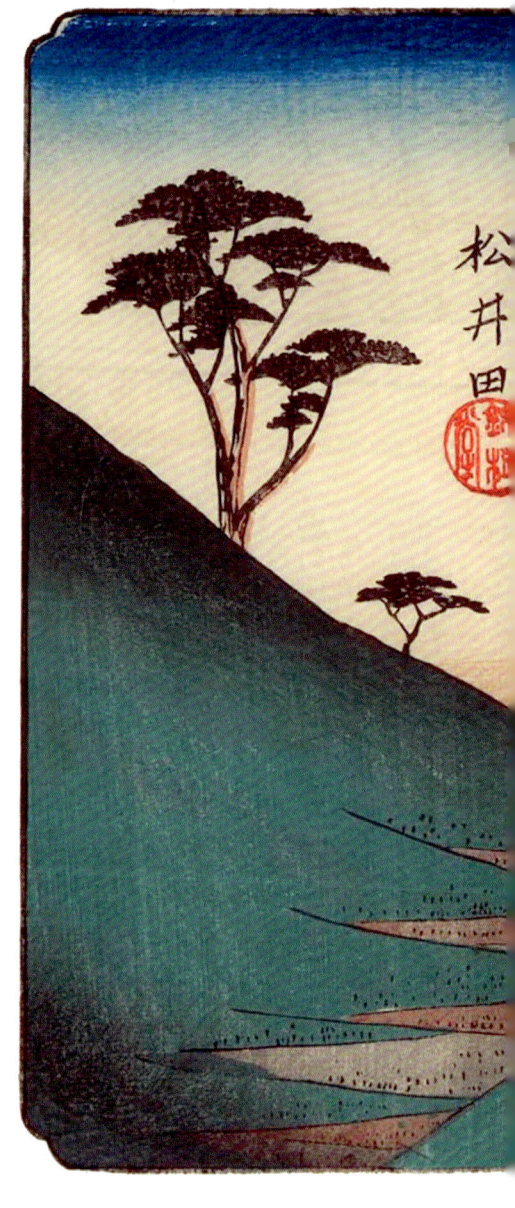

Matsuida, Station 17

Matsuida, relais 17

Matsuida, Station 17

Matsuida, Estación 17

Matsuida, stazione 17

Matsuida, halteplaats 17

Colour woodcut/Gravure sur bois en couleurs

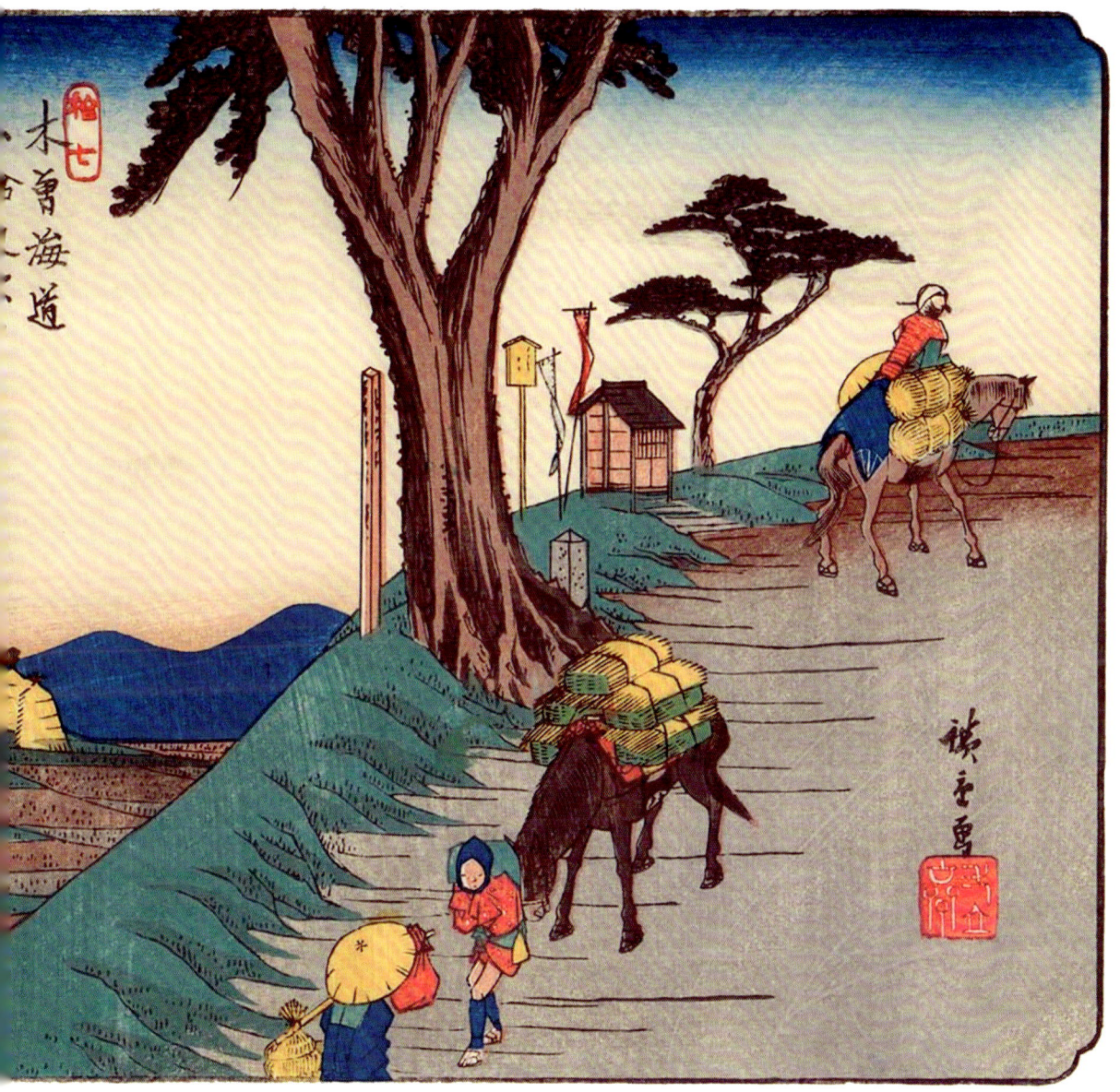

Karuizawa
Station 19

Karuizawa,
relais 19

Karuisawa
Station 19

Karuizawa,
Estación 19

Karuizawa
Stazione 19

Karuizawa
halteplaats 19

Colour woodcut/Gravure sur bois en couleurs

Hiroshige was also inspired by Western art in his representation of light and shadow. Fire illuminates the nocturnal path to the roadside inn. A paper lantern is attached to the horse's saddle and casts its glow on the travellers' luggage.

Hiroshige se laisse aussi inspirer par l'art occidental dans son traitement des ombres et des lumières. Un feu éclaire le chemin nocturne jusqu'à l'auberge. Accrochée à la selle du cheval, une lanterne en papier projette sa lumière sur les bagages du voyageur.

Für seine Darstellung von Licht und Schatten lässt sich Hiroshige auch durch westliche Kunst inspirieren. Feuer beleuchten den nächtlichen Weg zur Herberge. Am Sattel des Pferdes ist eine Papierlaterne angebracht, die ihren Schein auf das Gepäck des Reisenden wirft.

Hiroshige también se inspira en el arte occidental en su tratamiento de las luces y sombras. Las hogueras iluminan el camino nocturno al albergue. Una linterna de papel, colgada de la silla de montar del caballo, alumbra el equipaje del viajero.

Per la rappresentazione di luci ed ombre, Hiroshige si lasciò ispirare anche dall'arte occidentale. Fuochi illuminano il cammino notturno verso la locanda. Sulla sella del cavallo viene fissata una lanterna di carta, che illumina con il suo chiarore il bagaglio del viaggiatore.

Ook in zijn weergave van licht en donker wordt Hiroshige door westerse voorbeelden geïnspireerd. De weg naar de herberg wordt verlicht met nachtelijke vuren. Aan het zadel van het paard is een papieren lampion bevestigd, die zijn schijnsel op de bagage van de reiziger werp.

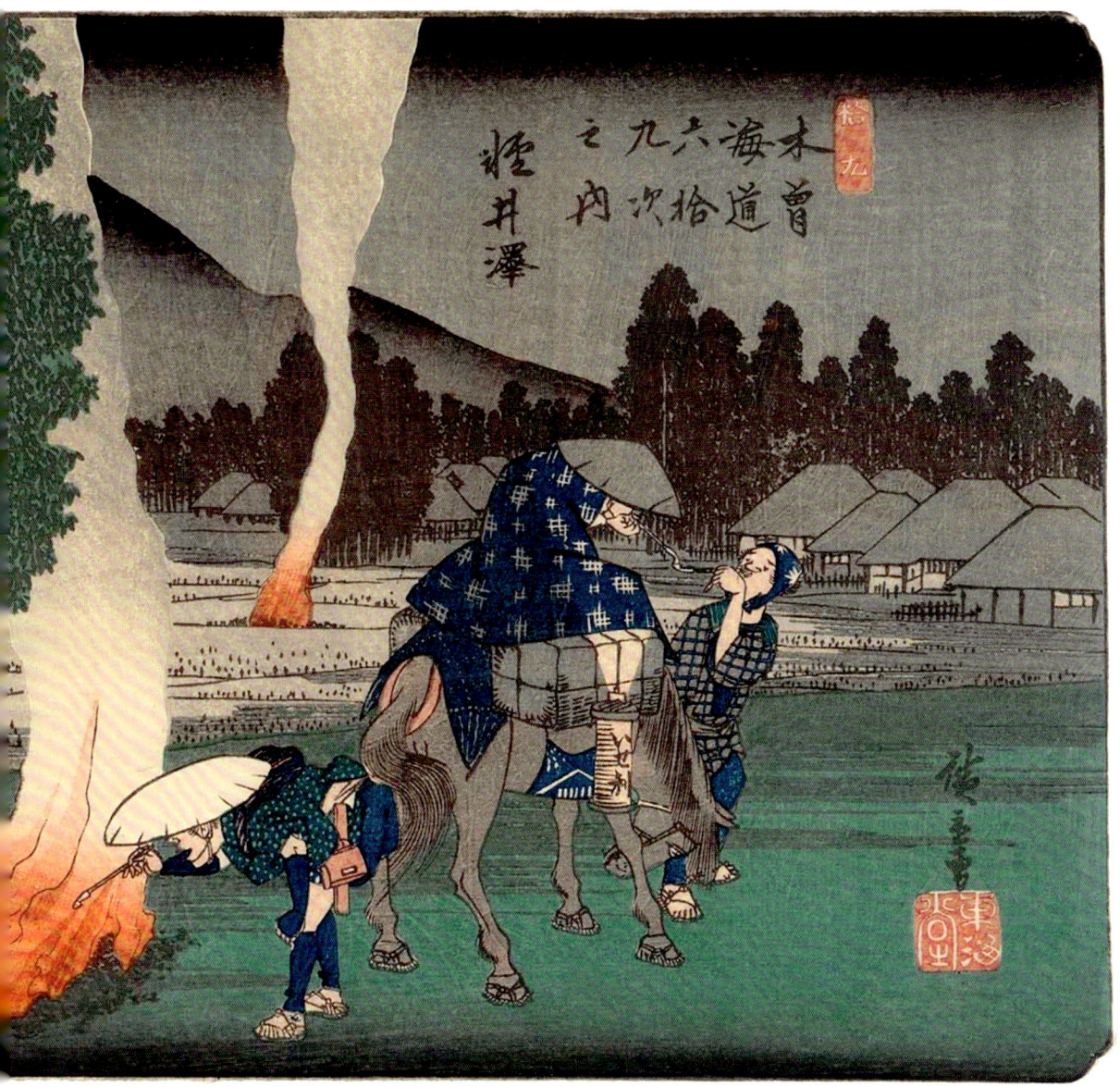

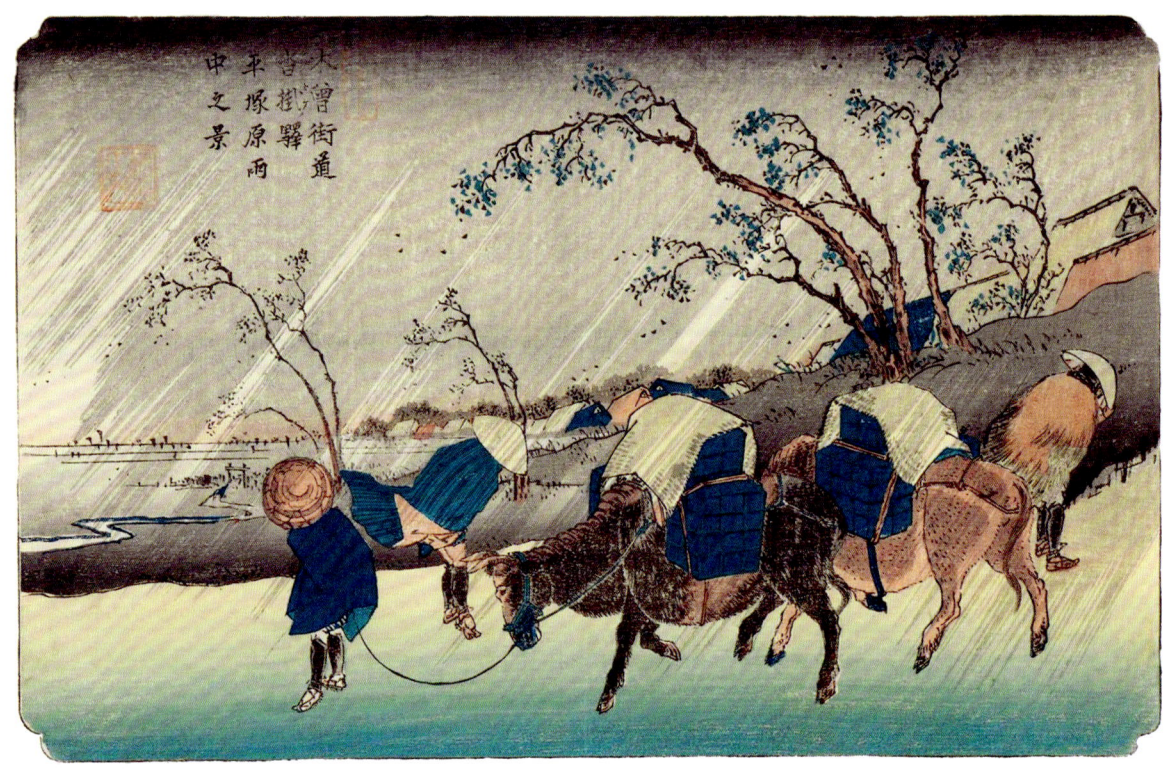

Kutsukake, Station 20

Kutsukake, relais 20

Kutsukake, Station 20

Kutsukake, Estación 20

Kutsukake, stazione 20

Kutsukake, halteplaats 20

Colour woodcut/Gravure sur bois en couleurs

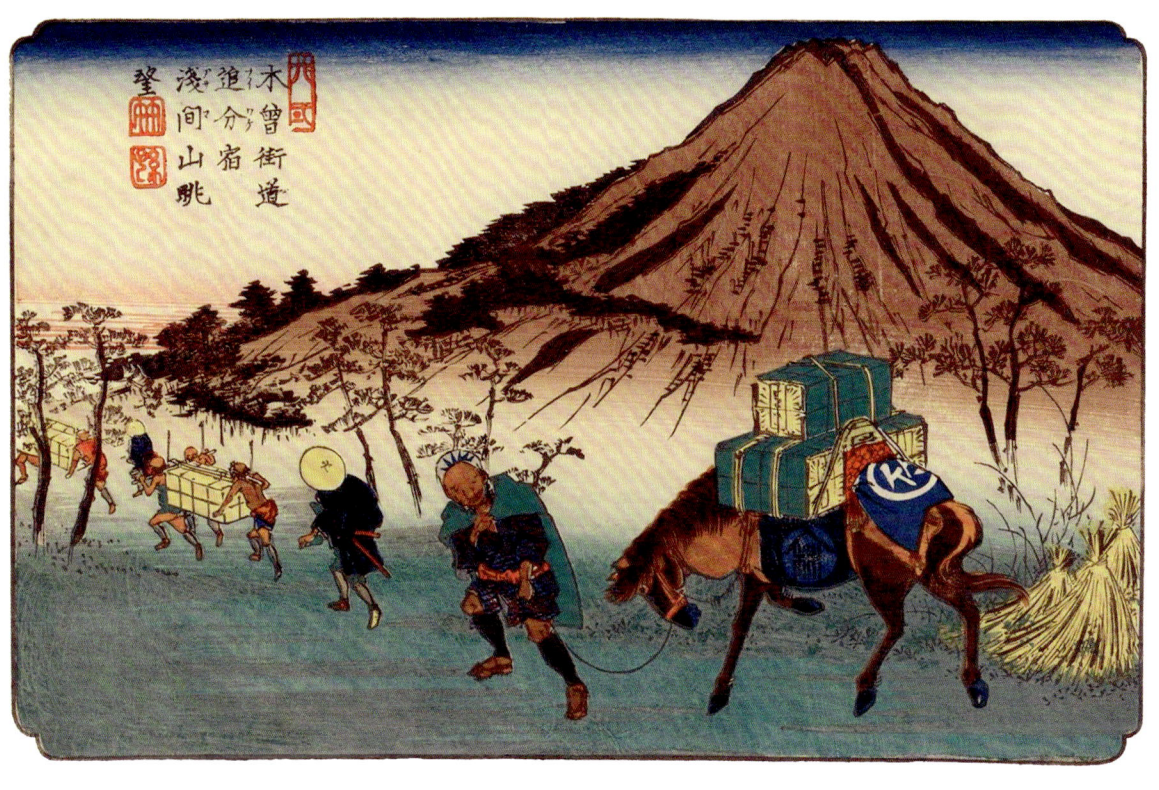

Keisai Eisen (1790-1848):

Oiwake, Station 21

Oiwake, relais 21

Oiwake, Station 21

Oiwake, Estación 21

Oiwake, stazione 21

Oiwake, halteplaats 21

Colour woodcut/Gravure sur bois en couleurs

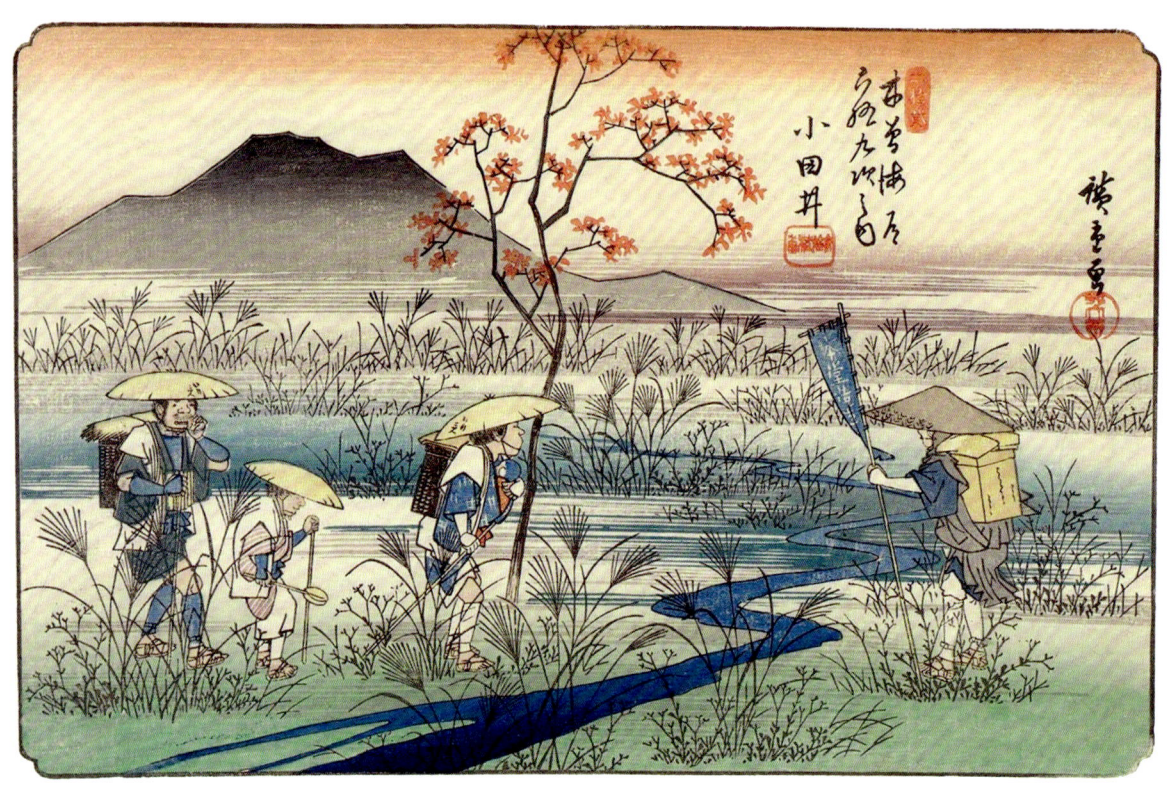

Otai, Station 22

Odai, relais 22

Otai, Station 22

Ota, Estación 22

Otai, stazione 22

Otai, halteplaats 22

Colour woodcut/Gravure sur bois en couleurs

Keisai Eisen

Iwamurada, Station 23

Iwamurata, relais 23

Iwamurada, Station 23

Iwamurada, Estación 23

Iwamurada, stazione 23

Iwamurada, halteplaats 23

Colour woodcut/
Gravure sur bois en couleurs

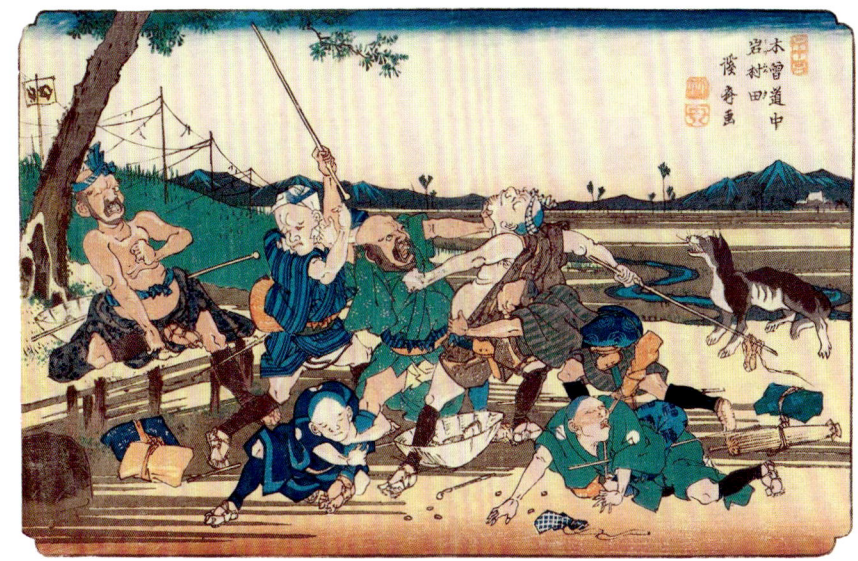

Shionada, Station 24

Shionata, relais 24

Shionada, Station 24

Shionada, Estación 24

Shionada, stazione 24

Shionada, halteplaats 24

Colour woodcut/
Gravure sur bois en couleurs

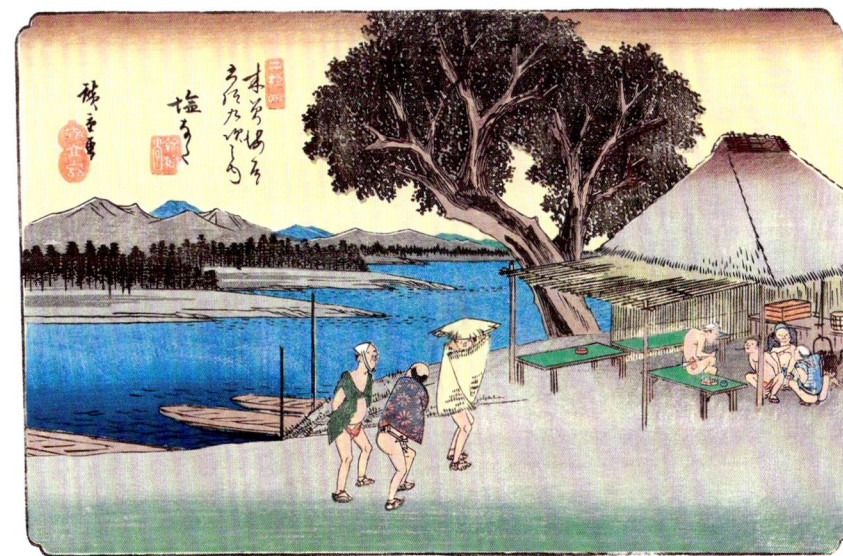

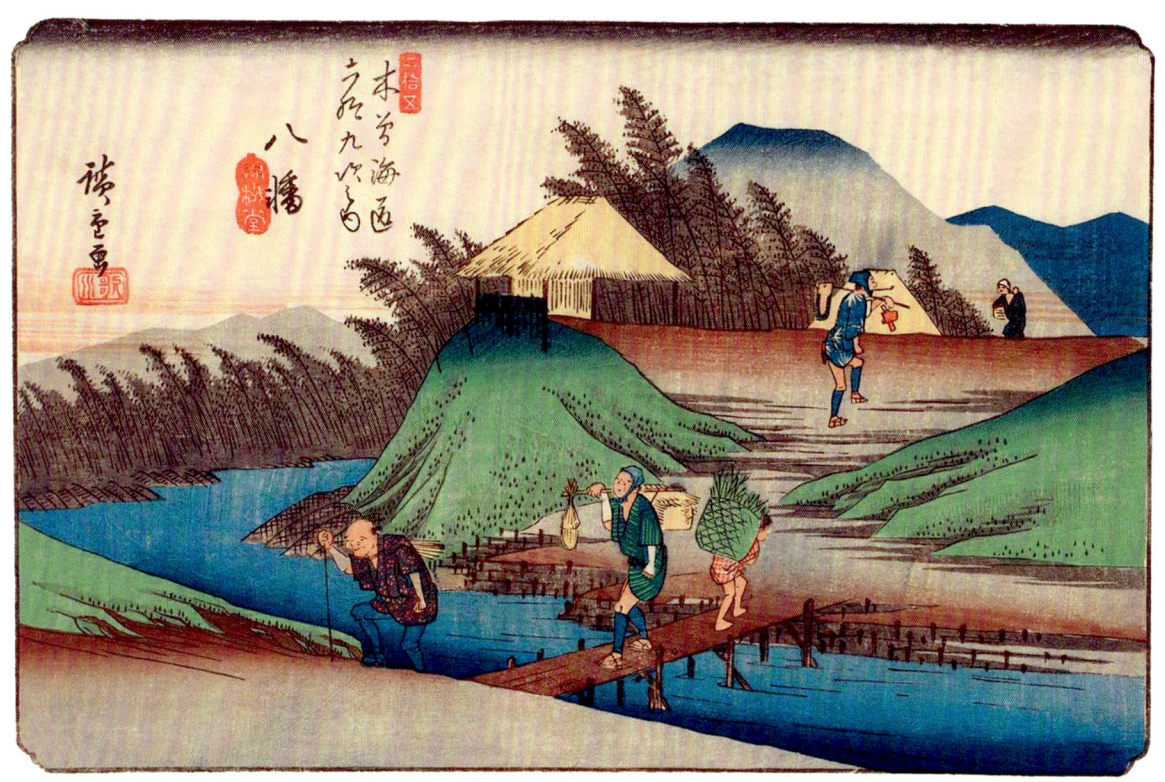

Yawata, Station 25

Yawata, relais 25

Yawata, Station 25

Yawata, Estación 25

Yawata, stazione 25

Yawata, halteplaats 25

Colour woodcut/Gravure sur bois en couleurs

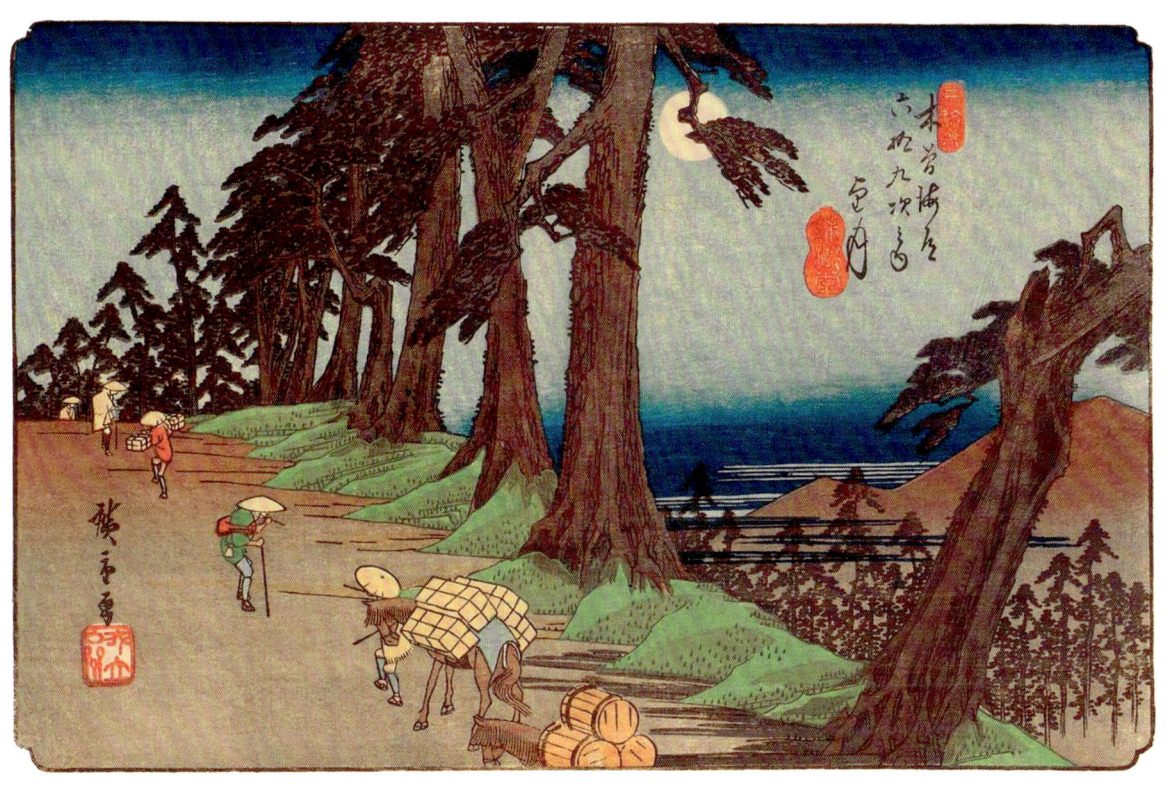

Mochizuki, Station 26
Mochizuki, relais 26
Mochizuki, Station 26
Mochizuki, Estación 26
Mochizuki, stazione 26
Mochizuki, halteplaats 26
Colour woodcut/Gravure sur bois en couleurs

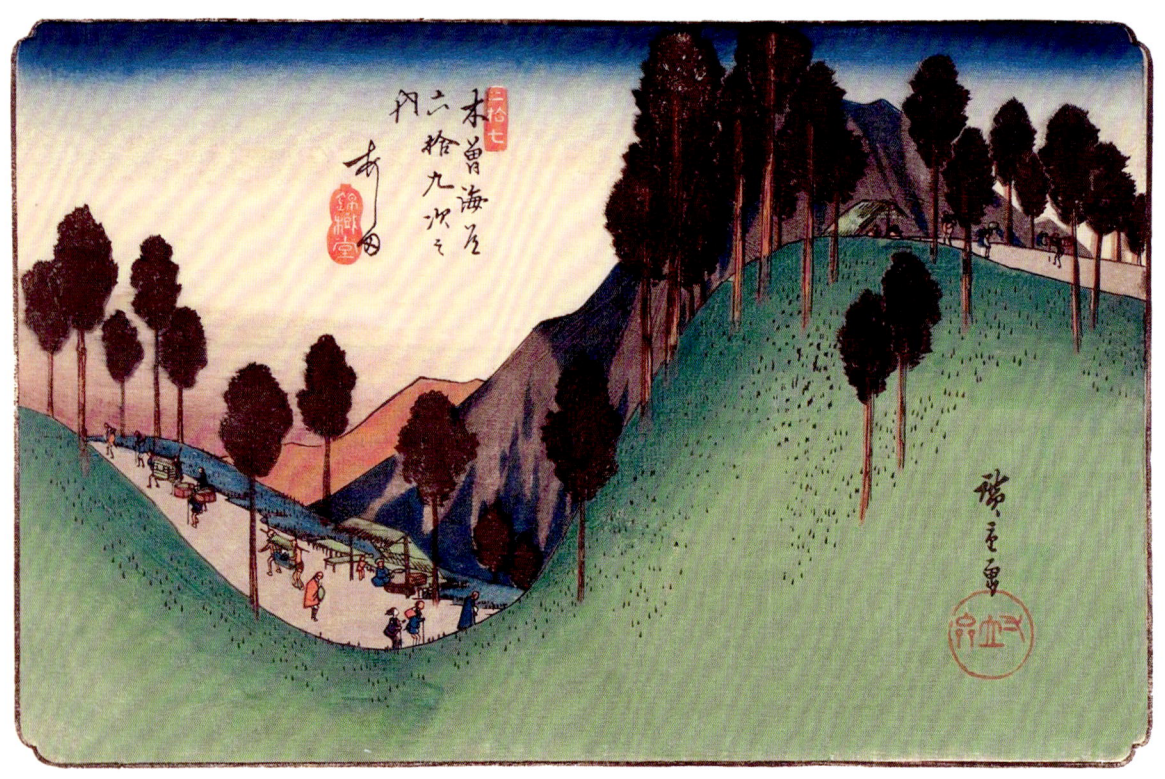

Ashida, Station 27

Ashida, relais 27

Ashida, Station 27

Ashida, Estación 27

Ashida, stazione 27

Ashida, halteplaats 27

Colour woodcut/Gravure sur bois en couleurs

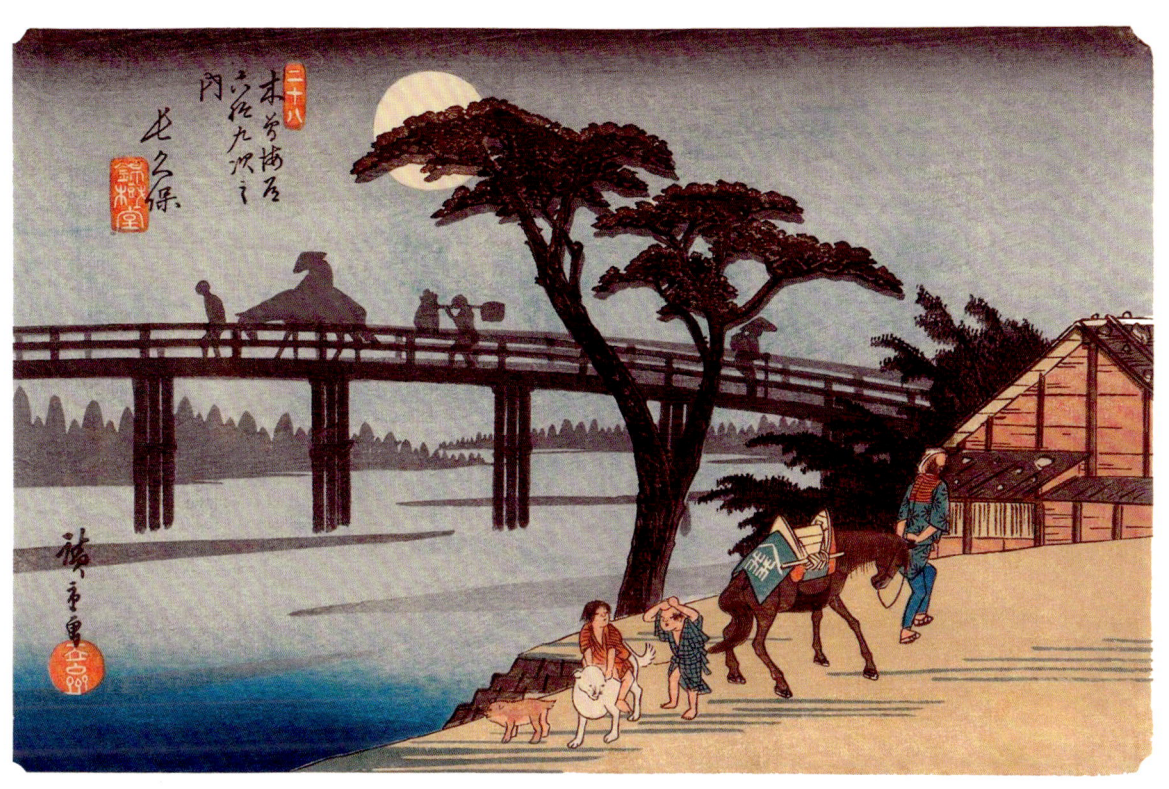

Nagakubo, Station 28

Nagakubo, relais 28

Nagakubo, Station 28

Nagakubo, Estación 28

Nagakubo, stazione 28

Nagakubo, halteplaats 28

Colour woodcut/Gravure sur bois en couleurs

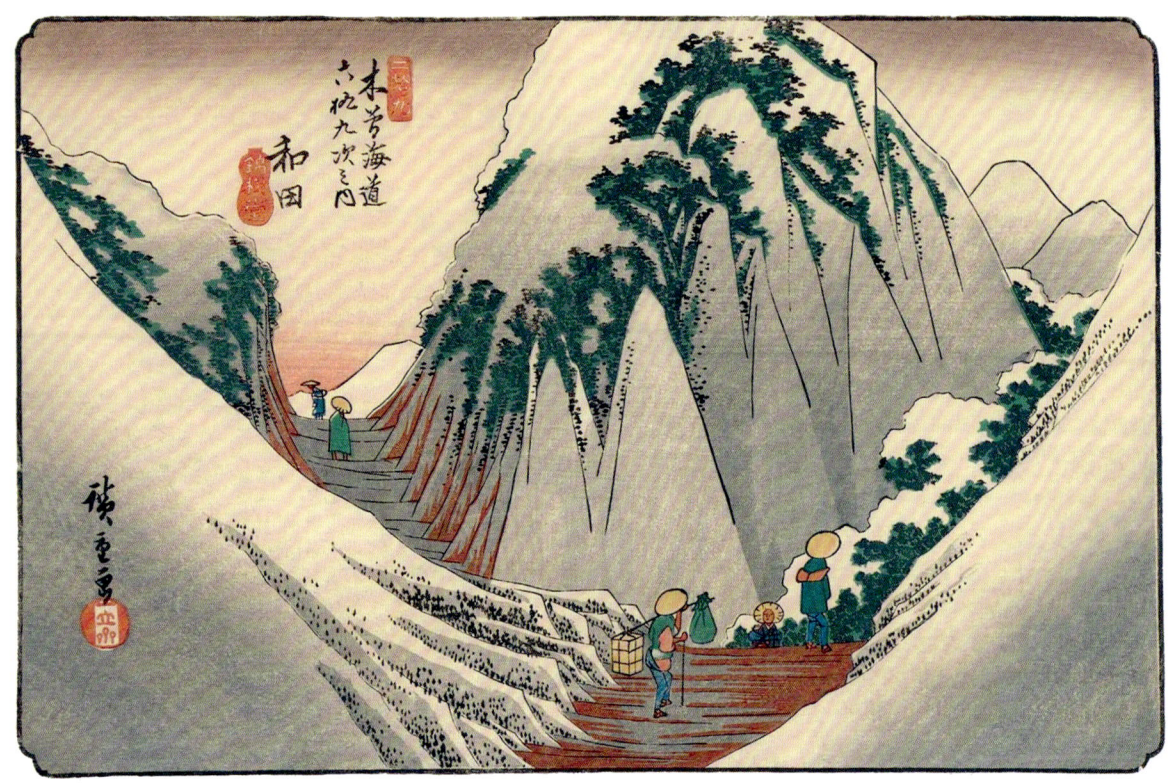

Wada, Station 29

Wada, relais 29

Wada, Station 29

Wada, Estación 29

Wada, stazione 29

Wada, halteplaats 29

Colour woodcut/Gravure sur bois en couleurs

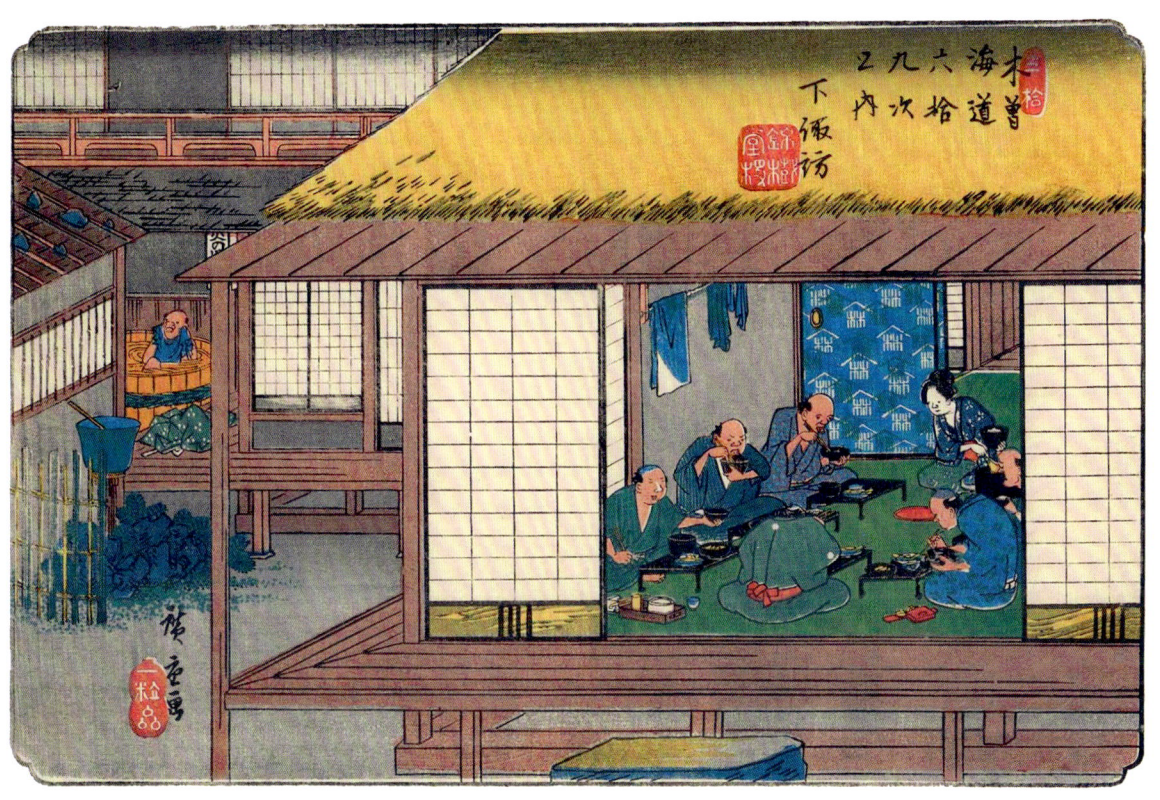

Shimosuwa, Station 30

Shimosuwa, relais 30

Shimosuwa, Station 30

Shimosuwa, Estación 30

Shimosuwa, stazione 30

Shimosuwa, halteplaats 30

Colour woodcut/Gravure sur bois en couleurs

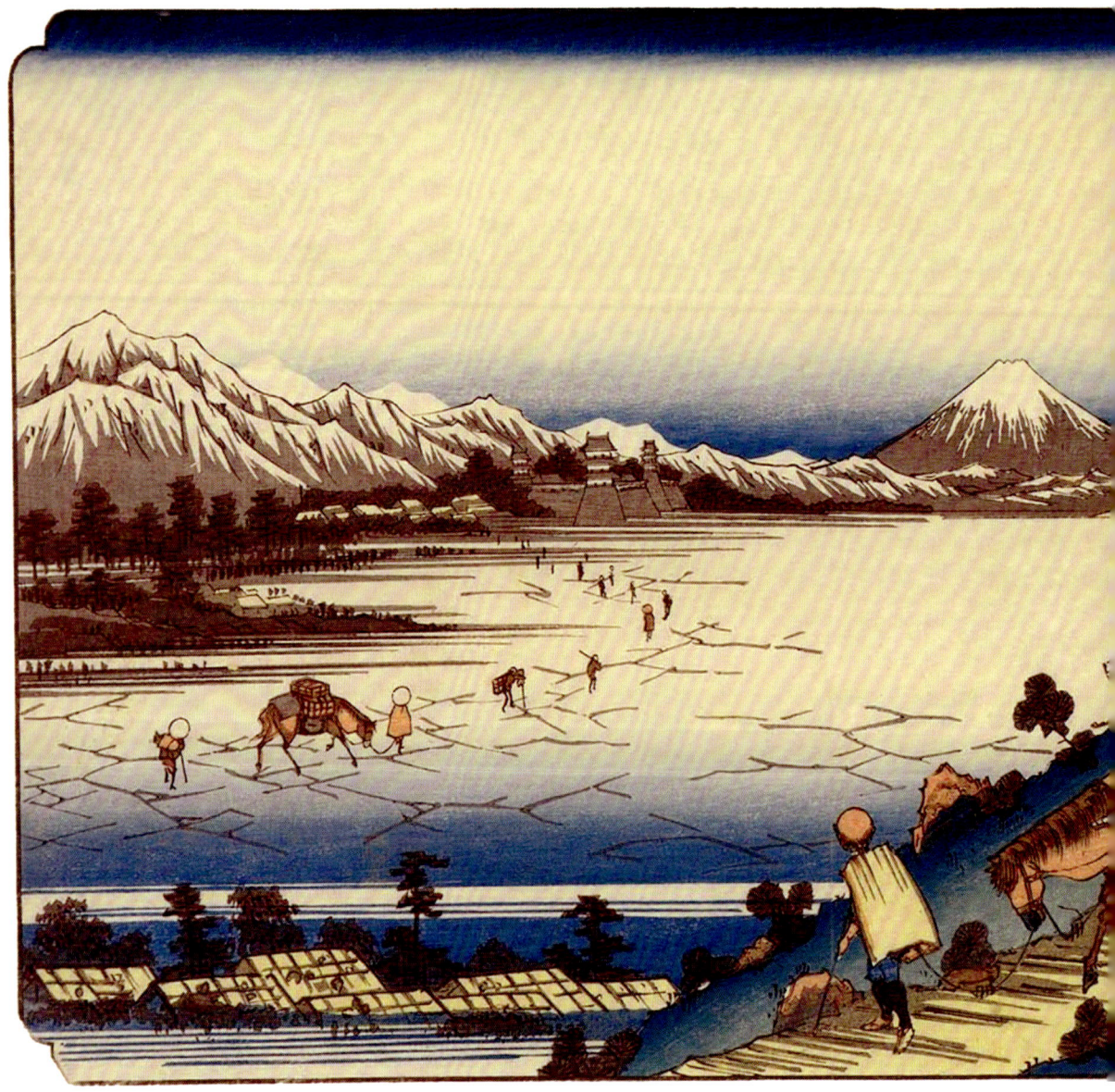

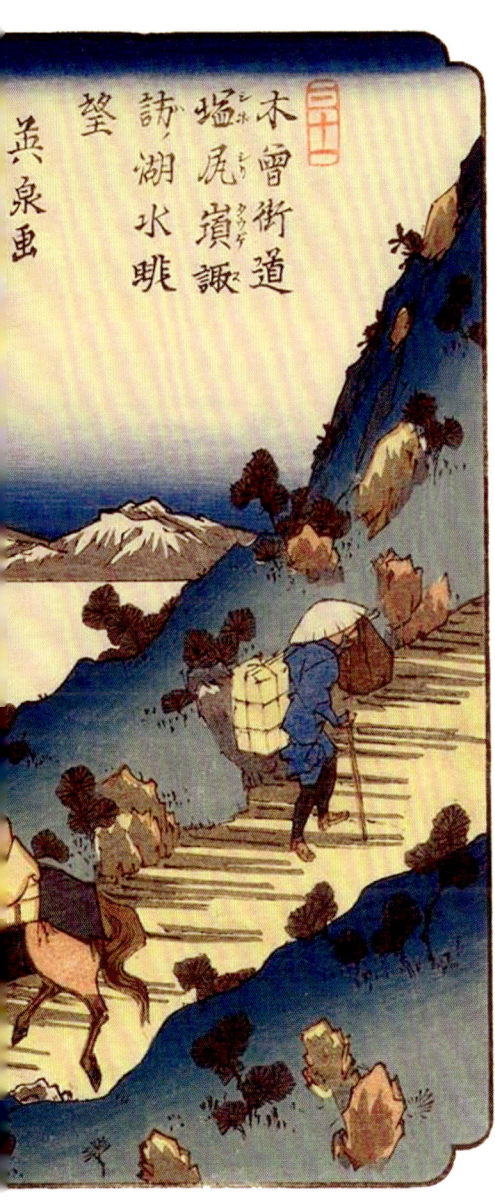

Keisai Eisen

Shiojiri, Station 31

Shiojiri, relais 31

Shiojiri, Station 31

Shiojiri, Estación 31

Shiojiri, stazione 31

Shiojiri, halteplaats 31

Colour woodcut/Gravure sur bois en couleurs

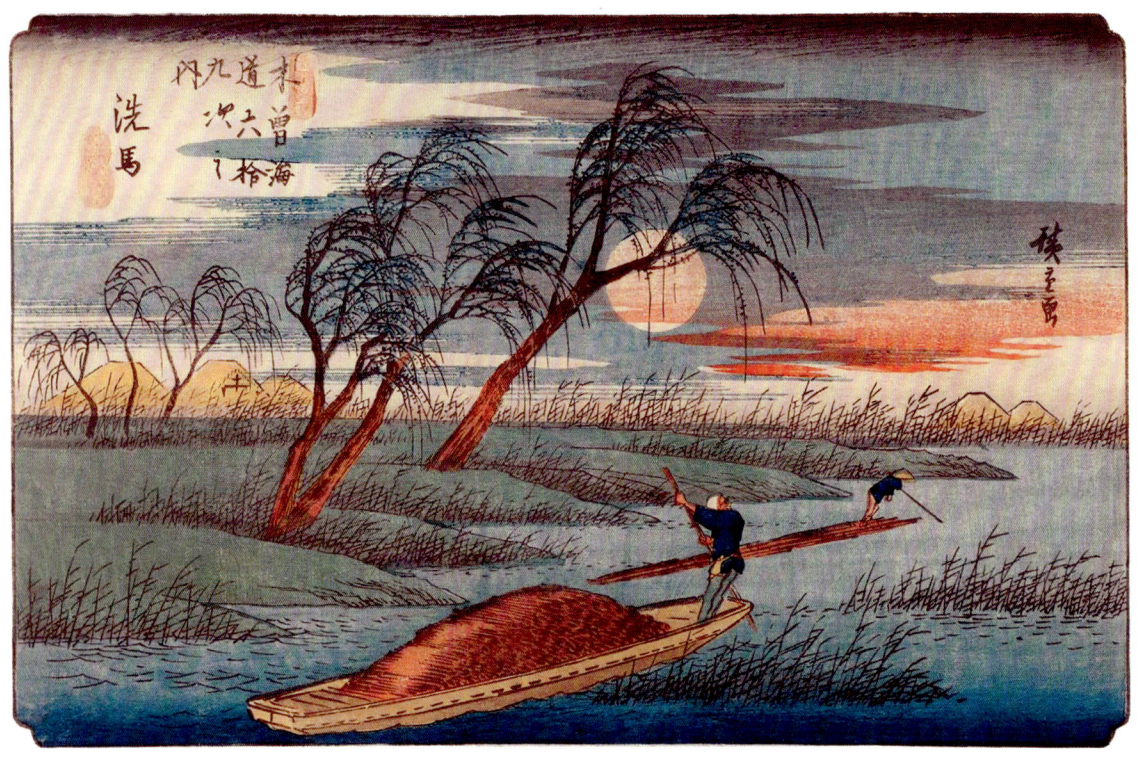

Seba, Station 32

Seba, relais 32

Colour woodcut/Gravure sur bois en couleurs

Weather and time of day play a central role in Hiroshige's work. Here the moon rises over the river Narai, turning the haze over the city a brilliant pink. The shading, which stands out particularly in the blues, bokashi.

Le temps et les moments de la journée jouent un rôle central chez Hiroshige. Ici, la lune se lève au-dessus du fleuve Narai et colore de rose la brume qui monte. Le dégradé qui ressort en particulier dans les nuances de bleu s'appelle techniquement bokashi.

Seba, Station 32

Seba, Estación 32

Wetter und Tageszeiten spielen bei Hiroshige eine zentrale Rolle. Hier geht der Mond über dem Fluss Narai am Himmel auf und färbt den aufsteigenden Dunst rosa. Die Schattierung, die besonders bei den blauen Farbnuancen hervorsticht, wird bokashi *genannt.*

El clima y los momentos del día juegan un papel fundamental para Hiroshige. Aquí, la luna aparece en el cielo detrás del río Narai, tiñendo la ingente neblina de color rosa. El sombreado, en especial en los matices azules, se conoce como bokashi.

Seba, stazione 32

Seba, halteplaats 32

Il tempo e le ore del giorno giocano un ruolo centrale per Hiroshige. Ecco la luna che sorge sul fiume Narai e colora di rosa la foschia che sale. L'ombra, evidenziata in particolare dalle sfumature di colore blu, è chiamata bokashi.

Het weer en het moment van de dag spelen bij Hiroshige een hoofdrol. Hier komt de maan op boven de rivier de Narai en kleurt de opstijgende nevel roze. De schaduwwerking die vooral in de blauwe kleurtonen naar voren komt, wordt bokashi *genoemd.*

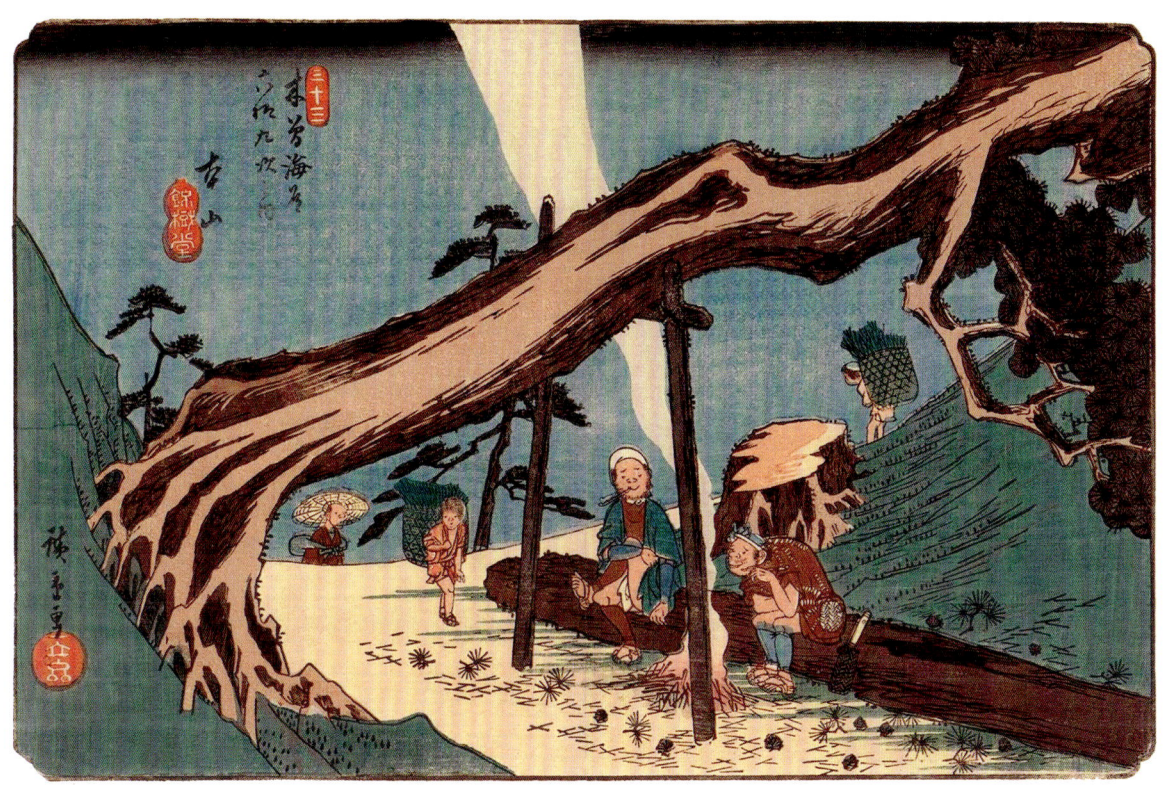

Motoyama, Station 33

Motoyama, relais 33

Motoyama, Station 33

Motoyama, Estación 33

Motoyama, stazione 33

Motoyama, halteplaats 33

Colour woodcut/Gravure sur bois en couleurs

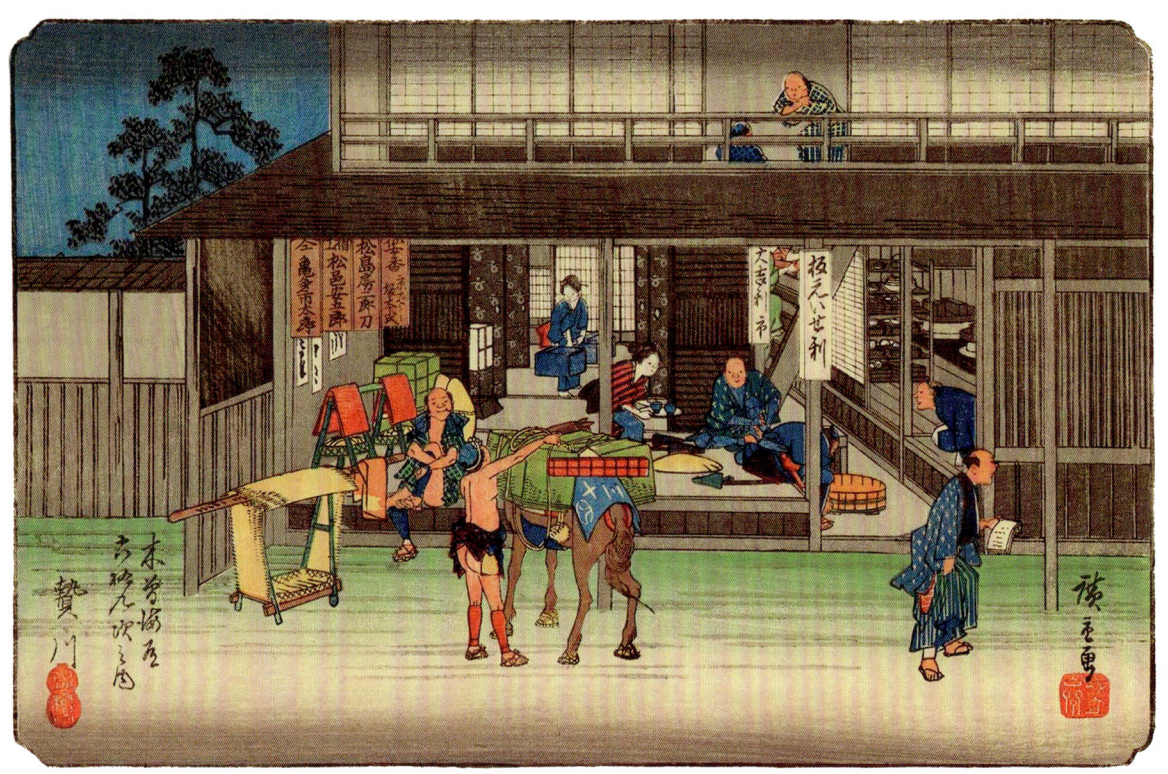

Niekawa, Station 34

Niekawa, relais 34

Niekawa, Station 34

Niekawa, Estación 34

Niekawa, stazione 34

Niekawa, halteplaats 34

Colour woodcut/Gravure sur bois en couleurs

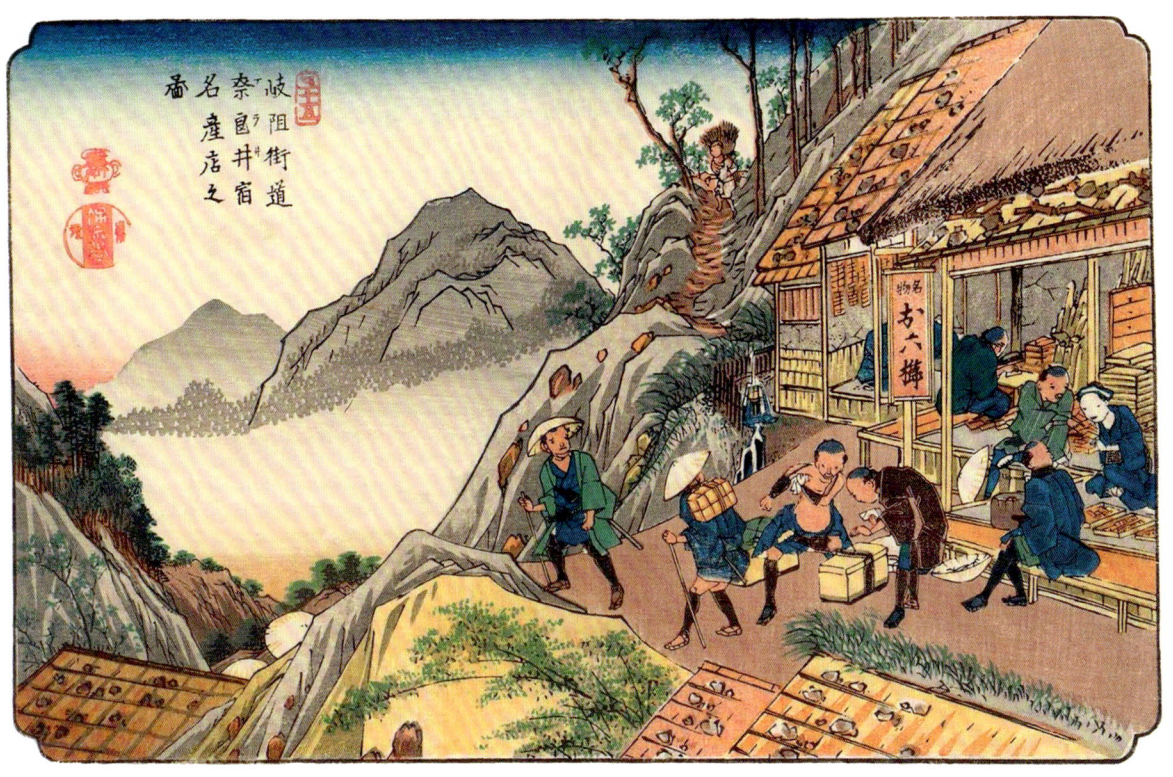

Keisai Eisen

Narai, Station 35

Narai, relais 35

Narai, Station 35

Narai, Estación 35

Narai, stazione 35

Narai, halteplaats 35

Colour woodcut/Gravure sur bois en couleurs

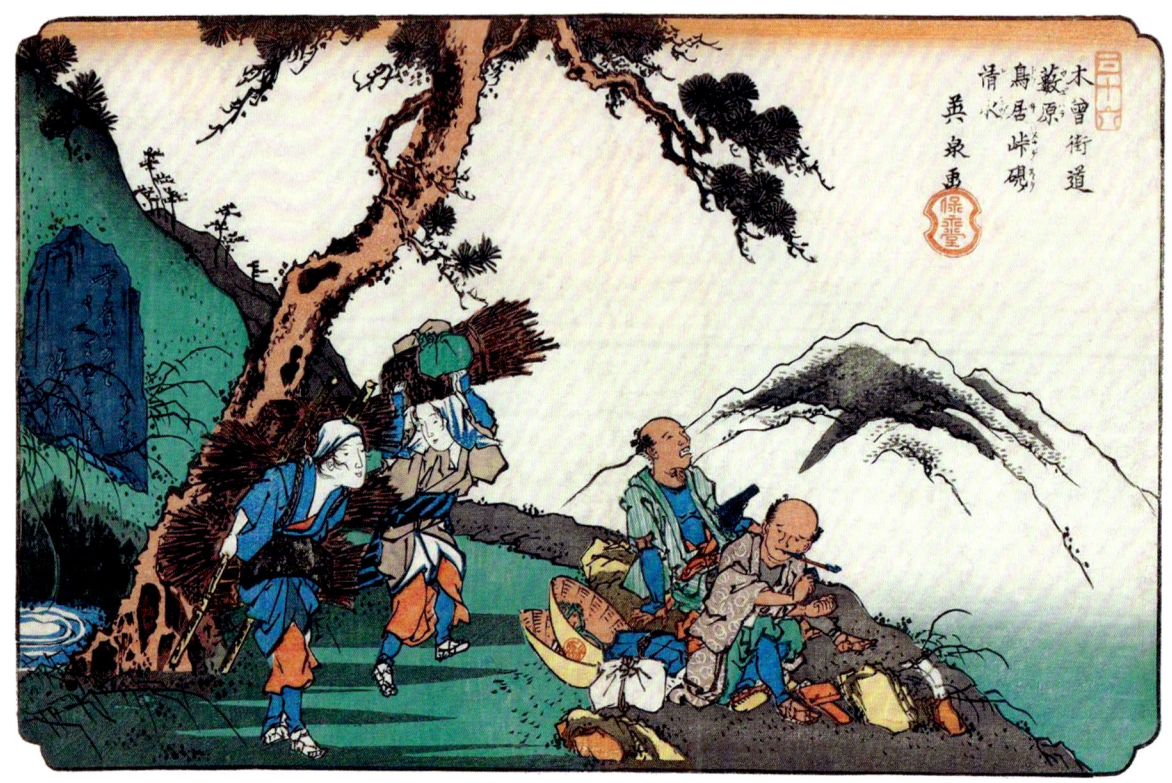

Keisai Eisen

Yabuhara, Station 36

Yabuhara, relais 36

Yabuhara, Station 36

Yabuhara, Estación 36

Yabuhara, stazione 36

Yabuhara, halteplaats 36

Colour woodcut/Gravure sur bois en couleurs

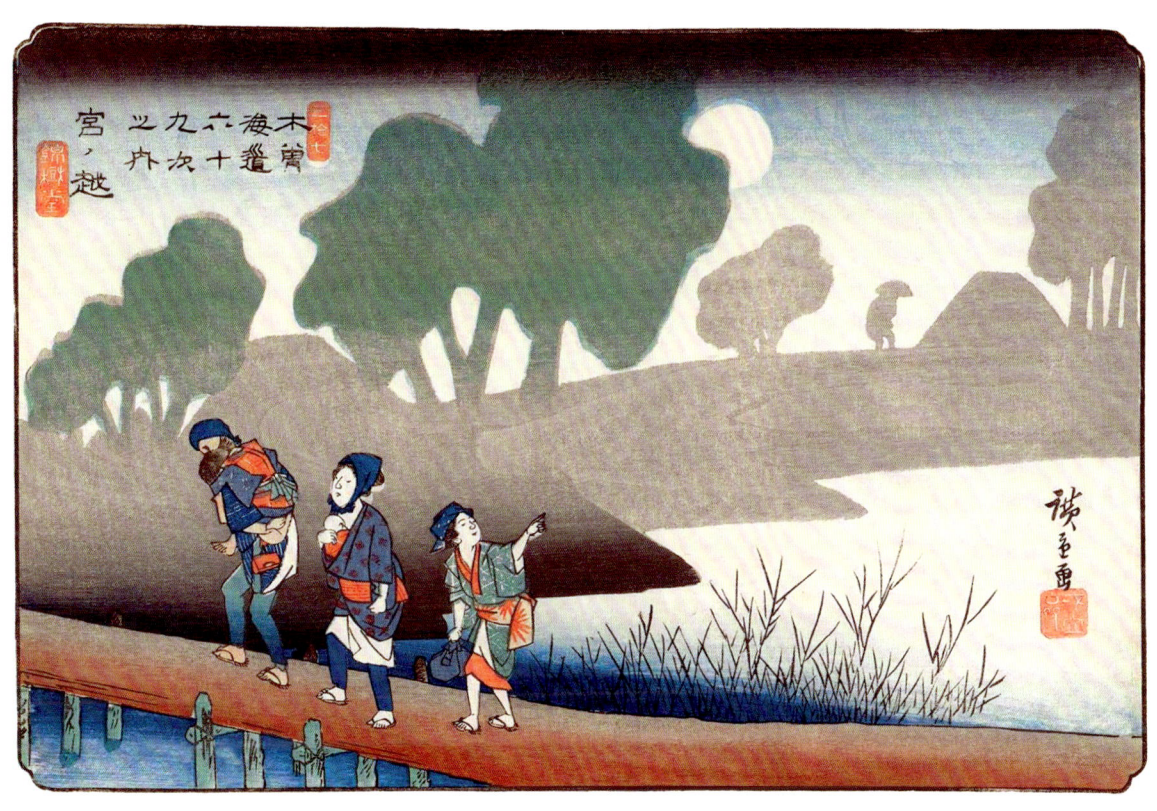

Miyanokoshi, Station 37

Miyanokoshi, relais 37

Miyanokoshi, Station 37

Miyanokoshi, Estación 37

Miyanokoshi, stazione 37

Miyanokoshi, halteplaats 37

Colour woodcut/Gravure sur bois en couleurs

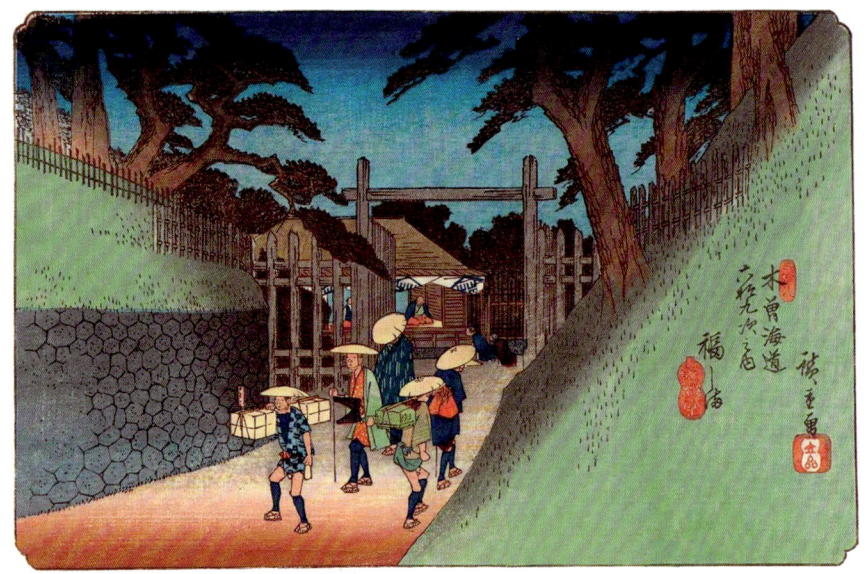

Fukushima, Station 38

Fukushima, relais 38

Fukushima, Station 38

Fukushima, Estación 38

Fukushima, stazione 38

Fukushima, halteplaats 38

Colour woodcut/Gravure sur bois
en couleurs, 24×36 cm

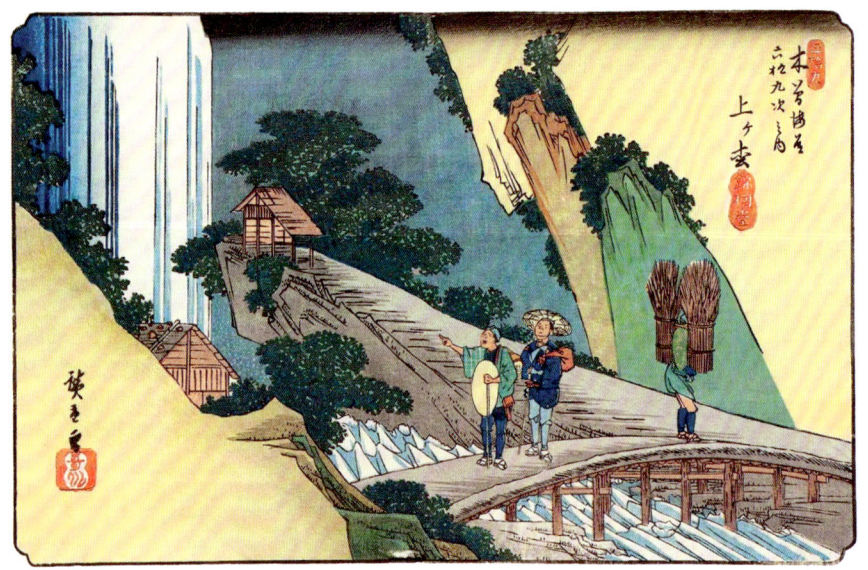

Agematsu, Station 39

Agematsu, relais 39

Agematsu, Station 39

Agematsu, Estación 39

Agematsu, stazione 39

Agematsu, halteplaats 39

Colour woodcut/Gravure sur bois
en couleurs

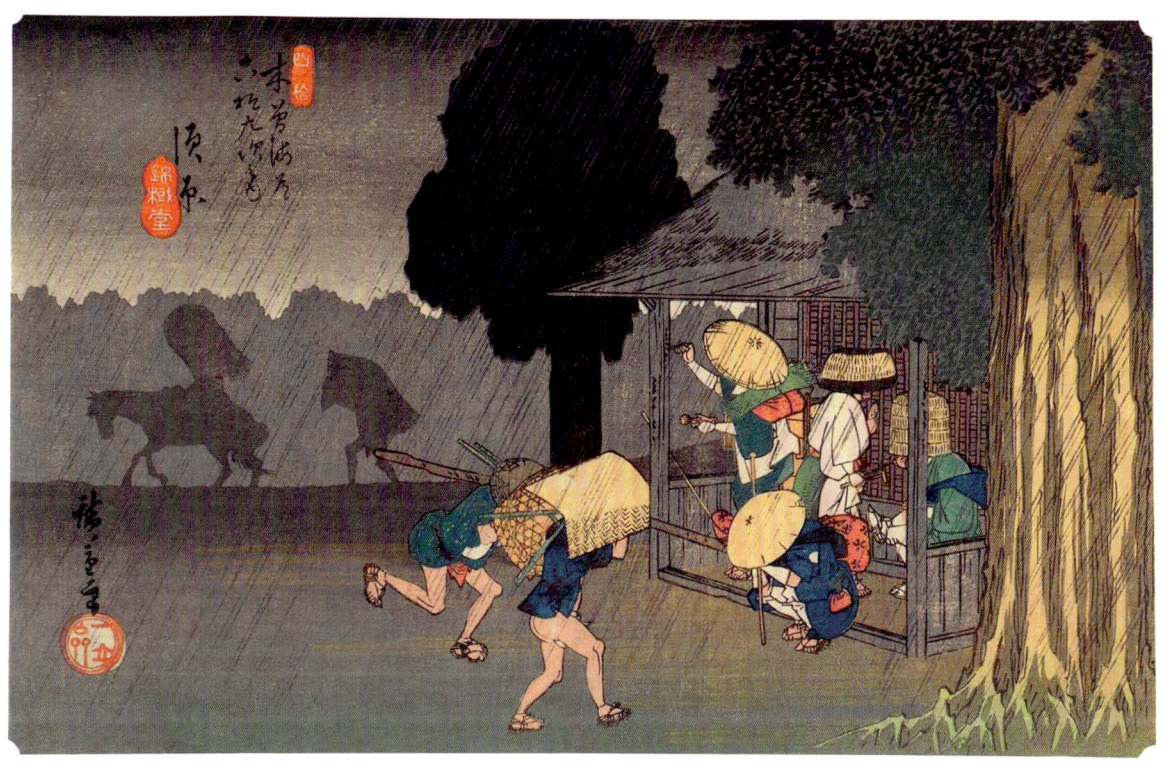

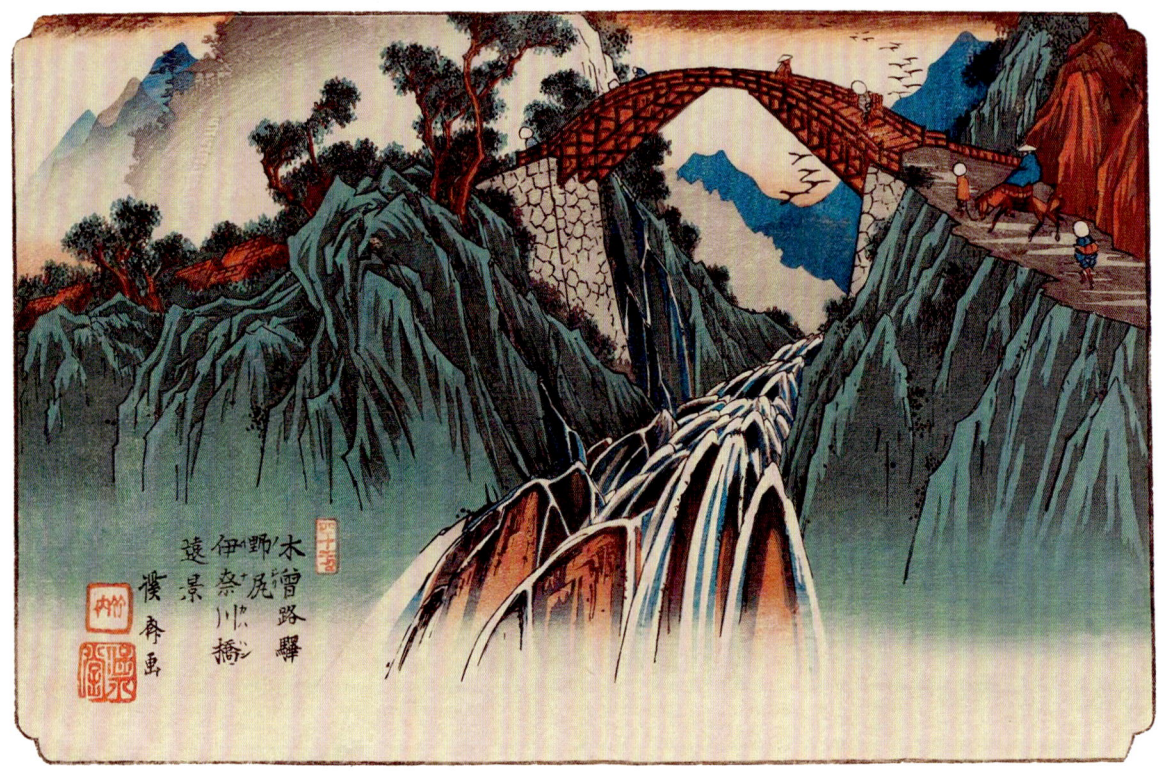

Keisai Eisen

Nojiri, Station 41

Nojiri, relais 41

Nojiri, Station 41

Nojiri, Estación 41

Nojiri, stazione 41

Nojiri, halteplaats 41

Colour woodcut/Gravure sur bois en couleurs

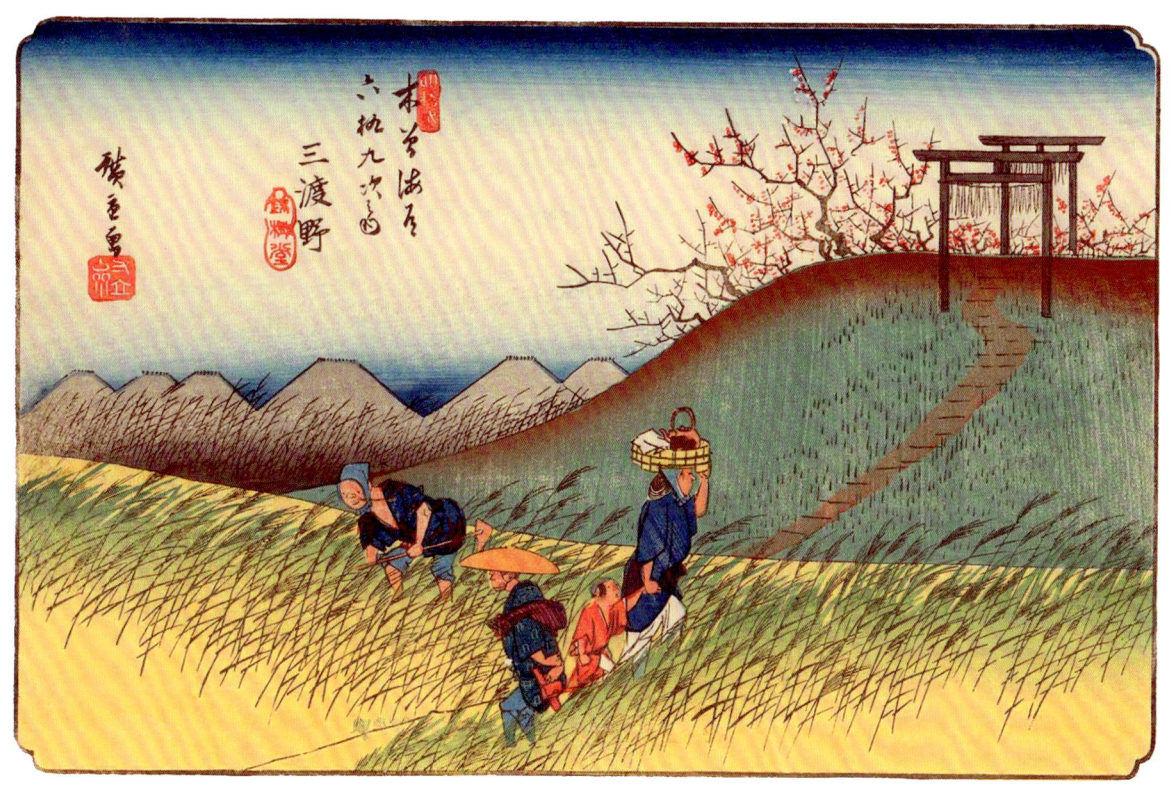

Midono, Station 42

Midono, relais 42

Midono, Station 42

Midono, Estación 42

Midono, stazione 42

Midono, halteplaats 42

Colour woodcut/Gravure sur bois en couleurs

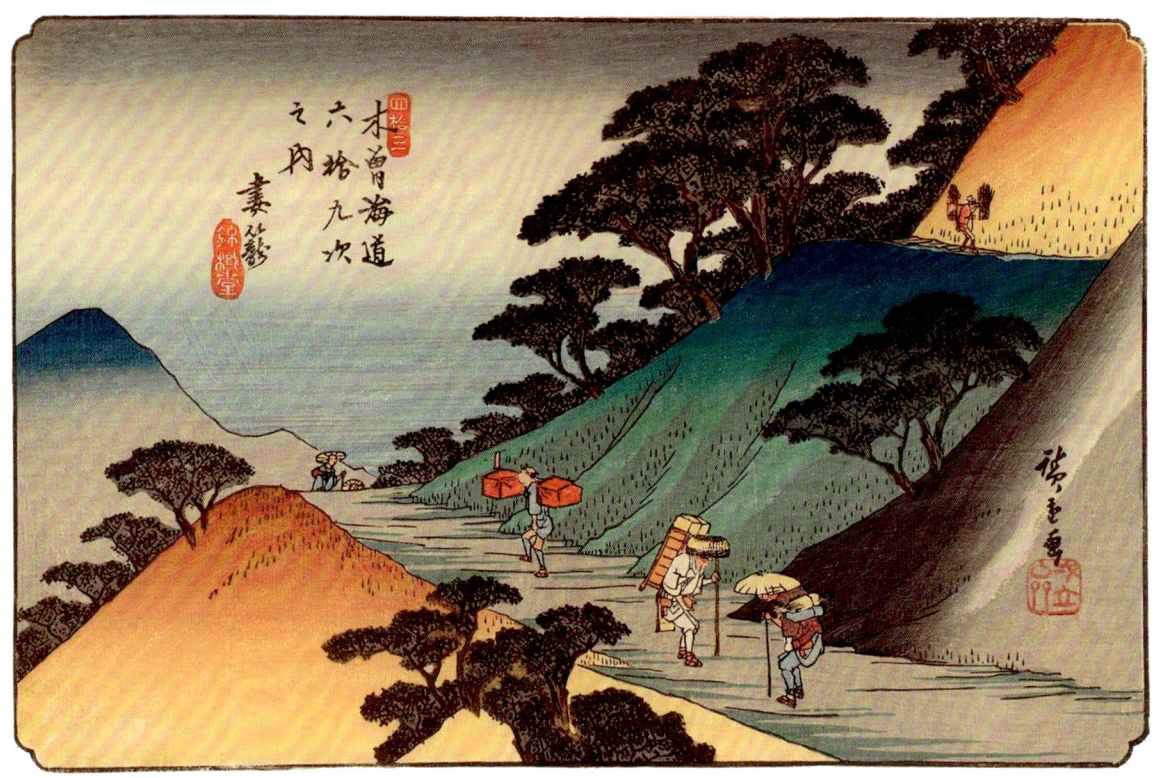

Tsumago, Station 43

Tsumago, relais 43

Tsumago, Station 43

Tsumago, Estación 43

Tsumago, stazione 43

Tsumago, halteplaats 43

Colour woodcut/Gravure sur bois en couleurs

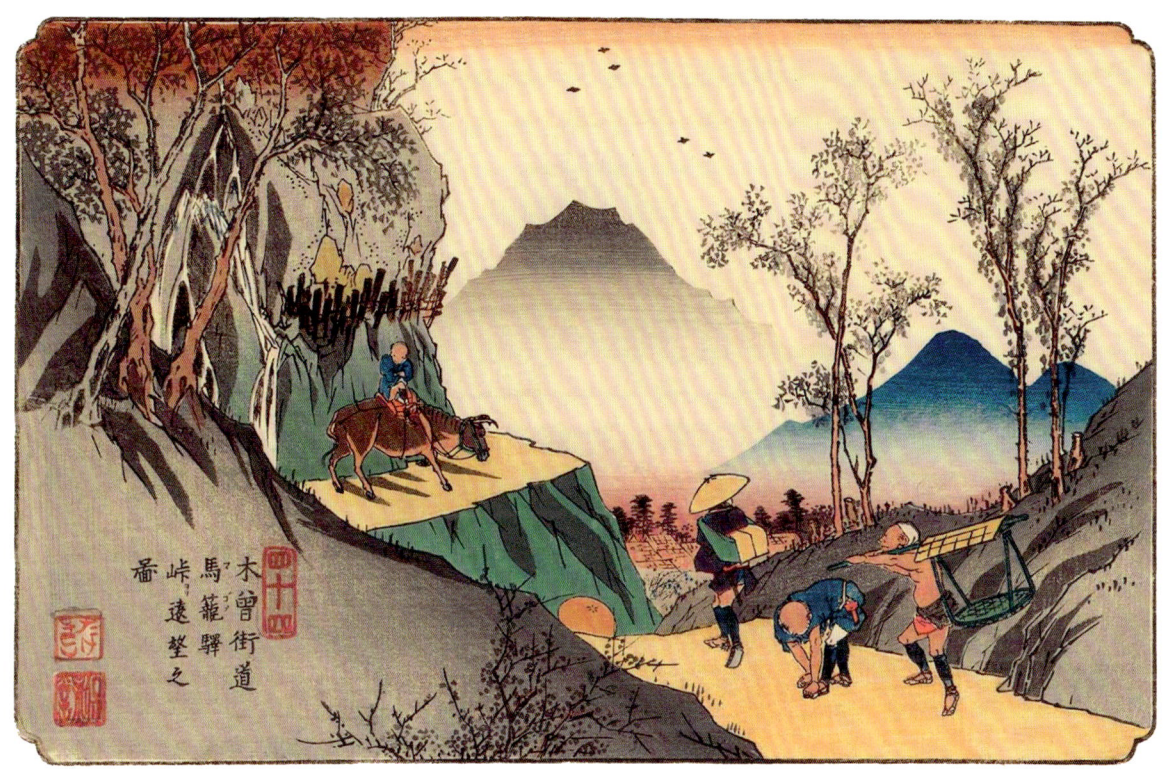

Keisai Eisen

Magome, Station 44

Magome, relais 44

Magome, Station 44

Magome, Estación 44

Magome, stazione 44

Magome, halteplaats 44

Colour woodcut/Gravure sur bois en couleurs

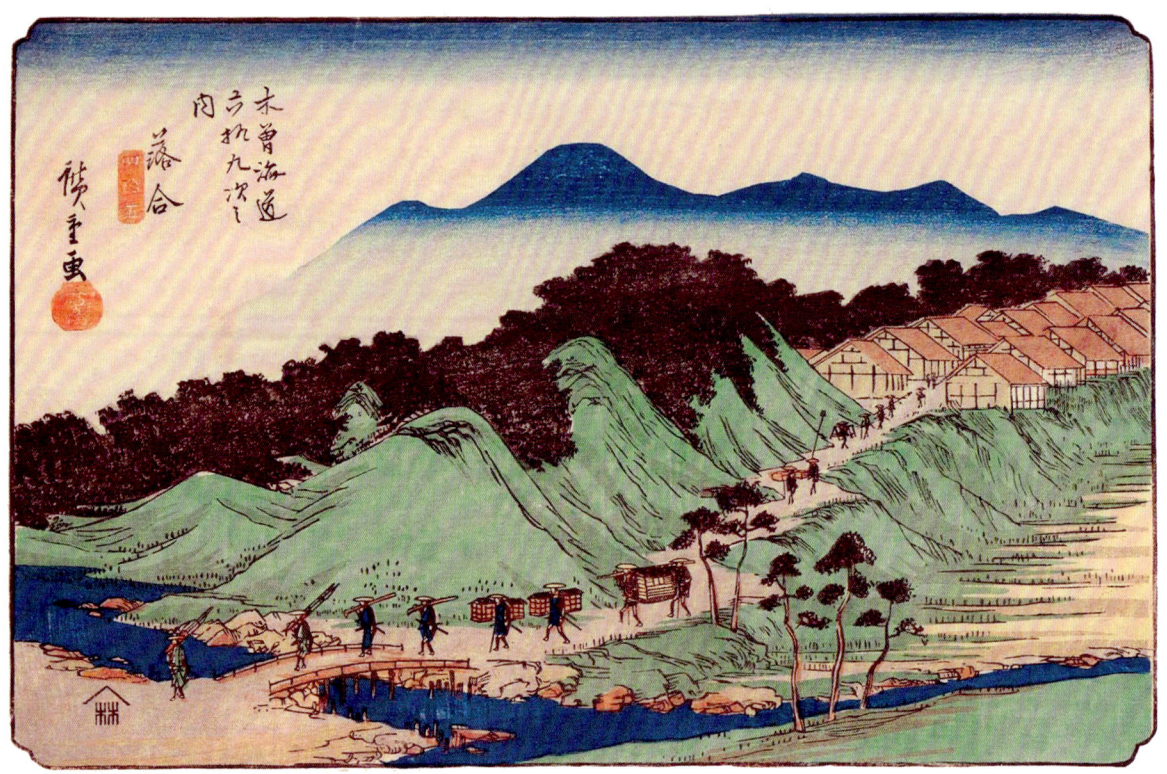

Ochiai, Station 45

Ochiai, relais 45

Ochiai, Station 45

Ochiai, Estación 45

Ochiai, stazione 45

Ochiai, halteplaats 45

Colour woodcut/Gravure sur bois en couleurs

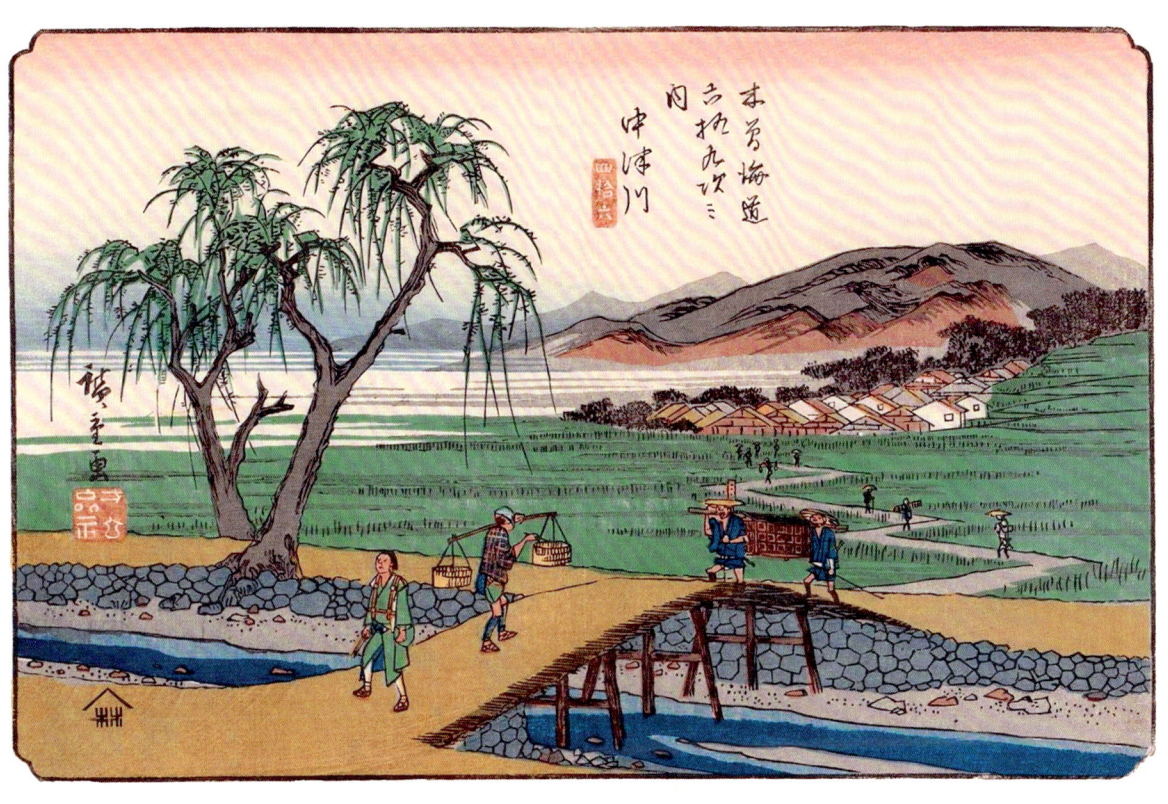

Nakatsugawa, Station 46, Version 2

Nakatsugawa, relais 46, Version 2

Nakatsugawa, Station 46, Version 2

Nakatsugawa, Estación 46, Versión 2

Nakatsugawa, stazione 46, versione 2

Nakatsugawa, halteplaats 46, Versie 2

Colour woodcut/Gravure sur bois en couleurs

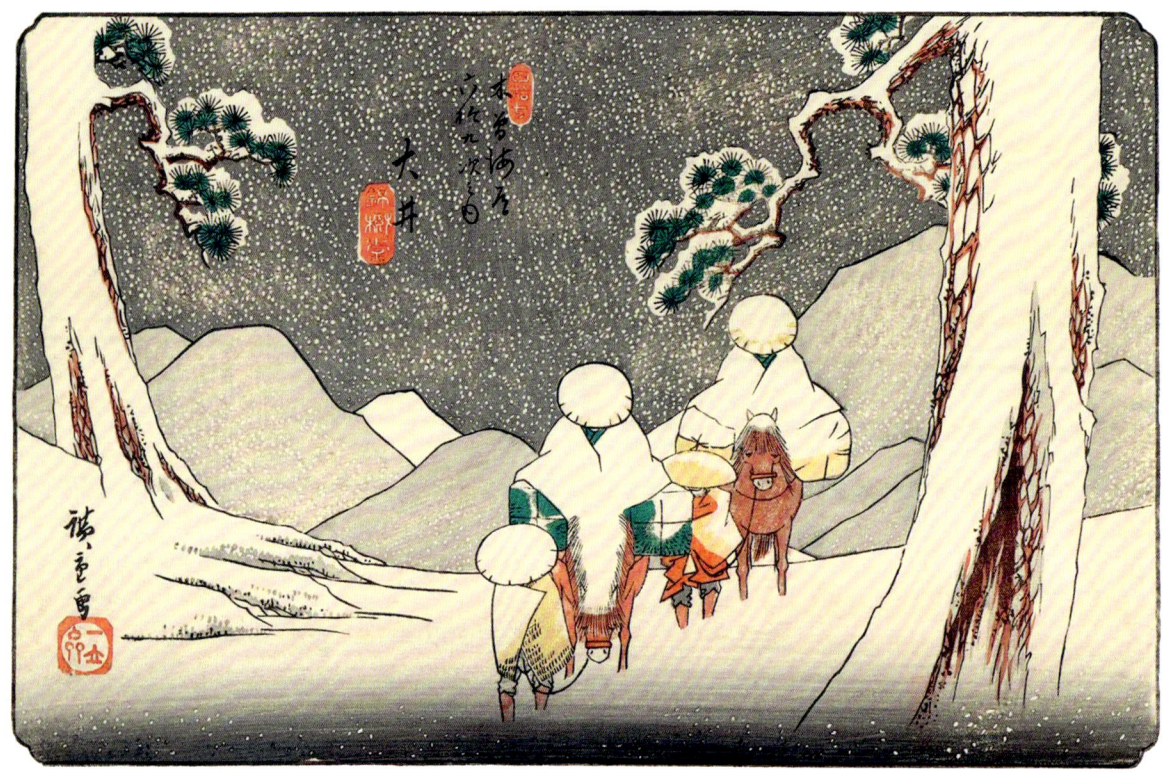

Oi, Station 47

Oi, relais 47

Oi, Station 47

Oi, Estación 47

Oi, stazione 47

Oi, halteplaats 47

Colour woodcut/Gravure sur bois en couleurs

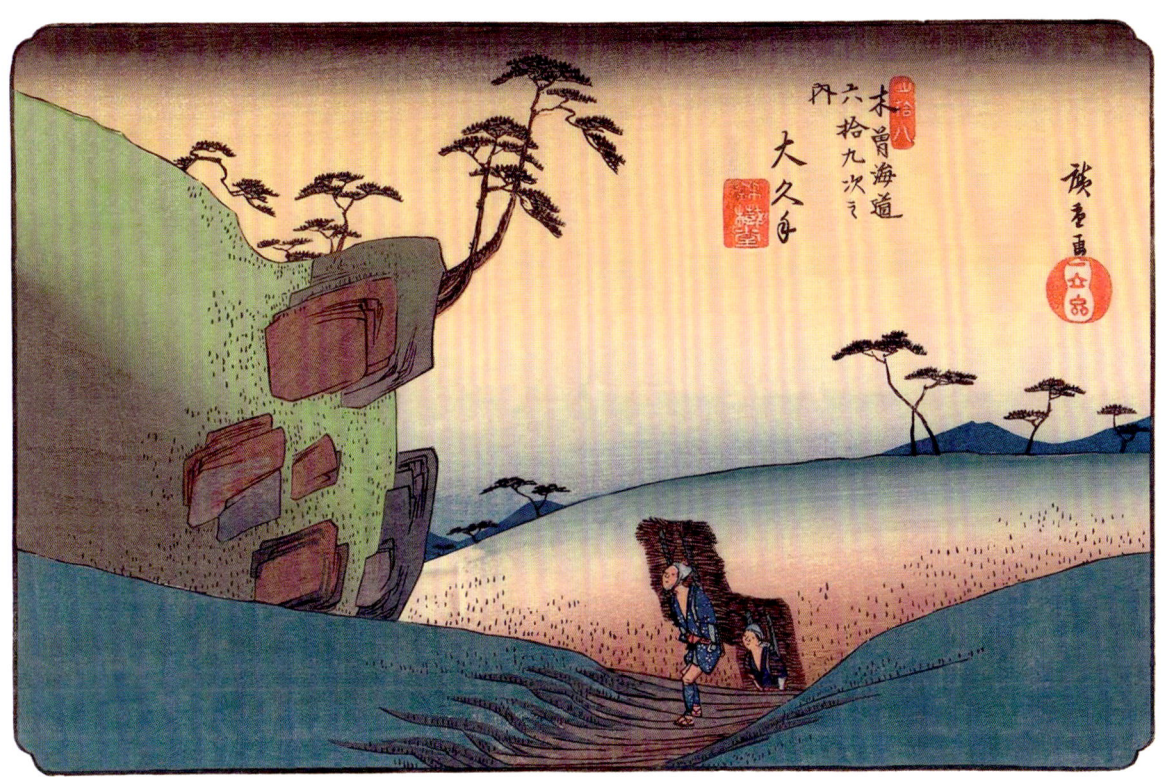

Okute, Station 48

Okute, relais 48

Okute, Station 48

Okute, Estación 48

Okute, stazione 48

Okute, halteplaats 48

Colour woodcut/Gravure sur bois en couleurs

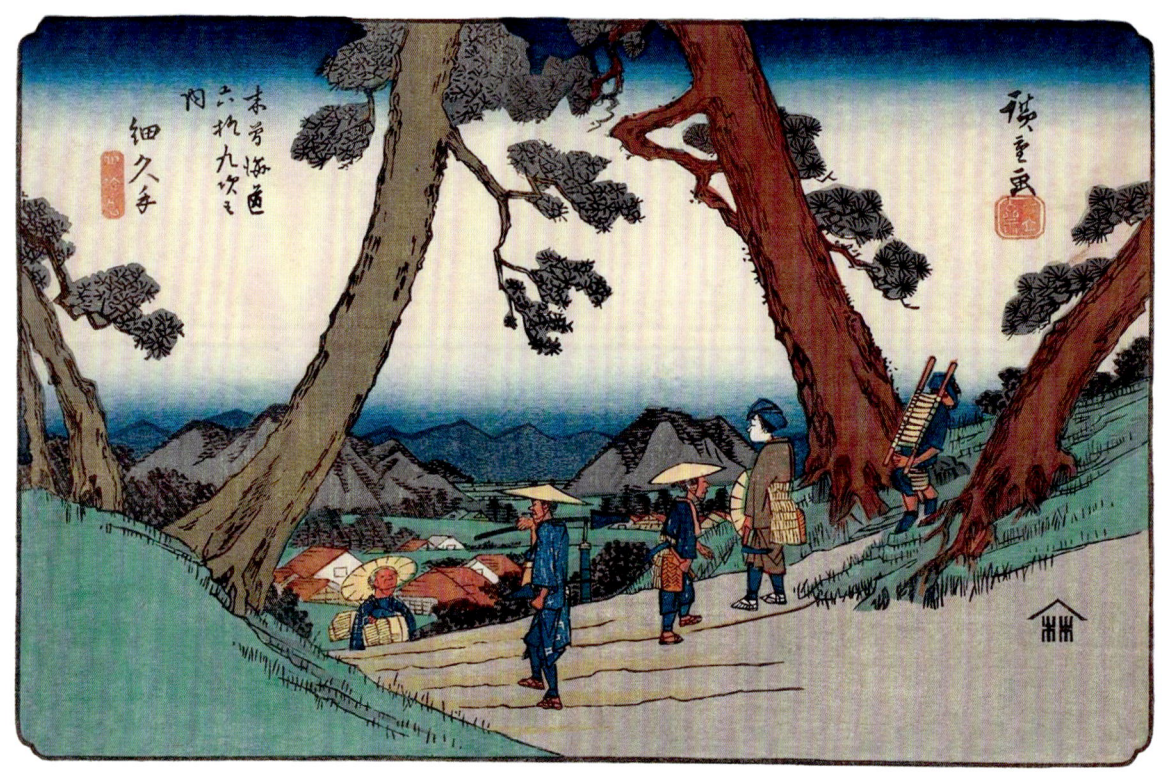

Hosokute, Station 49

Hosokute, relais 49

Hosokute, Station 49

Hosokute, Estación 49

Hosokute, stazione 49

Hosokute, halteplaats 49

Colour woodcut/Gravure sur bois en couleurs

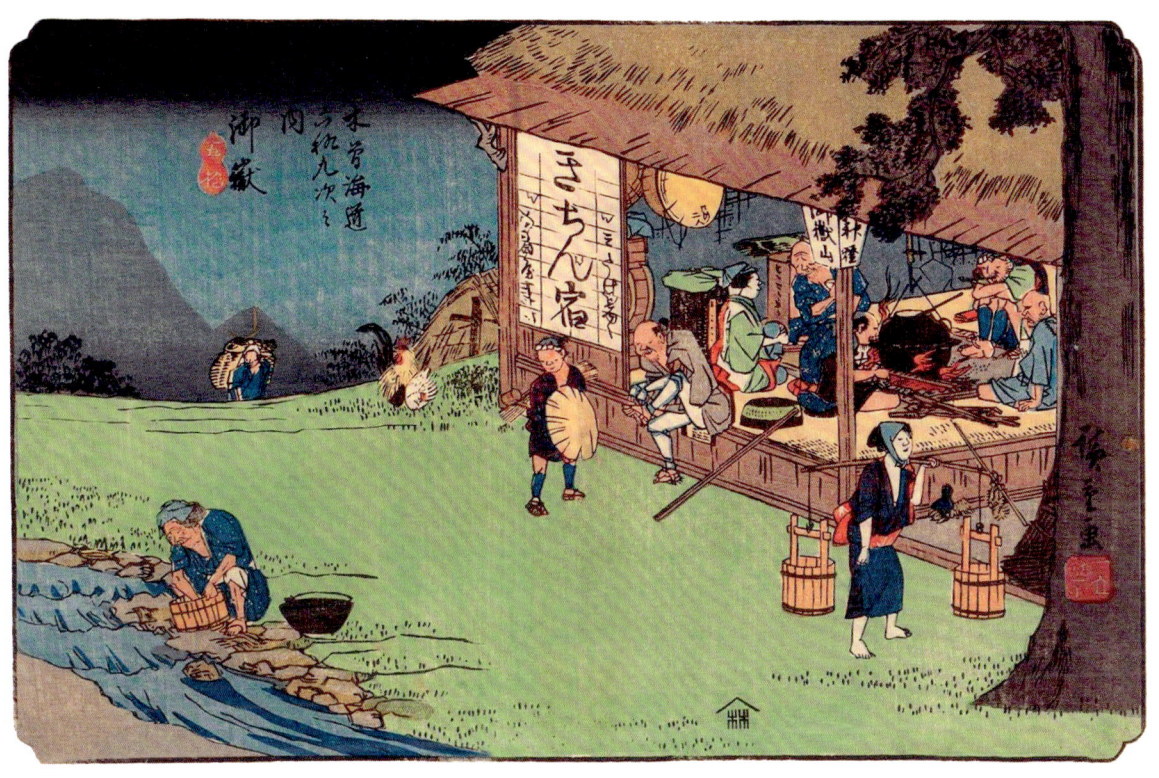

Mitake, Station 50

Mitake, relais 50

Mitake, Station 50

Mitake, Estación 50

Mitake, stazione 50

Mitake, halteplaats 50

Colour woodcut/Gravure sur bois en couleurs

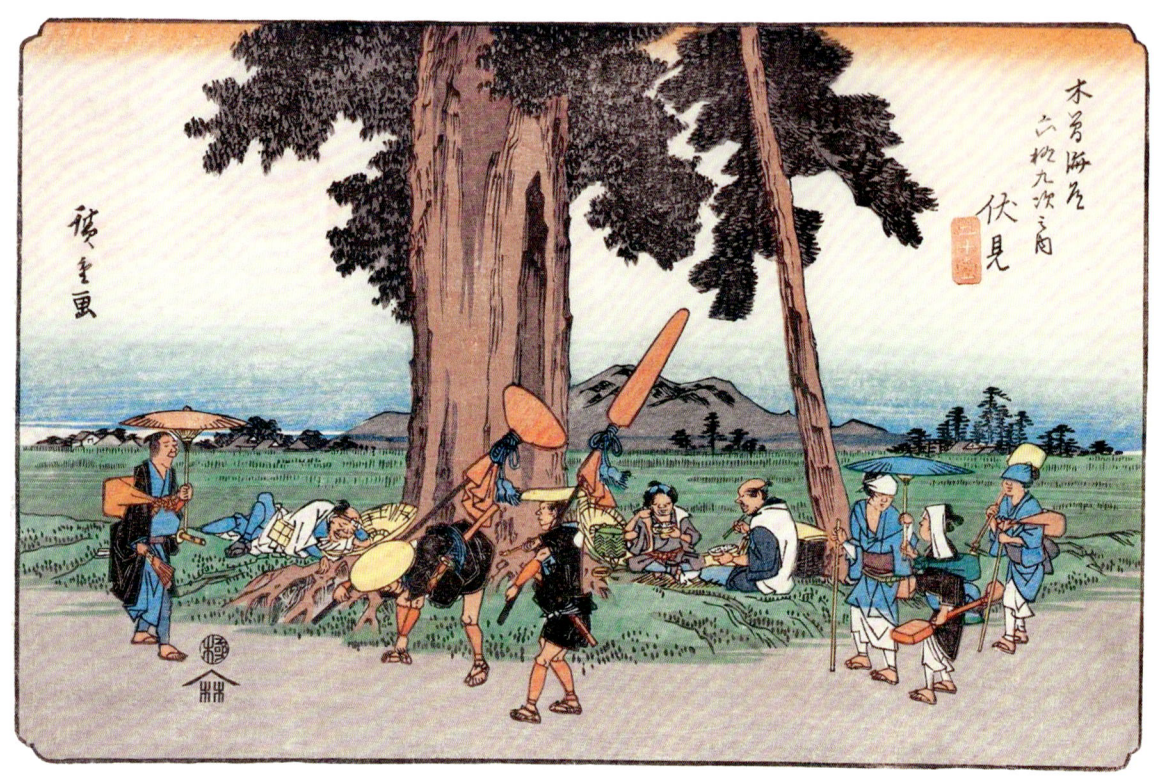

Fushimi, Station 51

Fushimi, relais 51

Fushimi, Station 51

Fushimi, Estación 51

Fushimi, stazione 51

Fushimi, halteplaats 51

Colour woodcut/Gravure sur bois en couleurs

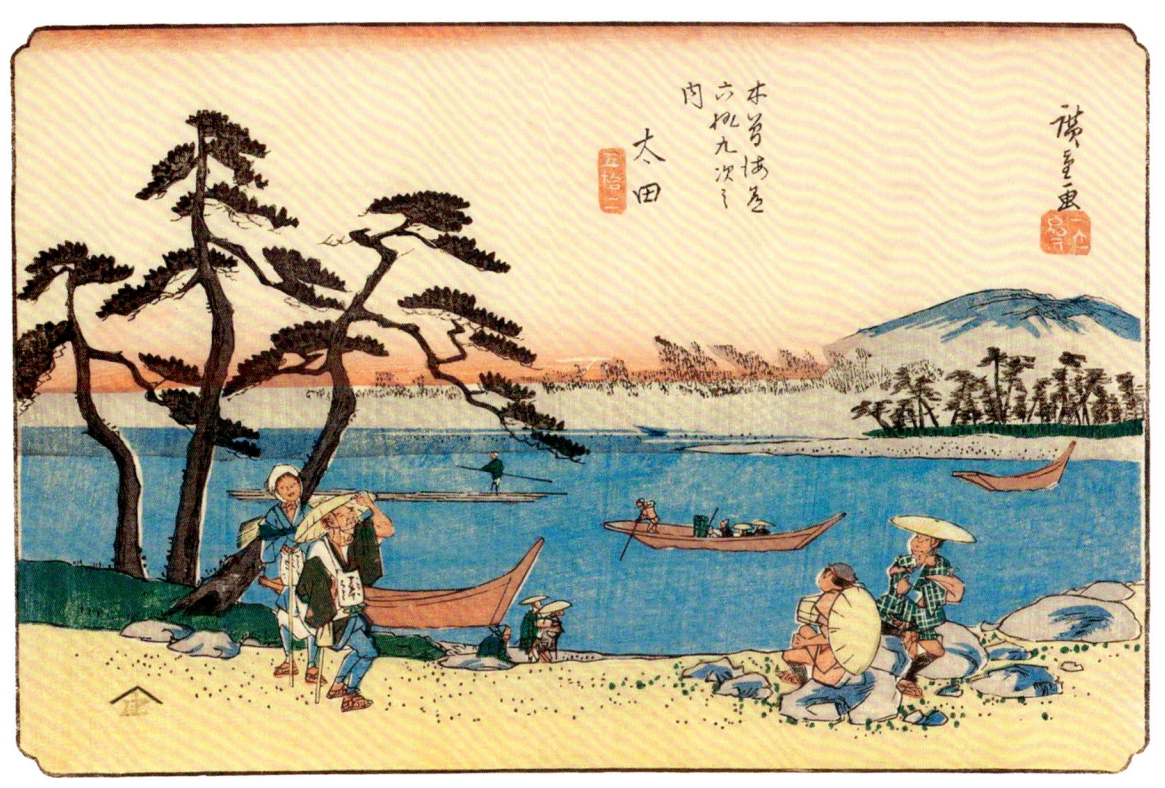

Ota, Station 52

Ota, relais 52

Ota, Station 52

Ota, Estación 52

Ota, stazione 52

Ota, halteplaats 52

Colour woodcut/Gravure sur bois en couleurs

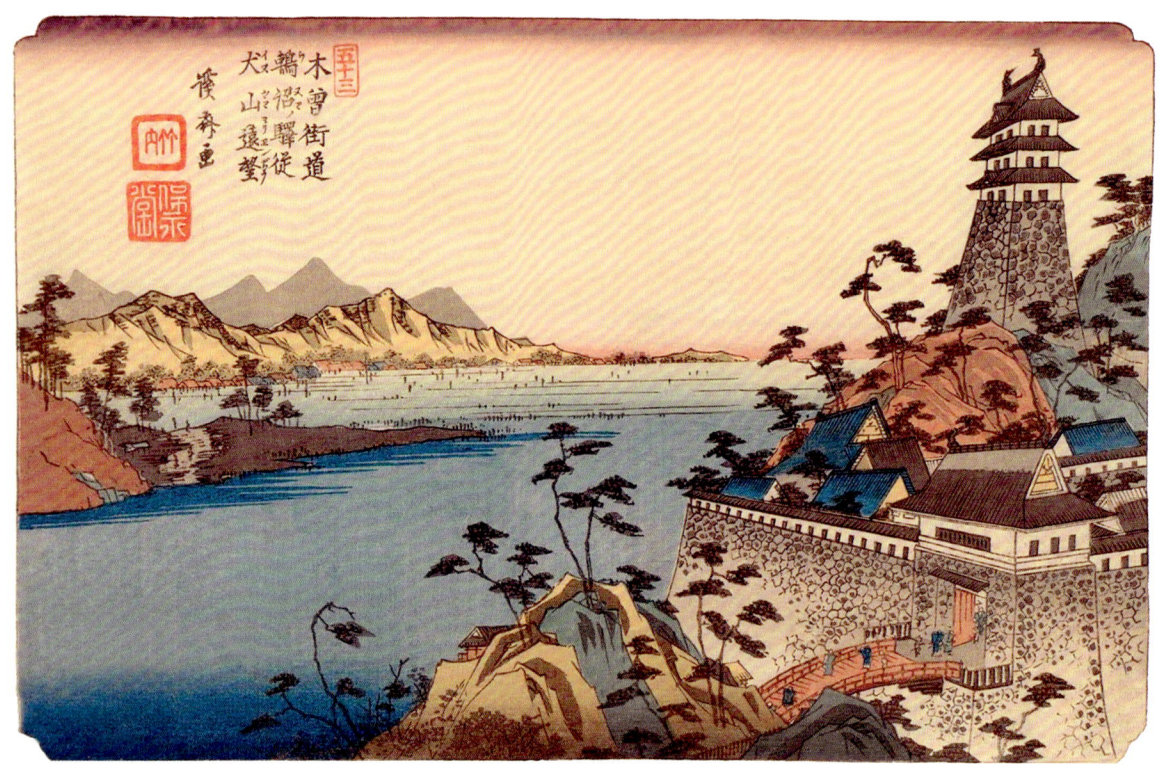

Keisai Eisen

Unuma, Station 53

Unuma, relais 53

Unuma, Station 53

Unuma, Estación 53

Unuma, stazione 53

Unuma, halteplaats 53

Colour woodcut/Gravure sur bois en couleurs

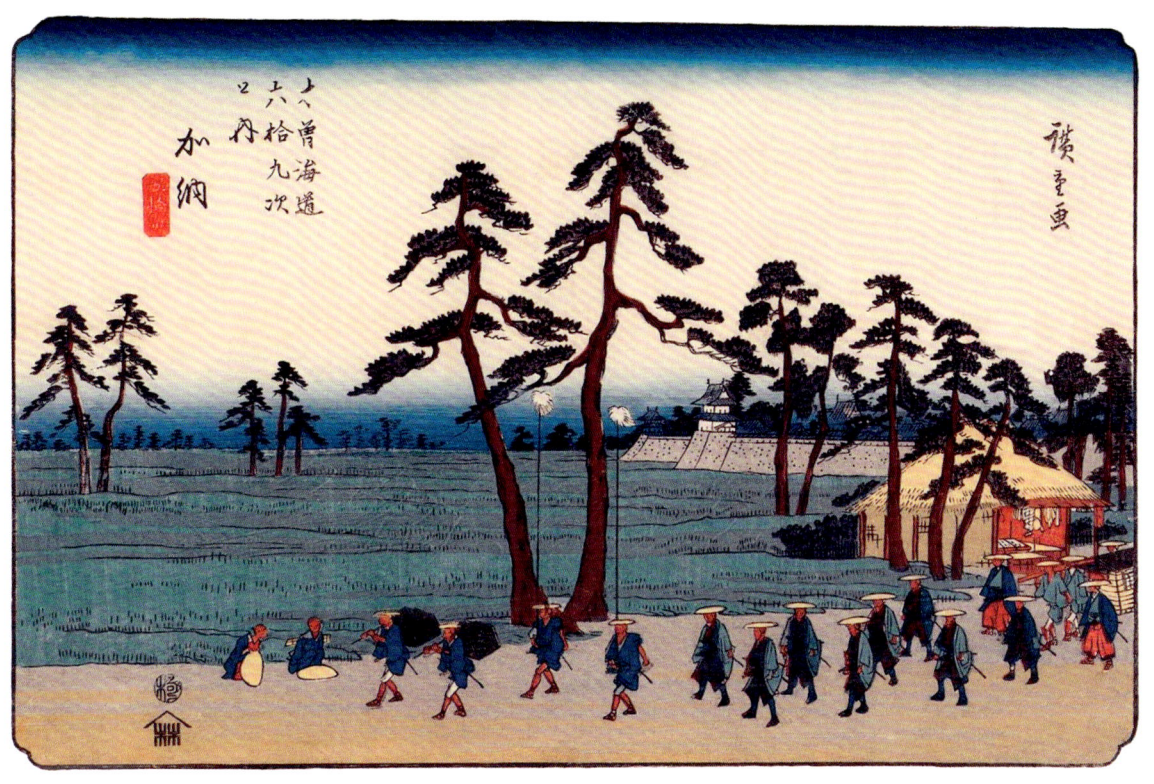

Kano, Station 54

Kano, relais 54

Kano, Station 54

Kano, Estación 54

Kano, stazione 54

Kano, halteplaats 54

Colour woodcut/Gravure sur bois en couleurs

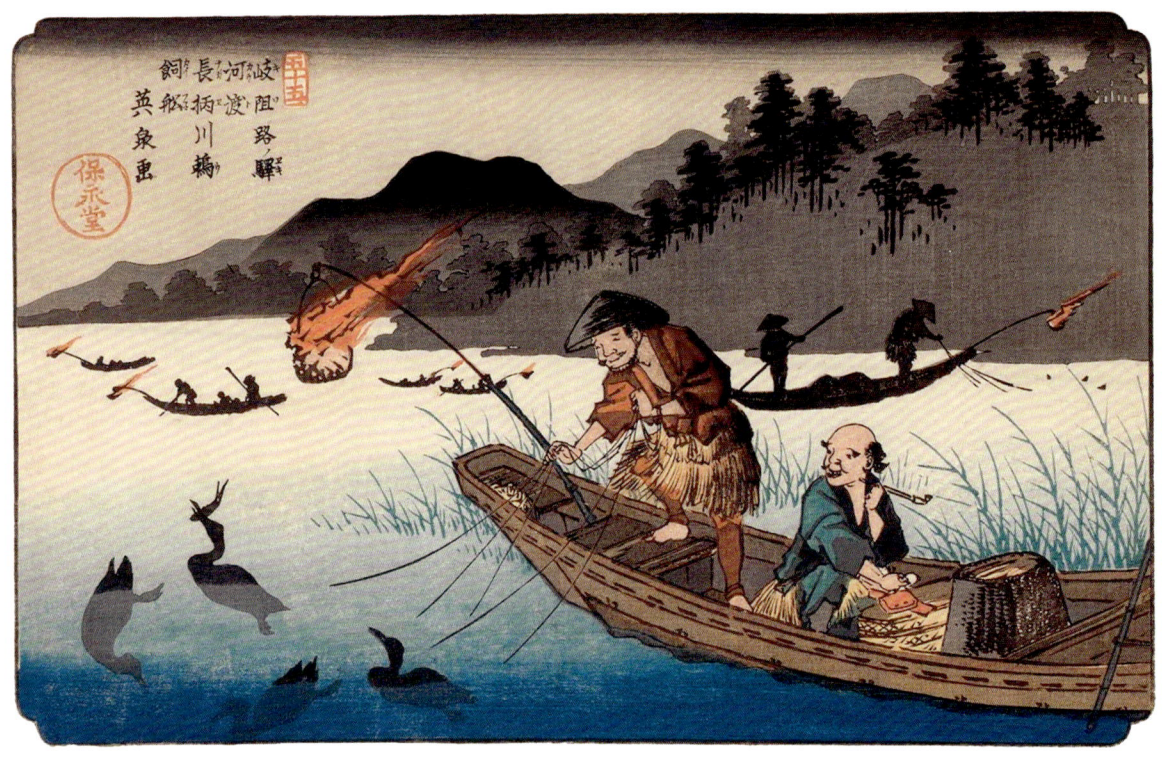

Keisai Eisen

Godo, Station 55

Godo, relais 55

Godo, Station 55

Godo, Estación 55

Godo, stazione 55

Godo, halteplaats 55

Colour woodcut/Gravure sur bois en couleurs

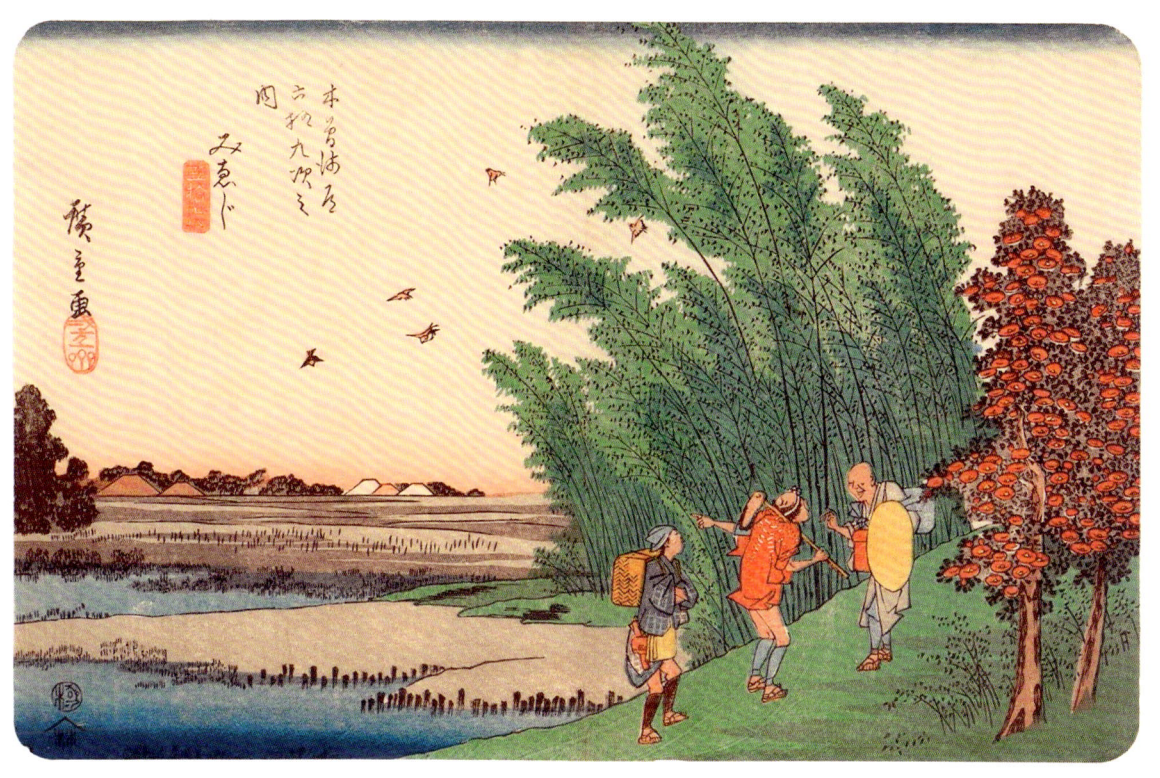

Mieji, Station 56
Mieji, relais 56
Mieji, Station 56
Mieji, Estación 56
Mieji, stazione 56
Mieji, halteplaats 56
Colour woodcut/Gravure sur bois en couleurs

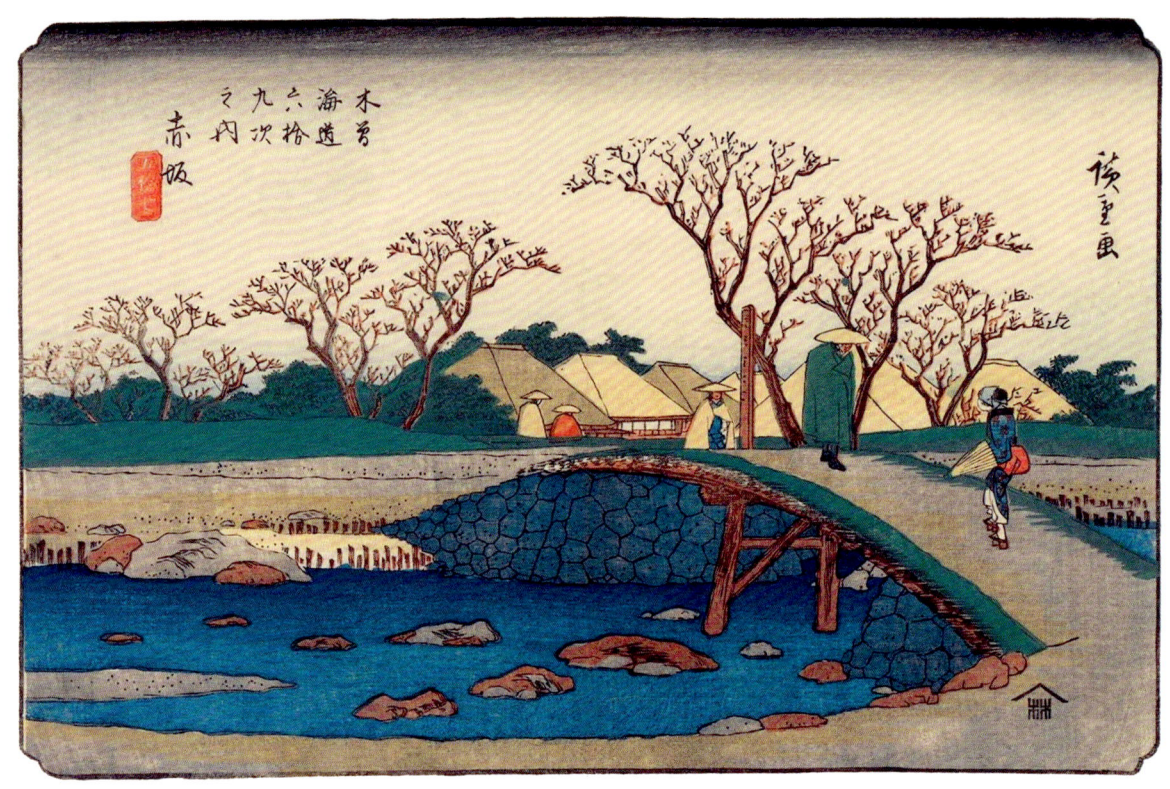

Akasaka, Station 57

Akasaka, relais 57

Akasaka, Station 57

Akasaka, Estación 57

Akasaka, stazione 57

Akasaka, halteplaats 57

Colour woodcut/Gravure sur bois en couleur

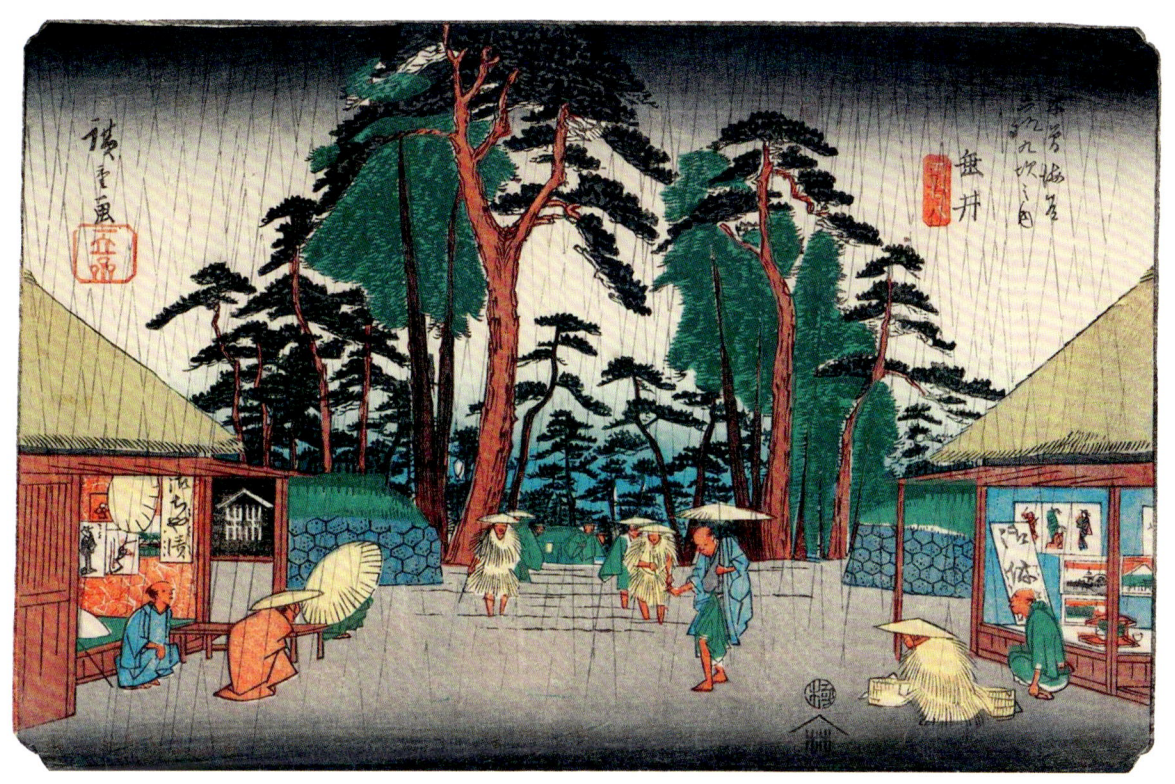

Tarui, Station 58

Tarui, relais 58

Tarui, Station 58

Tarui, Estación 58

Tarui, stazione 58

Tarui, halteplaats 58

Colour woodcut/Gravure sur bois en couleurs

121

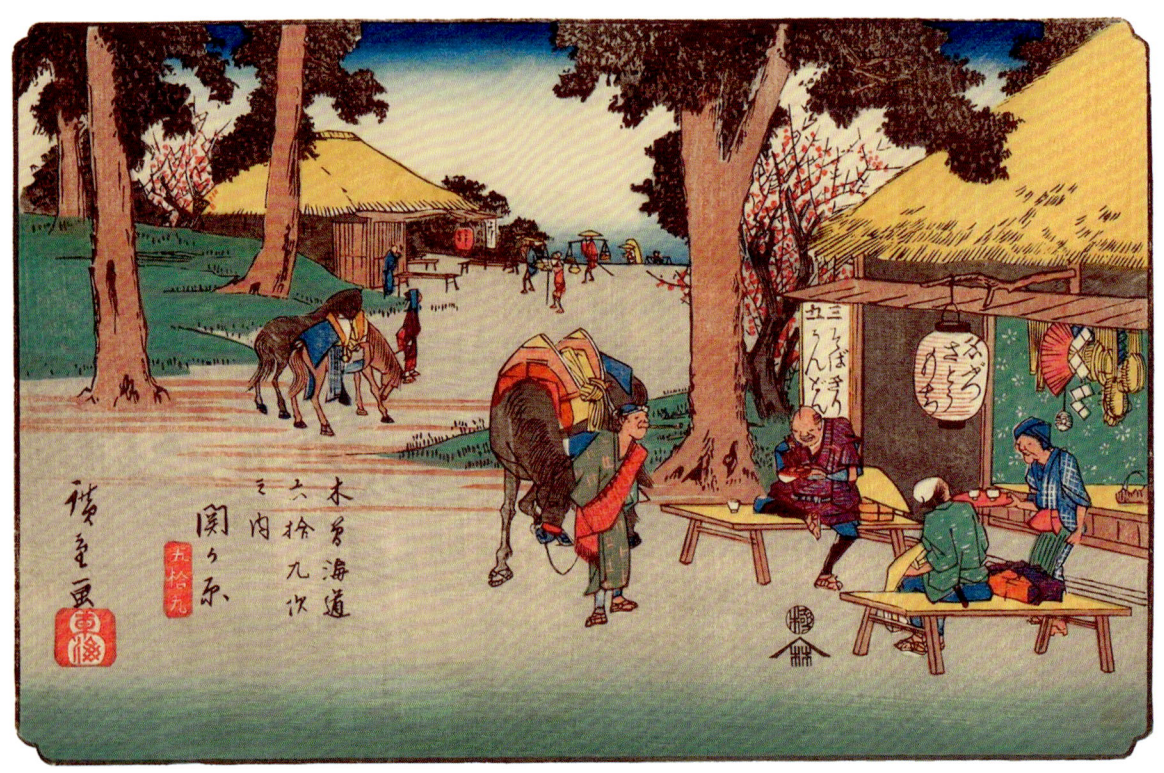

Sekigahara, Station 59

Sekigahara, relais 59

Sekigahara, Station 59

Sekigahara, Estación 59

Sekigahara, stazione 59

Sekigahara, halteplaats 59

Colour woodcut/Gravure sur bois en couleurs

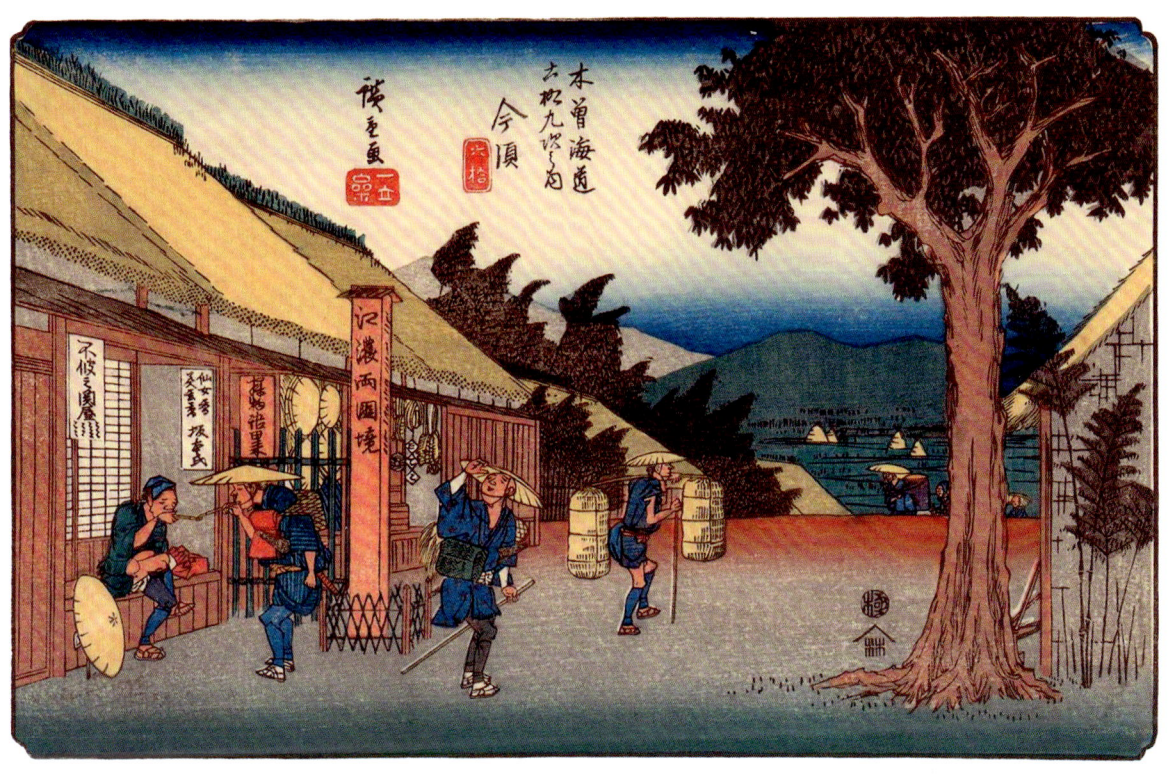

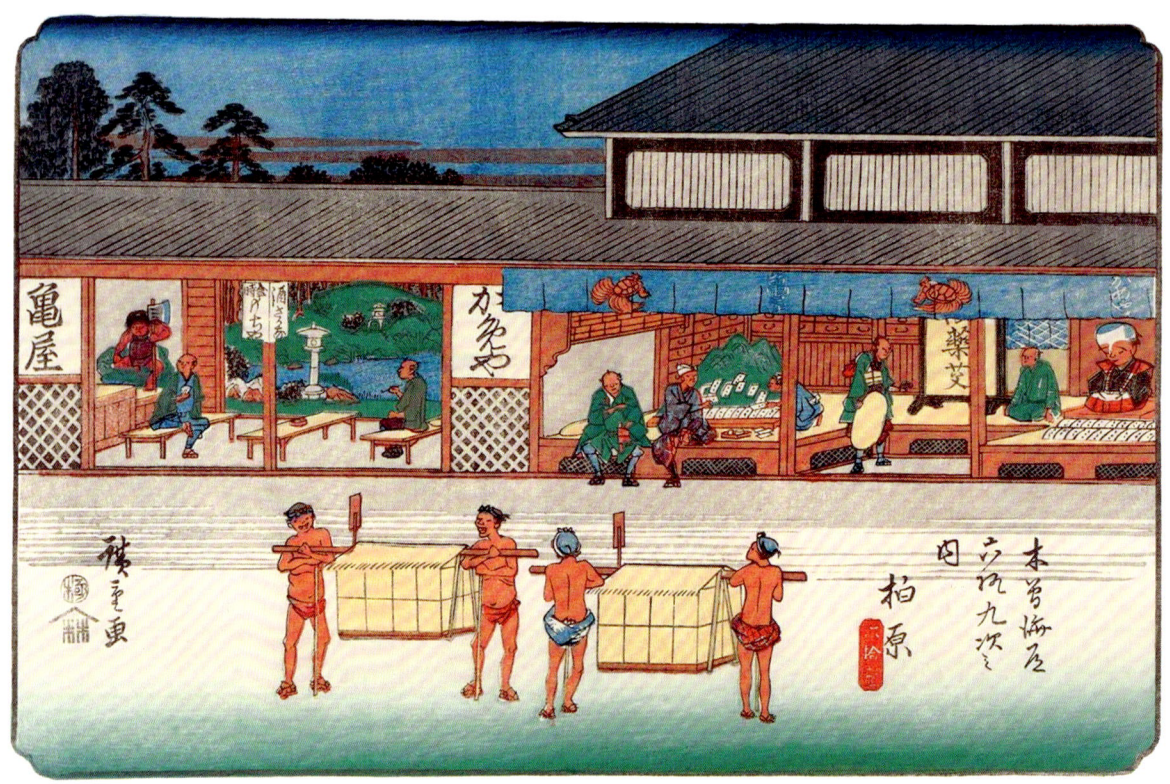

Kashiwabara, Station 61

Kashiwabara, relais 61

Kashiwabara, Station 61

Kashiwabara, Estación 61

Kashiwabara, stazione 61

Kashiwabara, halteplaats 61

Colour woodcut/Gravure sur bois en couleurs

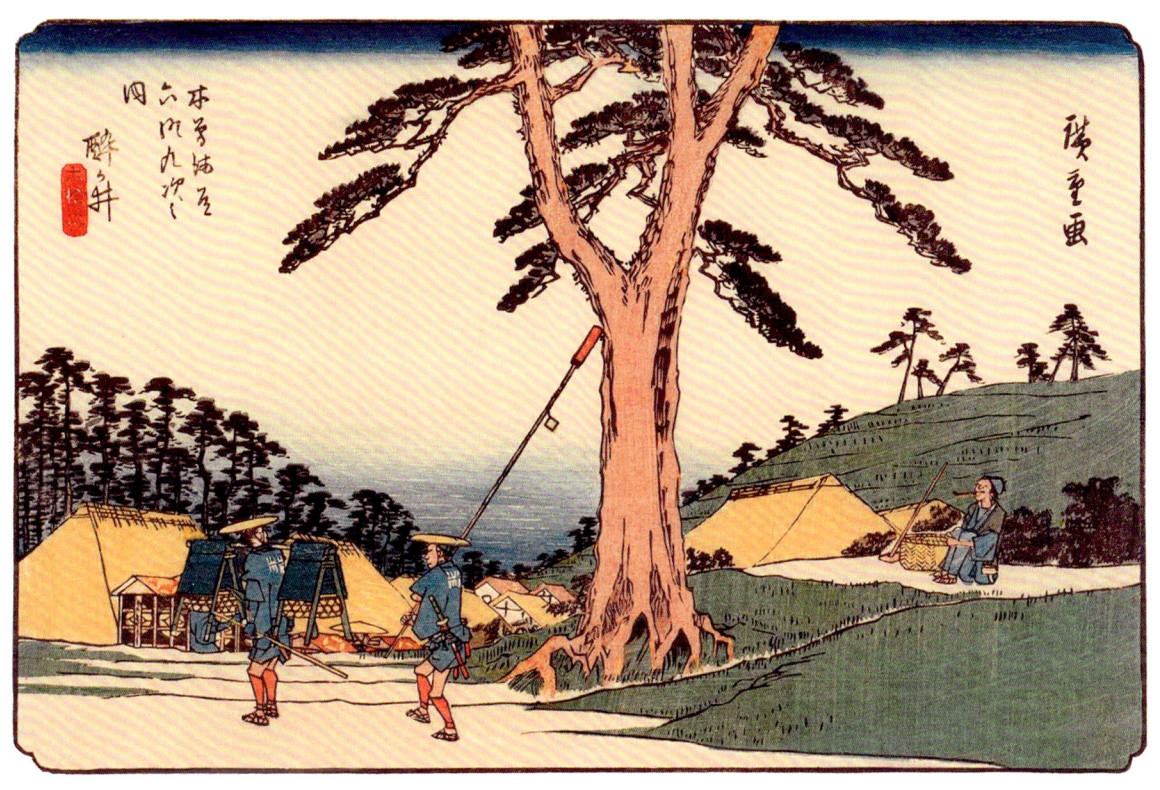

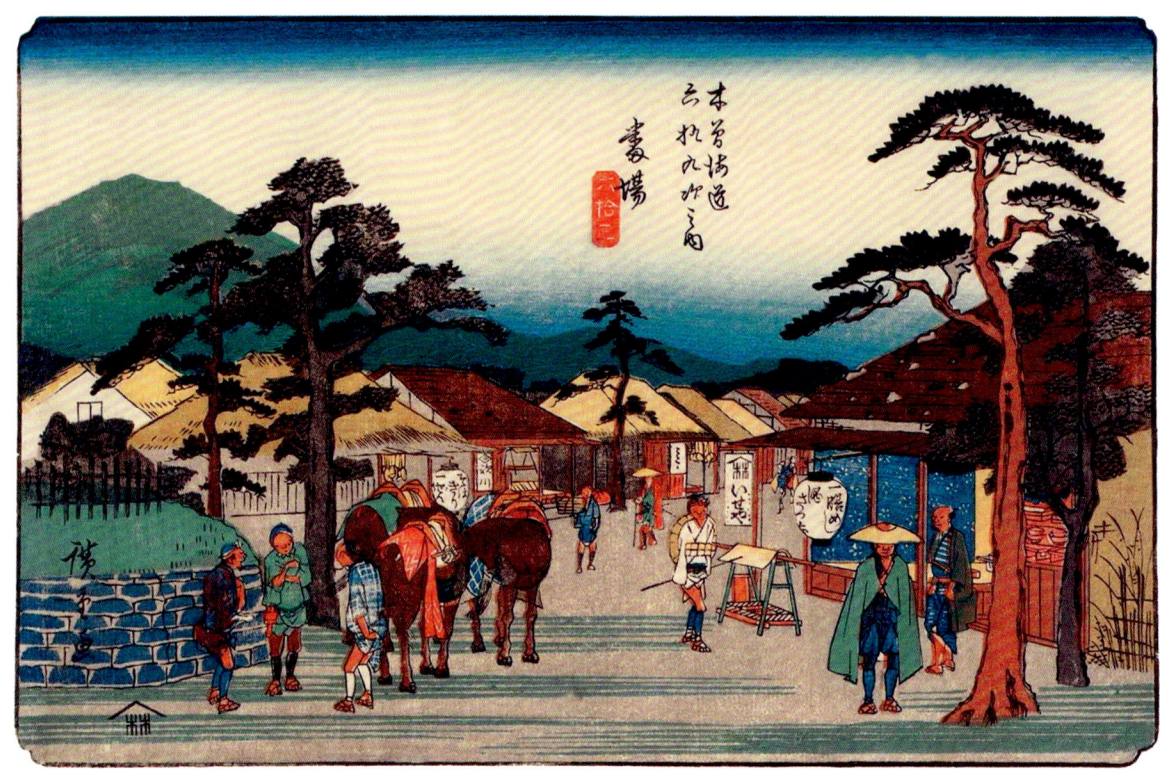

Banba, Station 63

Banba, relais 63

Banba, Station 63

Banba, Estación 63

Banba, stazione 63

Banba, halteplaats 63

Colour woodcut/Gravure sur bois en couleurs

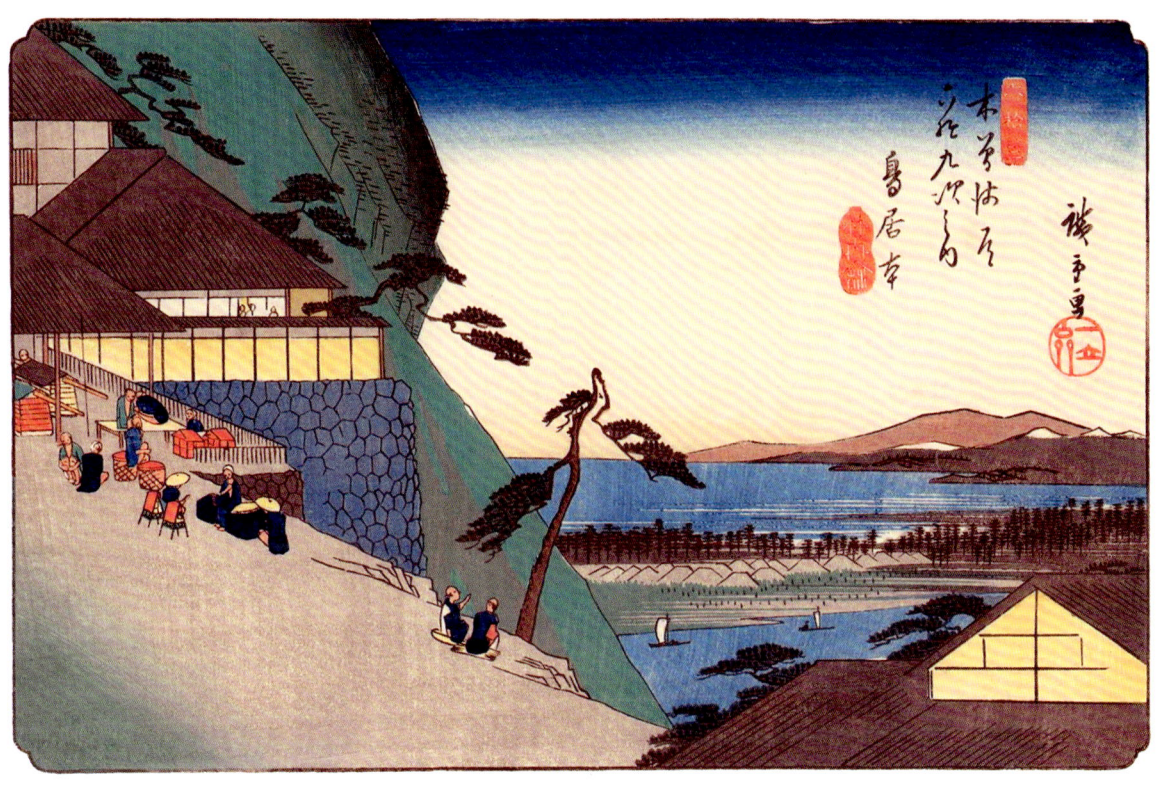

Toriimoto, Station 64

Toriimoto, relais 64

Toriimoto, Station 64

Toriimoto, Estación 64

Toriimoto, stazione 64

Toriimoto, halteplaats 64

Colour woodcut/Gravure sur bois en couleurs

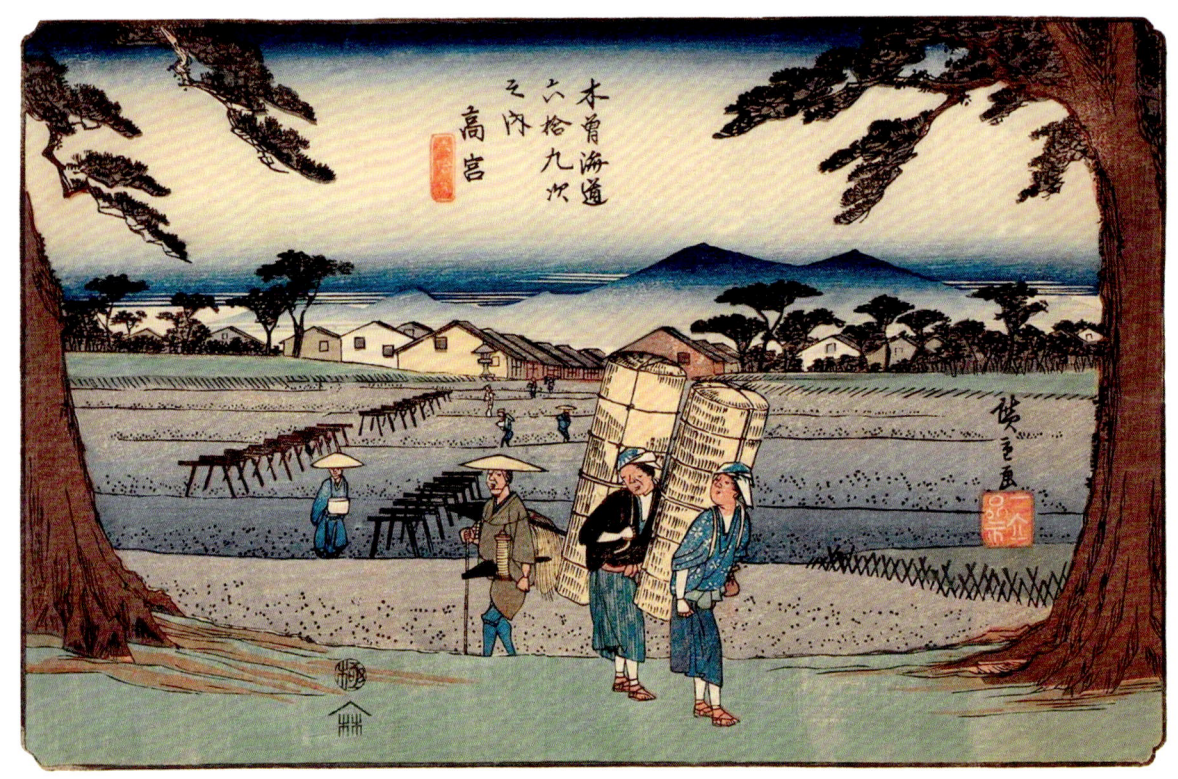

Takamiya, Station 65

Takamiya, relais 65

Takamiya, Station 65

Takamiya, Estación 65

Takamiya, stazione 65

Takamiya, halteplaats 65

Colour woodcut/Gravure sur bois en couleurs

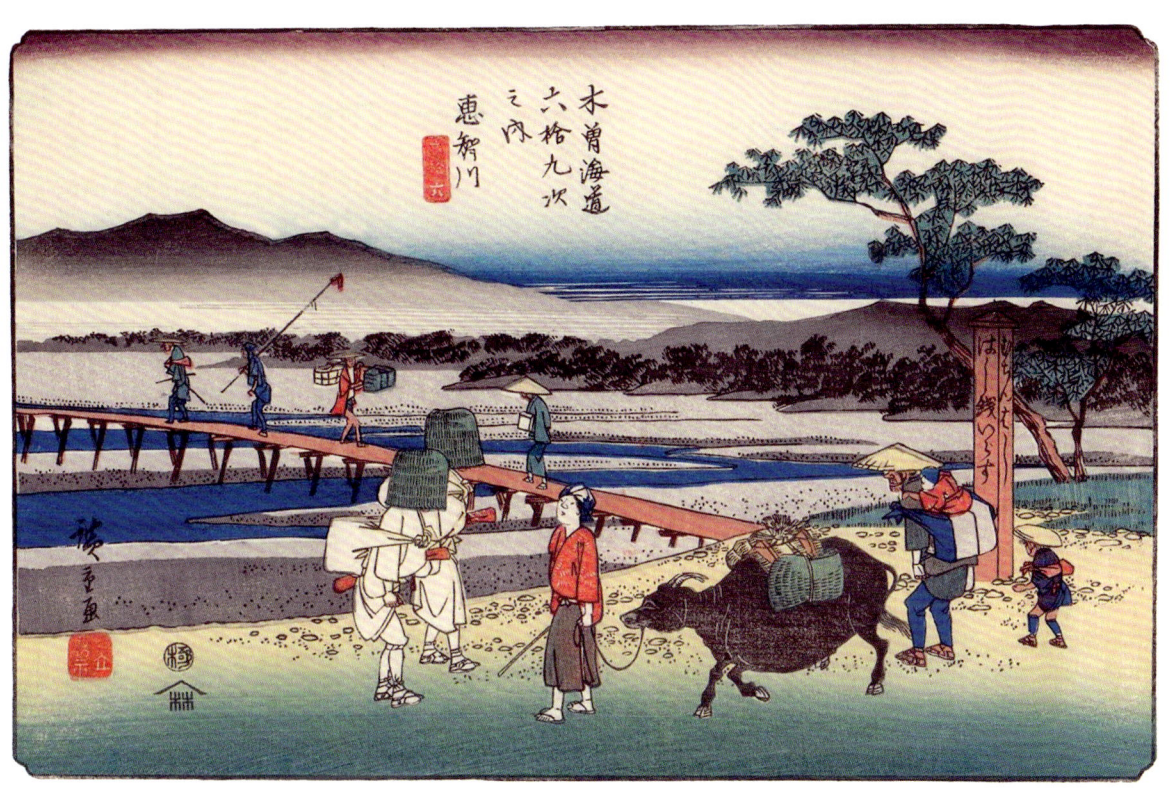

Echigawa, Station 66

Echigawa, relais 66

Echigawa, Station 66

Echigawa, Estación 66

Echigawa, stazione 66

Echigawa, halteplaats 66

Colour woodcut/Gravure sur bois en couleurs

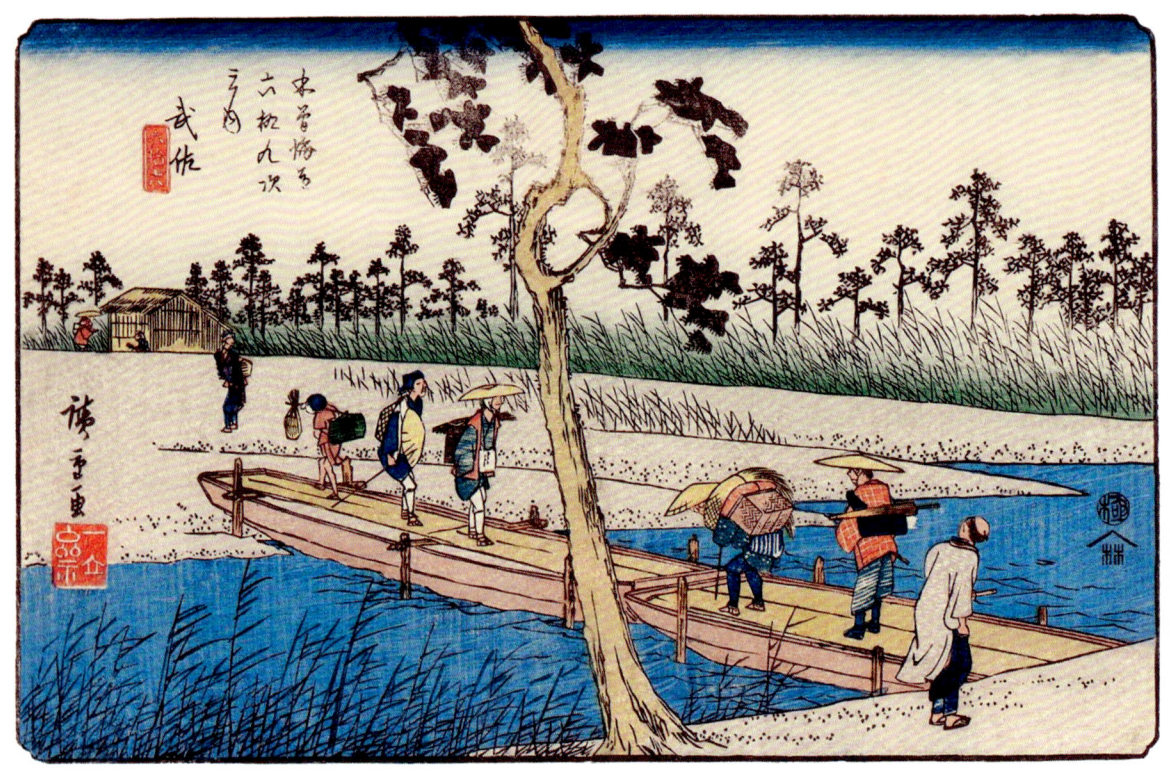

Musa, Station 67

Musa, relais 67

Musa, Station 67

Musa, Estación 67

Musa, stazione 67

Musa, halteplaats 67

Colour woodcut/Gravure sur bois en couleurs

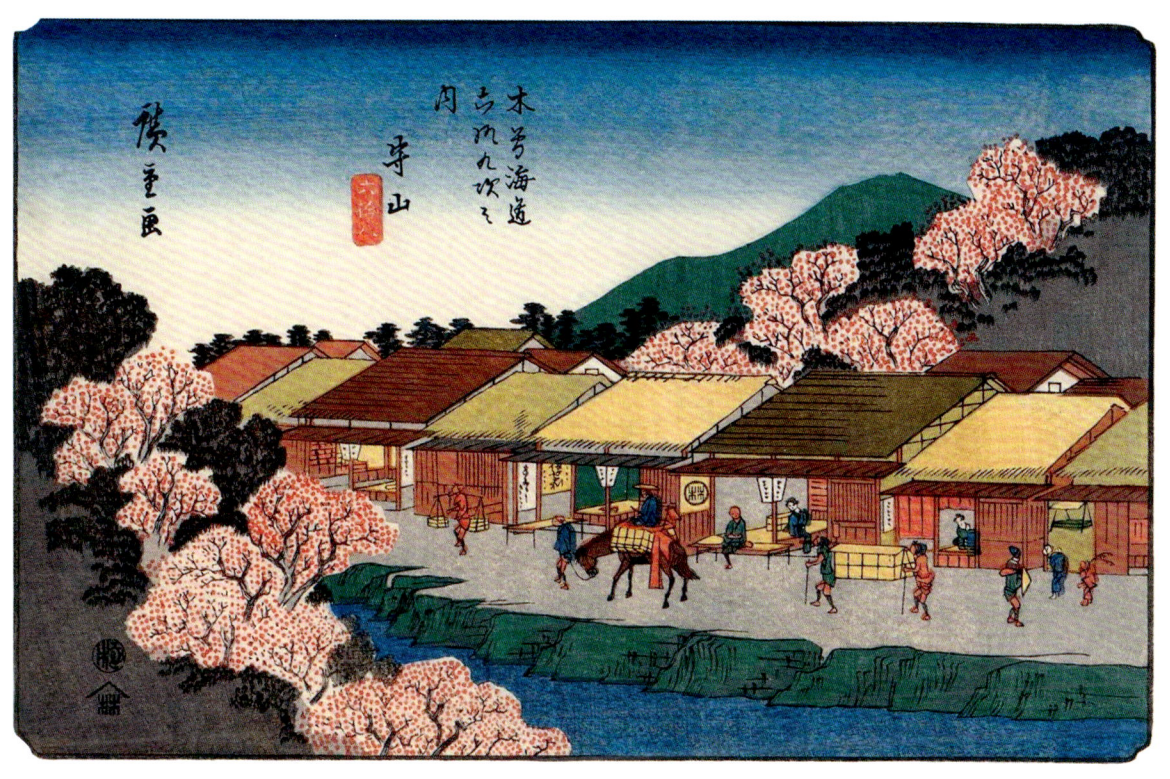

Moriyama, Station 68

Moriyama, relais 68

Moriyama, Station 68

Moriyama, Estación 68

Moriyama, stazione 68

Moriyama, halteplaats 68

Colour woodcut/Gravure sur bois en couleurs

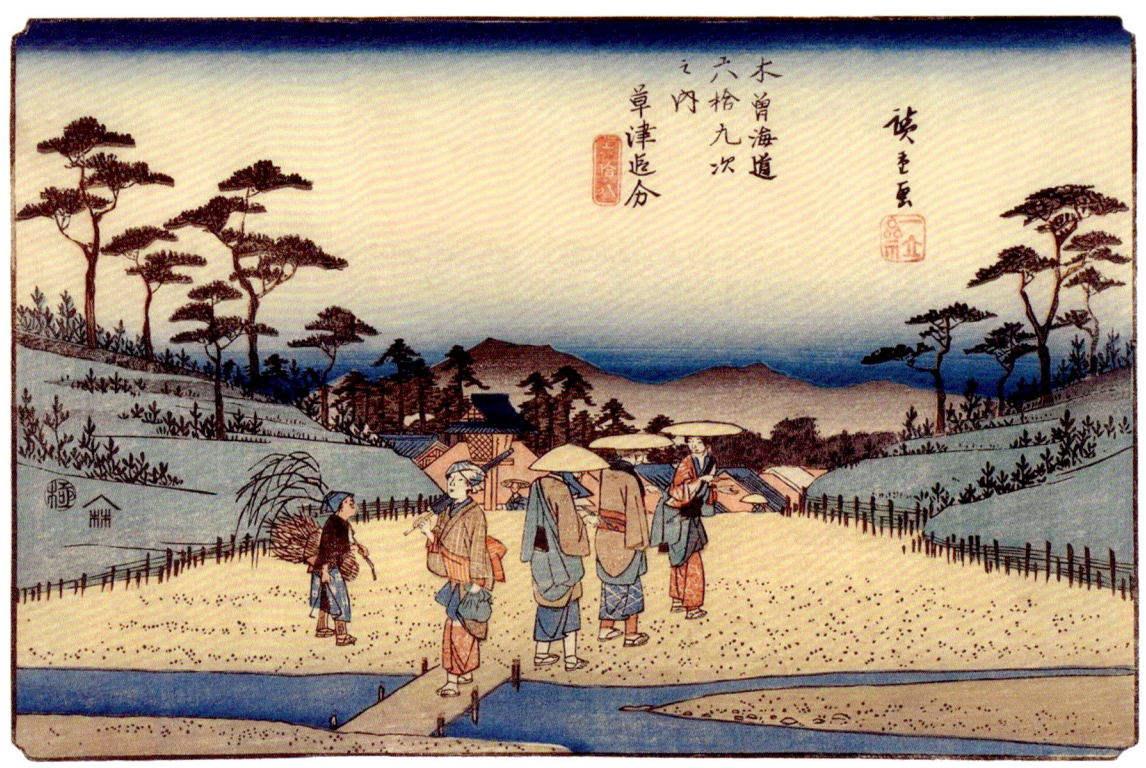

Kusatsu, Station 69

Kusatsu, relais 69

Kusatsu, Station 69

Kusatsu, Estación 69

Kusatsu, stazione 69

Kusatsu, halteplaats 69

Colour woodcut/Gravure sur bois en couleurs

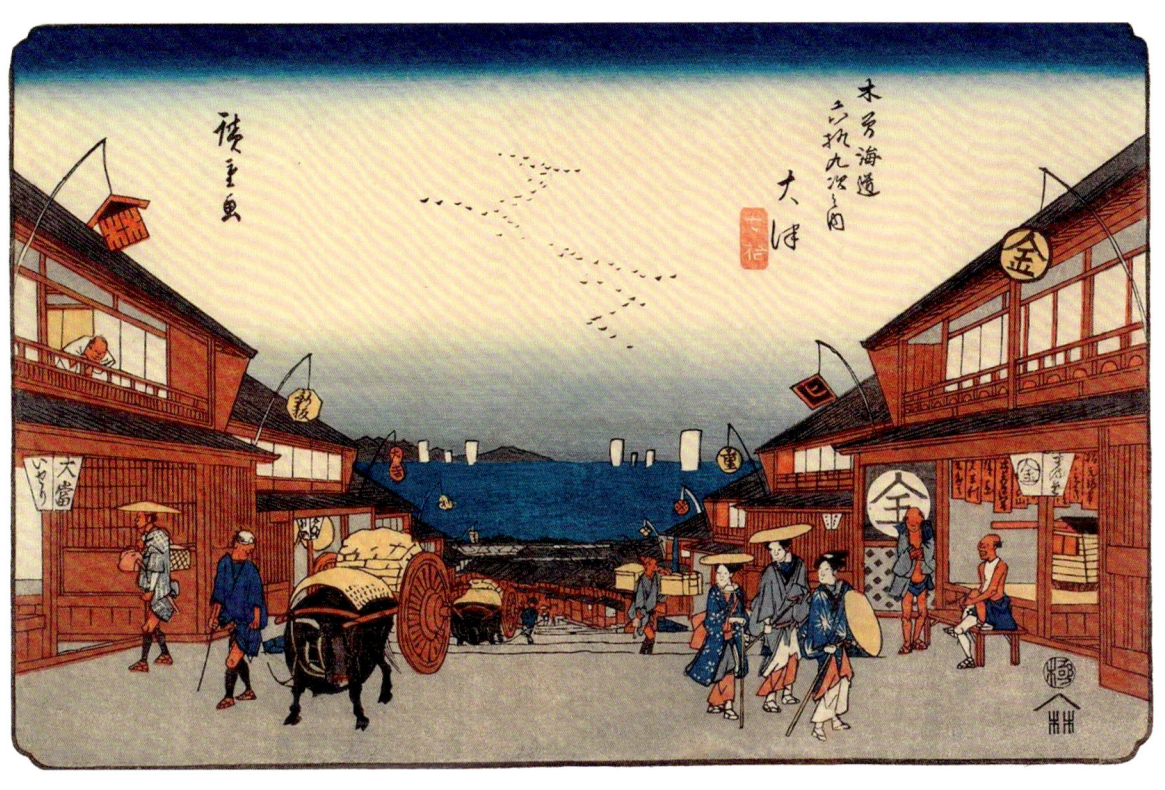

Otsu, End Station

Otsu, dernier relais

Otsu, Endstation

Otsu, Estación final

Otsu, stazione finale

Otsu, Endstation

Colour woodcut/Gravure sur bois en couleurs

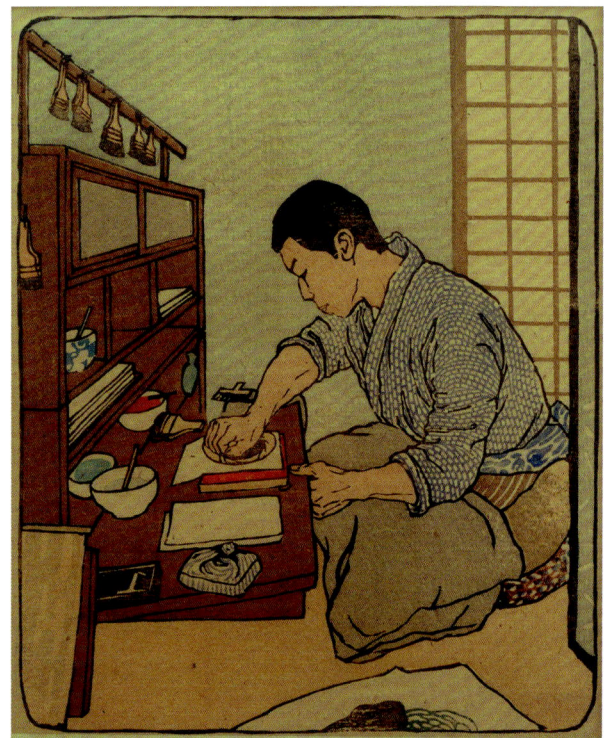

Emil Orlik (1870–1932)

Japanese Printer

L'imprimeur japonais

Japanischer Drucker

Impresor Japonés

Stampatore giapponese

Japanse drukker

1900, Colour woodcut/Gravure sur bois en couleurs, 19,5×16 cm,
Private collection

Inari Bridge and Minato Shrine in Teppozu

Le Pont d'Inari et le sanctuaire de Minato à Teppozu

Inari-Brücke und der Minato-Schrein in Teppozu

El puente Inari del santuario Minato en Teppozu

Ponte di Inari e il santuario di Minato a Teppozu

De Inari-brug en de Minato-schrijn in Teppozu

1850–1858, India ink on paper/Encre sur papier, 24,5×35 cm,
Private collection

The Japanese woodcut: a highly specialized industry

In the early days of the *ukiyo-e* woodblock prints, the prints were coloured by hand as required. But this method was time consuming and expensive. To meet the demand in the general population for affordable colour images, a highly specialised industry developed. With the perfecting of multi-colour printing, the production of woodprints was split among specialist shops by the mid-18th century. By Hiroshige's

L'estampe japonaise : une industrie hautement spécialisée

Dans les premiers temps de l'*ukiyo-e,* on colorie les tirages à la main – mais ce procédé est long et coûteux. Une industrie très spécialisée se met donc vite en place, pour satisfaire la demande de larges couches de la population en images coloriées, à des prix abordables : à partir du milieu du XVIIIᵉ siècle, le perfectionnement de l'impression polychrome permet de développer une production rationnelle reposant sur une division précise du

Der japanische Holzschnitt – eine hochspezialisierte Industrie

In der Anfangszeit des *Ukiyo-e-* Holzschnitts koloriert man die Drucke bei Bedarf von Hand. Doch dieses Verfahren ist zeitaufwendig und teuer. Um die Nachfrage breiter Bevölkerungsschichten nach preisgünstigen farbigen Bildern zu befriedigen, entwickelt sich eine hochspezialisierte Industrie. Mit der Perfektionierung des Vielfarbendruckes wird ab der Mitte des 18. Jahrhunderts eine arbeitsteilige Produktionsweise

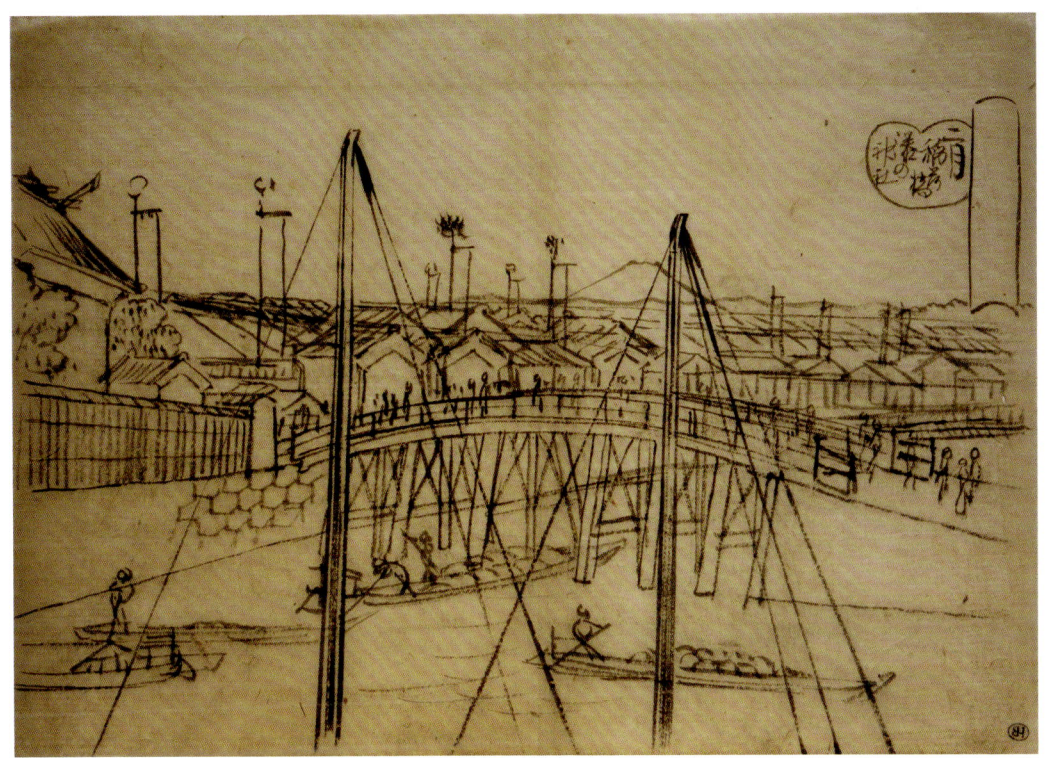

La xilografía japonesa, una industria de alta especialización

En los inicios de la xilografía *Ukiyo-e* los sellos se coloreaban, en caso de ser necesario, a mano. Este proceso sin embargo cuesta mucho tiempo y dinero. Para satisfacer la demanda de imágenes en color baratas por parte de clases populares más amplias se creó una industria altamente especializada. Con el perfeccionamiento de la impresión a color, a mediados del XVII, se llega a un producción en base a la división del trabajo. En tiempos de Hiroshige las

La xilografia giapponese: un'industria altamente specializzata

Nella fase iniziale della xilografia *ukiyo-e*, se necessario, le stampe venivano colorate a mano. Tuttavia questo procedimento richiedeva molto tempo ed era costoso. Per soddisfare la domanda di quadri colorati a un prezzo conveniente da parte di ceti più disparati della popolazione, fu sviluppata un'industria altamente specializzata. A partire dalla metà del XVIII secolo, con il perfezionamento della stampa multicolore si perseguì un metodo di

De Japanse houtsnede – een gespecialiseerde industrie

In de begintijd van de *ukiyo-e*-houtsneden worden de prenten naar behoefte ingekleurd. Maar dit procedé kost veel tijd en is duur. Om aan de vraag naar goedkopere kleurenprenten onder bredere lagen van de bevolking te kunnen voldoen, ontwikkelt zich een zeer gespecialiseerde industrie. Door de perfectionering van de kleurendruk ontstaat vanaf het midden van de achttiende eeuw een productieproces met werkverdeling. In Hiroshige's tijd

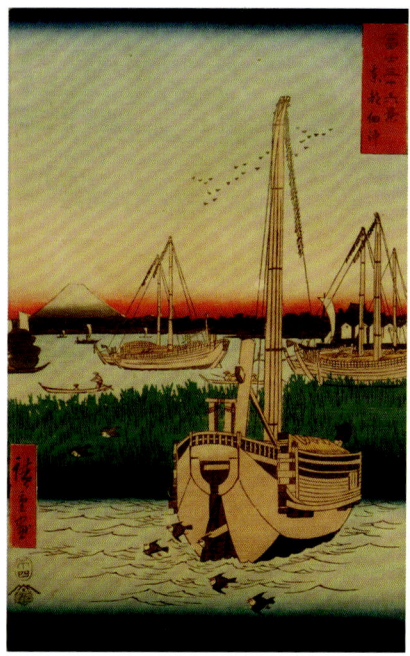

time, everyone's roles had been clearly defined. The publisher would commission an illustrator to draw a specific subject or series. Hiroshige, too, rarely created works without being commissioned first. The wooden printing block was not cut by the artist himself, but instead by a specially trained woodcutter. The woodcutter would first make a contour plate by gluing the drawing face down onto the printing block and then carving out the contour lines of the image in high relief. The illustrator would then receive several black-and-white proofs. Since the colours had to be printed consecutively, the illustrator needed

travail ; à l'époque, le rôle de tous les intervenants est clairement défini. C'est l'éditeur qui commande à l'artiste une estampe – ou une série d'estampes – sur un sujet déterminé ; même Hiroshige n'a créé que très peu d'œuvres personnelles, travaillant le plus souvent sur commande. L'artiste commence par exécuter un dessin-maître à l'encre, mais ne sculpte pas le bois lui-même. Un artisan-graveur colle ensuite ce dessin sur une planche de bois, afin d'évider avec différentes gouges les zones où le papier est blanc, pour créer le dessin en relief sur la planche (dite « de trait »). Celle-ci est alors encrée et imprimée en plusieurs épreuves. Lesdites épreuves sont à

verfolgt. Zu Hiroshiges Zeit sind die Rollen aller Beteiligten klar verteilt: Der Verleger beauftragt einen Zeichner mit dem Entwurf für ein bestimmtes Motiv oder eine Serie. Auch Hiroshige wird kaum freie Werke geschaffen, sondern zumeist im Auftrag der Verlage agiert haben. Der hölzerne Druckblock wird nicht vom Künstler selbst, sondern von einem eigens dafür ausgebildeten Holzschneider geschnitten. Dieser fertigt zunächst eine Umrissplatte an, indem er die Zeichnung mit der Vorderseite auf den Druckblock klebt und die Konturlinien des Bildes als Hochrelief herausschnitzt. Der Zeichner erhält nun mehrere schwarz-weiße Probeabzüge. Da die gewünschten Farben

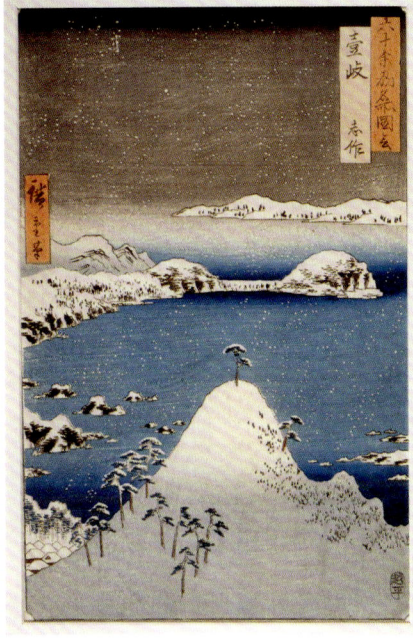

funciones de todos los involucrados están claramente distribuidas: El editor encarga a un dibujante el diseño de un determinado motivo o serie. Hiroshige no realiza casi trabajos por libre, sino que también él procede por encargo de editores la mayoría de las veces. El taco de madera no lo realiza el propio artista, sino un xilógrafo especialmente educado a tal efecto. Este crea primero una plancha, pegando el dibujo a la parte frontal del taco y tallando un altorrelieve con los contornos de la imagen. El dibujante recibe entonces varios duplicados de prueba en blanco y negro. Dado que los colores deseados se imprimen de forma consecutiva el dibujante debe entregar una plantilla

produzione basato sulla divisione del lavoro. Ai tempi di Hiroshige i ruoli di tutti i partecipanti erano chiaramente distribuiti: l'editore incaricava un disegnatore di progettare un motivo stabilito o una serie. Anche Hiroshige creò poche opere a soggetto libero, lavorando per lo più su incarico delle case editrici. Il blocco di stampa in legno non viene intagliato dall'artista stesso, bensì da uno scultore del legno specializzato. Questi fabbrica inizialmente una matrice, incollando il disegno con il lato inferiore sul blocco di stampa e intagliando le linee di contorno dell'immagine come altorilievo. Il disegnatore riceve quindi diverse bozze di prova in bianco e nero. Affinché

liggen de taken van de betrokkenen duidelijk vast: de uitgever geeft een kunstenaar de opdracht om een ontwerptekening van een bepaald onderwerp of voor een serie te maken; ook Hiroshige zal nauwelijks vrije kunst hebben gecreëerd maar meestal in opdracht van uitgevers hebben gewerkt. Het houten drukblok wordt niet door de kunstenaar zelf maar door een daarvoor speciaal opgeleide houtsnijder vervaardigd. Deze maakt eerst een contourblok, waarin hij de tekening met de voorzijde naar beneden op het blok plakt en de contouren van de tekening dan in hoog-reliëf uitsnijdt. De tekenaar ontvangt vervolgens meerdere drukproeven in zwart-wit. Omdat de

137

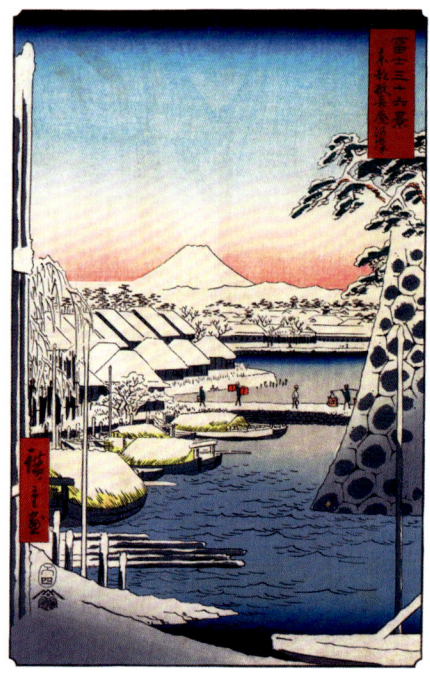

Sukiyagashi in the Eastern Capital, from the Series **36 Views of Mount Fuji**

Sukiyagashi dans la capitale de l'Est, de la série **Trente-six vues du mont Fuji**

Sukiyagashi in der Östlichen Hauptstadt, aus der Serie **36 Ansichten des Fuji**

Sukiyagashi en la capital del Este, de la serie **36 vistas del Fuji**

Sukiyagashi nella capitale orientale, della serie **36 vedute del monte Fuji**

Sukiyagashi in de Oostelijke Hoofdstad, uit de serie **36 gezichten op de Fuji**

1858, Colour woodcut/Gravure sur bois en couleurs, 35,9×24,5 cm

to create a template for each drawing, indicating the colour he had chosen for each section on the relevant proofs. Following these instructions, the woodcutter would then cut a separate block for each colour. Up to twelve wood blocks could be used to produce a single print. The printer mixed the colours. He did not use a printing press, but instead used a muller to print each by hand. The moistened paper was pressed in a circular motion onto the printing block. Hiroshige's sophisticated compositions were undoubtedly quite the challenge for the woodcutter and printer, especially with his use of such

leur tour collées sur d'autres planches de bois (une par couleur à obtenir) et les zones à colorier sont laissées en relief. On peut avoir jusqu'à douze planches de bois différentes pour une seule et même estampe. Les planches ainsi obtenues sont ensuite encrées individuellement, puis appliquées et imprimées successivement sur une feuille de papier humidifiée, à l'aide de repères précis pour éviter les décalages. Un autre artisan spécialisé procède au tirage final – sans utiliser de presse, mais avec un tampon de bambou pour frotter le papier sur chacune des planches de couleurs encrées, dans un ordre précis qui commence toujours

nacheinander gedruckt werden, muss der Zeichner für jede erforderliche Platte eine Vorlage anfertigen. Dazu trägt er die gewünschte Farbe in die einzelnen Flächen auf den jeweiligen Vordrucken ein. Nach diesen Anweisungen entsteht für jede Farbe ein eigener Block. Bis zu zwölf solcher Holzplatten kommen für einen Druck zum Einsatz. Das Mischen der Farben übernimmt der Drucker. Er verwendet keine Druckerpresse, sondern stellt den Abzug von Hand mit dem Reiber her. Das befeuchtete Papier wird in kreisenden Bewegungen auf die Druckplatte gedrückt. Hiroshiges anspruchsvolle Kompositionen stellen den Holzschneider und den

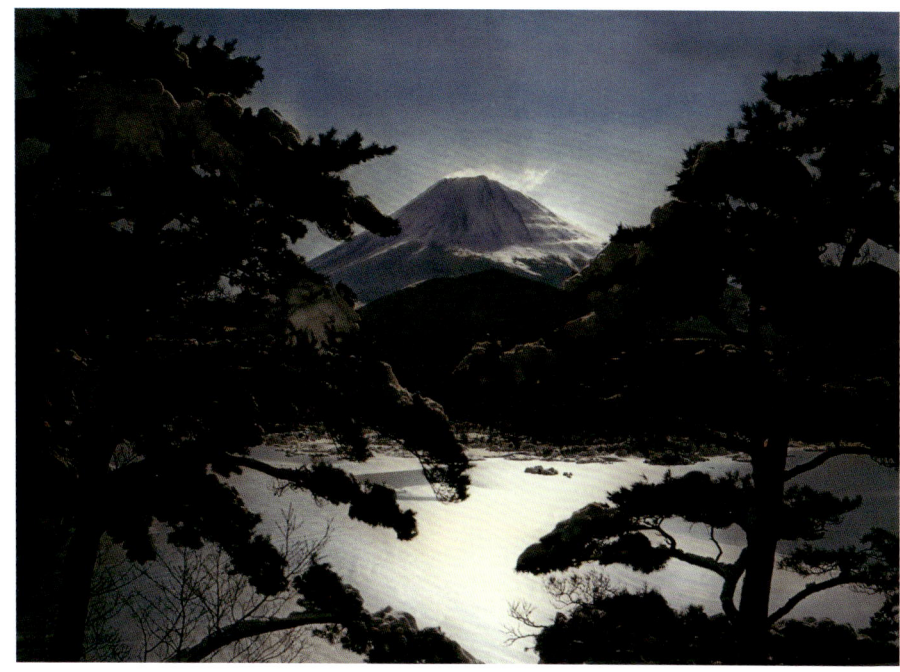

*View of Mount Fuji
covered in snow*

Le Mont Fuji sous la neige

Blick auf den Fuji im Schnee

Vista del Fuji nevado

*Vista sul monte
Fuji nella neve*

*Gezicht op de Fuji
in de sneeuw*

1905, Photograph, coloured/
Photographie colorée

para cada plancha necesaria. Allí introduce el color que se desee en las superficies particulares de las diversas plantillas. Con estas indicaciones se crea un sello para cada color. Para realizar una impresión llegan a usarse hasta 12 planchas de madera. El impresor se encarga de realizar la mezcla de los colores. No utiliza para ello una prensa, sino que la copia se obtiene de manera manual con un bruñidor. El papel, húmedo, se estampa frotándolo en movimientos circulares sobre el taco. Las exigentes composiciones de Hiroshige suponen sin duda un gran reto para el xilógrafo y el impresor, por ejemplo en las representaciones de lluvia o los

i colori desiderati siano stampati uno dopo l'altro, il disegnatore deve realizzare un modello per ogni matrice occorrente. A questo scopo inserisce i colori desiderati sulle singole superfici sul rispettivo modello. Seguendo questo procedimento si forma un blocco per ogni colore. Per ogni stampa vengono utilizzate fino a dodici tavole di legno di questo tipo. Allo stampatore spetta la miscelazione dei colori. Egli non utilizza alcun torchio per stampa, bensì realizza la bozza a mano con il raschietto. La carta inumidita viene stampata sulla lastra con movimenti circolari. Le impegnative composizioni di Hiroshige rappresentano senza dubbio una grande

vereiste kleuren na elkaar worden gedrukt, moet de kunstenaar voor elke drukgang een aparte tekening maken. Daarbij vult hij de gewenste kleur in de afzonderlijke vlakken op de drukproeven in. Met deze werkwijze ontstaat voor elke kleur een apart drukblok. Bij het drukken worden soms wel twaalf verschillende drukblokken gebruikt. Het mengen van de kleuren op het papier is de taak van de drukker. Hij gebruikt geen drukpers, maar vervaardigt de prent met de hand door met een inkttampon te werken. Het bevochtigde papier wordt in cirkelvormige bewegingen op het drukblok gewreven. De veeleisende composities van Hiroshige vormen

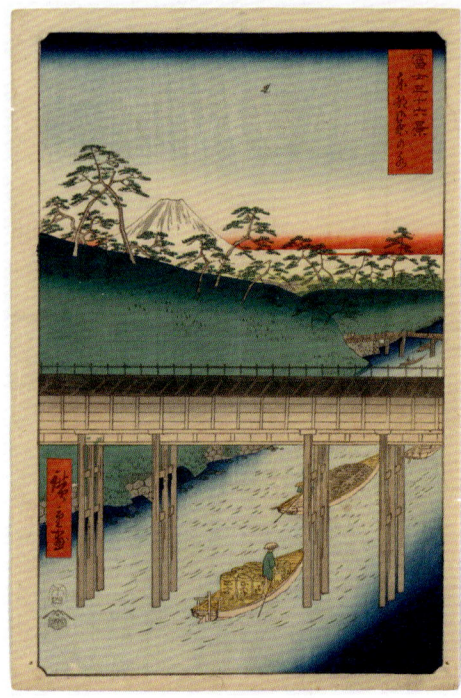

elements as rain or shading gradients. Despite all of the craftsmanship that went into the *ukiyo-e* woodcuts, at the time, it was considered a "low" form of art and Hiroshige was considered a craftsman at his time.

par le noir, avec des mouvements circulaires. Les compositions élaborées de Hiroshige posent au graveur comme à l'imprimeur des planches de gros problèmes de précision, en particulier pour les hachures de la pluie et les dégradés de couleur (ces derniers étant réalisés à l'aide de plusieurs passages sur la même planche de couleur). Toutefois, quel que soit le degré de raffinement et d'habileté artistiques et artisanales ici déployées, les estampes de l'*ukiyo-e* sont considérées à l'époque comme une forme d'art « inférieure » : aux yeux de ses contemporains, Hiroshige reste un artisan.

Drucker zweifelsohne vor große Herausforderungen, zum Beispiel bei der Darstellung von Regenschauern oder schattierenden Farbverläufen. Bei aller Kunstfertigkeit, die aus den *Ukiyo-e*-Holzschnitten spricht, handelt es sich nach damaliger Ansicht jedoch um eine „niedere" Kunstform, und Hiroshige gilt für seine Zeitgenossen als Handwerker.

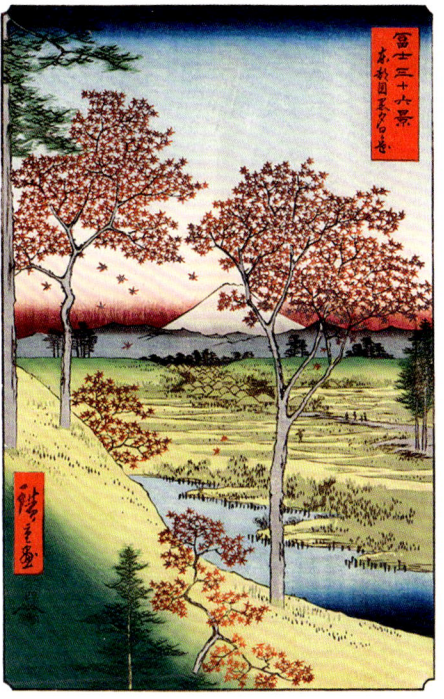

cambios de color sombreados. A pesar de la belleza artesanal que se desprende de las xilografías *Ukiyo-e* estas se consideraban en el momento una disciplina artística menor, y Hiroshige era visto como un artesano por sus coetáneos.

sfida per l'incisore e lo stampatore, ad esempio nella rappresentazione di temporali o sfumature di colore ombreggiate. Nonostante l'abilità che caratterizza le xilografie *ukiyo-e,* si tratta tuttavia di una forma d'arte "bassa", secondo l'opinione dell'epoca, e Hiroshige era considerato dai suoi contemporanei un artigiano.

voor de houtsnijders en de drukker ongetwijfeld een grote uitdaging, bijvoorbeeld in de weergave van regenbuien of in verlopende schaduwen. Ondanks het grote kunstenaarschap dat uit de *ukiyo-e*-houtsneden blijkt, wordt het medium in de tijd van Hiroshige toch als een 'lagere' vorm van kunstnijverheid gezien en is Hiroshige voor zijn tijdgenoten dus een gewone ambachtsman.

Yamabushi Gorge in Mimasaka Province, Famous Views of the 60-odd Provinces

La Gorge de Yamabushi dans la province de Mimasaka, de la série **Vues des sites célèbres des 60 et quelques provinces**

Yamabushi-Schlucht in der Provinz Mimasaka, aus der Serie **Berühmte Gegenden der mehr als 60 Provinzen**

El cañón Yamabushi en la provincia Mimasaka, de la serie **Famosas vistas de las más de 60 provincias**

Gola di Yamabushi nella provincia di Mimasaka, della serie **Luoghi famosi delle oltre 60 province**

De Yamabushi-kloof in de provincie Mimasaka, uit de serie **Beroemde streken van de meer dan 60 provincies**

1853, Colour woodcut/Gravure sur bois en couleurs, 34,3×22,9 cm, Museum of Art, San Diego

The cascading rain is here represented by broad diagonal lines, acting like a curtain in front of the landscape. This creates the dynamic impression of a particularly lashing storm. The effect is enhanced by the vertical format.

La pluie qui tombe est figurée par de larges diagonales, posées devant le paysage comme un rideau. Ce traitement communique l'impression dynamique d'un déluge de pluie battante. L'effet est encore accentué par le format vertical de la feuille.

Der herabstürzende Regen ist hier durch breite Diagonalen dargestellt, die wie ein Vorhang vor die Landschaft gesetzt sind. Dadurch entsteht der dynamische Eindruck eines peitschenden Sturms. Der Effekt wird durch das Hochformat zusätzlich verstärkt.

La lluvia torrencial se representa aquí por medio de amplias diagonales que se anteponen al paisaje como una suerte de cortina. Así se genera una impresión dinámica de una fuerte tormenta. El efecto se incrementa además por el formato vertical.

La pioggia che cade viene qui rappresentata attraverso ampie diagonali, che sono posizionate come un sipario davanti al paesaggio. In questo modo nasce l'impressione dinamica di una tempesta sferzante. L'effetto viene rafforzato ulteriormente dal formato verticale.

De stortbui is hier in brede diagonalen uitgebeeld, die als een gordijn voor het landschap zijn geplaatst. Daardoor ontstaat de dynamische indruk van een hevige regenstorm, een effect dat door het langgerekte, staande formaat nog wordt versterkt.

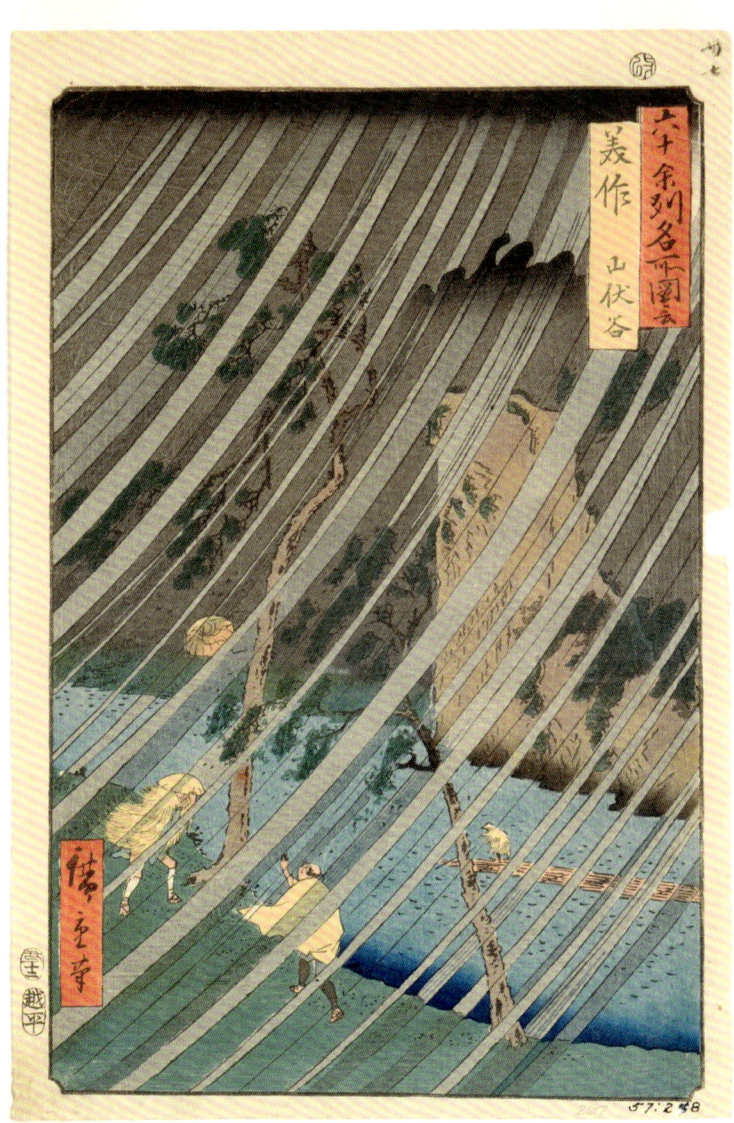

The 36 Views of Mount Fuji *were created shortly before Hiroshige's death and were completed by his student Hiroshige II. They show the mountain at different times of the day and in different seasons from different angles and distances. The particularly finely tuned gradients are typical of Hiroshige's late work.*

Les Trente-six vues du mont Fuji, *commencées peu avant la mort d'Hiroshige, seront achevées par son élève, Hiroshige II. Elles représentent la mythique montagne à différents moments du jour et des saisons, vue sous différents angles et à différentes distances. Les dégradés particulièrement délicats y sont typiques de la production tardive de Hiroshige.*

Die 36 Ansichten des Fuji *entstehen kurz vor Hiroshiges Tod und werden von seinem Schüler Hiroshige II zu Ende geführt. Sie zeigen den Berg zu verschiedenen Tages- und Jahreszeiten aus unterschiedlichen Blickwinkeln und Entfernungen. Die besonders fein abgestuften Farbverläufe sind typisch für Hiroshiges Spätwerk.*

Las 36 vistas del monte Fuji *fueron creadas poco antes de la muerte de Hiroshige, y fueron de hecho acabadas por su alumno Hiroshige II. Muestran el monte en diversos momentos del día y diversas estaciones, desde perspectivas y distancias diferentes. Los cambios de color, gradados de manera extremadamente fina, son típicos de la etapa tardía de Hiroshige.*

Le 36 vedute del monte Fuji *furono realizzate poco prima della morte di Hiroshige e portate a termine dal suo allievo Hiroshige II. Mostrano il monte in diverse ore del giorno e stagioni dell'anno da differenti angolature e distanze. Le sfumature di colore particolarmente raffinate sono tipiche delle ultime opere di Hiroshige.*

De 36 gezichten op de berg Fuji *ontstaan kort voor Hiroshige's dood en worden door zijn leerling Hiroshige II voltooid. Ze tonen de berg op verschillende momenten van de dag, in verschillende seizoenen, vanuit verschillende gezichtspunten en van verschillende afstanden. De uiterst subtiel verlopende kleurschakeringen zijn kenmerkend voor Hiroshige's latere werk.*

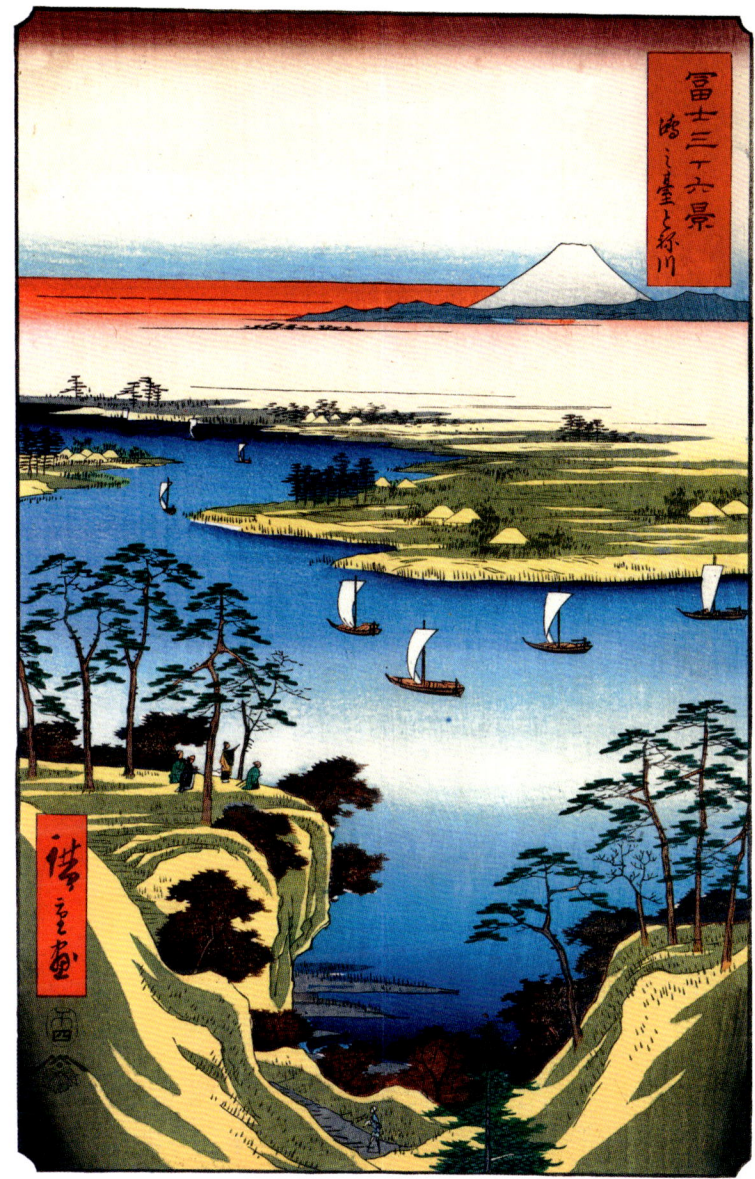

冨士三十六景

鴻之臺とね川

145

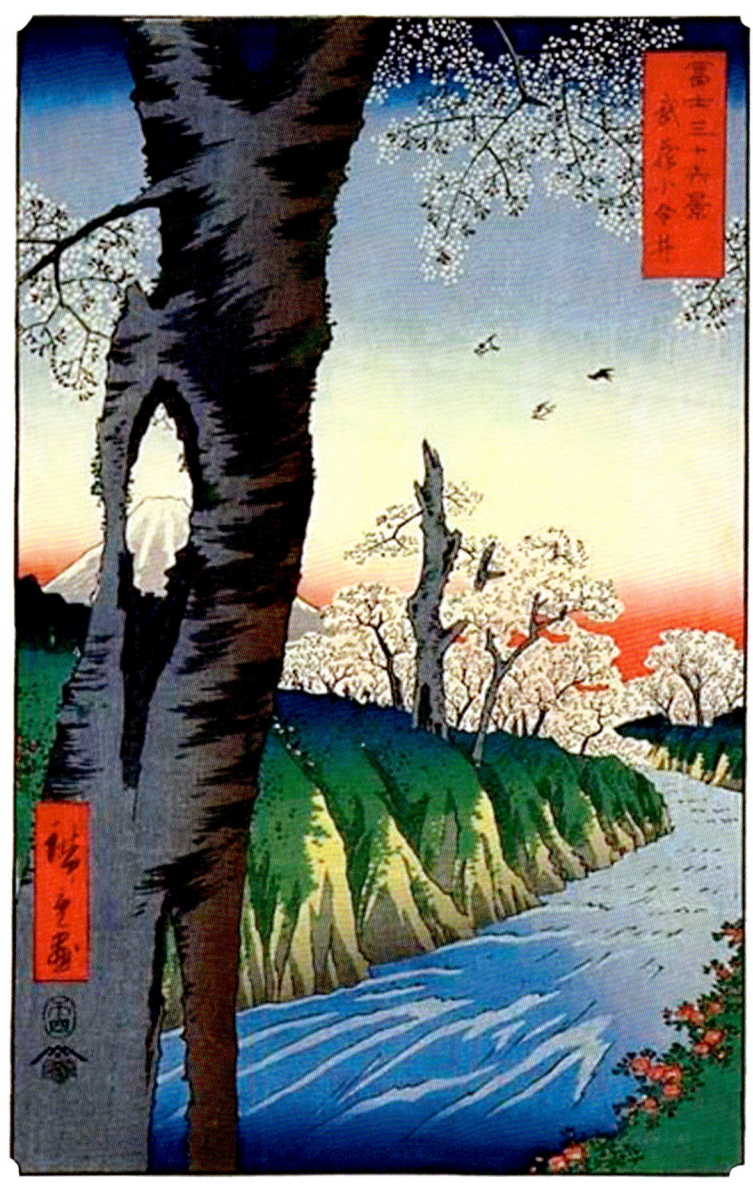

Koganei in Musashi Province
Koganei dans la province de Musashi
Koganei in der Provinz Musashi
Koganei en la provincia de Musashi
Koganei nella provincia di Musashi
Koganei in de provincie Musashi
Colour woodcut/Gravure sur bois en couleurs

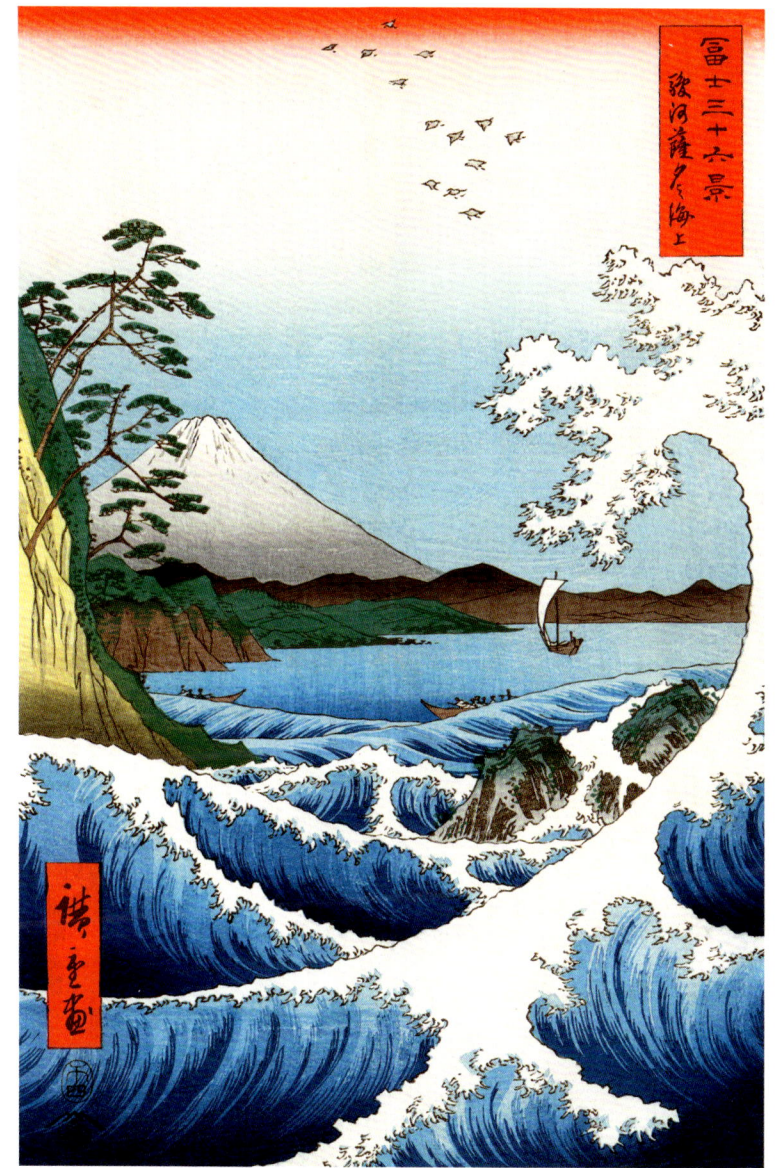

The sea near Satta in Suruga Province
La Mer à Satta dans la province de Suruga
Das Meer bei Satta in der Provinz Suruga
El mar en Satta, provincia de Suruga
Il mare a Satta nella provincia di Suruga
De zee bij Satta, in de provincie Suruga
Colour woodcut/Gravure sur bois en couleurs

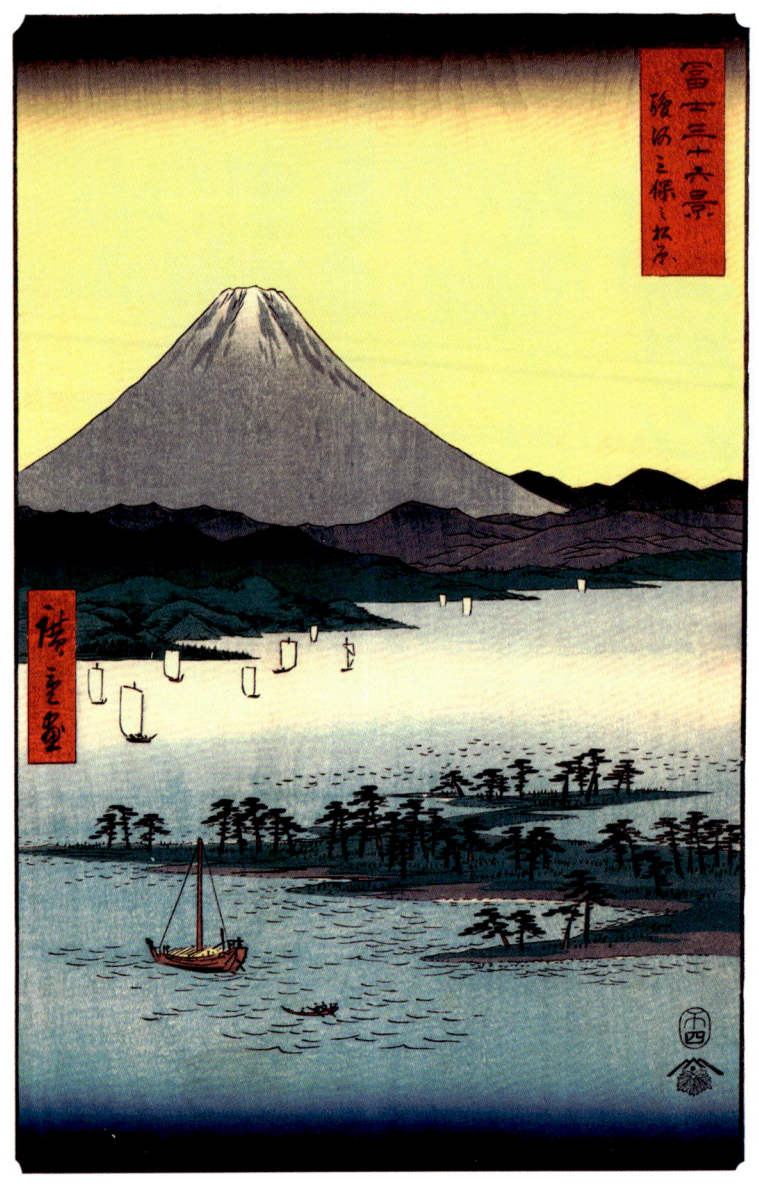

Miho pine forest in Suruga Province
La Pinède de Miho dans la province de Suruga
Pinienwald von Miho in der Provinz Suruga
Bosque de pinos de Miho en la provincia Suruga
Pineta a Miho nella provincia di Suruga
Dennebos van Miho in de provincie Suruga
Colour woodcut/Gravure sur bois en couleurs

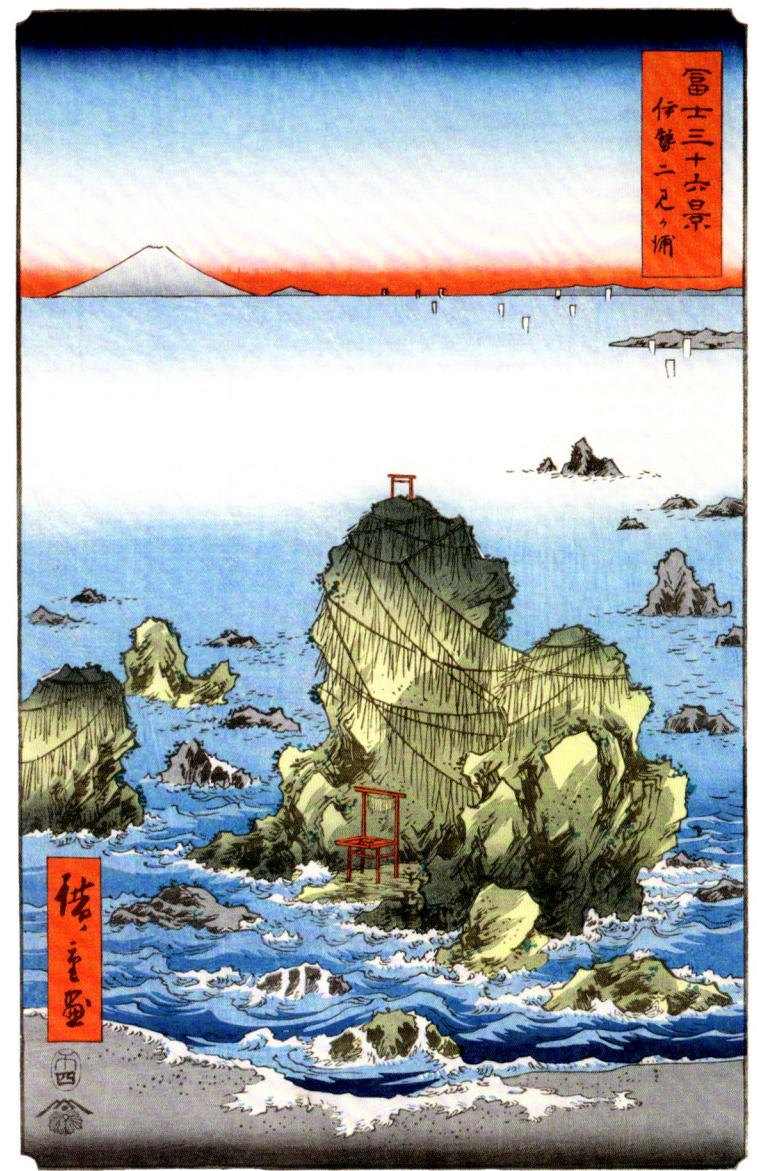

Bay of Futami in Ise Province
La Baie de Futami dans la province d'Ise
Bucht von Futami in der Provinz Ise
Bahía de Futami en la provincia Ise
Baia di Futami nella provincia di Ise
Bocht van Futami in de provincie Ise
Colour woodcut/Gravure sur bois en couleurs

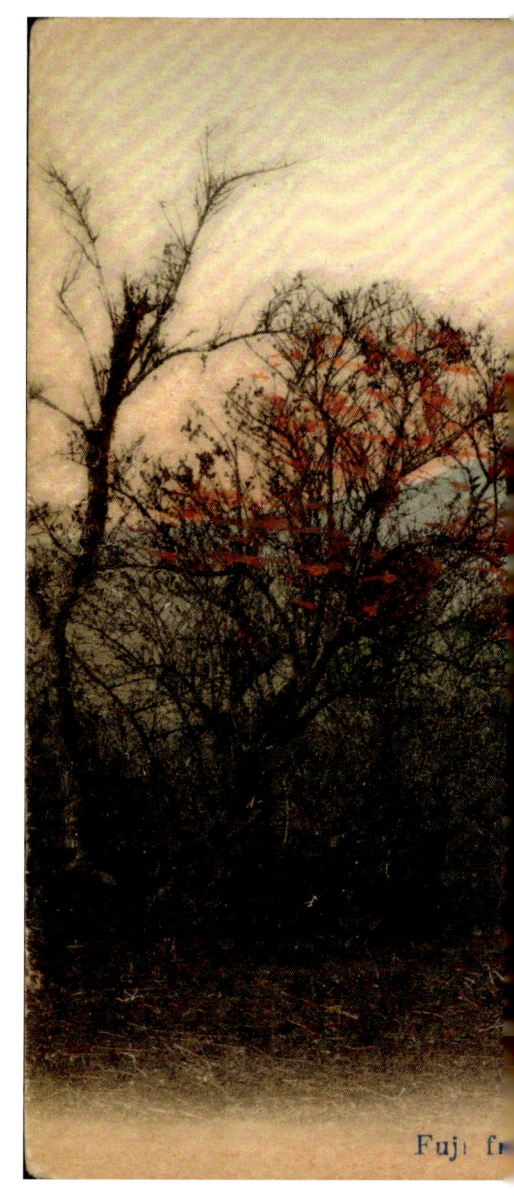

Fuji seen from Otometoge
Le mont Fuji vu d'Otometoge
Fuji von Otometoge aus gesehen
Fuji visto desde Otometoge
Il monte Fuji visto da Otometoge
De Fuji gezien vanuit Otometoge
1935, Postcard/Carte postale

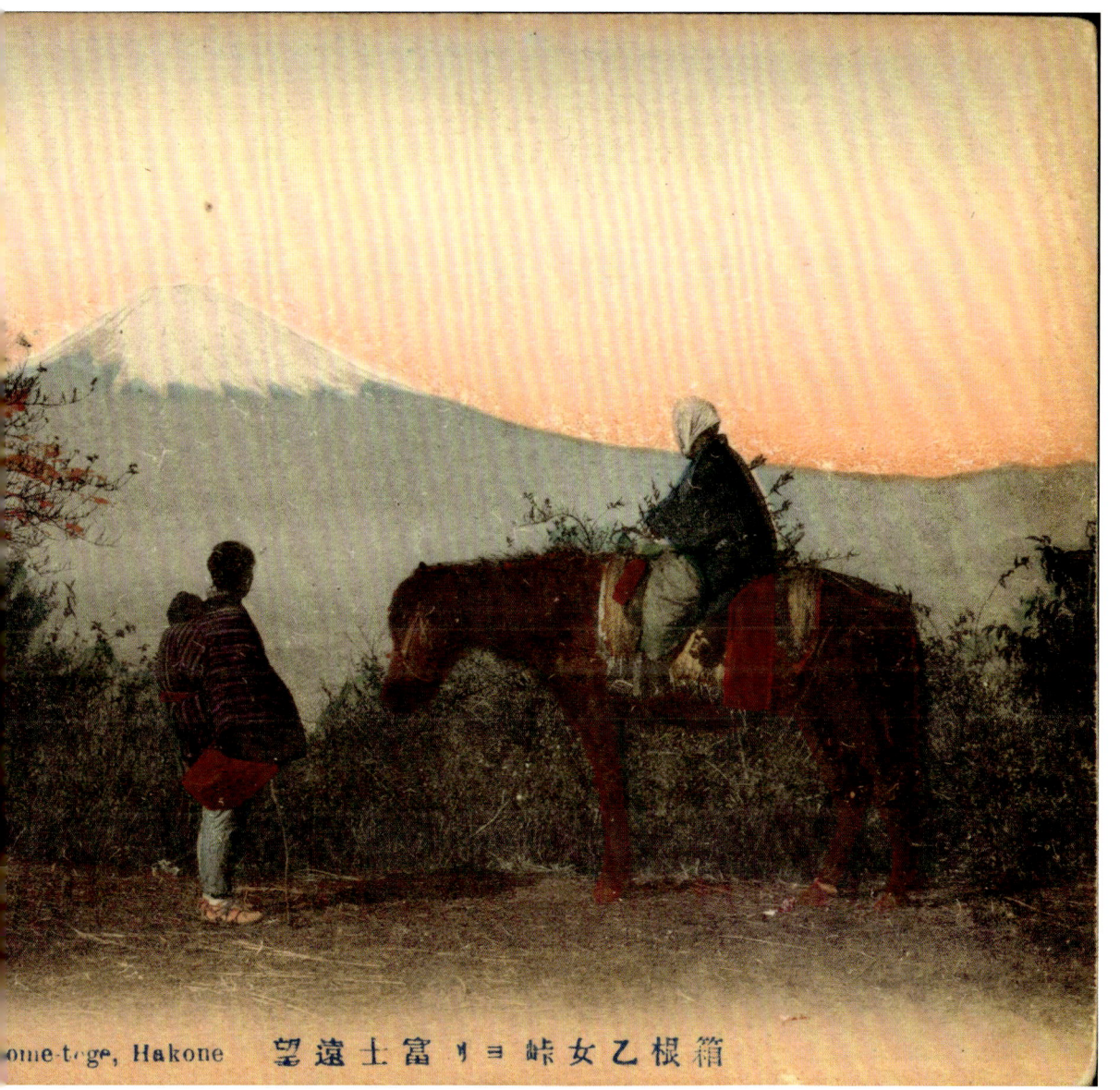

ome-tõge, Hakone　望遠士富リヨ峠女乙根箱

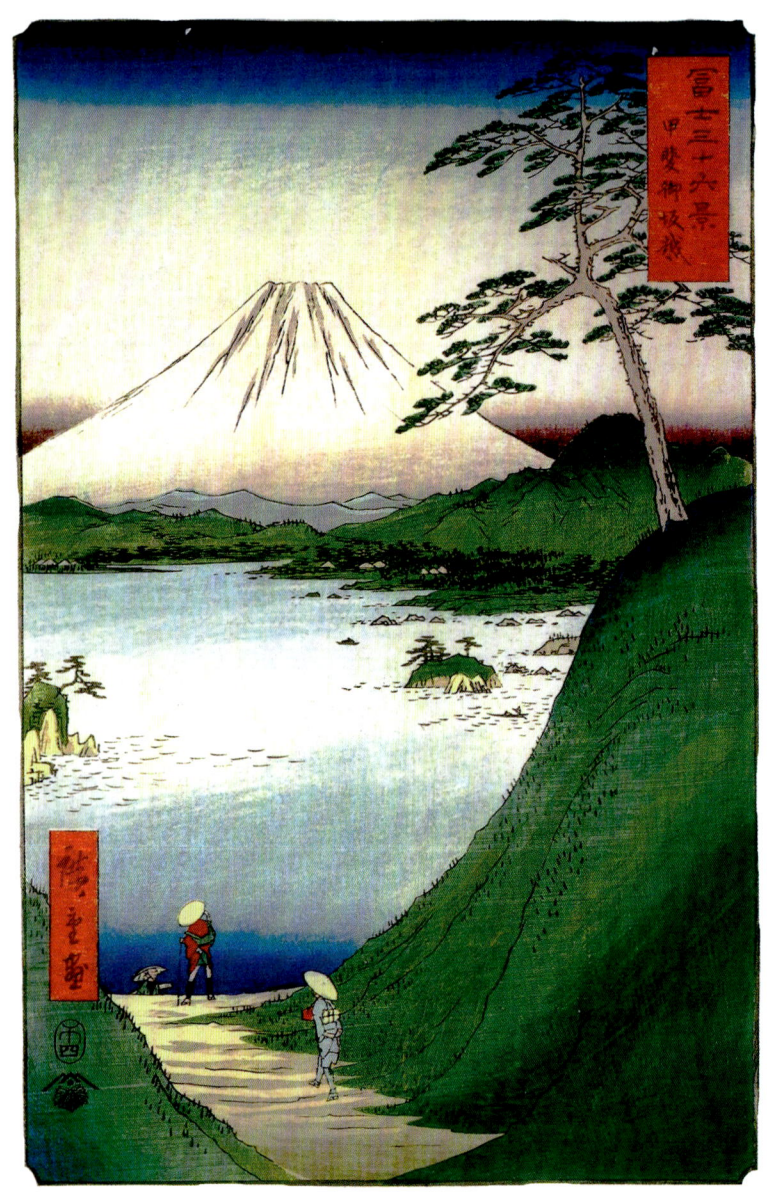

Misaka Pass in Kai Province
La Passe de Misaka dans la province de Kai
Misaka Pass in der Provinz Kai
Paso de Misaka en la provincia Kai
Il passo di Misaka nella provincia di Kai
De Misaka-pas in de provincie Kai
Colour woodcut/Gravure sur bois en couleurs

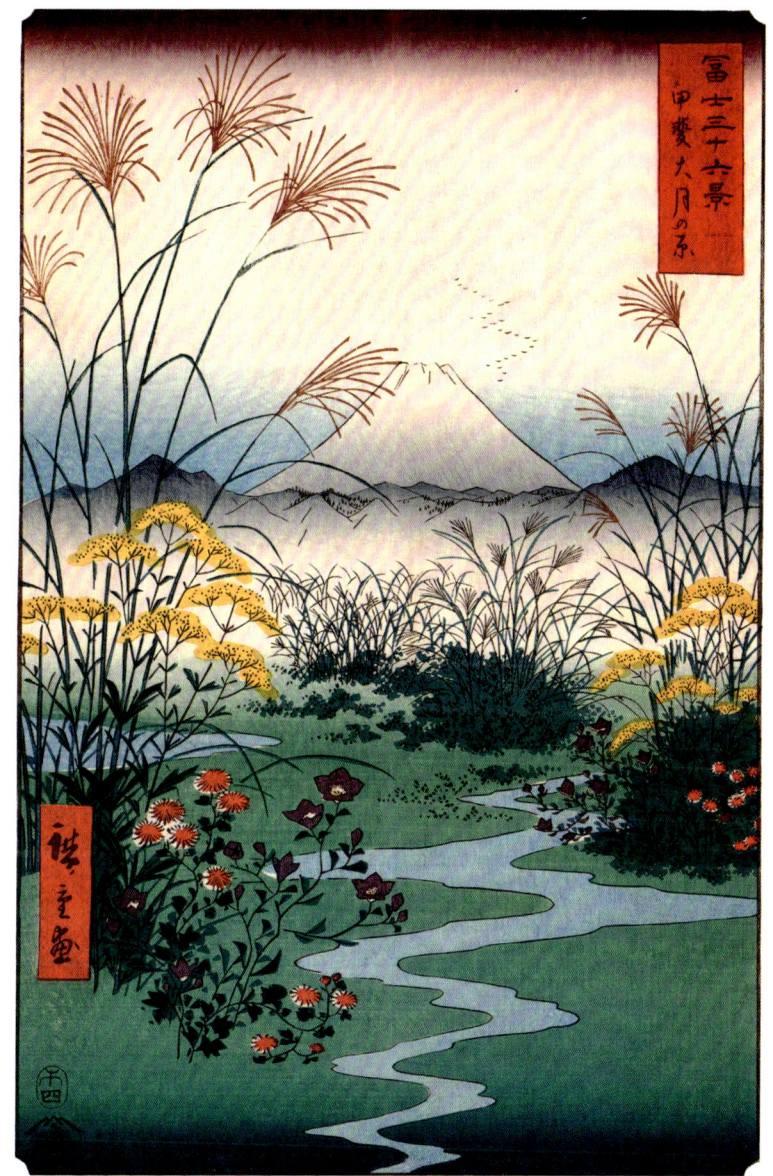

Plain of Otsuki in Kai Province
La Plaine d'Otsuki dans la province de Kai
Ebene von Otsuki in der Provinz Kai
El llano de Otsuki en la provincia Kai
La pianura di Otsuki nella provincia di Kai
Vlakte van Otsuki in de provincie Kai
Colour woodcut/Gravure sur bois en couleurs

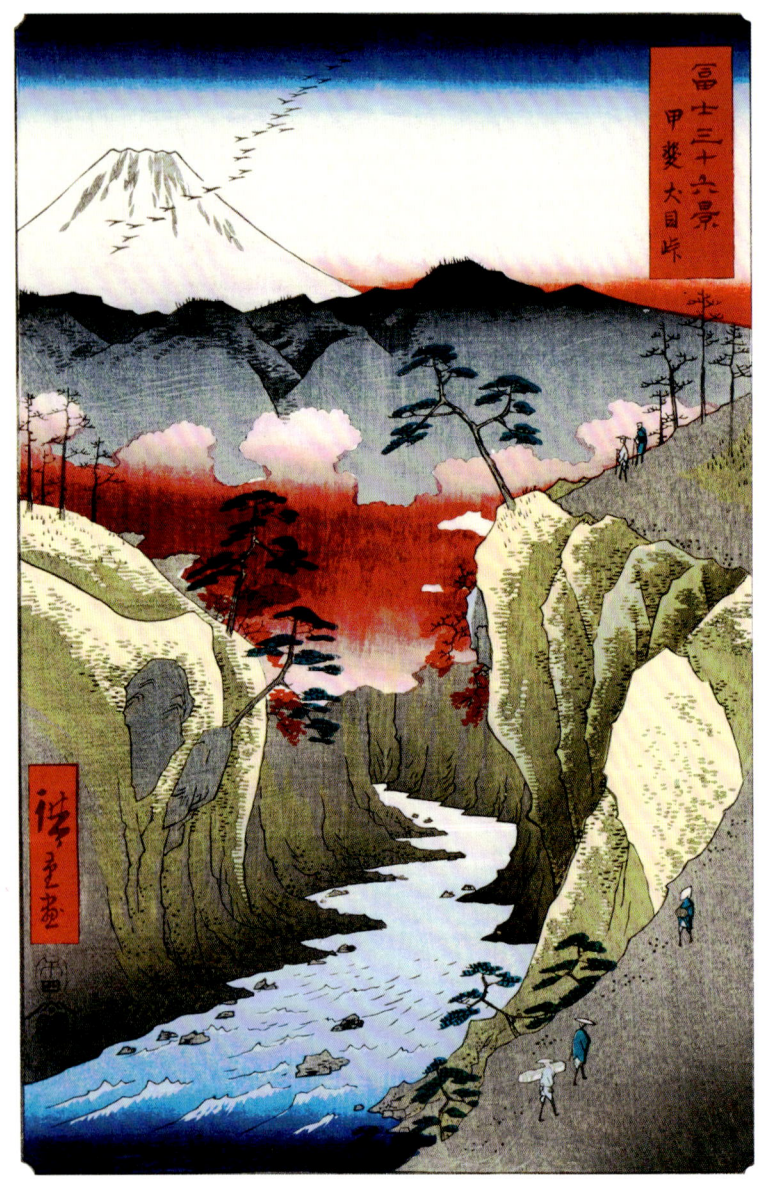

Dog Eye Pass in Kai Province

*La Passe des yeux de chiens
dans la province de Kai*

Hundeaugen-Pass in der Provinz Kai

El Paso de Ojo de Perro en la provincia Kai

Il passo di Hundeaugen nella provincia di Kai

Hundeaugen-pas in de provincie Kai

Colour woodcut/Gravure sur bois en couleurs

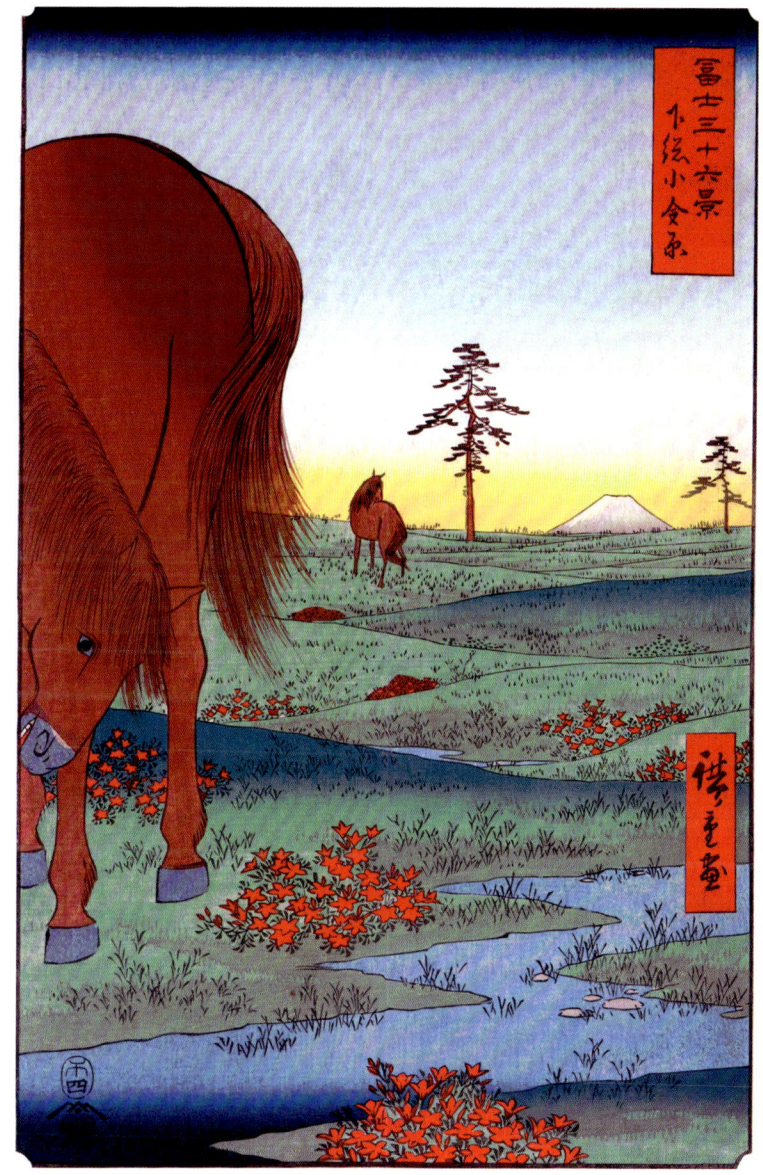

Plain of Kogane in Shimosa Province

*La Plaine de Kogane dans la
province de Shimosa*

Ebene von Kogane in der Provinz Shimosa

El llano de Kogane en la provincia Shimosa

*La pianura di Kogane nella
provincia di Shimosa*

Vlakte van Kogane in de provincie Shimosa

Colour woodcut/Gravure sur bois en couleurs

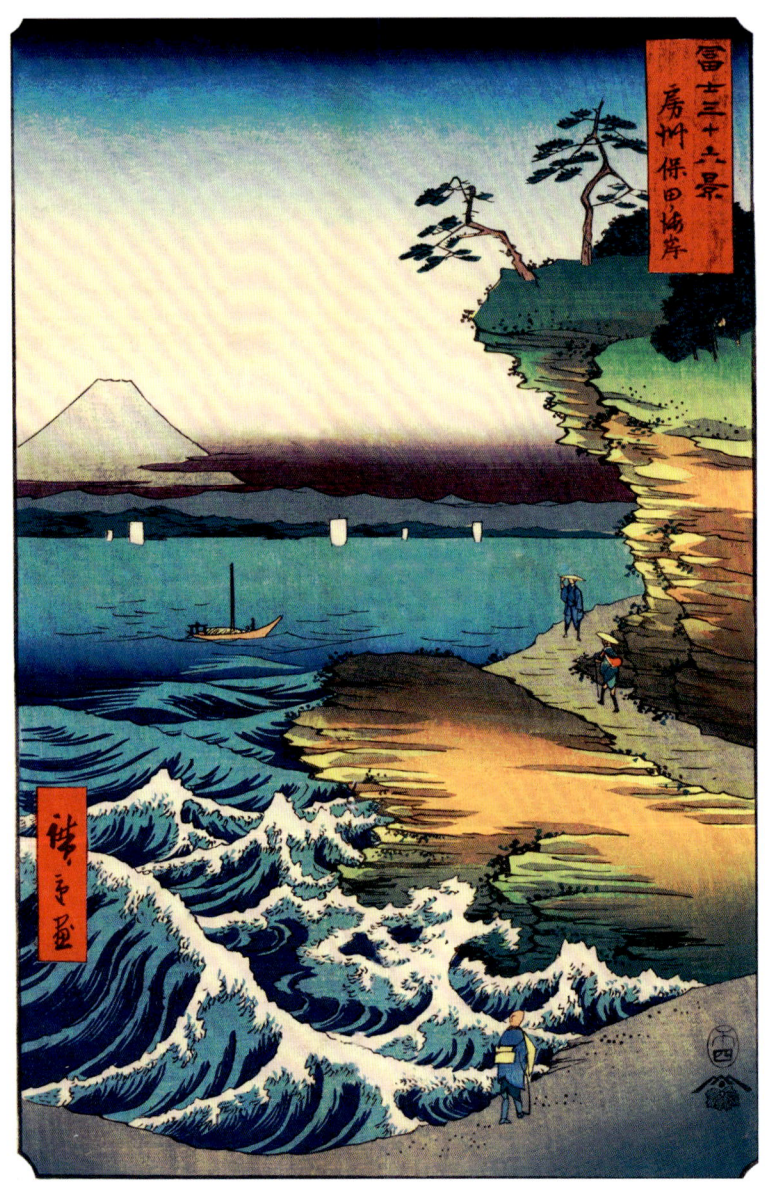

Coast near Hota in Awa Province
La Côte près de Hota dans la province d'Awa
Küste bei Hota in der Provinz Awa
La costa de Hota en la provincia Awa
Costa vicino a Hota nella provincia di Awa
De kust bij Hota, in de provincie Awa
Colour woodcut/Gravure sur bois en couleurs

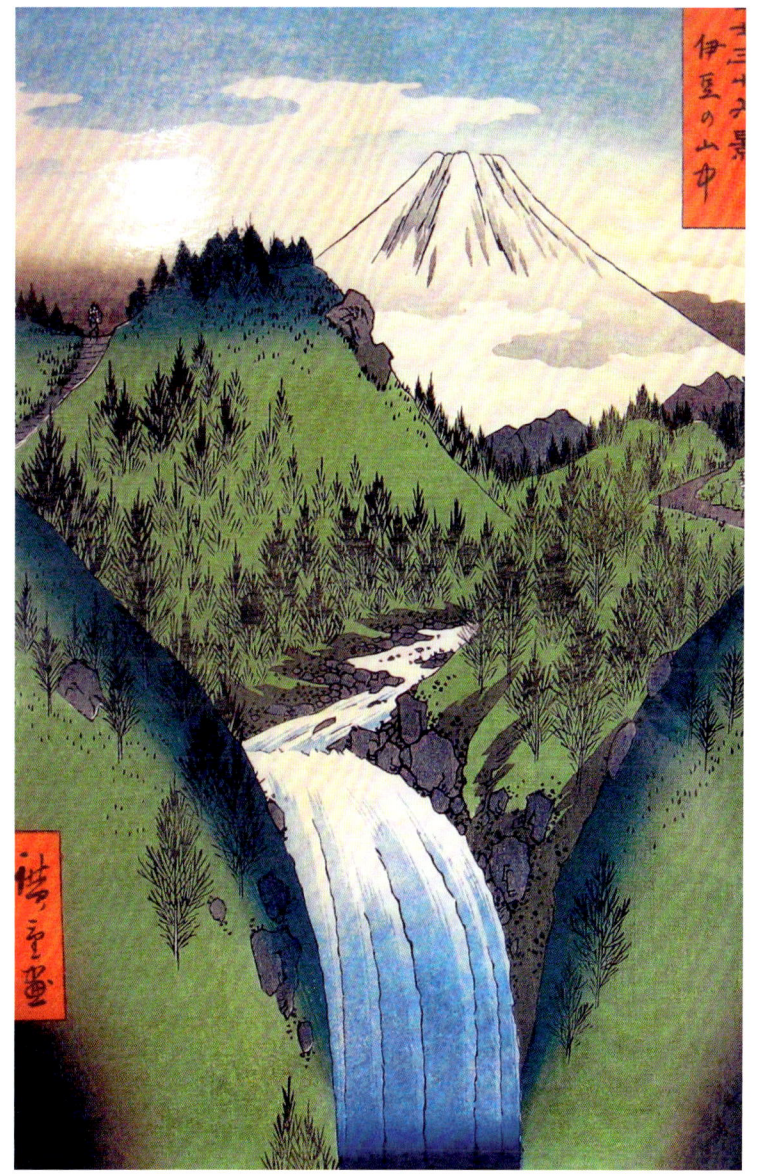

Mountains near Isu

Les Montagnes près d'Isu

Berge bei Isu

Montañas en Isu

Montagne di Isu

Bergen bij Isu

Colour woodcut/Gravure sur bois en couleurs

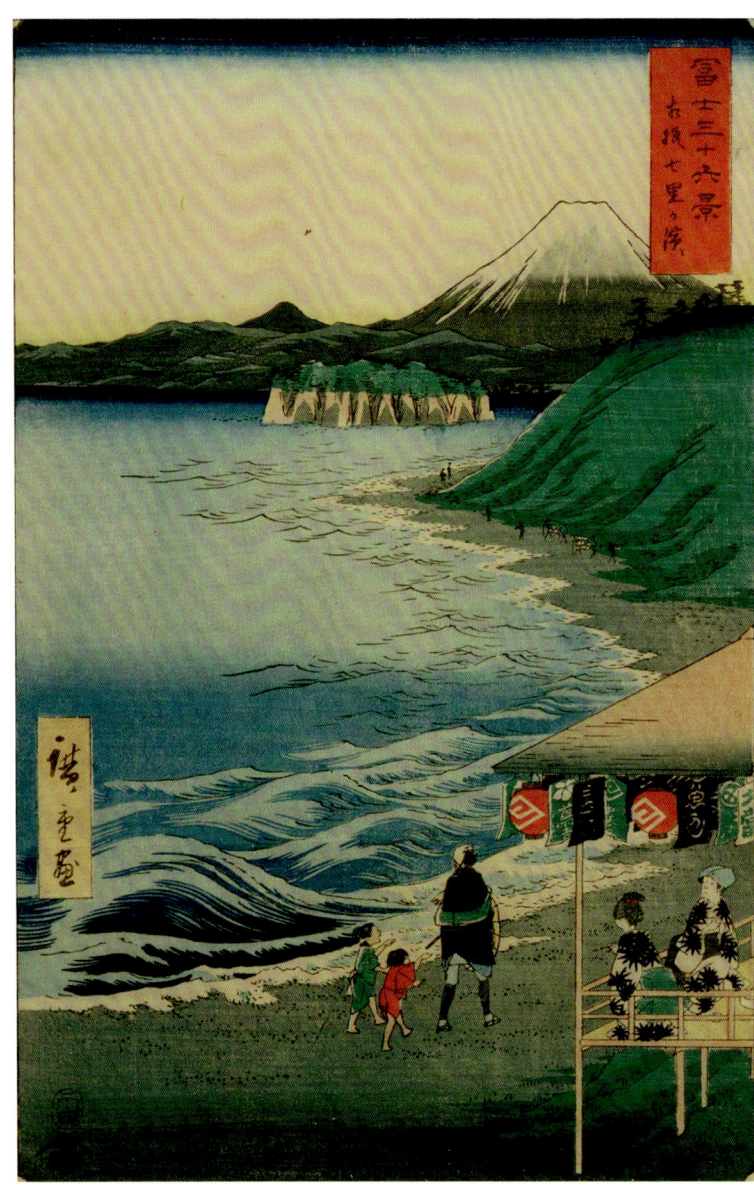

Shichirighama in Sagami

Shichirighama à Sagami

Shichirighama in Sagami

Shichirighama en Sagami

Shichirighama a Sagami

Shichirighama in Sagami

Colour woodcut/Gravure sur bois en couleurs,
36 × 24,2 cm, Universität, Trier

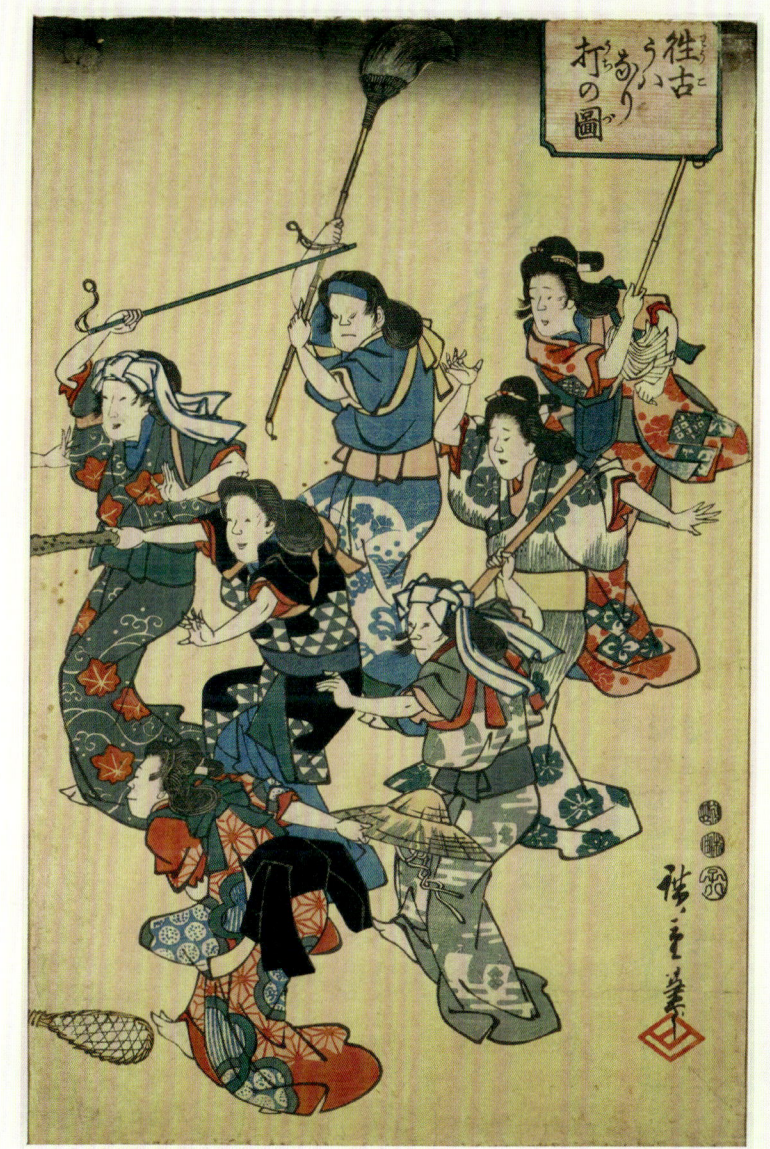

Oko Uwanare Uchi Nozu,
right sheet of a triptych

Oko Uwanare Uchi Nozu, feuille
droite d'un triptyque

Oko Uwanare Uchi Nozu, rechtes
Blatt eines Triptychons

Oko Uwanare Uchi Nozu, estampa
derecha de un tríptico

Oko Uwanare Uchi Nozu, stampa
diritta di un trittico

Oko Uwanare Uchi Nozu,
rechterblad van een triptiek

*Colour woodcut/Gravure sur bois
en couleurs, Private collection*

Fish
Poissons
Fische
Peces
Pesci
Vissen

Colour woodcut/*Gravure sur bois en couleurs, 9,6 × 10,8 cm*

Ukiyo-e: **Pictures of the floating world**
Ukiyo-e literally means something like "pictures of the floating world". The notion of the "floating world" in Buddhism initially had a pessimistic sense, not unlike the Christian vanitas, but this interpretation shifted in the late 17th century. Instead of reflecting on the finiteness of life, the idea evolved to one of enjoying the moment, precisely because of the transience of everything. The "pictures of the floating world" initially showed everyday life, festivals, and especially the world of courtesans and actors. The works reflect the lifestyles of the emerging middle class in the big cities, especially in Edo. Later, landscapes and animal and floral motifs become common in *ukiyo-e* as the woodcuts replace painting as the main medium of art distribution.

Ukiyo-e : **Images du monde flottant**
Ukiyo-e signifie littéralement « images du monde flottant ». Le « monde flottant » est d'abord un concept bouddhique, lié à la notion fondamentale de « l'impermanence » du monde. Vers la fin du XVIIe siècle, cette signification évolue de façon paradoxalement positive : au lieu de méditer sombrement sur la finitude éphémère du monde et en raison même de celle-ci, il convient de jouir de l'instant ; on passe ainsi de la *vanitas vanitatum* religieuse au *carpe diem* épicurien. Les « images du monde flottant » ont à présent pour sujets la vie quotidienne et surtout les fêtes, spécialement le monde des courtisanes et du théâtre. Les estampes représentent ainsi le plaisir de vivre de la bourgeoisie en pleine ascension dans les grandes villes, notamment à Edo. Les paysages seront ensuite intégrés à l'*ukiyo-e,* de même que les motifs de fleurs et d'animaux, et l'estampe remplace la peinture comme moyen de diffusion.

Ukiyo-e: **Bilder der fließenden Welt**
Ukiyo-e bedeutet wörtlich so viel wie „Bilder der fließenden Welt". Die Vorstellung der „fließenden Welt" hat im Buddhismus zunächst eine pessimistische, der christlichen Vanitas verwandte Ausrichtung. Im ausgehenden 17. Jahrhundert wandelt sich jedoch die Bedeutung. Anstelle der Besinnung auf die Endlichkeit des Lebens tritt nun die Idee, gerade angesichts der Vergänglichkeit alles Irdischen den Augenblick zu genießen. Die „Bilder der fließenden Welt" thematisieren anfangs vor allem das alltägliche Leben, Feste und speziell die Welt der Kurtisanen und der Schauspieler. Die Werke treffen damit das Lebensgefühl des aufkommenden Bürgertums in den großen Städten, besonders in Edo. Später werden auch die Landschaften sowie Tier- und Blumenmotive zu *ukiyo-e* gerechnet, und der Holzschnitt löst die Malerei als Verbreitungsmedium ab.

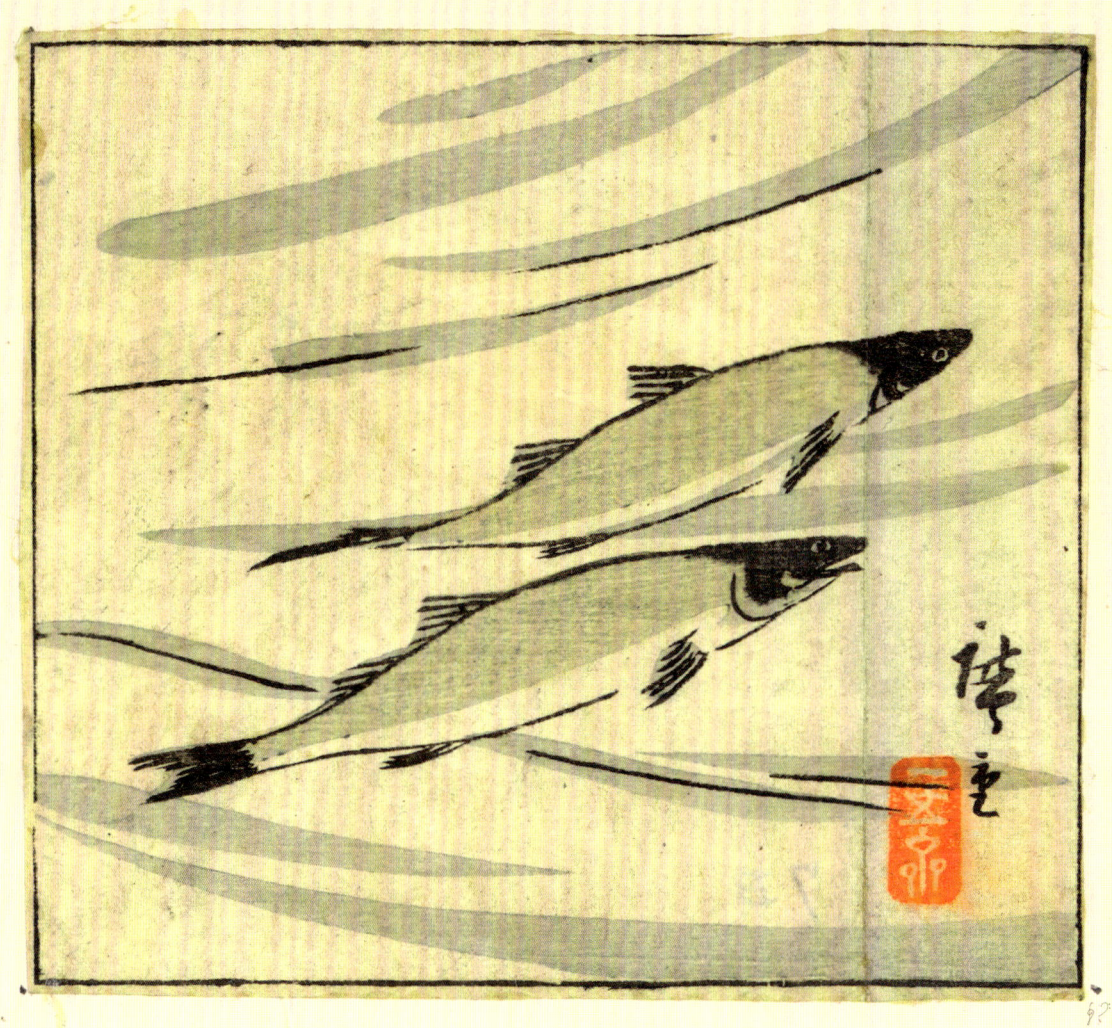

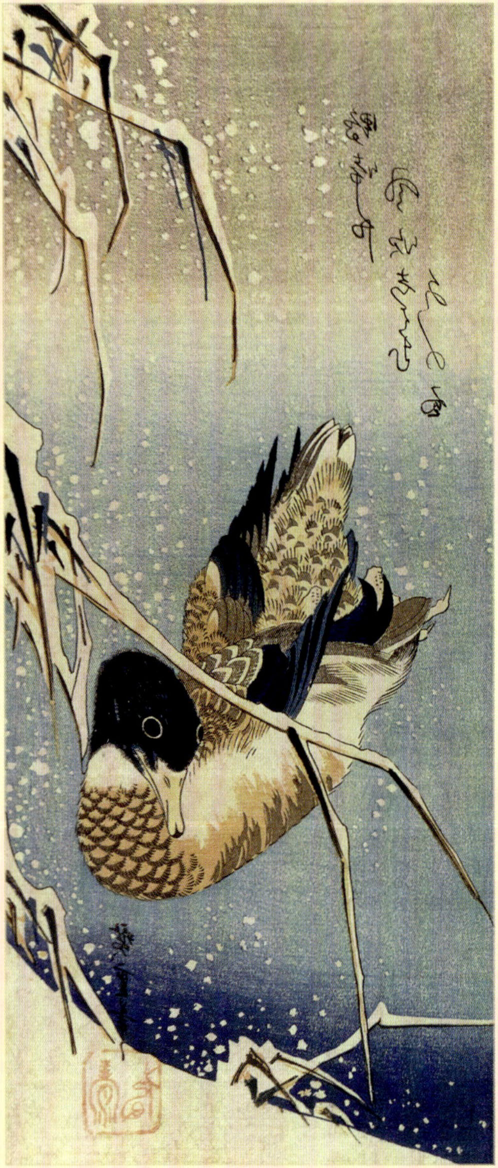

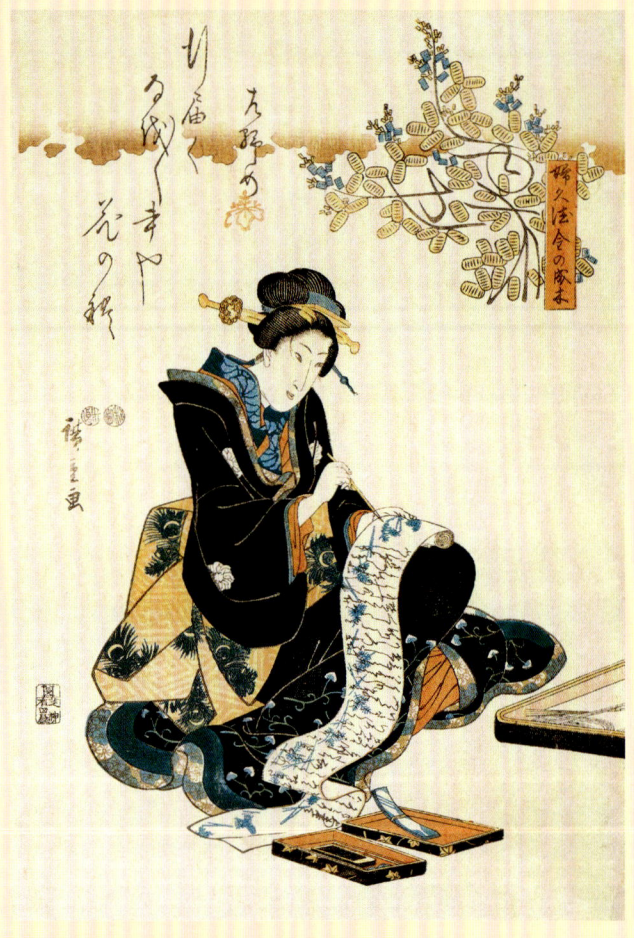

Wild duck in a snowy pond among the reeds

Canards sauvages dans une mare enneigée sous les roseaux

Wildente in einem verschneiten Teich unter Schilf

Patos salvajes entre juncos en un estanque nevado

Anatra selvatica in uno stagno innevato tra i canneti

Wilde eend onder het riet in een besneeuwde vijver

Colour woodcut/Gravure sur bois en couleurs

Courtesan writing a letter

Courtisane écrivant une lettre

Kurtisane einen Brief schreibend

Cortesana escribiendo una carta

Cortigiana che scrive una lettera

Courtisane bij het schrijven van een brief

Colour woodcut/Gravure sur bois en couleurs, 37,5 × 26,2 cm, Private collection

Ukiyo-e: Imágenes del mundo flotante

Ukiyo-e significa, literalmente, algo así como "imágenes del mundo flotante". La idea del "mundo flotante" tiene en el budismo en principio una connotación pesimista, relacionada con la Vanitas cristiana. A finales del XVII sin embargo este significado cambia. En vez de centrarse en la reflexión sobre la finitud de la vida aparece ahora la idea de, precisamente por la temporalidad de lo terrestre, disfrutar de cada momento. Las "imágenes del mundo flotante" trabajan en sus inicios sobre todo con temas de la vida cotidiana, fiestas y en concreto el mundo de los cortesanos y los actores. Así, las obras se adaptan al sentir vital de la creciente burguesía de las grandes ciudades, especialmente Edo. Más tarde llegarán también al *ukiyo-e* los temas de paisajes, animales y plantas, sustituyendo entonces la xilografía a la pintura como medio de difusión.

Ukiyo-e: immagini del mondo fluttuante

Ukiyo-e letteralmente significa qualcosa come "immagini del mondo fluttuante". Il concetto del "mondo fluttuante" ha un orientamento inizialmente pessimistico nel buddismo, affine a quello della vanità cristiana. Tuttavia verso la fine del XVII secolo il significato cambia. Invece di riflettere sulla caducità della vita, si fa strada l'idea di godere il momento, proprio a causa della fugacità di tutto ciò che è terreno. Le "immagini del mondo fluttuante" all'inizio tematizzano soprattutto la vita quotidiana, le feste e specialmente il mondo dei cortigiani e degli attori. Le opere incontrano il sentimento della vita della borghesia nascente delle grandi città, soprattutto di Edo. Più tardi nei *ukiyo-e* si annoverano anche paesaggi e motivi di animali e fiori, e la xilografia sostituisce la pittura come mezzo di diffusione.

Ukiyo-e: beelden van de vlietende wereld

Ukiyo-e betekent letterlijk "prenten van de vlietende wereld". Het idee van een altijd veranderende wereld heeft in het boeddhisme aanvankelijk een negatieve ondertoon, vergelijkbaar met de christelijke vanitas of ijdelheid. Maar eind zeventiende eeuw verandert de betekenis ervan, waarbij niet meer de bezinning op de eindigheid van het leven centraal staat maar het idee dat het, juist met het oog op de vergankelijkheid van al het aardse, belangrijk is om van het leven en het ogenblik te genieten. Aanvankelijk wordt in de "prenten van de vlietende wereld" vooral het alledaagse leven uitgebeeld, naast feestdagen en de wereld van courtisanes en toneelspelers. De werken weerspiegelen daarmee het levensgevoel van de opkomende burgerij in de grote steden, met name in Edo. Later worden ook landschappen en dier- en bloemmotieven tot de *ukiyo-e* gerekend en neemt de houtsnijkunst als medium voor een groter publiek de plaats van de schilderkunst in.

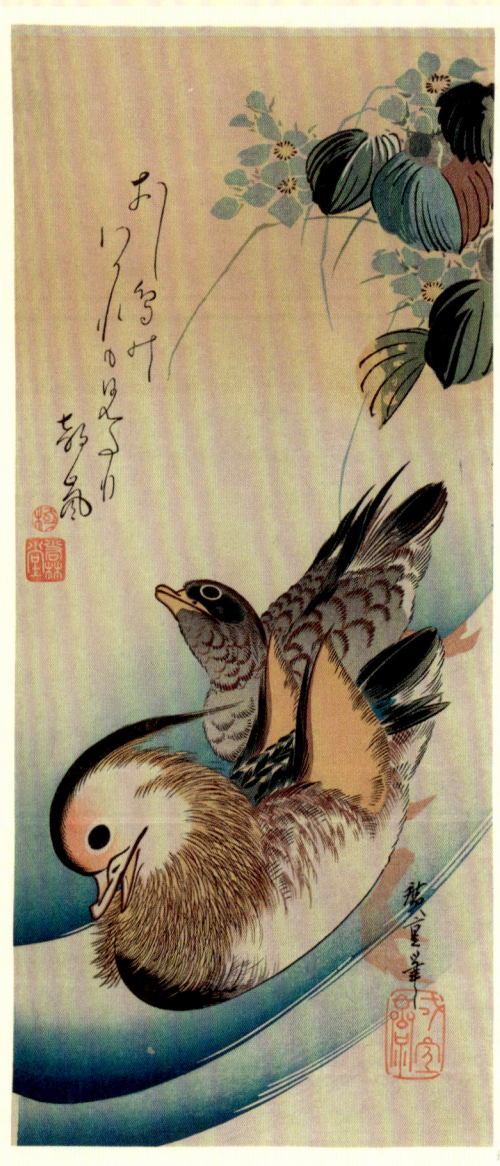

Pair of Mandarin Ducks

Couple de canards mandarins

Mandarinentenpaar

Par de patos mandarines

Coppia di anatre mandarine

Een koppel mandarijneenden

c. 1835, Colour woodcut/Gravure sur bois en couleurs, 36,9×13 cm

Mandarin ducks are a symbol of marital harmony in China. They also are native to Japan. Hiroshige has accurately observed a pair of ducks in this drawing. The drakes only have their show plumage during the mating and breeding season, moulting before moving to their winter quarters in the autumn.

Les canards mandarins sont en Chine le symbole de l'harmonie conjugale ; ces volatiles sont aussi chez eux au Japon. Pour cette représentation, Hiroshige a soigneusement observé un couple de ces canards qui n'ont leur plumage de prestige que pendant la parade et la nidification. Ils muent en automne, avant de prendre leurs quartiers d'hiver.

Mandarinenten stehen in China als Symbol für eheliche Harmonie. Die Vögel sind auch in Japan beheimatet. Hiroshige hat ein Entenpaar für diese Darstellung genau beobachtet: Die Erpel besitzen ihr Prachtgefieder nur während der Paarungs- und Brutzeit. Bevor sie im Herbst in ihr Winterquartier übersiedeln, mausern sie sich.

Los patos mandarines en China son un símbolo de armonía conyugal. Estos pájaros también pueden encontrarse en Japón. Hiroshige ha observado con detalle a una pareja para su representación: Los patos macho solo presentan su plumaje vistoso durante las épocas de celo y apareamiento. Antes de desplazarse a su morada de invierno, mudan el plumaje.

In Cina le anatre mandarine sono il simbolo dell'armonia coniugale. Questi uccelli si possono trovare anche in Giappone. Per questa rappresentazione Hiroshige ha osservato attentamente una coppia di anatre: il maschio possiede il suo magnifico piumaggio soltanto durante l'accoppiamento e il periodo della cova. Prima che in autunno emigri nel suo ricovero invernale, cambia le penne.

De mandarijneend is in China het symbool voor de harmonie tussen echtgenoten. De vogel is ook in Japan inheems. Voor deze tekening heeft Hiroshige een eendenpaar zeer goed bestudeerd: woerden tonen hun prachtige verenkleed alleen in de paar- en broedtijd. Voordat ze in de herfst naar hun wintergronden verhuizen, komen ze in de rui.

White heron and purple iris

Héron blanc et iris violets

Weißer Reiher und violette Iris

Caballero blanco e iris violeta

Airone bianco e iris violetti

Witte reiger en paarse irissen

c. 1830, Colour woodcut/Gravure sur bois en couleurs, Victoria and Albert Museum, London

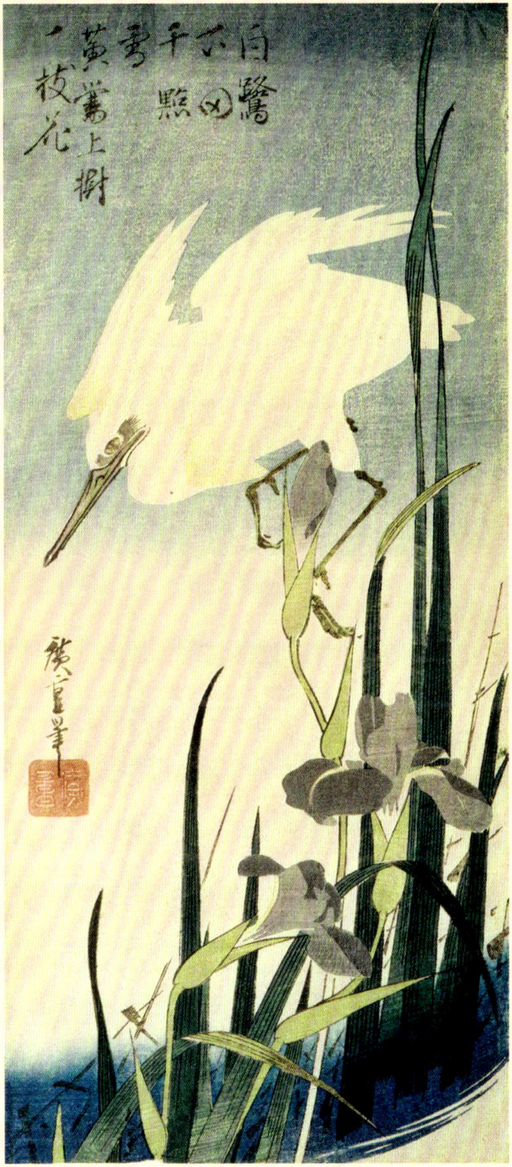

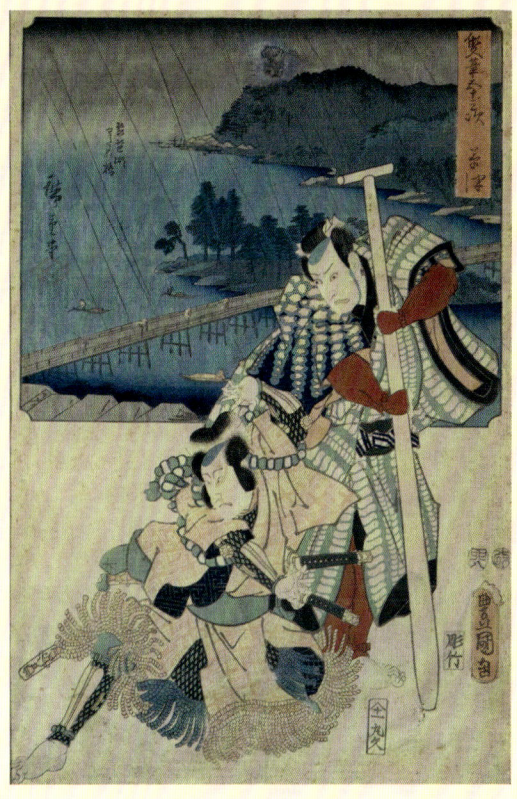

With Utagawa Kunisada: Two actors in front of a landscape,
from the series *53 Stations from Two Paintbrushes*

*Avec Utagawa Kunisada : Deux acteurs devant un paysage,
de la série Les 53 relais par deux pinceaux*

*Mit Utagawa Kunisada: Zwei Schauspieler vor einer Landschaft,
aus der Serie 53 Stationen von zwei Pinseln*

*Con Utagawa Kunisada: Dos actores frente a un paisaje,
de la serie 53 estaciones de Dos Pinceles*

*Con Utagawa Kunisada: due attori davanti a un paesaggio,
della serie Le 53 stazioni a due pennelli*

*Met Utagawa Kunisada: Twee toneelspelers voor een landschap,
uit de serie 53 halteplaatsen van twee penselen*

1857, Colour woodcut/Gravure sur bois en couleurs

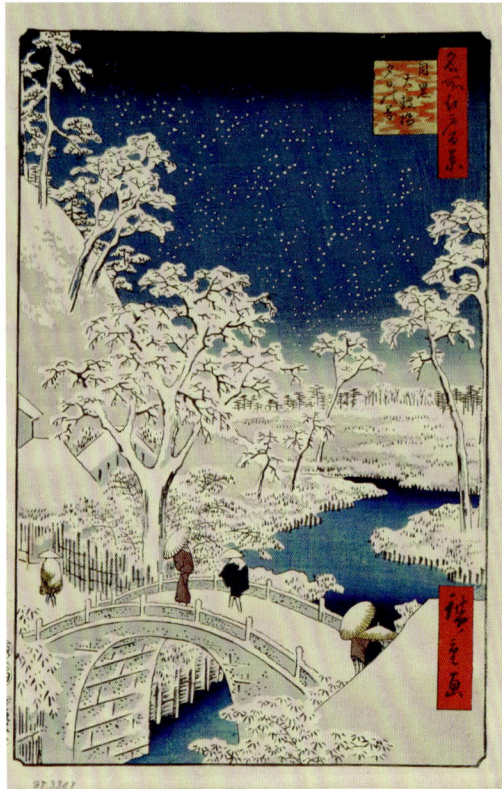

The Drum Bridge at Meguro, from the series *100 Famous Views of Edo*

Le Pont de Drum près de Meguro, de la série *Cent vues d'Edo*

Die Drum Brücke bei Meguro, aus der Serie *100 berühmte Ansichten von Edo*

El punte Drum en Meguro, de la serie *100 vistas famosas de Edo*

Ponte del tamburo a Meguro, della serie *100 vedute famose di Edo*

De maanbrug bij Meguro, uit de serie *100 beroemde gezichten op Edo*

1856–1858, Colour woodcut/Gravure sur bois en couleurs, 39 × 26 cm, State Hermitage, St. Petersburg

Views of Edo

Views of Edo form the second focus in Hiroshige's work alongside his highway scenes. During his lifetime, there were about one and a half million people living in the metropolis. In several series, the artist shows urban life in all its facets. The turbulent street life, the merchants, the tea houses, and theatres are shown as are nearby destinations for excursions outside the city. Hiroshige's last series *100 Views of Edo* is considered his artistic

Cent vues d'Edo

À côté des grandes voies de communication, les vues de la capitale Edo constituent le second thème principal de l'œuvre de Hiroshige. De son temps, la métropole compte environ un million et demi d'habitants. Dans plusieurs séries d'estampes, l'artiste montre la vie de la métropole sous toutes ses facettes : l'animation trépidante des rues, les marchands, les maisons de thé et les théâtres

Ansichten von Edo

Ansichten der Hauptstadt Edo bilden neben den Reiserouten den zweiten Schwerpunkt in Hiroshiges Schaffen. Zu seinen Lebzeiten wohnen rund anderthalb Millionen Menschen in der Metropole. Der Künstler zeigt in mehreren Serien das großstädtische Leben in allen Facetten. Das turbulente Straßenleben, die Händler, die Teehäuser und Theater kommen ebenso zur Darstellung wie die Ausflugsziele vor

Iris in Horikiri

Iris à Horikiri

Iris in Horikiri

Iris en Horikiri

Iris a Horikiri

Irissen in Horikiri

*Colour woodcut/Gravure sur bois en couleurs, 39×26 cm,
State Hermitage, St. Petersburg*

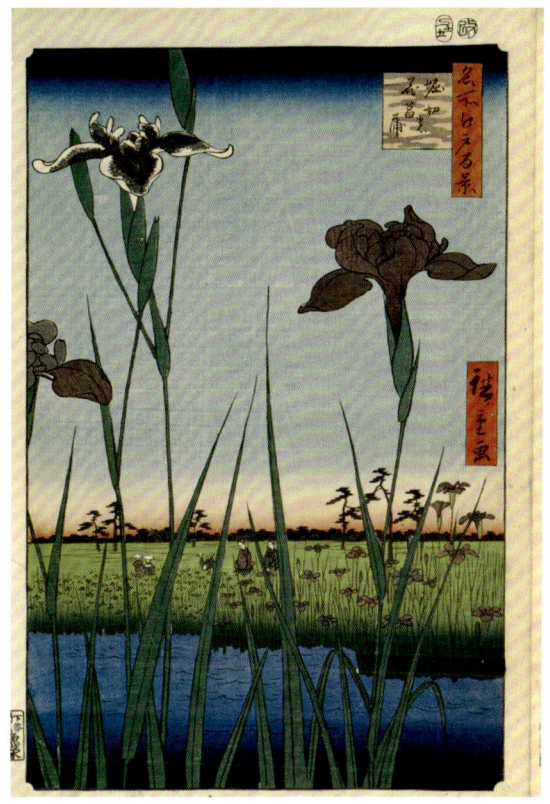

Vistas de Edo

Las vistas de la capital Edo constituyen, junto a las rutas de viaje, el segundo tema principal del trabajo de Hiroshige. Durante su época la metrópolis albergaba alrededor de un millón y medio de habitantes. El artista muestra en diferentes series la vida de la gran ciudad en todas sus facetas. La turbulenta vida de las calles, los comerciantes, las teterías y teatros forman parte de las representaciones,

Vedute di Edo

Oltre alle rotte di viaggio, le vedute della capitale Edo costituiscono il secondo tema delle creazioni di Hiroshige. Alla sua epoca, nella metropoli, vivevano circa un milione e mezzo di persone. L'artista mostra in diverse serie la vita delle grandi città in tutte le sue sfaccettature. La turbolenta vita sulla strada, i commercianti, le case da tè e i teatri vengono rappresentati come le mete di escursioni davanti alle porte

Gezichten op Edo

Naast de reisseries zijn de gezichten op de hoofdstad Edo het tweede belangrijke thema in Hiroshige's werk. Tijdens zijn leven telt de metropool rond anderhalf miljoen inwoners. In meerdere series toont de kunstenaar het leven van de grote stad in al zijn facetten. Het drukke straatleven, de kooplieden, de theehuizen en de theaters worden net levendig uitgebeeld als uitstapjes buiten de poorten van de stad. De laatste

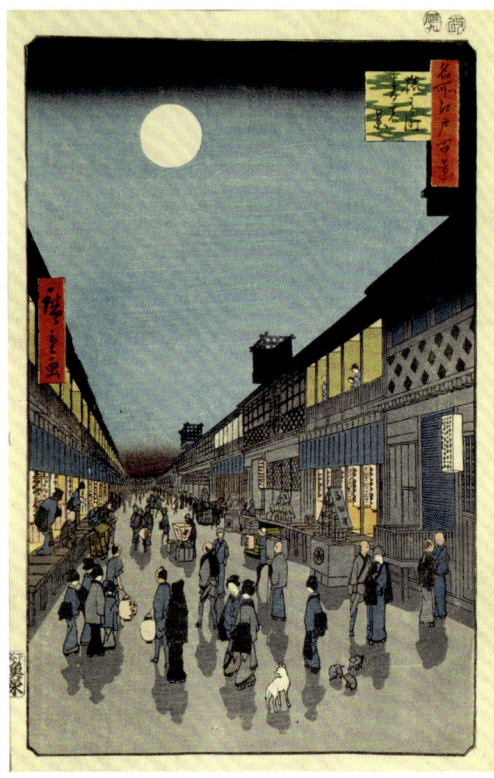

Saruwaka-machi at night
Saruwaka-machi la nuit
Saruwaka-machi bei Nacht
Saruwaka-machi por la noche
Saruwaka-machi di notte
Saruwaka-machi bij nacht

Colour woodcut/Gravure sur bois en couleurs, 39×26 cm,
State Hermitage, St. Petersburg

legacy, an outstanding and particularly extensive work created at the end of his life. It is the night scenes in this series that particularly stand out, with the sky full of stars and fireworks. The numerous views from windows and balconies are among the highlights of the series. Here Hiroshige is applying a compositional scheme in which a seemingly incidental motif such as a railing or a lantern is moved extremely close to the viewer. The actual landscape, however, is only seen in the distance as a backdrop. Bird's

figurent aussi souvent que les lieux de divertissement et d'excursion, aux portes de la ville. La dernière série d'estampes de Hiroshige – *Cent vues d'Edo* – est considérée comme son testament artistique, point d'orgue et conclusion exceptionnellement riches d'une vie de créateur infatigable. Dans ces feuilles se distinguent particulièrement les vues nocturnes, avec des ciels éclairés par les étoiles ou des feux d'artifice. Les nombreuses vues prises depuis une fenêtre ou un balcon comptent

den Toren der Stadt. Hiroshiges letzte Serie, die *100 Ansichten von Edo* gilt als sein künstlerisches Vermächtnis, mit dem er am Ende seines Lebens noch einmal ein herausragendes und besonders umfangreiches Werk schafft. Aus diesen Blättern stechen besonders die Nachtansichten heraus, bei denen der Himmel von Sternen und Feuerwerk erhellt wird. Auch die zahlreichen Ausblicke aus Fenstern und von Balkonen gehören zu den Höhepunkten der Serie. Hier wendet Hiroshige ein

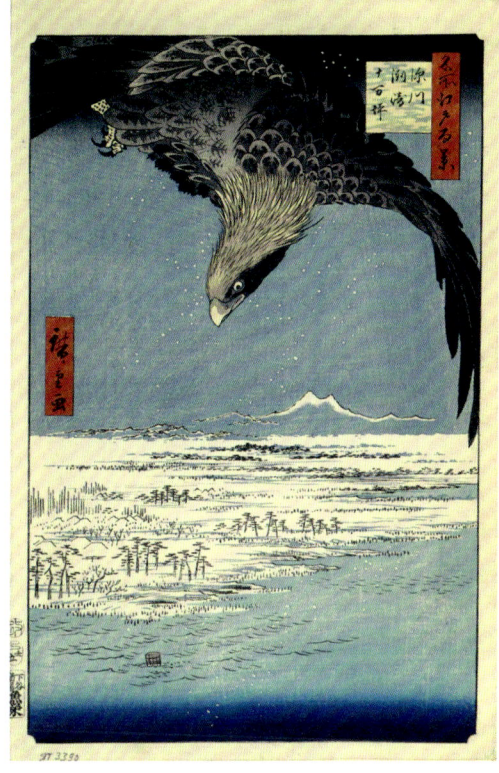

tanto como lugares de excursión
o las puertas de la ciudad. La última
serie de Hiroshige *100 famosas vistas
de Edo* es considerada su testamento
artístico, con el que crea al final de su
vida una última extensa obra de gran
originalidad y excepcionalidad. De estas
estampas se destacan especialmente
las vistas nocturnas, en las que el
cielo se ve iluminado por estrellas y
fuegos artificiales. También son puntos
culminantes de la serie las vistas desde
balcones y ventanas. En ellas, Hiroshige

della città. Le *cento vedute di Edo* è
l'ultima serie di Hiroshige e anche il suo
testamento artistico, con il quale alla fine
della sua vita crea ancora una volta un
mondo straordinario e particolarmente
vasto. In queste stampe spiccano
specialmente le vedute notturne, nelle
quali il cielo viene illuminato dalle
stelle e dai fuochi d'artificio. Anche
i numerosi panorami dalle finestre
e dai balconi sono tra i soggetti
principali di questa serie. Qui Hiroshige
utilizza uno schema compositivo con

serie van Hiroshige, *100 gezichten op
Edo*, wordt gezien als zijn artistieke
nalatenschap, waarmee hij aan het
einde van zijn leven nog eenmaal een
opmerkelijk en omvangrijk meesterwerk
creëert. Op deze bladen vallen vooral
de avondscènes op, waarin de donkere
hemel wordt verlicht door de sterren
en vuurwerk. Ook de vele uitzichten
vanuit ramen en vanaf balkons behoren
tot de hoogtepunten van de serie. Hier
past Hiroshige een compositieschema
toe waarin hij een ogenschijnlijk

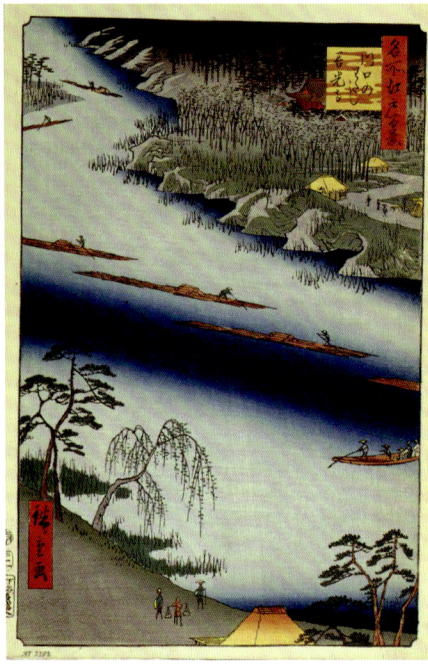

eye views of the city are also frequently featured in Hiroshige's *100 Views of Edo*. Hiroshige once again shows off the whole spectrum of his artistic talent to perfection, so it is no wonder that this series has shaped our present image of Hiroshige like no other.

également au nombre des sommets de la série. L'artiste utilise ici un schéma de composition installant tout près du spectateur un motif apparemment secondaire – par exemple une balustrade ou un lampion ; le paysage proprement dit n'est en revanche visible que comme un décor éloigné. Les vues verticales, qui présentent au spectateur le monde vu à vol d'oiseau, sont particulièrement fréquentes dans la série des Cent vues. Hiroshige déploie ici, une fois encore, toute la palette d'un art parvenu à son point de perfection. Rien d'étonnant à ce que cette ultime série d'estampes marque comme nulle autre l'image que nous avons de son créateur.

Kompositionsschema an, bei dem ein scheinbar nebensächliches Motiv, zum Beispiel eine Brüstung oder ein Lampion, extrem nah an den Betrachter herangerückt ist. Die eigentliche Landschaft ist hingegen nur in der Ferne als Kulisse zu sehen. Auch die steilen Aufsichten, die dem Betrachter die Welt aus der Vogelperspektive präsentieren, finden sich in den *100 Ansichten von Edo* besonders häufig. Hiroshige zeigt hier noch einmal das gesamte Spektrum seiner Kunst in Perfektion – kein Wunder, dass diese Serie unser heutiges Bild von Hiroshige wie keine andere prägt.

Asakusa Rice Fields and Torinomachi Festival

Les Rizières d'Asakusa et la fête de Torinomachi

Asakusa-Reisfelder und Torinomachi-Fest

Los campos de arroz de Asakusa y la fiesta de Torinomachi

Campi di riso di Asakusa e la festa di Torinomachi

De rijstvelden van Asakusa en het feest van Torinomachi

Colour woodcut/Gravure sur bois en couleurs, 39 × 26 cm,
State Hermitage, St. Petersburg

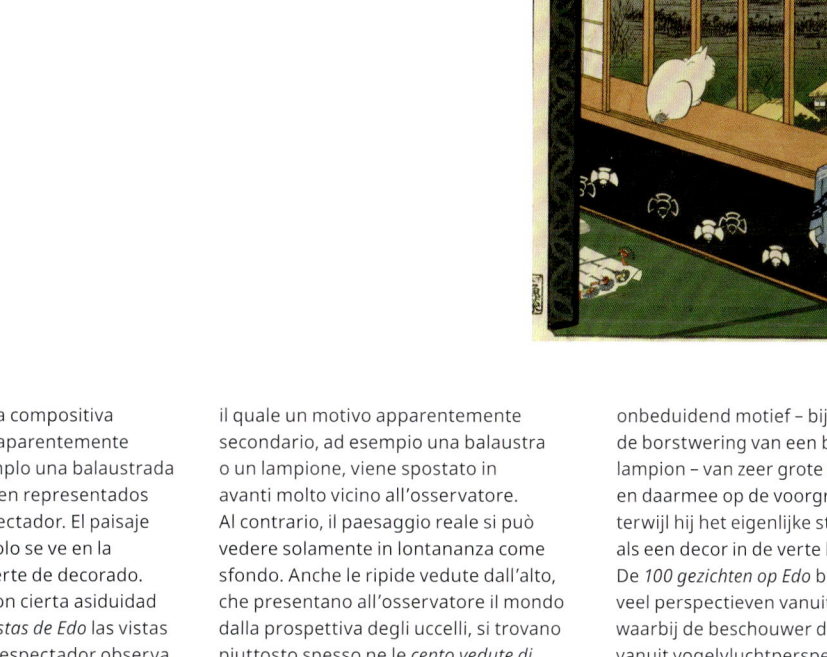

utiliza una estructura compositiva
en la que un motivo aparentemente
secundario, por ejemplo una balaustrada
o un farolillo, aparecen representados
muy cercanos al espectador. El paisaje
en sí, por su parte, solo se ve en la
lejanía como una suerte de decorado.
También aparecen con cierta asiduidad
en las *100 famosas vistas de Edo* las vistas
aéreas, en las que el espectador observa
el mundo desde la perspectiva de un
pájaro. Hiroshige muestra aquí todo el
rango de su arte con total perfección;
no puede por tanto sorprender que esta
serie defina como ninguna otra nuestra
imagen actual de Hiroshige.

il quale un motivo apparentemente
secondario, ad esempio una balaustra
o un lampione, viene spostato in
avanti molto vicino all'osservatore.
Al contrario, il paesaggio reale si può
vedere solamente in lontananza come
sfondo. Anche le ripide vedute dall'alto,
che presentano all'osservatore il mondo
dalla prospettiva degli uccelli, si trovano
piuttosto spesso ne le *cento vedute di
Edo*. Qui Hiroshige presenta ancora
una volta l'intero spettro della sua arte
nella perfezione; non c'è dunque da
meravigliarsi che questa serie influenzi
la nostra immagine odierna di Hiroshige
come nessun'altra.

onbeduidend motief – bijvoorbeeld
de borstwering van een balkon of een
lampion – van zeer grote nabijheid tekent
en daarmee op de voorgrond plaatst,
terwijl hij het eigenlijke stadslandschap
als een decor in de verte behandelt.
De *100 gezichten op Edo* bevatten ook
veel perspectieven vanuit de hoogte,
waarbij de beschouwer de wereld
vanuit vogelvluchtperspectief overziet.
Hiroshige toont hier nog eenmaal en
in alle perfectie het hele scala van zijn
meesterschap – geen wonder dat deze
serie ons huidige beeld van Hiroshige's
oeuvre als geen ander bepaalt.

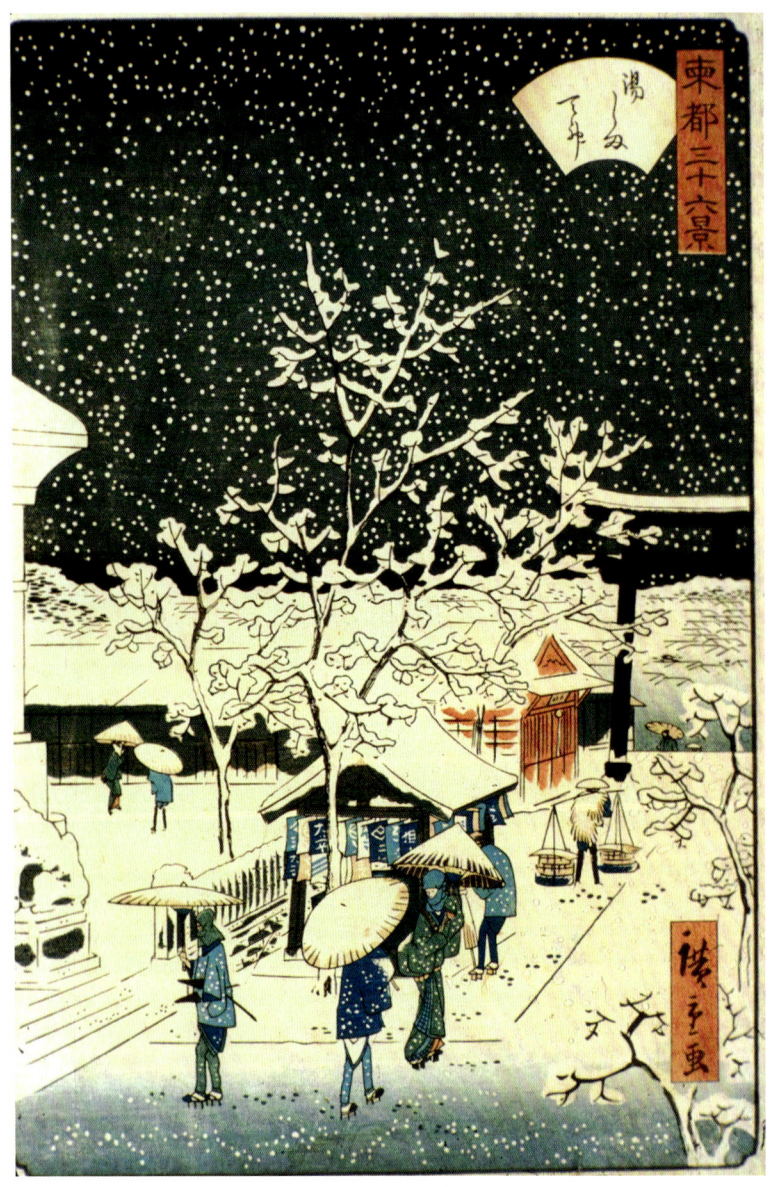

Yushima Tenjin shrine in the snow
Le Sanctuaire de Yushima-Tenjin sous la neige
Yushima-Tenjin-Schrein im Schnee
Santuario Yushima-Tenjin nevado
Santuario di Yushima-Tenjin sotto la neve
Yushima-Tenjin-schrijn in de sneeuw

Colour woodcut/Gravure sur bois en couleurs,
State Hermitage, St. Petersburg

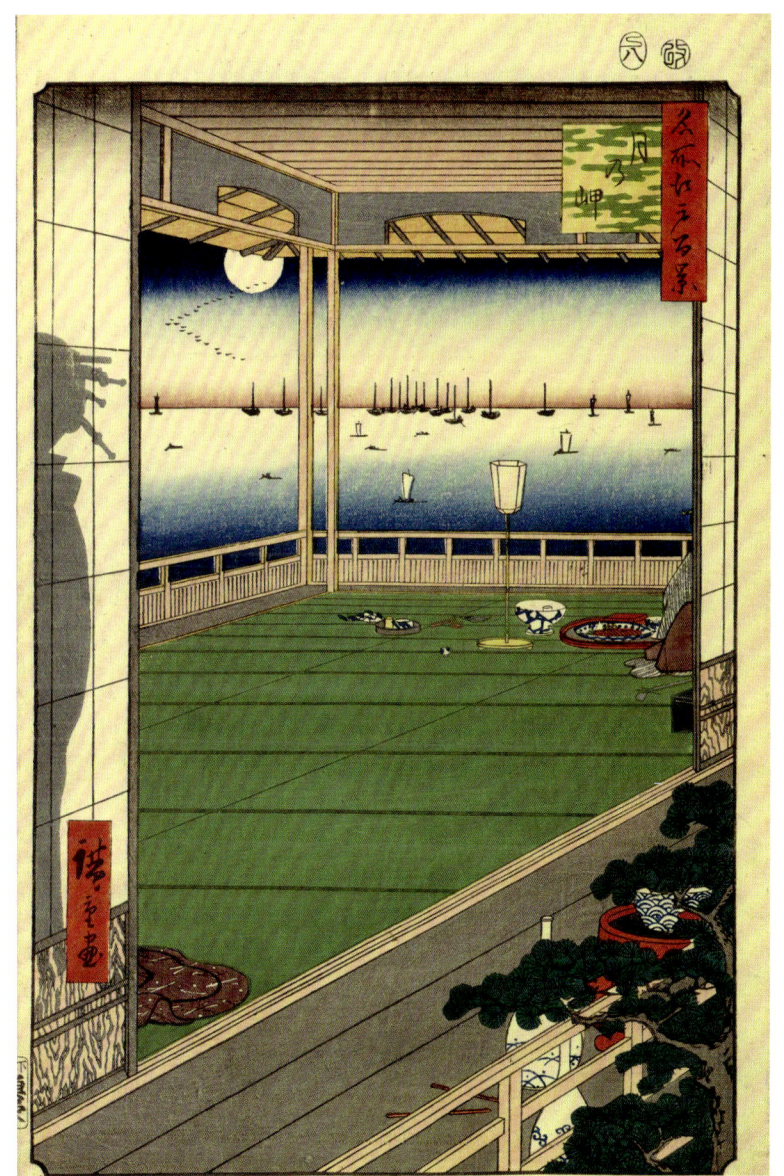

Moonlight

Clair de lune

Mondlicht

Luz de luna

Chiaro di luna

Maanlicht

Colour woodcut/Gravure sur bois en couleurs,
39×26 cm, State Hermitage, St. Petersburg

173

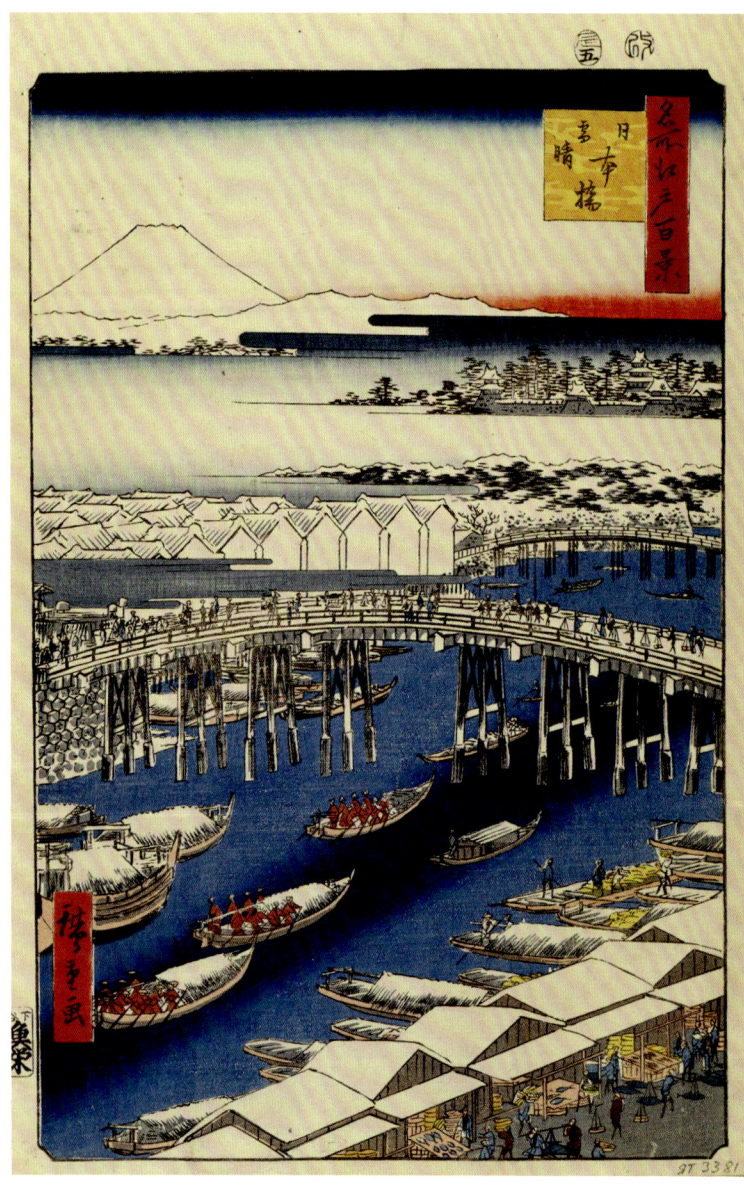

Nihonbashi, clear sky after the snowfall

Nihonbashi, ciel clair après une chute de neige

Nihonbashi, klarer Himmel
nach dem Schneefall

Nihonbashi con cielo descubierto
tras la nevada

Nihonbashi, cielo sereno dopo la nevicata

Nihonbashi, heldere hemel na sneeuwval

Colour woodcut/Gravure sur bois en couleurs,
39×26 cm, State Hermitage, St. Petersburg

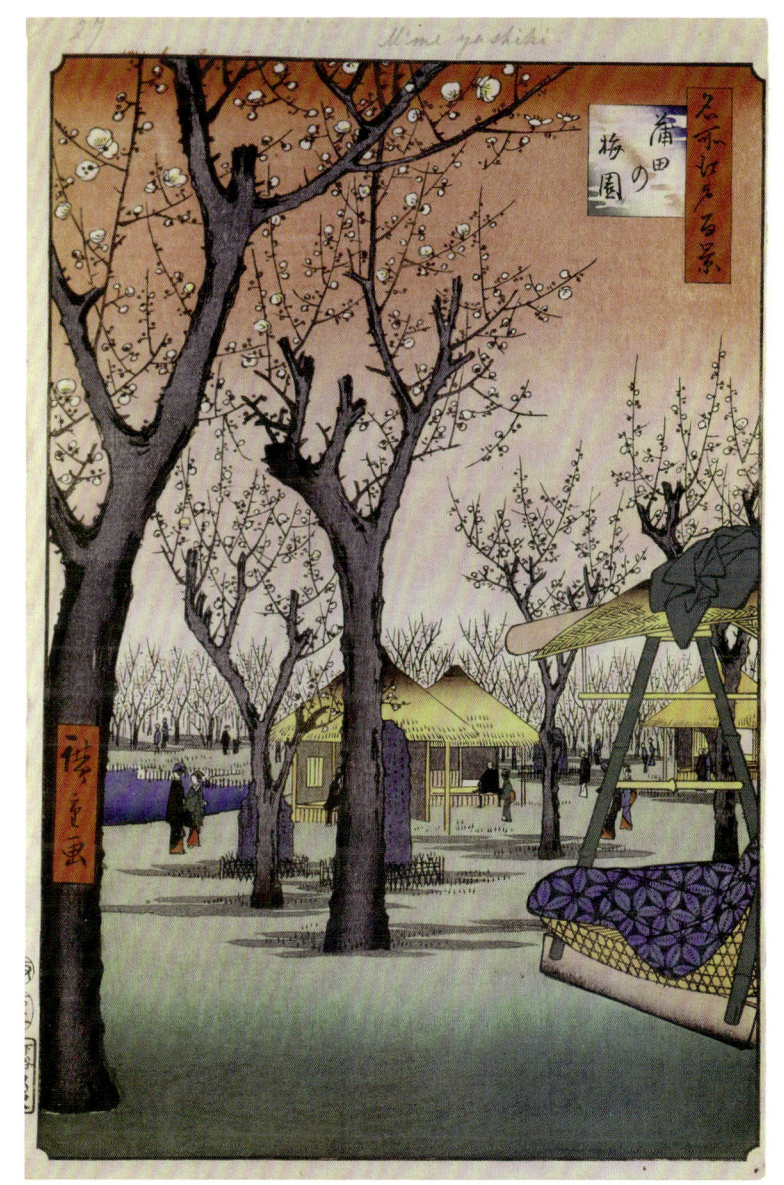

The Plum Garden at Kamata

Pruneraie à Kamata

Der Pflaumengarten bei Kamata

El jardín de ciruelos en Kamata

Il giardino dei susini a Kamata

De pruimentuin bij Kamatat

Colour woodcut/Gravure sur bois en couleurs,
39×26 cm, State Hermitage, St. Petersburg

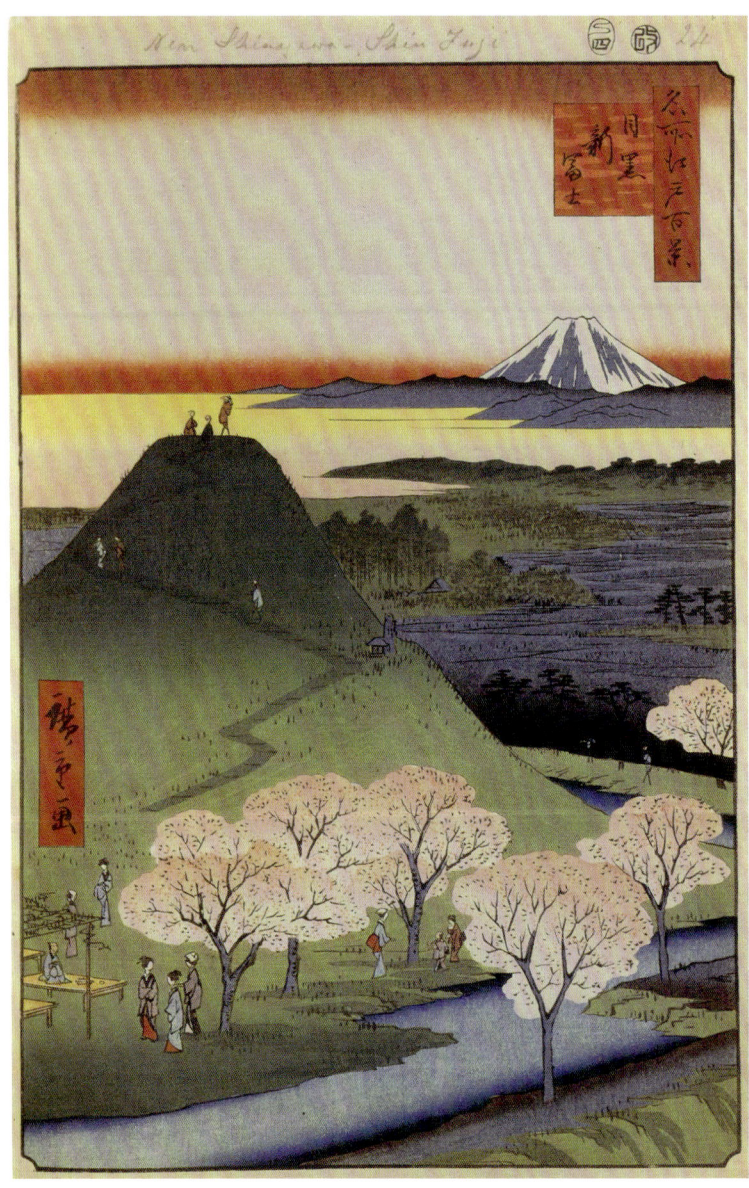

The New Fuji in Meguro
Le Nouveau Fuji à Meguro
Der Neue Fuji in Meguro
El nuevo Fuji en Meguro
Il nuovo Fuji a Meguro
Der Nieuwe Fuji in Meguro

*Colour woodcut/Gravure sur bois en couleurs,
39 × 26 cm, State Hermitage, St. Petersburg*

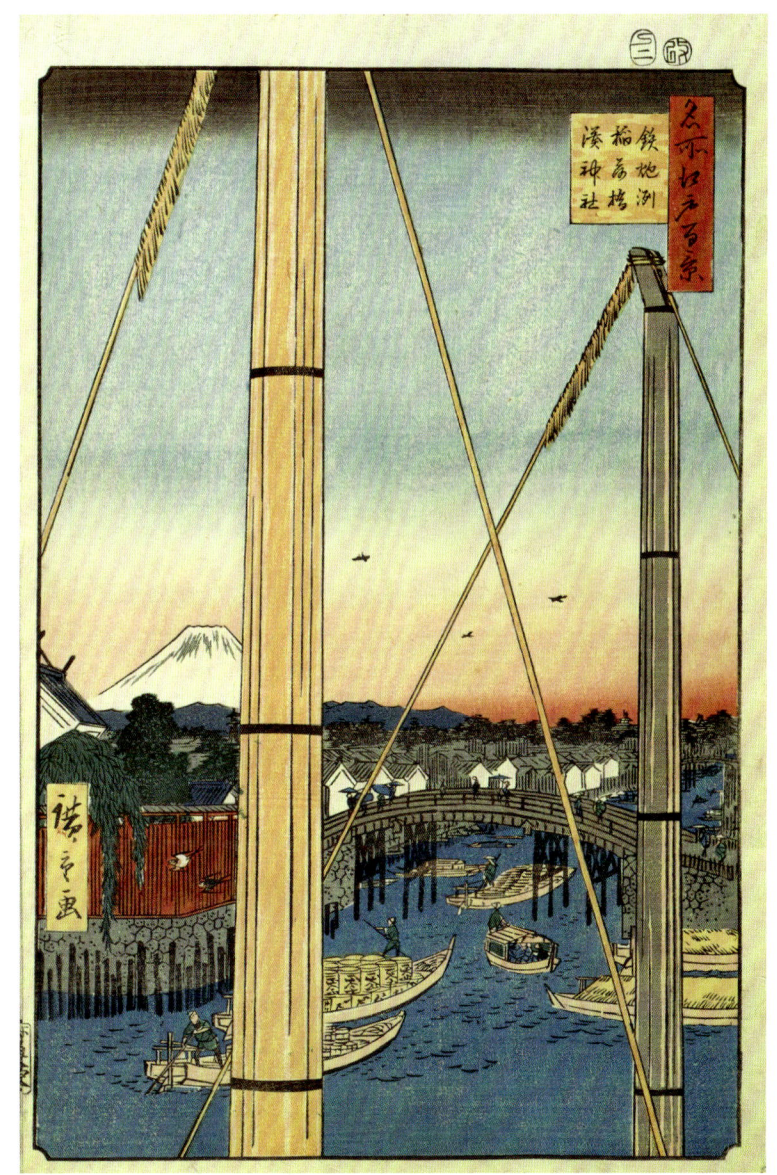

Inari Bridge and Minato Shrine in Teppozu

*Le Pont d'Inari et le sanctuaire
de Minato à Teppozu*

Inari-Brücke und Minato-Schrein in Teppozu

*El puente Inari y el santuario
Minato en Teppozu*

*Il ponte di Inari e il santuario
di Minato a Teppozu*

De Inari-brug en de Minato-schrijn in Teppozu

Colour woodcut/Gravure sur bois en couleurs,
39×26 cm, State Hermitage, St. Petersburg

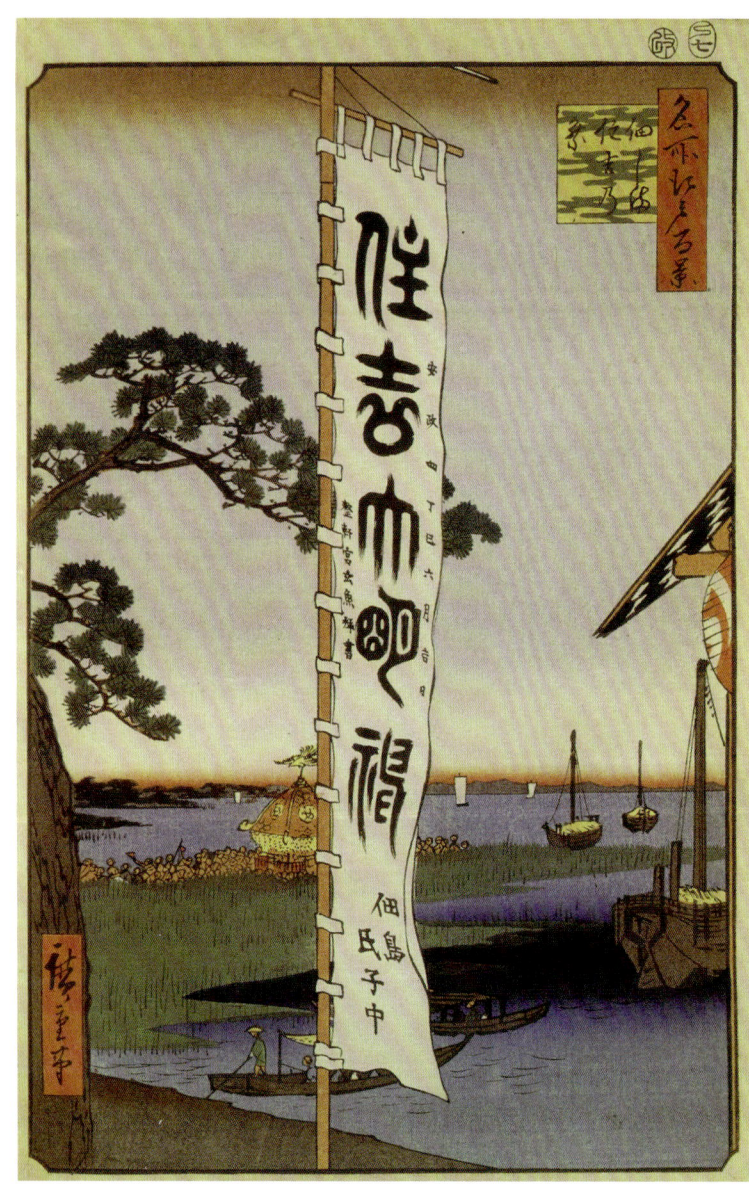

The Sumiyoshi Festival on Tsukuda Island
La Fête de Sumiyoshi sur l'île de Tsukuda
Das Sumiyoshi-Fest auf der Insel Tsukuda
La fiesta Sumiyoshi en la isla Tsukuda
La festa di Sumiyoshi sull'isola di Tsukuda
Het Sumiyoshi-feest op het eiland Tsukuda

*Colour woodcut/Gravure sur bois en couleurs,
39×26 cm, State Hermitage, Sankt Petersburg*

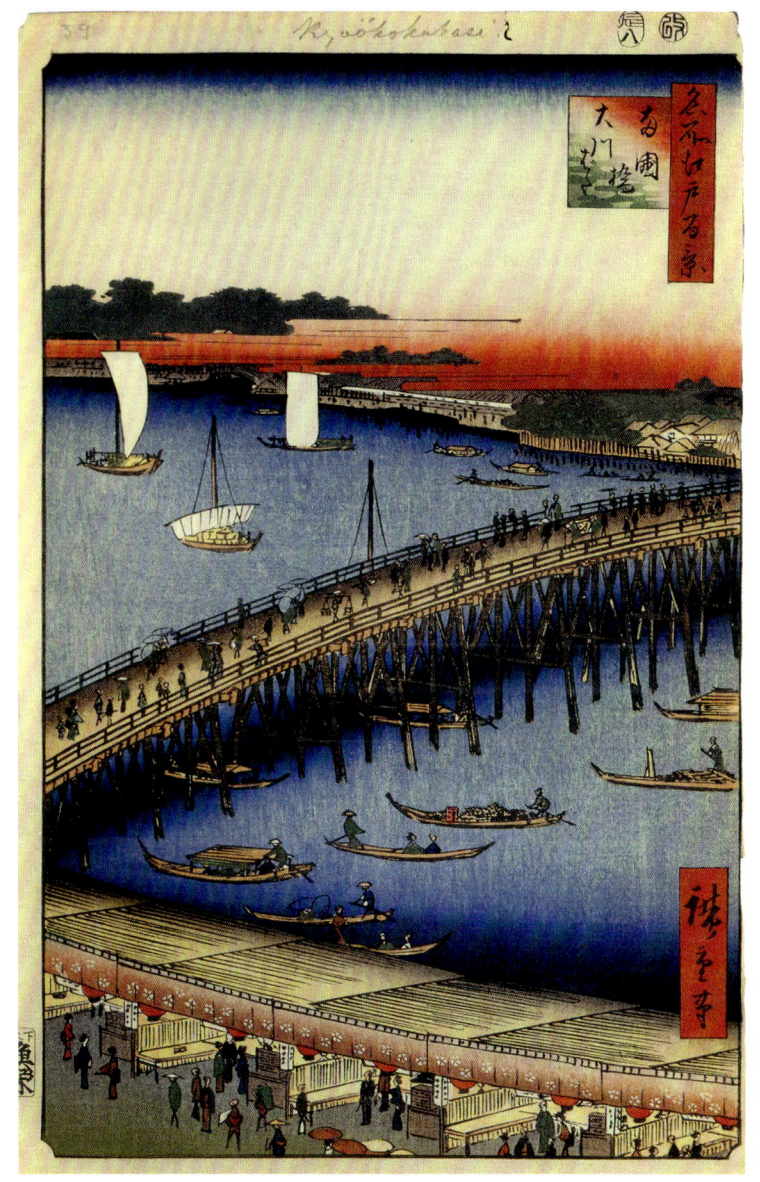

Ryogoku Bridge and Okawabata
Le Pont de Ryogoku et Okawabata
Ryogoku-Brücke und Okawabata
El puente Ryogoku y Okawabata
Il ponte di Ryogoku e Okawabata
Ryogoku-brug en Okawabata

Colour woodcut/Gravure sur bois en couleurs,
39×26 cm, State Hermitage, Sankt Petersburg

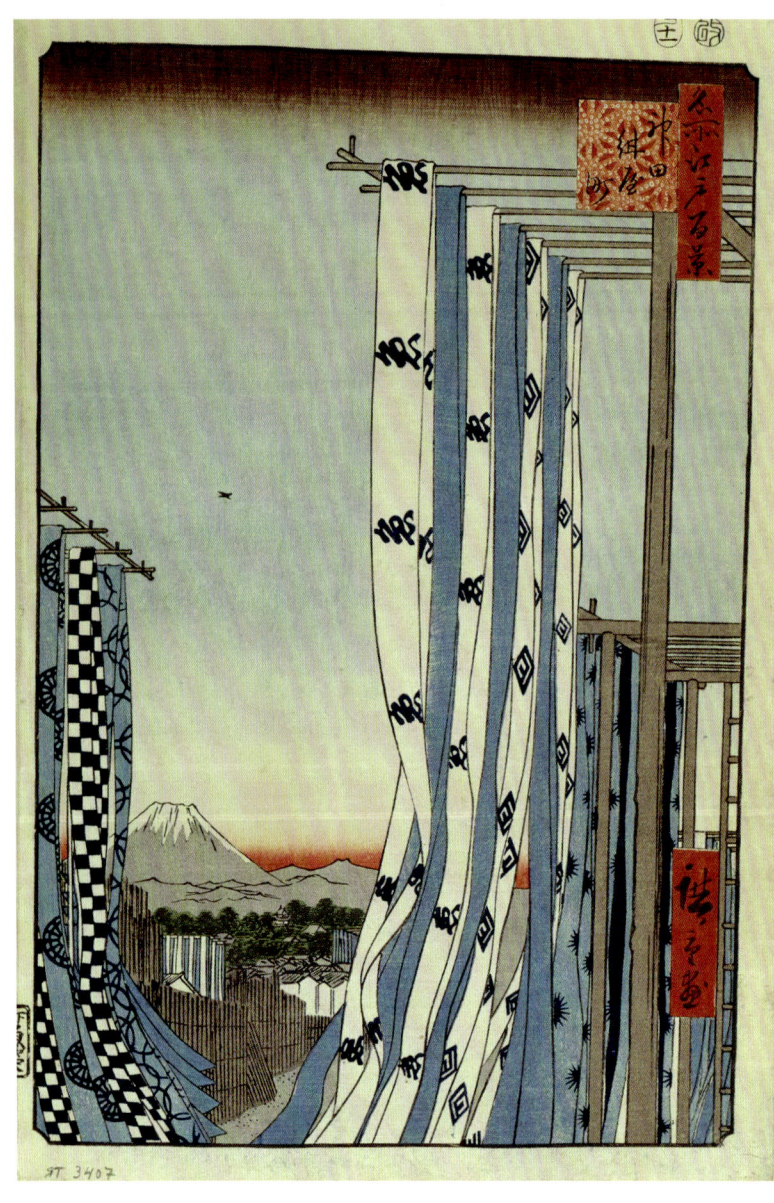

The Dyers District in Kanda

Le Quartier des teinturiers à Kanda

Das Färberviertel in Kanda

El barrio de teñidores en Kanda

Il quartiere dei tintori a Kanda

De stofververswijk in Kanda

Colour woodcut/Gravure sur bois en couleurs,
39×26 cm, State Hermitage, St. Petersburg

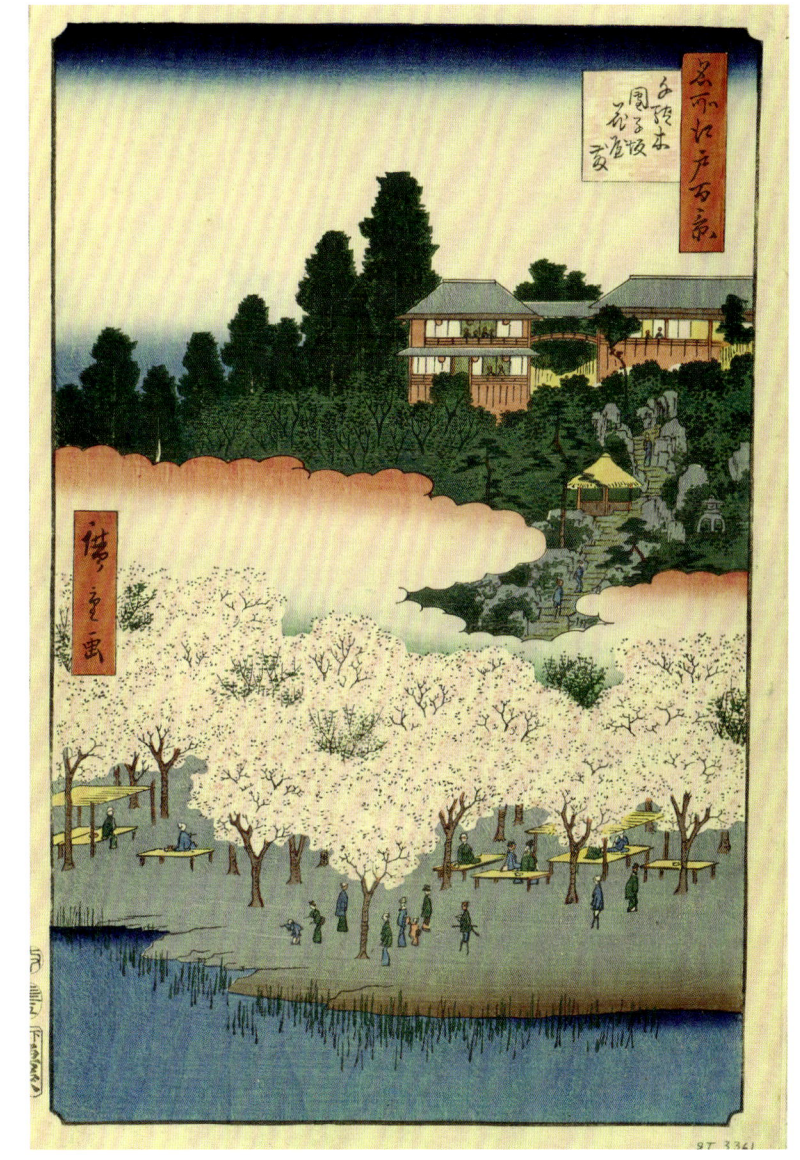

*The Flower House
on Dango Hill in Sendagi*

*Le Pavillon des fleurs sur la
colline Dang à Sendagi*

*Das Blumenhaus auf dem
Dango-Hügel in Sendagi*

*El pabellón de las flores en la
colina Dango, Sendagi*

*La casa dei fiori sulla collina
di Dango a Sendagi*

*Het bloemenhuis op de
Dango-heuvel in Sendagi*

*Colour woodcut/Gravure sur bois en couleurs,
39×26 cm, State Hermitage, St. Petersburg*

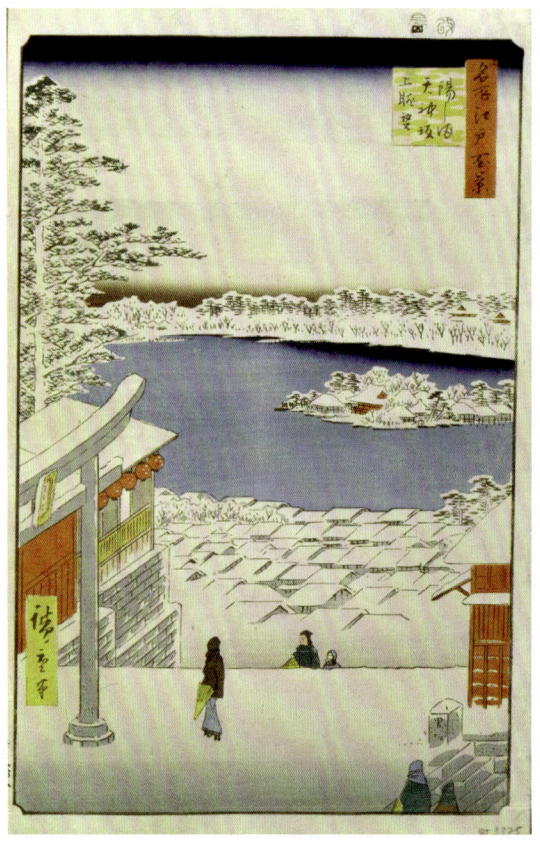

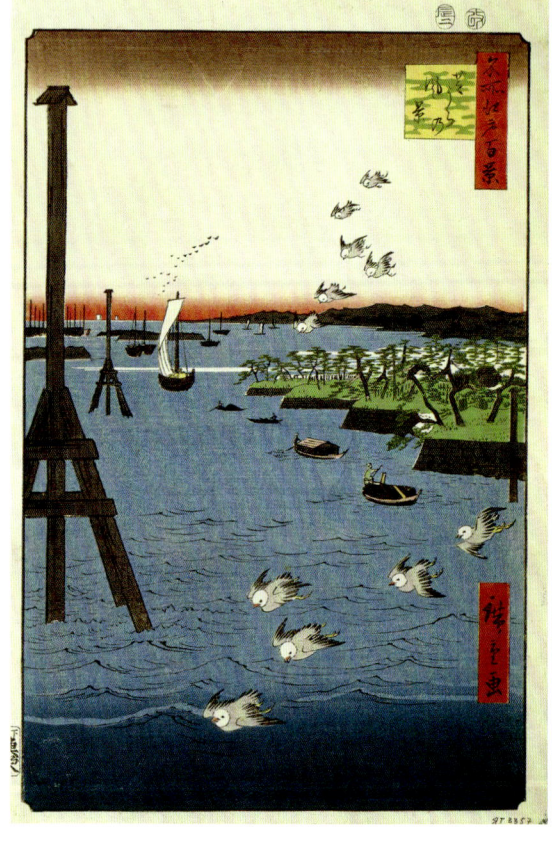

Overlooking the bay at Shiba

Vue sur la baie de Shiba

Blick auf die Bucht bei Shiba

Vista de la bahía de Shiba

Vista sulla baia di Shiba

Uitzicht over de baai bij Shiba

Colour woodcut/Gravure sur bois en couleurs,
39×26 cm, State Hermitage, St. Petersburg

View from above the Yushima Tenjin Shrine

Vue d'une hauteur sur le sanctuaire de Yushima-Tenjin

Blick von der Anhöhe auf den Yushima-Tenjin-Schrein

Vista del santuario Yushima-Tenjin desde la colina

Vista dall'altura sul santuario di Yushima-Tenjin

Uitzicht vanaf de Yushima-Tenjin-schrijn

Colour woodcut/Gravure sur bois en couleurs,
39×26 cm, State Hermitage, St. Petersburg

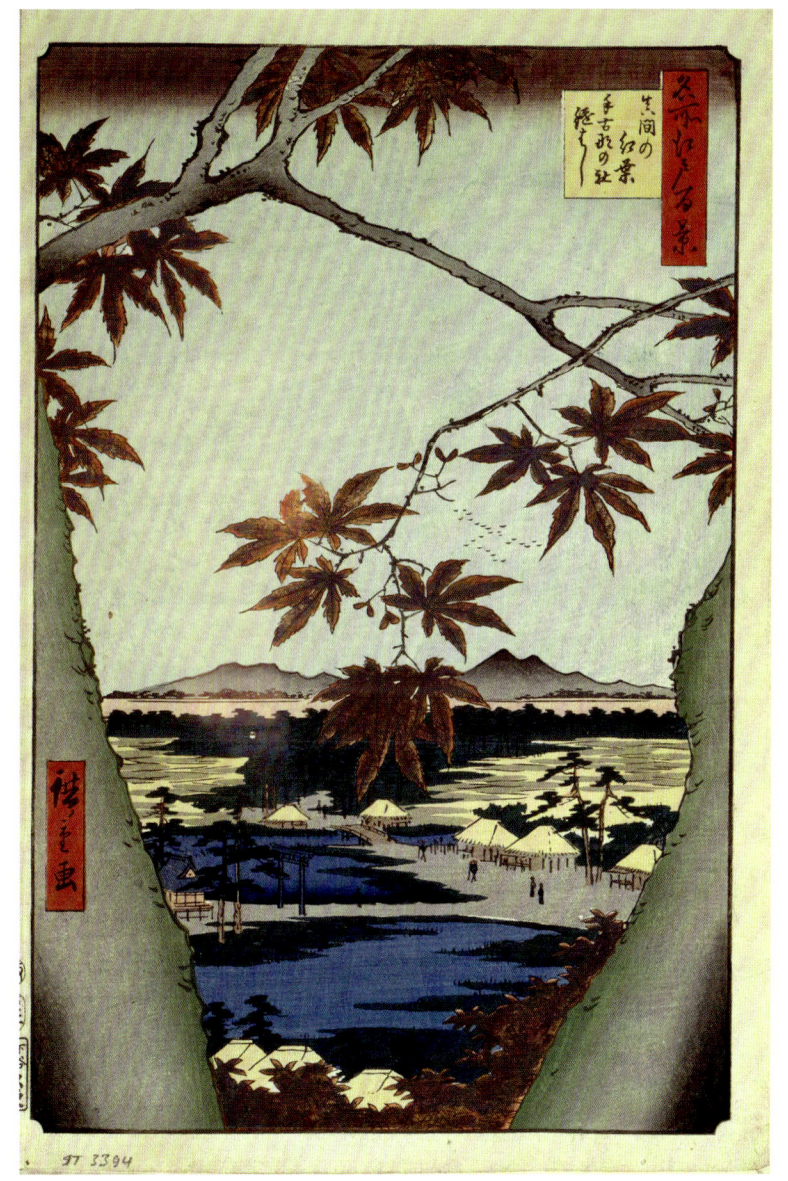

Maples, Tekona, and the Bridge at Mama
Erables, Tekona et le pont de Mama
Ahornbäume, Tekona und Brücke bei Mama
Arces, Tekona y puente en Mama
Aceri, Tekona e il ponte di Mama
Esdoorns, Tekona en brug bij Mama

Colour woodcut/Gravure sur bois en couleurs,
39×26 cm, State Hermitage, St. Petersburg

183

The Kannon Temple at Asakusa

Le Temple de Kannon à Asakusa

The open entrance to the temple provides a clear
view of the snow-covered courtyard, across which
the faithful tread carefully. The door and the
lantern in the foreground are heavily cut and give
the impression that the viewer is also about to
cross the threshold at this very moment.

*Le portail d'entrée du sanctuaire, ouvert, donne
à voir le parvis enneigé que les fidèles traversent
avec précaution. La porte et la lanterne au premier
plan, visuellement très présentes, donnent au
spectateur l'impression qu'il est lui-même à ce
moment-là sur le seuil et qu'il s'apprête à entrer.*

Der Kannon-Tempel von Asakusa

El templo Kannon de Asakusa

Das geöffnete Eingangstor zum Tempel gibt den
Blick auf den verschneiten Vorplatz frei, den die
Gläubigen vorsichtig überqueren. Die Tür und die
Laterne im Vordergrund sind stark angeschnitten
und vermitteln so den Eindruck, dass der
Betrachter gerade in diesem Augenblick selbst auf
der Schwelle steht, um ebenfalls einzutreten.

*La puerta de entrada al templo, abierta, nos
permite vislumbrar el patio nevado que los
creyentes atraviesan respetuosamente. La puerta
y el farolillo en primer plano están abruptamente
cortados, transmitiendo así la sensación de que el
propio espectador se encuentra en este momento
en el umbral, a punto de entrar.*

Il tempio di Kannon ad Asakusa

De Kannon-tempel van Asakusa

Colour woodcut/Gravure sur bois en couleurs

La porta di entrata aperta del tempio apre la vista
sul piazzale innevato, che i fedeli attraversano
con cautela. La porta e la lanterna in primo piano
sono intagliati profondamente e trasmettono
l'impressione che l'osservatore si trovi proprio in
quel momento sulla soglia per entrare.

*Door de geopende tempelpoort valt de blik op een
winterse binnenplaats waar gelovigen voorzichtig
door de sneeuw schuifelen. De deur en de lampion
op de voorgrond zijn zwaar aangezet en wekken
zo de indruk dat de beschouwer op het punt staat
zelf de binnenplaats te betreden.*

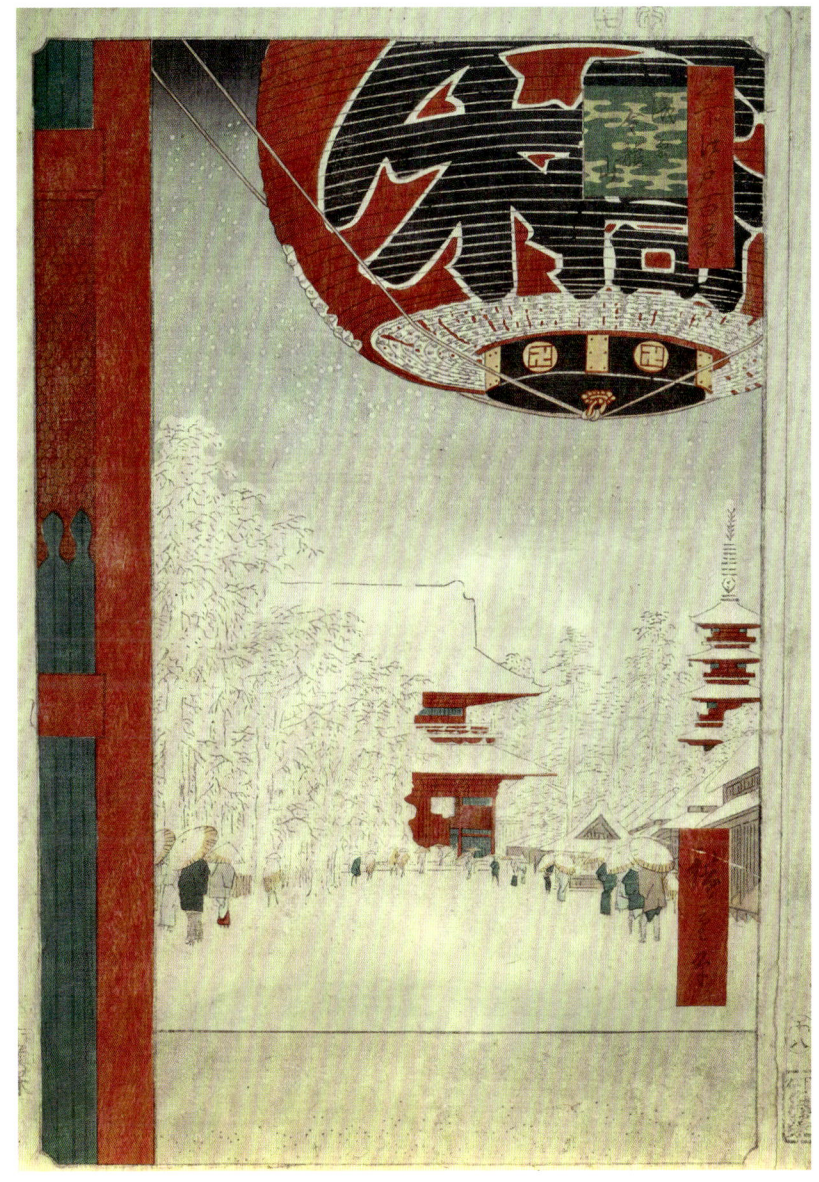

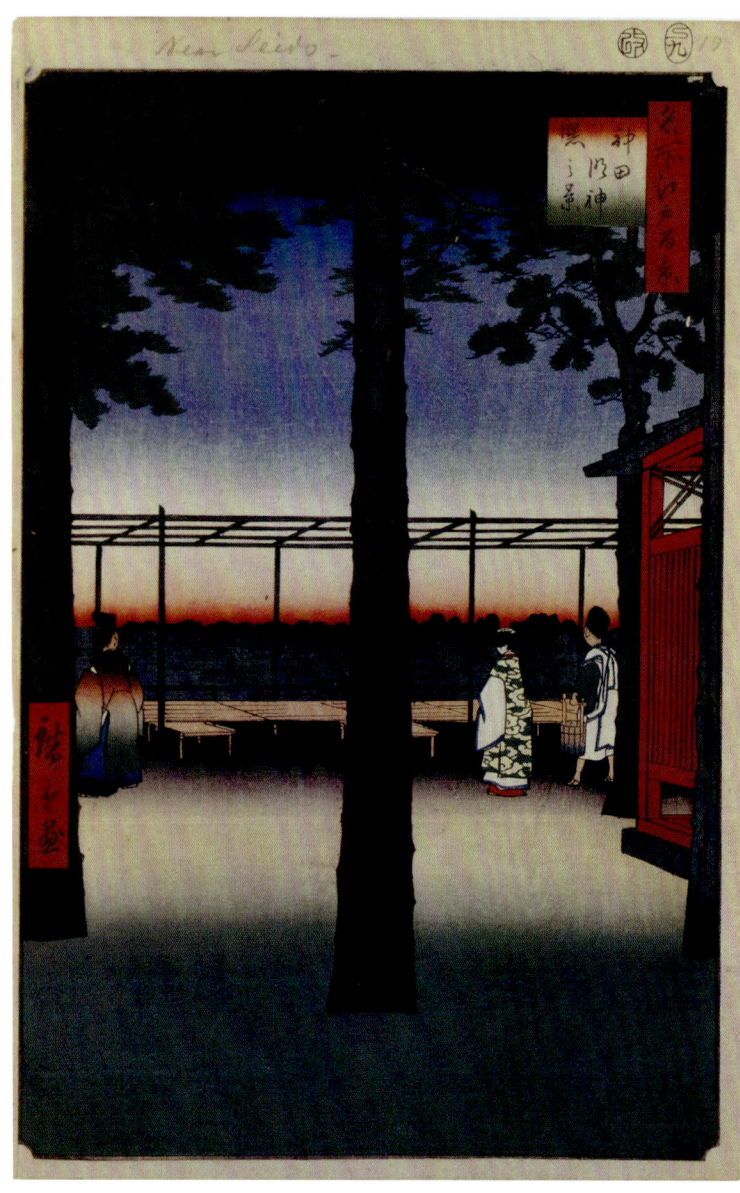

The Kanda-Myojin shrine at dawn

Le Sanctuaire de Kanda-Myojin au lever du jour

Der Kanda-Myojin-Schrein bei Tagesanbruch

El santuario Kanda-Myojin al amanecer

Alba al santuario di Kanda-Myojin

De Kanda-Myojin-schrijn bij het ochtendgloren

Colour woodcut/Gravure sur bois en couleurs,
39×26 cm, State Hermitage, St. Petersburg

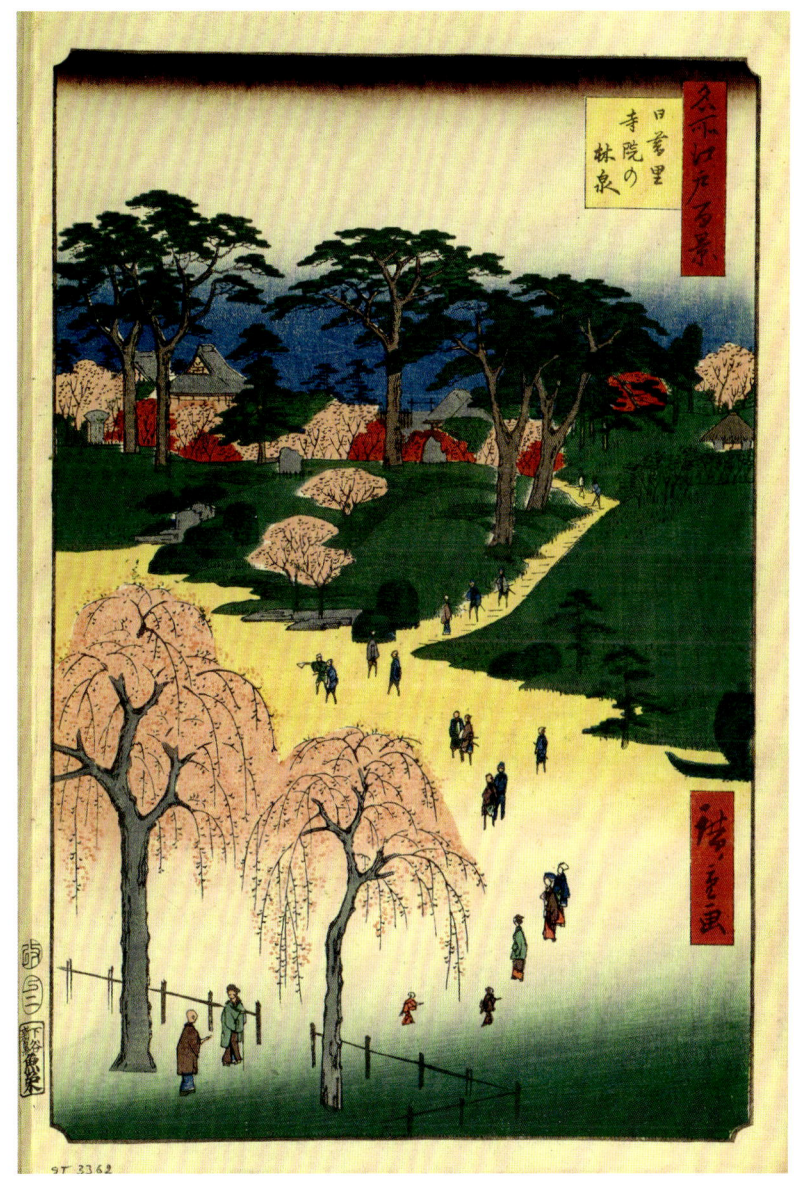

The temple garden in Nippori

Le Jardin du temple à Nippori

Der Tempelgarten in Nippori

El jardín del templo en Nippori

Il giardino del tempio di Nippori

De tempeltuin in Nippori

*Colour woodcut/Gravure sur bois en couleurs,
39×26 cm, State Hermitage, St. Petersburg*

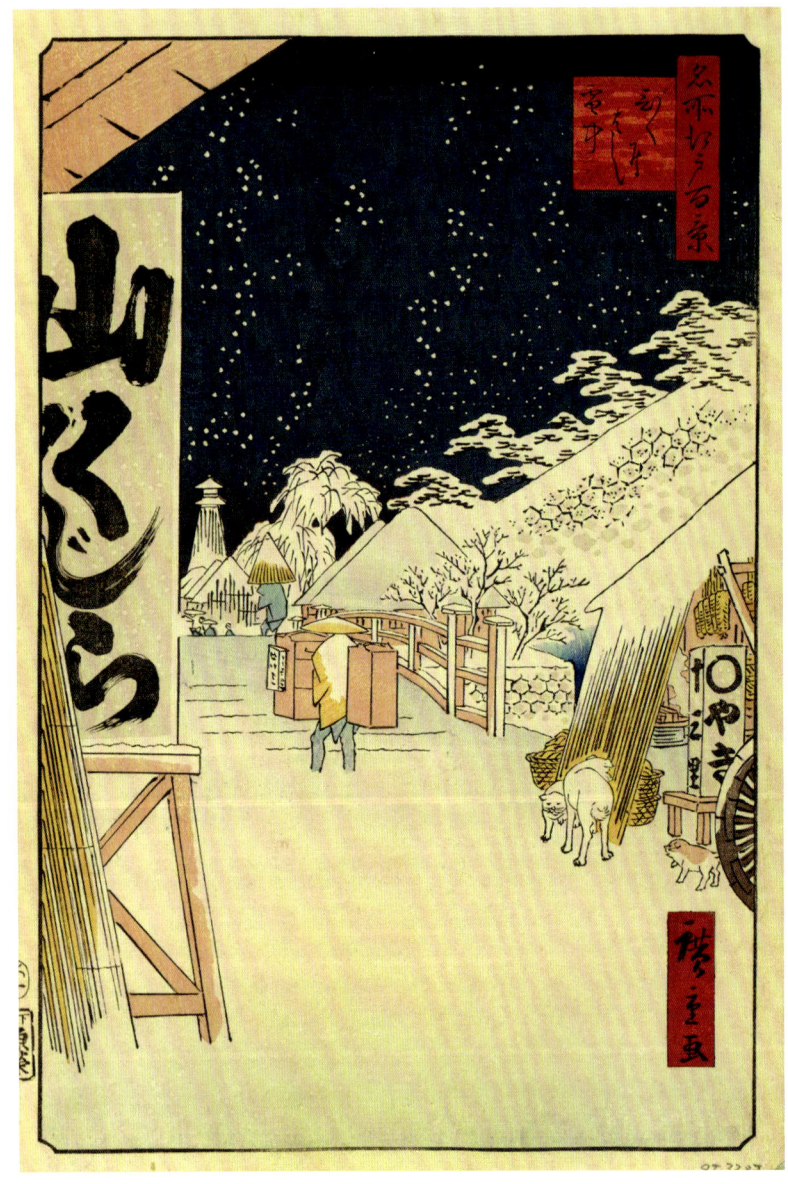

The Bikuni bridge in the snow
Le Pont de Bikuni dans la neige
Die Bikuni-Brücke im Schnee
El puente Bikuni bajo la nieve
Il ponte di Bikuni sotto la neve
De Bikuni-brug in de sneeuw

Colour woodcut/Gravure sur bois en couleurs,
39×26 cm, State Hermitage, St. Petersburg

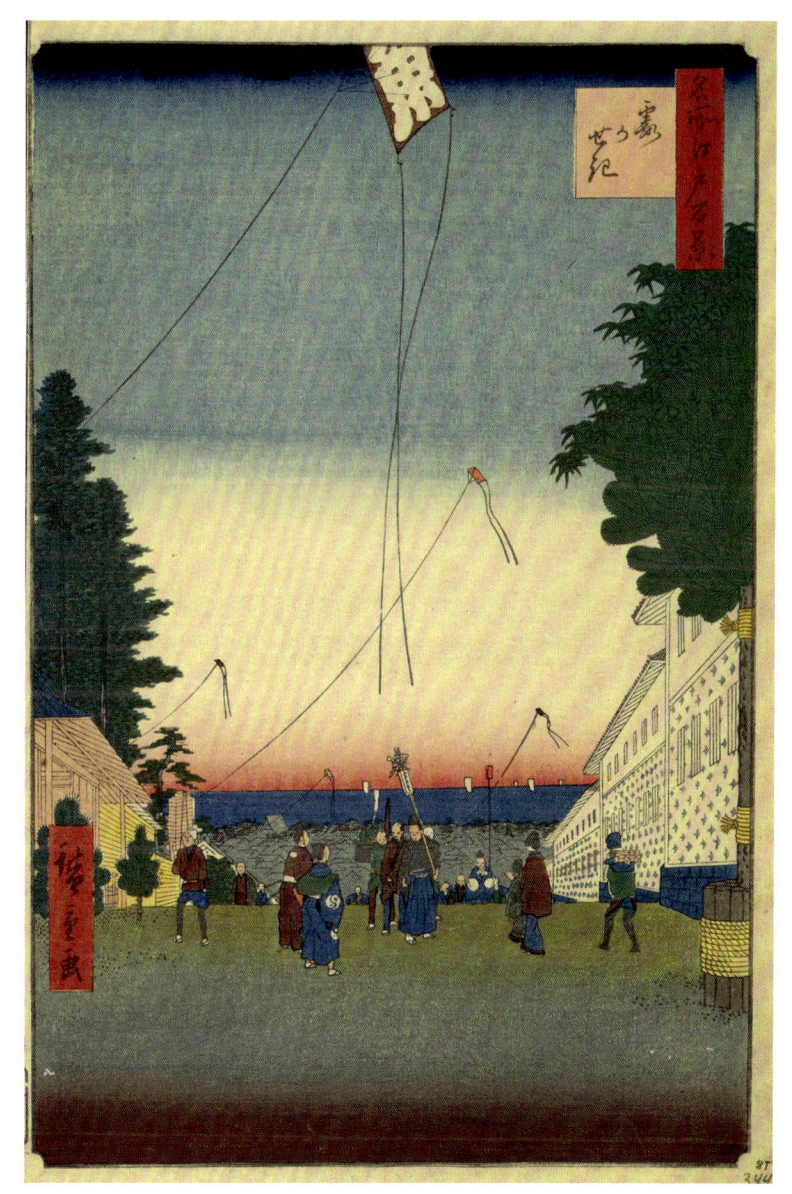

Kasumigaseki

Colour woodcut/Gravure sur bois en couleurs,
39×26 cm, State Hermitage, St. Petersburg

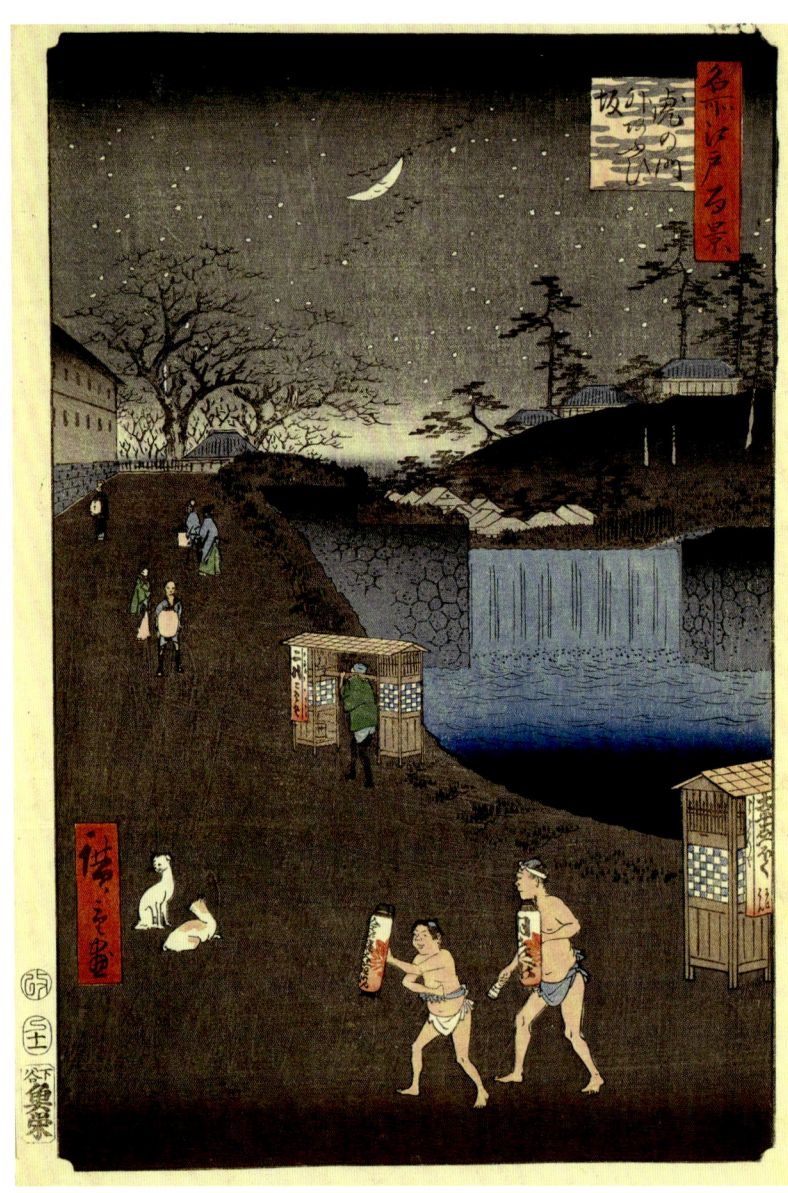

The Suruga Highway

La Route de Suruga

Die Suruga-Straße

El Camino Suruga

La strada Suruga

De Suruga-weg

Colour woodcut/Gravure sur bois
en couleurs, 39×26 cm,
State Hermitage, St. Petersburg

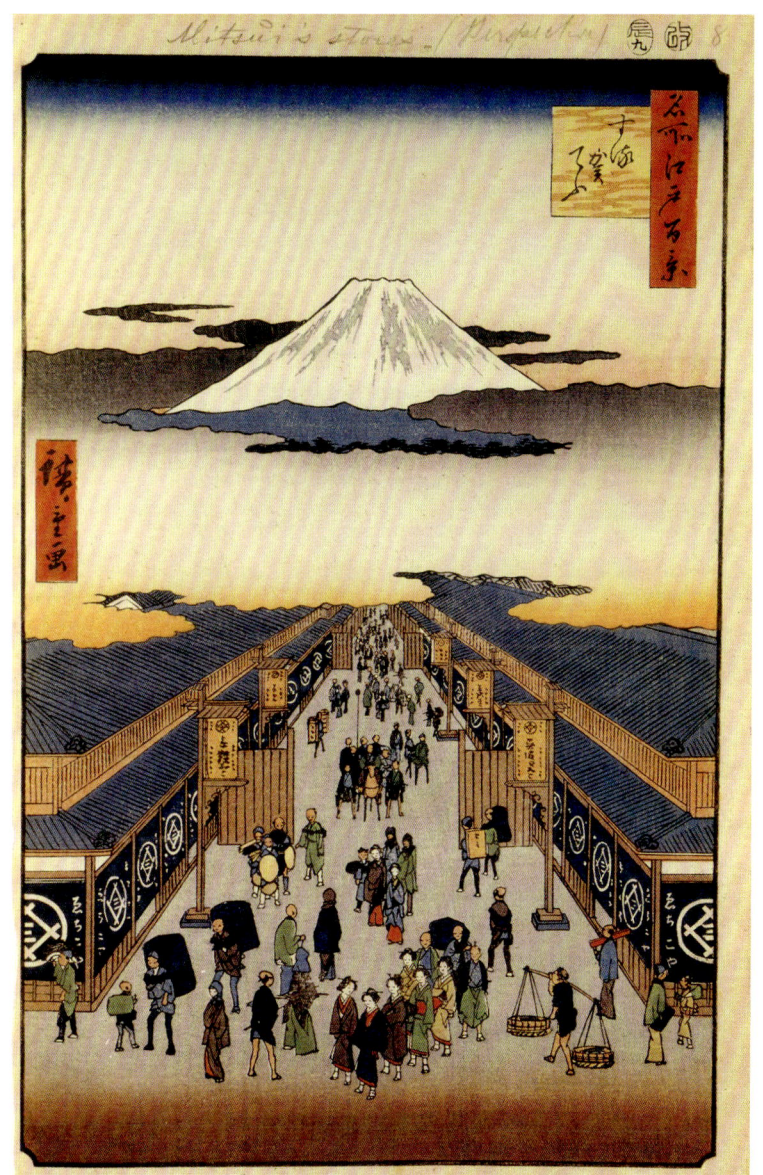

Aoi behind the Toranomon Gate

Aoi derrière la porte de Toranomon

Aoi hinter dem Tor Toranomon

Aoi tras la puerta Toranomon

Aoi fuori la porta Toranomon

Aoi achter de Toranomon-poort

Colour woodcut/Gravure sur bois en couleurs,
39×26 cm, State Hermitage, St. Petersburg

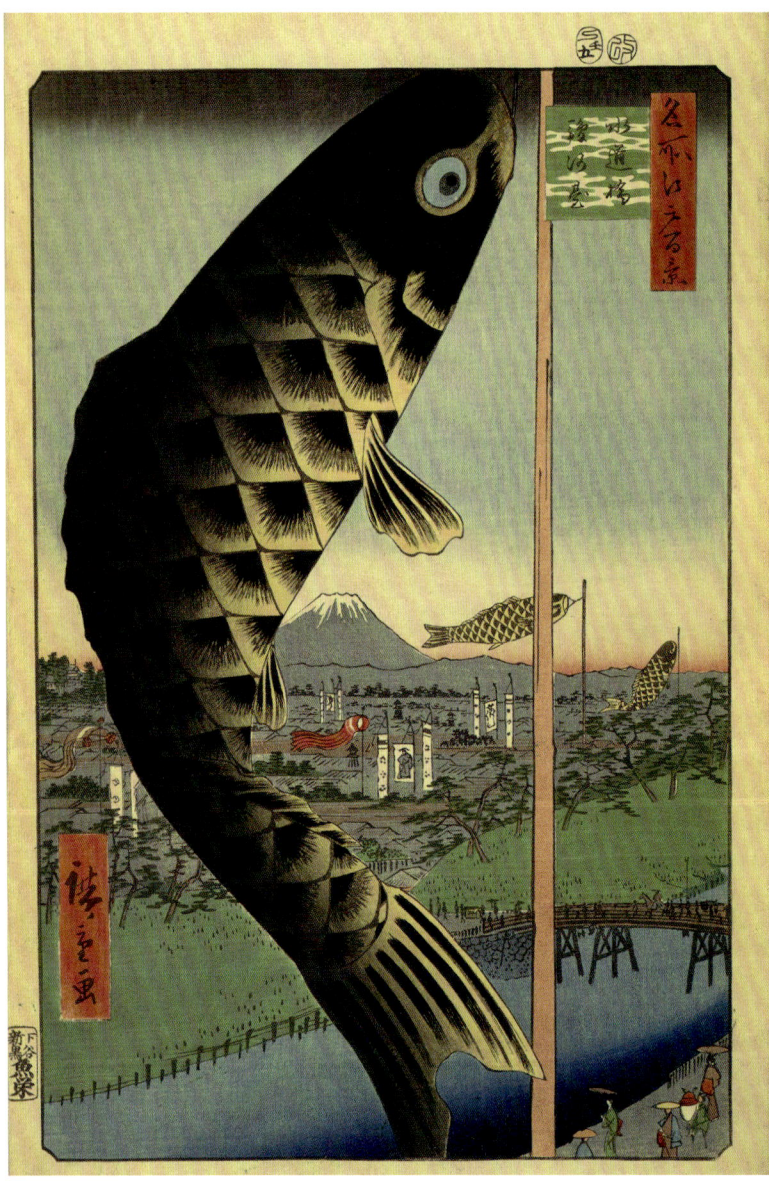

*Seido and the River Kanda
from the Shohei Bridge*

*Seido et le fleuve Kanda depuis
le pont de Shohei*

*Seido und der Fluss Kanda
von der Shohei-Brücke*

Seido y el río Kanda desde el puente Shohei

Seido e il fiume Kanda dal ponte di Shohei

*Seido en de rivier de Kanda
gezien vanaf de Shohei-brug*

*Colour woodcut/Gravure sur bois en couleurs,
39×26 cm, State Hermitage, St. Petersburg*

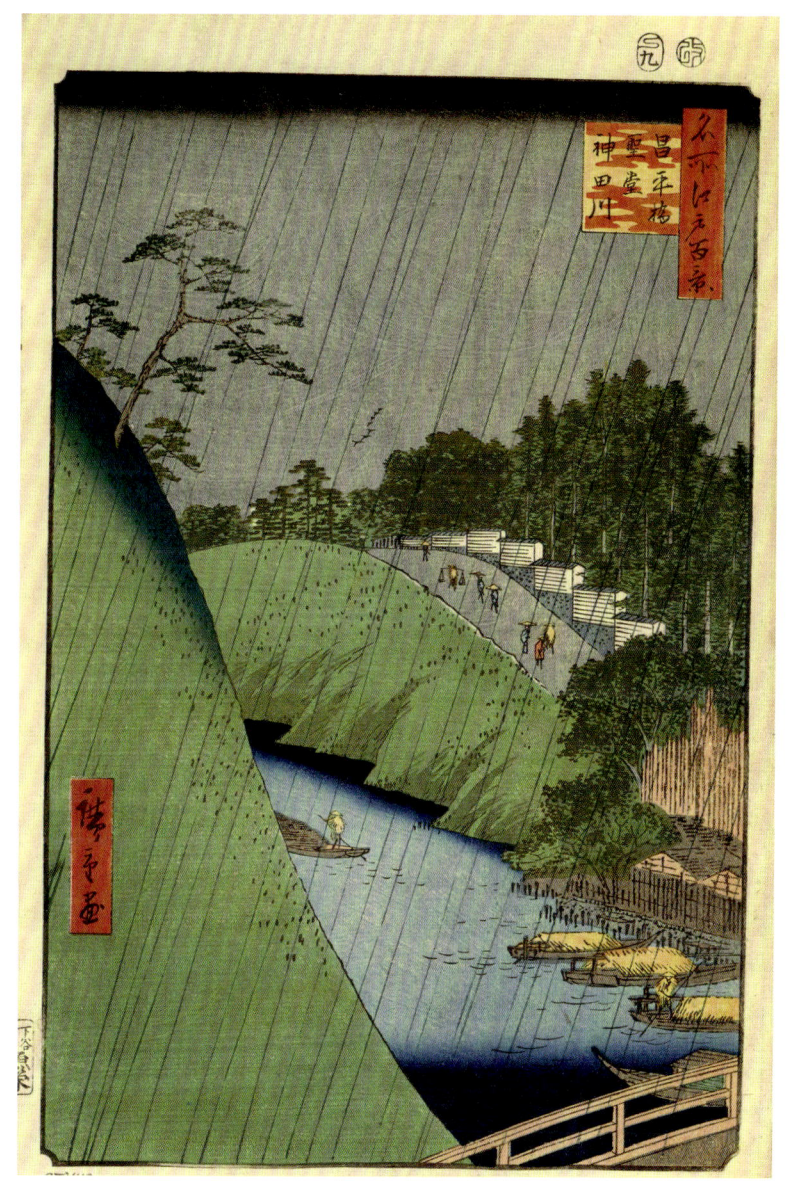

Suido Bridge and Surugadai

Le Pont de Suido et Surugadai

Suido-Brücke und Surugadai

El puente Suido y Surugadai

Ponte di Suido e Surugadai

De Suido-brug en Surugadai

Colour woodcut/Gravure sur bois en couleurs,
39×26 cm, State Hermitage, St. Petersburg

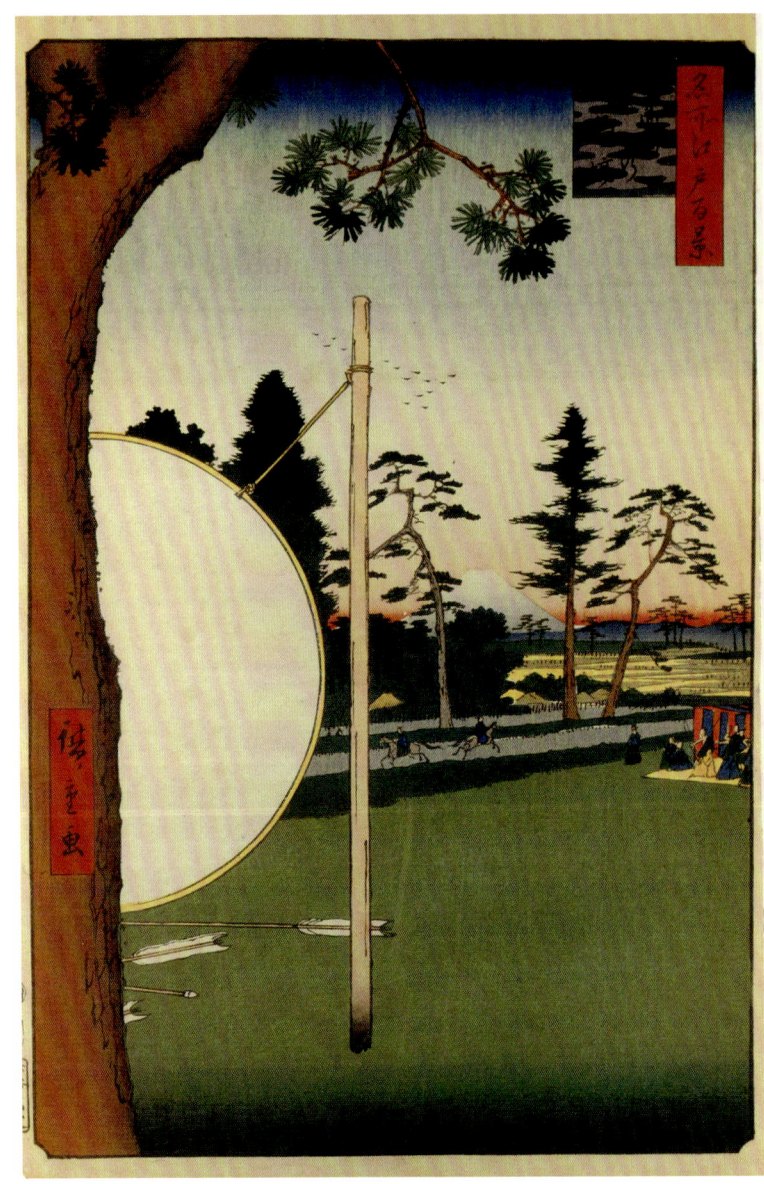

The Takata Track

L'Hippodrome de Takata

Die Takata-Reitbahn

La pista en Takata

Il maneggio di Takata

De Takata-rijbaan

Colour woodcut/Gravure sur bois en couleurs,
39×26 cm, State Hermitage, St. Petersburg

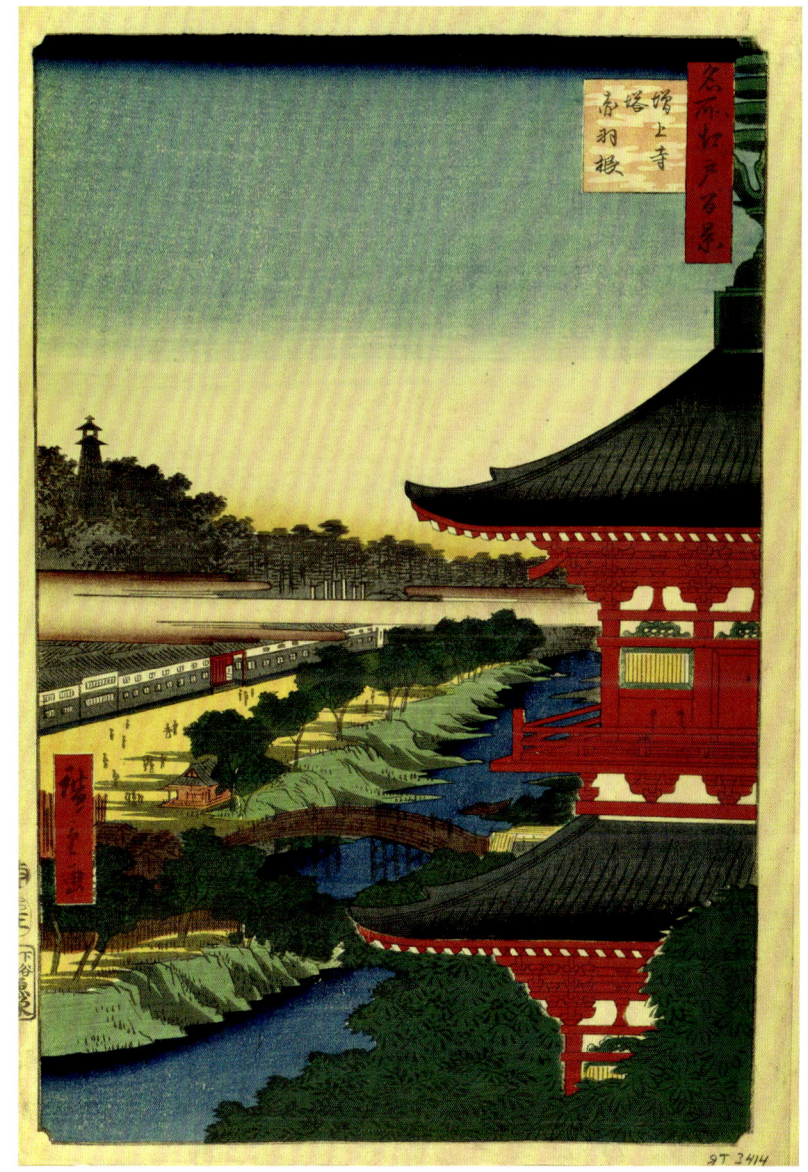

Zojoji Pagoda and Akabane

La Pagode de Zojoji et Akabane

Zojoji-Pagode und Akabane

La Pagoda Zojoji y Akabane

Pagoda di Zojoji e Akabane

De Zojoji-pagode en Akabane

Colour woodcut/Gravure sur bois en couleurs, 39×26 cm, State Hermitage, St. Petersburg

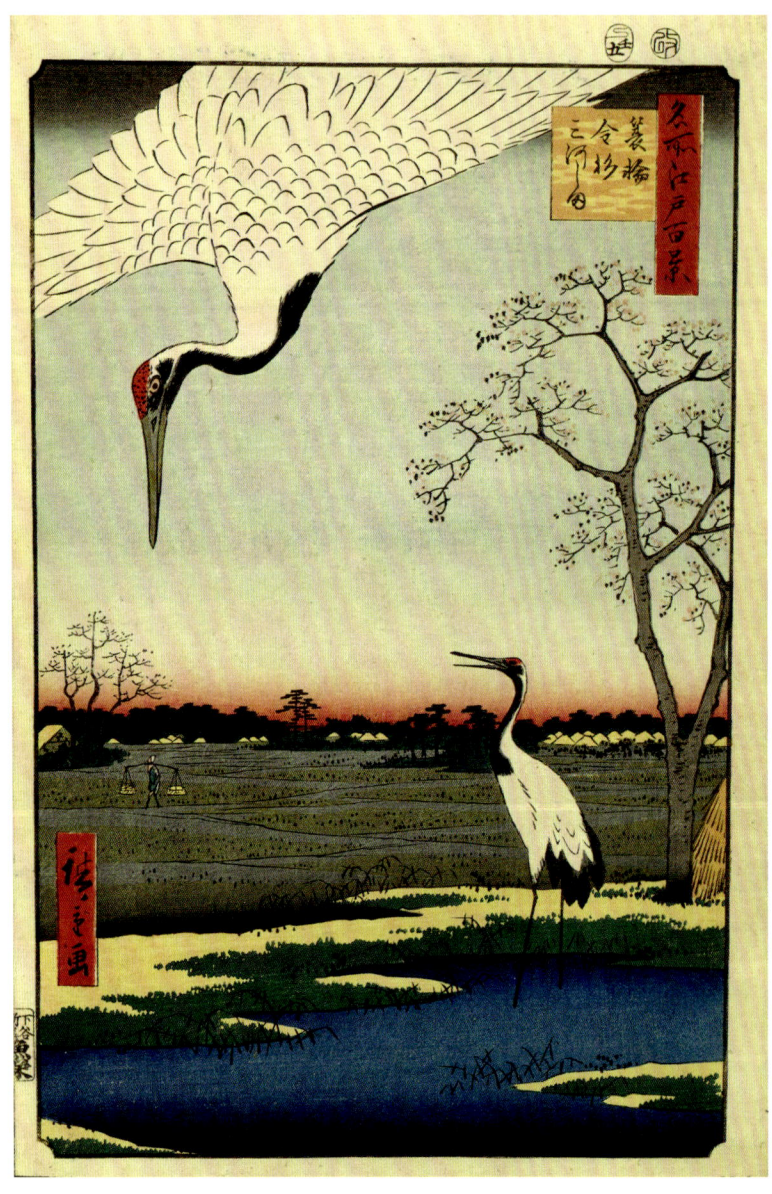

Minowa, Kanasugi and Mikawashima

Minowa, Kanasugi et Mikawashima

Minowa, Kanasugi und Mikawashima

Minowa, Kanasugi y Mikawashima

Minowa, Kanasugi e Mikawashima

Minowa, Kanasugi en Mikawashima

Colour woodcut/Gravure sur bois en couleurs,
39×26 cm , State Hermitage, St. Petersburg

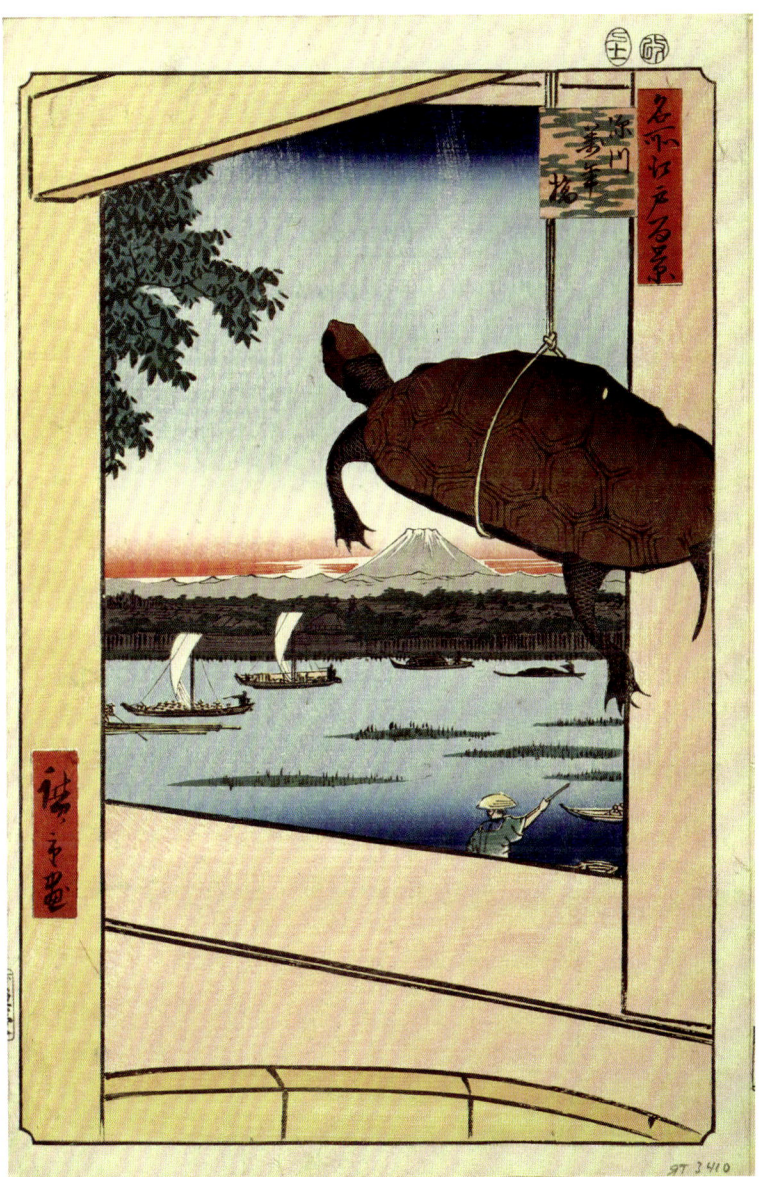

The Mannen Bridge in Fukagawa

Le Pont de Mannen à Fukagawa

Die Mannen-Brücke in Fukagawa

El puente Mannen en Fukagawa

Il ponte di Mannen a Fukagawa

De Mannenbrug in Fukagawai

Colour woodcut/Gravure sur bois en couleurs,
39×26 cm, State Hermitage, St. Petersburg

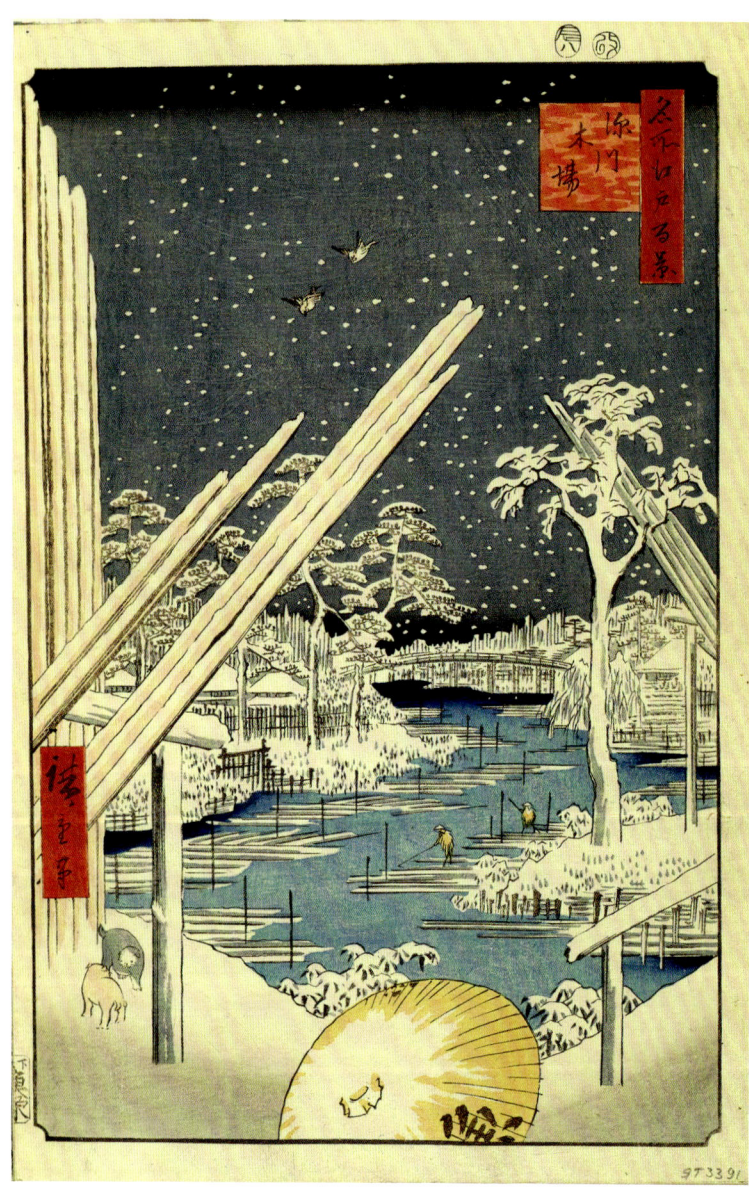

The carpenter district in Fukagawa
Le Quartier des charpentiers à Fukagawa
Das Zimmermannsviertel in Fukagawa
El barrio de los carpinteros en Fukagawa
Il quartiere dei carpentieri a Fukagawa
De timmermanswijk in Fukagawa

Colour woodcut/Gravure sur bois en couleurs,
39×26 cm, State Hermitage, St. Petersburg

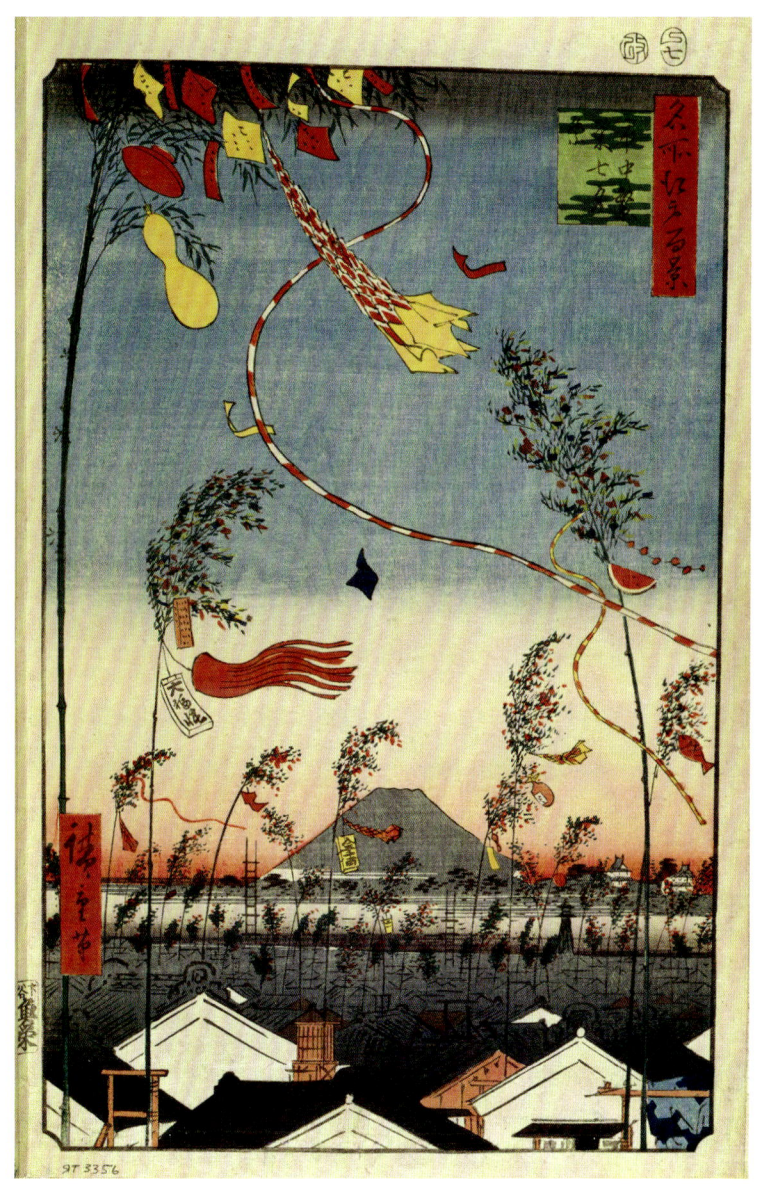

The city in bloom during the Tanabata festival

La Ville fleurie pendant la fête de Tanabata

*Die blühende Stadt während
des Tanabata-Festes*

La ciudad floreciente durante la fiesta Tanabata

La città adornata durante la festa di Tanabata

De bloeiende stad tijdens het Tanabata-feest

*Colour woodcut/Gravure sur bois en couleurs,
39 × 26 cm, State Hermitage, St. Petersburg*

*New Year's Gathering of Foxes
near the Ōji-Inari Shrine*

*Réunion de renards le jour de l'an
près du sanctuaire d'Ōji-Inari*

*Fuchstreffen zu Neujahr nahe
des Ōji-Inari-Schreins*

*Reunión de zorros en el año nuevo
junto al santuario Ōji-Inari*

*Incontro di volpi a Capodanno
vicino al santuario di Ōji-Inari*

*Vossenbijeenkomst op Oudejaarsnacht
bij de Ōji-Inari-schrijn*

Colour woodcut/Gravure sur bois en couleurs, 39 × 26 cm, State Hermitage, St. Petersburg

*A Japanese legend attributes foxes with magical
powers, seen here gathering for New Year's Eve
under the enoki tree at Shōzoku. Their breath
almost looks like flames. Behind the pines is the
Ōji shrine of the rice god Inari, whose sacred
animal is the white fox.*

*Selon une légende japonaise locale, des renards
phosphorescents dotés de pouvoirs magiques se
réunissent la nuit du Nouvel An, autour du grand
micocoulier (enoki) de Shōzoku (alias Ōji). Leur
haleine est matérialisée par de petites flammes.
En arrière-plan, derrière les pins, se trouve le
sanctuaire d'Inari, divinité shintō du riz, dont les
renards blancs sont les animaux sacrés.*

*Nach einer japanischen Sage treffen sich die
mit Zauberkräften ausgestatteten Füchse in
der Neujahrsnacht bei dem Nesselbaum (enoki)
von Shōzoku. Ihre Atemwolken sehen aus wie
Flammen. Hinter den Kiefern ist der Schrein des
Reisgottes Inari von Ōji verborgen, dem die weißen
Füchse als heilige Tiere dienen.*

*Según una leyenda japonesa en la noche del año
nuevo zorros con poderes mágicos se reúnen
alrededor del celtis (enoki) de Shōzoku. Su aliento
tiene apariencia de llamas. Detrás de los pinos
está escondido el santuario del dios del arroz
Inari de Ōji, para quien los zorros blancos son
considerados animales sagrados.*

*Secondo una leggenda giapponese, nella notte
di Capodanno le volpi dotate di poteri magici si
incontrano vicino all'albero delle ortiche (enoki)
di Shōzoku. Il respiro esce dalle loro bocche come
fiamme. Dietro ai pini è nascosto il santuario
del dio del riso Inari di Ōji, che venera le volpi
bianche come animali sacri.*

*Volgens een Japanse sage komen vossen met
toverkracht op Oudejaarsnacht bijeen onder de
netelboom (enoki) van Shōzoku. De ademwolkjes
die de vossen uitstoten, zien eruit als vlammen.
Achter de boom ligt de schrijn van de rijstgod
Inari in Ōji verscholen, waar de witte vossen
als dienaren verblijven.*

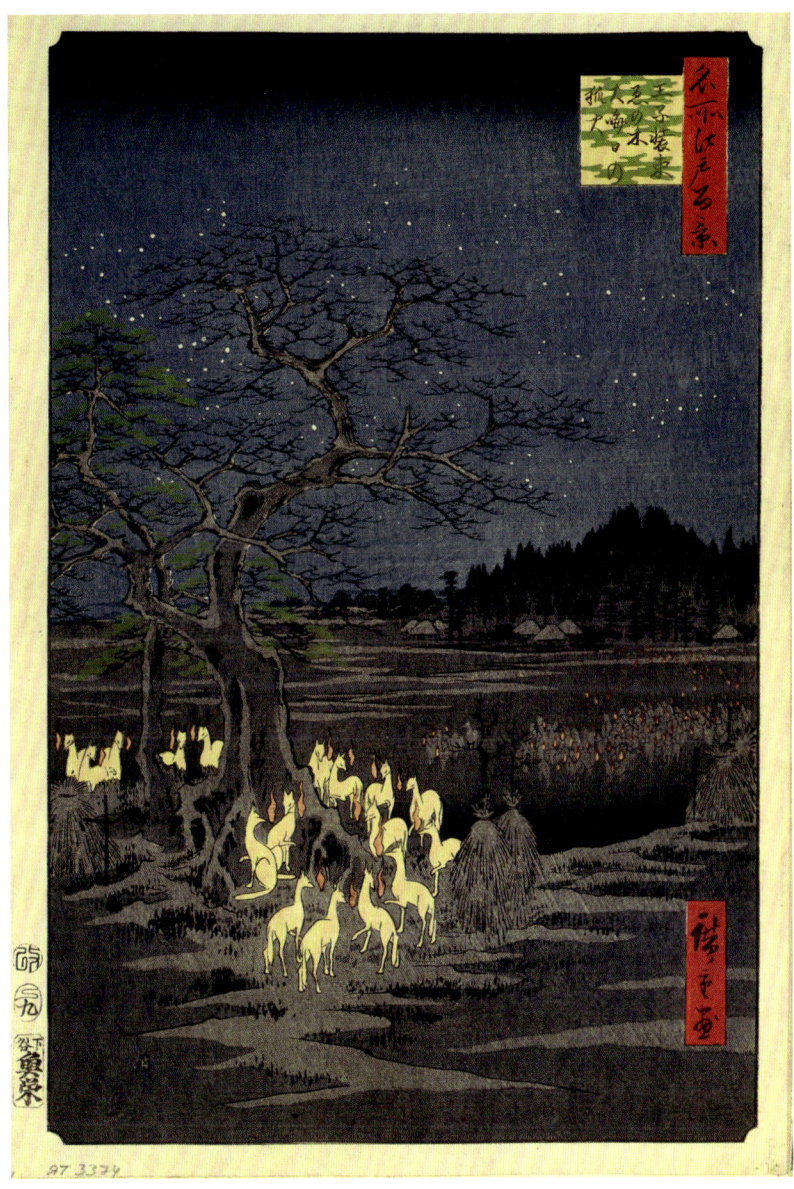

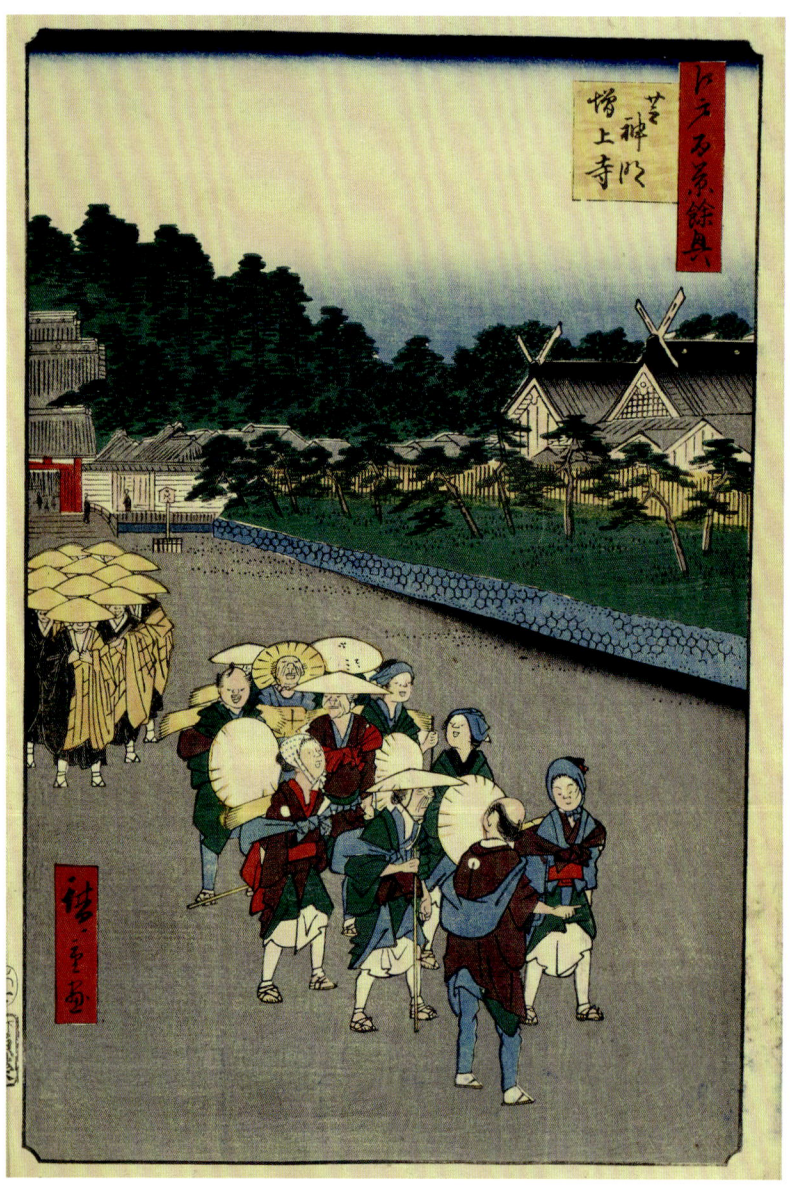

Shinmei Shrine and Zojoji Temple in Shiba

Le Sanctuaire de Shinmei et le temple de Zojoji à Shiba

Shinmei-Schrein und Zojoji-Tempel in Shiba

Santuario Shinmei y templo Zojoji en Shiba

Il santuario di Shinmei e il tempio di Zojoji a Shiba

Shinmei-schrijn en Zojoji-tempel in Shiba

Colour woodcut/Gravure sur bois en couleurs, 39×26 cm, State Hermitage, St. Petersburg

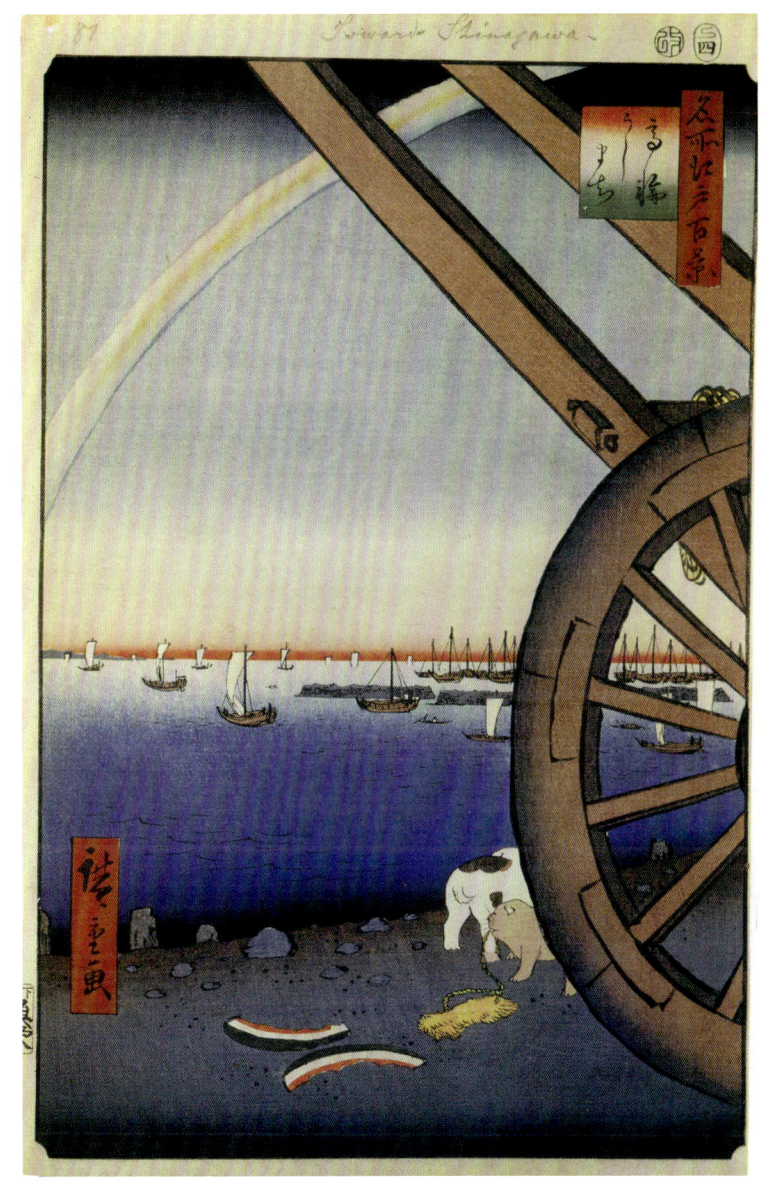

Ushimachi, Takanawa

Colour woodcut/Gravure sur bois en couleurs,
39 × 26 cm, State Hermitage, St. Petersburg

View of the first street in Nihonbashidori

Vue de la rue Itchome à Nihonbashidori

Blick auf die Erste Straße von Nihonbashidori

Vista de la Calle Primera de Nihonbashidori

Vista sulla prima strada di Nihonbashidori

Gezicht op de Eerste Straat van Nihonbashidori

Colour woodcut/Gravure sur bois en couleurs, 39×26 cm, State Hermitage, St. Petersburg

Numerous restaurants on Nihonbashi in the cotton traders' quarter. To the right, we see a barely clad servant carrying a tray of food. We also see equally poor-looking hawkers selling fruit, while the remaining passers-by protect themselves against the sun with umbrellas.

Dans la rue de Nihonbashi, au cœur du quartier des marchands de laine, se trouvent de nombreux restaurants. À droite de l'image, un serveur à peine vêtu porte un plateau avec des mets. Un marchand ambulant – d'allure presque aussi misérable – vend des fruits, tandis que les autres passants se protègent du soleil avec des ombrelles.

Auf der Nihonbashi-Straße im Viertel der Baumwollhändler befinden sich zahlreiche Restaurants. Rechts im Bild trägt ein kaum bekleideter Bote ein Tablett mit Speisen. Ein ebenso ärmlich aussehender Straßenhändler verkauft Früchte, während die übrigen Passanten sich vor der Sonne mit Schirmen schützen.

En la Calle Nihonbashi, en el barrio de los comerciantes de algodón, encontramos multitud de restaurantes. En la parte derecha de la imagen podemos ver un portador casi desnudo llevando una bandeja de comida. Un vendedor callejero de apariencia igualmente pobre vende frutas, mientras que el resto de paseantes se protege del sol con parasoles.

Nel quartiere dei commercianti di cotone della strada di Nihonbashi si trovano numerosi ristoranti. Sulla destra del quadro un fattorino non ben vestito porta un vassoio con del cibo. Un commerciante dall'aspetto povero vende della frutta, mentre gli altri passanti si proteggono dal sole con i parasoli.

In de Nihonbashi-straat, in de wijk van de katoenhandelaren, bevinden zich talloze restaurants. Rechts draagt een schaars geklede dienaar een blad met gerechten. Een even armoedig ogende straatventer verkoopt fruit, terwijl de voorbijgangers zich met parasols tegen de zon beschermen.

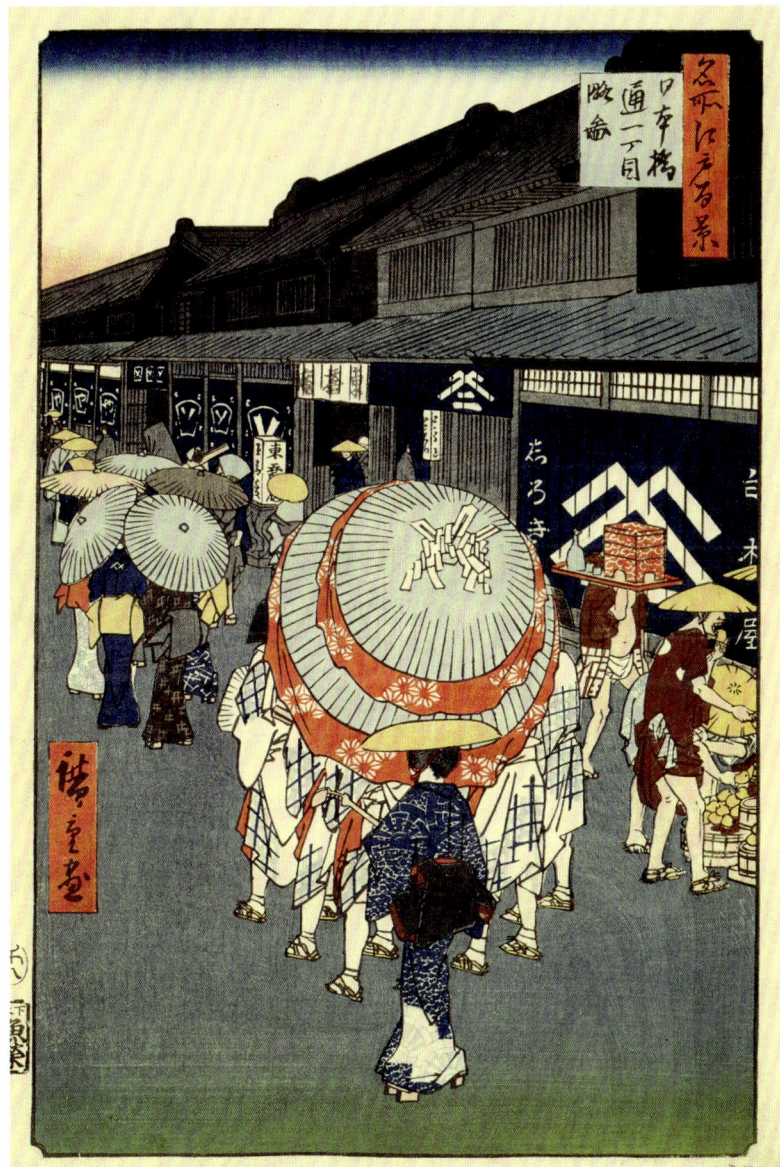

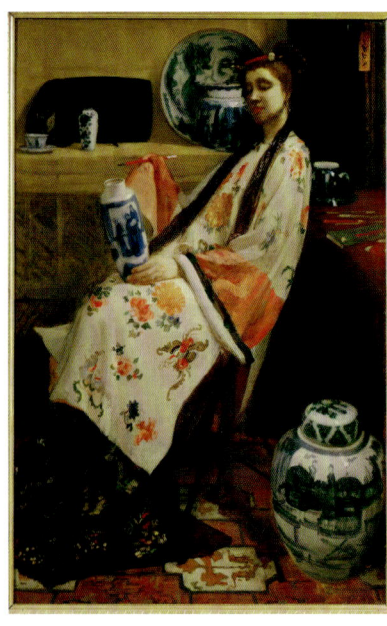

James Abbott McNeill Whistler (1834–1903)

Purple and Rose
Pourpre et rose
Purpur und Rosa
Púrpura y Rosa
Viola e rosa
Paars en roze

1864, Oil on canvas/Huile sur toile, 91×61 cm, Philadelphia Museum of Art, Philadelphia

Vincent van Gogh (1853–1890)

Tree roots and Tree trunks
Troncs et racines
Baumwurzeln und Baumstämme
Raíces y troncos de árboles
Radici e tronchi d'albero
Boomwortels

1890, Oil on canvas/Huile sur toile, 50×100 cm, Van Gogh Museum, Amsterdam

Hiroshige and the European enthusiasm for Japanese art

In the second half of the 19th century, many Europeans became quite enthusiastic for Japanese art. For centuries, the country had been closed off and had only opened its doors in 1853 under Western pressure. After the opening of Japan, a flood of Japanese art and crafts made its way to Europe, creating a real euphoria for all things Japanese. In art, this so-called Japonism is first seen in the various Japanese props that turn up in European figure paintings and portraits. Artists like Claude Monet, James Abbott McNeill Whistler, and Vincent van Gogh collected Japanese woodblocks, especially those by Hokusai and Hiroshige, and

Hiroshige et la passion du « japonisme » en Europe

Dans la seconde moitié du xixᵉ siècle, de nombreux Européens se prennent de passion pour l'art du Japon. Resté fermé pendant des siècles, le pays ne renonce qu'en 1853 à cette politique d'isolement, sous la pression des Occidentaux. À la suite de cette ouverture, les produits de l'art et de l'artisanat japonais arrivent en nombre sur le marché européen, déclenchant un véritable engouement pour le Japon : le « japonisme ». Cette vogue se manifeste d'abord par les multiples accessoires qu'on remarque sur les personnages et les portraits, puis par la fièvre des amateurs d'estampes. Des artistes comme Claude Monet, James Abbott McNeil Whistler

Hiroshige und die Japanbegeisterung in Europa

In der zweiten Hälfte des 19. Jahrhunderts begeistern sich viele Europäer für Kunst aus Japan. Über Jahrhunderte hatte sich das Land abgeschottet und gab erst ab 1853 auf Druck des Westens seine Isolationspolitik auf. Nach der Öffnung Japans kommt nun erstmalig auch japanische Kunst und Kunsthandwerk in größerem Umfang nach Europa. Es bricht eine regelrechte Japaneuphorie aus. In der Kunst wirkt sich der sogenannte Japonismus zunächst durch die zahlreichen japanischen Requisiten aus, mit denen Figurenbilder und Porträts ausgestattet werden. Künstler wie Claude Monet, James Abbott

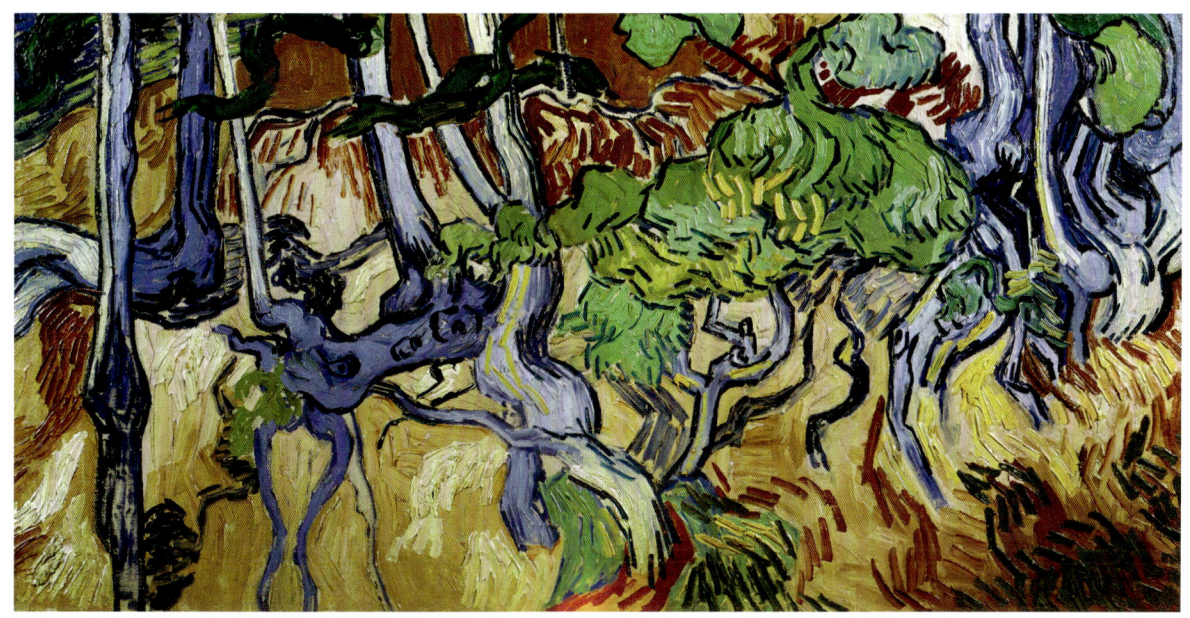

Hiroshige y la fascinación por Japón en Europa

En la segunda mitad del XIX muchos europeos se entusiasmaron con el arte japonés. Durante muchos siglos el país se había mantenido excluido y solo a partir del 1853, y a raíz de la presión de occidente, abandona su política de aislamiento. Tras la apertura de Japón llegan a Europa por primera vez el arte y la artesanía japonesas en grandes cantidades, desatando una verdadera euforia por Japón. Al principio el llamado Japonismo se expresa en el arte por la multitud de objetos japoneses que adornan retratos y escenas. Artistas como Claude Monet, James Abbott McNeill Whistler o Vincent van Gogh coleccionaron xilografías japonesas,

Hiroshige e l'entusiasmo giapponese in Europa

Nella seconda metà del XIX secolo, molti europei si entusiasmarono per l'arte proveniente dal Giappone. Nel corso dei secoli il paese si era isolato e solo dal 1853 rinunciò alla sua politica di isolamento, a causa della pressione dei paesi occidentali. Dopo l'apertura del Giappone anche l'arte e l'artigianato giapponesi arrivarono per la prima volta su larga scala in Europa. Scoppiò una vera e propria euforia per il Giappone. Nell'arte, il cosiddetto "giapponismo" agiva inizialmente attraverso i numerosi requisiti giapponesi, dei quali erano dotati immagini figurative e ritratti. Artisti come Claude Monet, James Abbott McNeill Whistler e Vincent van

Hiroshige en het Europese enthousiasme voor de Japanse kunst

In de tweede helft van de negentiende eeuw worden veel Europeanen gegrepen door een groot enthousiasme voor kunst uit Japan. Eeuwenlang heeft het land zich afgeschermd en pas in 1853 geeft het onder druk van het Westen zijn politiek van isolatie op. Na de openstelling van Japan bereiken Japanse kunstwerken voor het eerst in grote hoeveelheden Europa en breekt er een regelrechte Japan-gekte uit. In de kunst blijkt dit uit het zogenaamde "japonisme", waarbij Japanse voorwerpen in veel schilderijen en portretten als rekwisieten worden opgevoerd. Kunstenaars als Claude Monet, James Abbott McNeill Whistler en Vincent van Gogh verzamelen Japanse

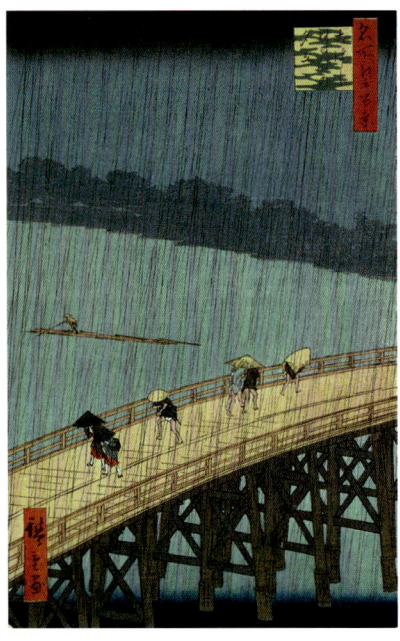

Ohashi Bridge in the rain, from the series **100 Famous Views of Edo**

Le Pont d'Ohashi sous la pluie, de la série *Cent vues d'Edo*

Ohashi-Brücke im Regen, aus der Serie *100 berühmte Ansichten von Edo*

El puente Ohashi bajo la lluvia, de la serie *100 vistas famosas de Edo*

Ponte di Ohashi sotto la pioggia, della serie *100 vedute famose di Edo*

De Ohashi-brug in de regen, uit de serie *100 beroemde gezichten op Edo*

*1857, Colour woodcut/Gravure sur bois en couleurs,
39×26 cm, State Hermitage, St. Petersburg*

were deeply impressed by the foreign compositions. The concentration on line and surface as the main design element opened the artists' eyes to the opportunities for representing the world beyond the natural image. The colours and perspectives that seemed unusual to Western eyes also provided crucial inspiration for the development of modern art. Van Gogh, one of the most radical pioneers in this way, shared ownership of more than forty woodcuts of Hiroshige with his brother, even copying them for study purposes. In an 1888 letter, Van Gogh expressed his admiration for the Japanese art and described the unique quality of Hiroshige's work: "I envy the Japanese the extreme clarity that everything in

ou Vincent van Gogh les collectionnent à l'envi – surtout celles de Hokusai et de Hiroshige. La focalisation sur la ligne et la surface comme principaux éléments de représentation ouvrent aux artistes occidentaux la perspective d'un mode de figuration du monde au-delà de la reproduction naturaliste. Les couleurs et les perspectives inhabituelles pour les esprits occidentaux fournissent aussi des inspirations extrêmement importantes pour le développement de l'art moderne. Van Gogh – un des pionniers les plus radicaux dans ce domaine – possédait en commun avec son frère Theo plus de quarante estampes de Hiroshige, qu'il copia même pour s'entraîner. Dans une lettre de 1888, Vincent exprime son admiration pour l'art japonais,

McNeill Whistler und Vincent van Gogh sammeln japanische Farbholzschnitte, vor allem von Hokusai und Hiroshige, und sind tief beeindruckt von den fremdartigen Kompositionen. Die Konzentration auf Linie und Fläche als Hauptgestaltungsmittel öffnet den Künstlern die Augen für eine Darstellung der Welt jenseits der naturgetreuen Abbildung. Die für westliche Begriffe ungewöhnlichen Farben und Perspektiven liefern ebenfalls äußerst wichtige Inspirationen für die Entwicklung der modernen Kunst. Van Gogh, einer der radikalsten Pioniere auf diesem Weg, besaß gemeinsam mit seinem Bruder über vierzig Holzschnitte von Hiroshige, die er zu Studienzwecken sogar kopierte. In einem Brief bringt

Vincent van Gogh

Bridge in Rain (after Hiroshige)

Le Pont sous la pluie (d'après Hiroshige)

Brücke im Regen (nach Hiroshige)

El puente bajo la lluvia (copia de Hiroshige)

Ponte sotto la pioggia (dopo Hiroshige)

Brug in de regen (naar Hiroshige)

1887, Oil on canvas/Huile sur toile, 73 × 54 cm, Van Gogh Museum, Amsterdam

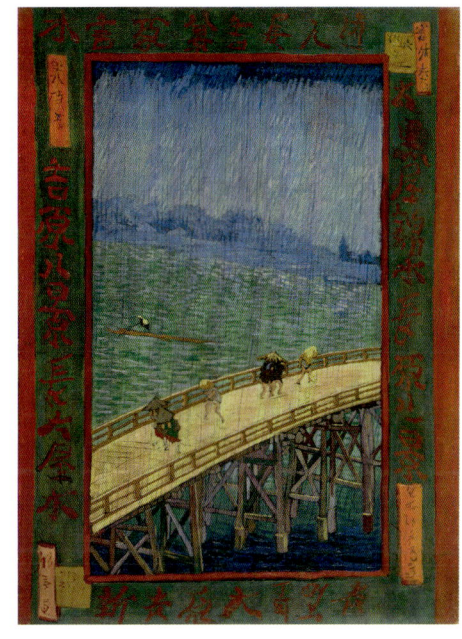

especialmente de Hokusai e Hiroshige, y se muestran profundamente impactados por las extrañas composiciones. La concentración sobre la línea y el punto como principales medios de expresión abre los ojos de estos artistas a una representación del mundo alejada de la ilustración naturalista. Los colores y perspectivas poco habituales a ojos europeos proporcionaron igualmente una inspiración importante para el desarrollo del arte moderno. Van Gogh, uno de los pioneros más radicales en esta dirección, poseía junto con su hermano más de 40 xilografías de Hiroshige, algunas de las cuales llegó a copiar con motivo de su estudio. En una carta de 1888 van Gogh expresa su admiración por

Gogh collezionarono xilografie a colori giapponesi, soprattutto di Hokusai e Hiroshige, rimanendo profondamente impressionati dalle composizioni insolite. La concentrazione su linee e superficie come metodo principale di composizione aprì gli occhi degli artisti ad una rappresentazione del mondo che oltrepassasse l'illustrazione conforme all'originale. I colori e le prospettive insolite per i concetti occidentali fornivano anche ispirazioni estremamente importanti per lo sviluppo dell'arte moderna. Van Gogh, uno dei pionieri più radicali in questo senso, possedeva con suo fratello oltre quaranta xilografie di Hiroshige, che copiò persino a scopo di studio. In una lettera del 1888, van Gogh espresse la

kleurenhoutsneden, vooral van Hokusai en Hiroshige, en zijn diep onder de indruk van de vernuftige composities. De grote rol in de Japanse prentkunst van de lijn en het vlak als de voornaamste compositorische structuren maakt de Europese kunstenaars meer ontvankelijk voor een weergave van de werkelijkheid die losstaat van de natuurgetrouwe afbeelding. Ook de naar westerse begrippen ongebruikelijke kleuren en perspectieven zijn uiterst belangrijke inspiratiebronnen voor de ontwikkeling van de moderne kunst. Een van de meest radicale pioniers in dat opzicht, Vincent van Gogh, bezit samen met zijn broer Theo ruim veertig houtsneden, die hij zelfs bestudeert door ze te kopiëren. In een brief uit 1888 drukt Van Gogh zijn

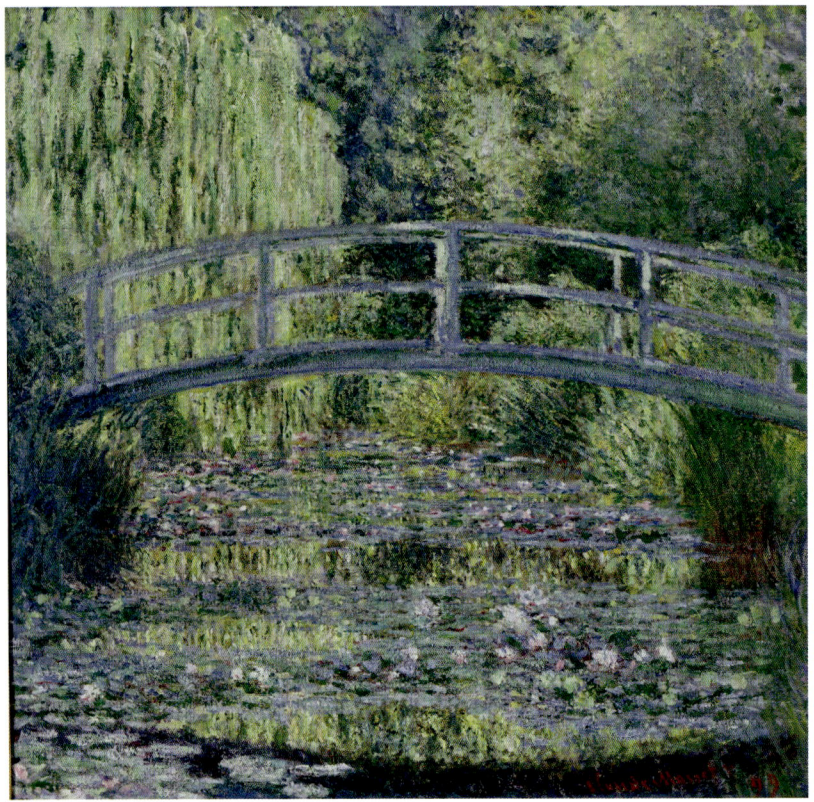

Claude Monet (1840–1926)

The Water Lily Pond (Green Harmony)

Le Bassin aux nymphéas,
(harmonie verte)

Der Seerosenteich (Harmonie in Grün)

El estanque de nenúfares
(armonía verde)

Lo stagno delle ninfee (armonia verde)

Vijver met waterlelies
(Harmonie in groen)

1899, Oil on canvas/Huile sur toile,
89×93 cm, Musée d'Orsay, Paris

their work has. It's never dull, and never appears to be done too hastily. Their work is as simple as breathing, and they do a figure with a few confident strokes with the same ease as if it was as simple as buttoning your waistcoat."

en commentant aussi la qualité unique du travail d'Hiroshige : « J'envie les Japonais à cause de l'extraordinaire clarté que l'on trouve partout dans leurs œuvres. [...] Leur travail est aussi simple que de respirer et ils font une figure en quelques traits sûrs avec la même aisance, comme si c'était aussi simple que de boutonner son gilet. »

van Gogh 1888 seine Bewunderung für die japanische Kunst zum Ausdruck und beschreibt damit auch die einzigartige Qualität von Hiroshiges Werk: „Ich beneide die Japaner wegen ihrer unglaublichen Klarheit. Es ist nie langweilig und man hat nie den Eindruck, dass sie in Eile arbeiten. Es ist so einfach wie atmen. Sie malen mit ein paar Strichen eine Figur mit solch unfehlbarer Leichtigkeit, als wäre es so einfach wie das Zuknöpfen einer Jacke."

Vincent van Gogh

Flowering Plum Tree (after Hiroshige)

L'Arbre Prunier en fleur (d'après Hiroshige)

Blühender Pflaumenbaum (nach Hiroshige)

Ciruelo en flor (copia de Hiroshige)

Il susino in fiore (copia di Hiroshige)

Bloeiende pruimenboom (naar Hiroshige)

1887, Oil on canvas/Huile sur toile, 55×46 cm,
Van Gogh Museum, Amsterdam

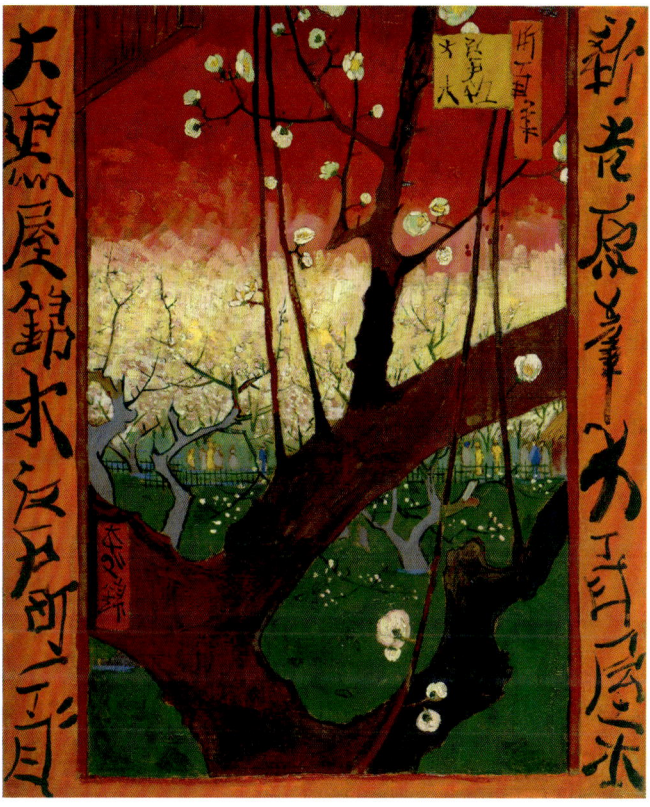

el arte japonés y describe así también la particular calidad del trabajo de Hiroshige: "Envidio a los japoneses su increíble claridad. En ningún momento son aburridos y nunca tiene uno la impresión de que trabajen con prisa. Es tan sencillo como respirar: con un par de trazos firmes dibujan una figura con una ligereza tal que parece tan sencillo como atarse los botones de un chaleco."

sua ammirazione per l'arte giapponese e descrisse anche la straordinaria qualità delle opere di Hiroshige: "Invidio i giapponesi per la loro incredibile chiarezza. Non è mai noiosa e non si ha mai l'impressione che lavorino in fretta. È tanto facile quanto respirare. Con un paio di tratti dipingono una figura con una semplicità talmente infallibile che è facile come abbottonare una giacca."

bewondering voor de Japanse kunst uit en beschrijft daarmee ook de unieke kwaliteit van Hiroshige's werk: "Ik benijd de Japanners de buitengewone duidelijkheid die alle dingen bij hen hebben. Nooit is het vervelend en nooit lijkt het haastig gedaan. Hun werk is even simpel als ademhalen en zij maken een figuur in enkele zekere trekken met hetzelfde gemak alsof het zoiets eenvoudigs betrof als het dichtknopen van je vest."

Plum garden in Kameido, from the series **100 Famous Views of Edo**

Pruneraie à Kameido, de la série **Cent vues d'Edo**

The plum blossom in Kameido was famous in Hiroshige's time for being especially fragrant. A stunning barrier stands in front of this tree, the "plum of the sleeping dragon". We look through its branches into the plum orchard, which receives spatial depth with all of the colour gradients.

La floraison des pruniers à Kameido est réputée à l'époque de Hiroshige en raison de leurs fleurs particulièrement odorantes. Cet arbre – le « prunier du dragon dormant » – forme au premier plan une saissante barrière. À travers ses branches, on aperçoit la pruneraie à laquelle les dégradés de couleur donnent une étonnante profondeur spatiale.

Pflaumengarten in Kameido, aus der Serie **100 berühmte Ansichten von Edo**

Jardín de ciruelos en Kameido, de la serie **100 vistas famosas de Edo**

Die Pflaumenblüte in Kameido ist zu Hiroshiges Zeit wegen eines besonders duftenden Pflaumenbaumes berühmt. Diesen Baum, die „Pflaume des schlafenden Drachen", bildet im Vordergrund eine reizvolle Barriere. Durch seine Äste blicken wir auf den Pflaumengarten, der durch die Farbverläufe räumliche Tiefe erhält.

La floración del ciruelo en Kameido era famosa en tiempos de Hiroshige por un ciruelo particularmente fragante. Este árbol, el "ciruelo del dragón durmiente", forma en primer plano una atractiva barrera. A través de sus ramas observamos el jardín de ciruelos, que gracias a la gradación de color gana una profundidad espacial.

Giardino dei susini a Kameido, della serie **100 vedute famose di Edo**

Pruimentuin in Kameido, uit de serie **100 beroemde gezichten op Edo**

1857, Colour woodcut/Gravure sur bois en couleurs

Ai tempi di Hiroshige la fioritura dei susini di Kameido era famosa grazie ad un susino particolarmente profumato. Questo albero, il "susino del drago dormiente", crea un'affascinante barriera in primo piano. Attraverso i suoi rami possiamo osservare il giardino dei susini, che ottiene profondità spaziali grazie alle sfumature di colore.

De pruimenbloei van Kameido is in Hiroshige's tijd beroemd vanwege de heerlijk ruikende "pruimenboom van de slapende draak". De boom vormt op de voorgrond een bekoorlijke barrière. Door de takken heen valt onze blik op de pruimenboomgaard, die door het verloop van de kleuren ruimtelijke diepte krijgt.

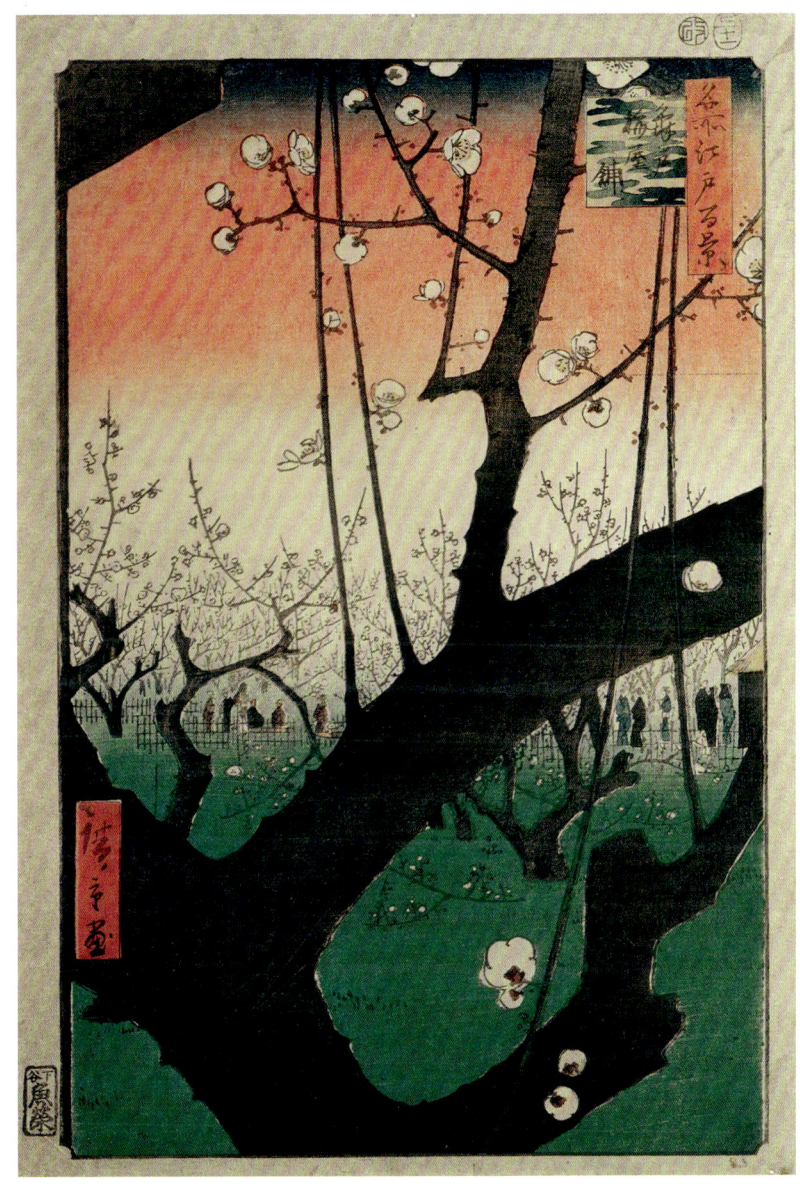

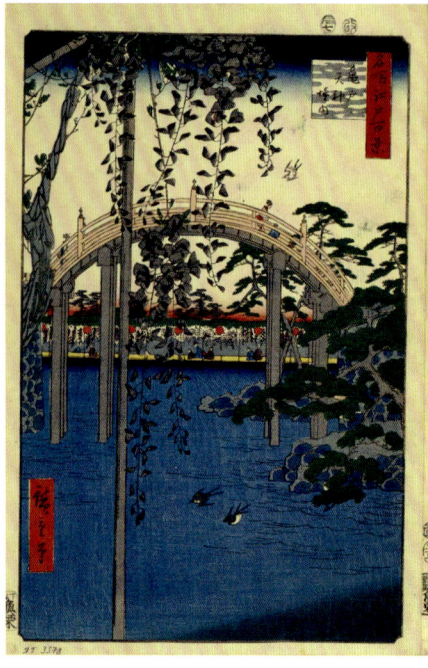

The Tenjin Shrine in Kameido, from the series Famous Views of Edo

Le Sanctuaire de Tenjin à Kameido, de la série Cent vues d'Edo

Der Tenjin-Schrein in Kameido, aus der Serie 100 berühmte Ansichten von Edo

El santuario Tenjin en Kameido, de la serie Vistas famosas de Edo

Santuario di Tenjin a Kameido, della serie 100 vedute famose di Edo

De Tenjin-schrijn in Kameido, uit de serie 100 beroemde gezichten op Edo

1856–1858, Colour woodcut/Gravure sur bois en couleurs, 39×26 cm,
State Hermitage, St. Petersburg

James Abbott McNeill Whistler

Nocturne in Blue and Gold:
Old Battersea Bridge

Nocturne en bleu et or : Le Vieux
Pont de Battersea

Nocturne in Blau und Gold:
ld Battersea Bridge

Nocturno en azul y oro:
Old Battersea Bridge

Notturno in blu e oro:
Old Battersea Bridge

Nocturne in blauw en goud:
Old Battersea Bridge

1872–1875, Oil on canvas/Huile sur toile, 67×49 cm, Tate Britain, London

Whistler was sharply criticised for his Nocturnes. His contemporaries found the bold compositions and gradients too foreign and too abstract. Whistler's pictures of the Thames were especially strongly influenced by Hiroshige's woodcuts.

Les Nocturnes de Whistler lui valent de sévères critiques. Ses contemporains en jugent les compositions et les dégradés trop « exotiques » et trop abstraits. Les visions de la Tamise par Whistler, surtout, sont fortement influencées par les estampes de Hiroshige.

Mit seinen Nachtansichten, den Nocturnes, erntet Whistler herbe Kritik. Zu fremd und von der Wirklichkeit abstrahierend empfinden seine Zeitgenossen die kühnen Kompositionen und Farbverläufe. Vor allem Whistlers Bilder der Themse sind stark von Hiroshiges Holzschnitten beeinflusst.

Las escenas de noche de Whistler, sus Nocturnos, le valieron feroces críticas. Sus coetáneos consideraron estas audaces composiciones con sus gradaciones de colores demasiado extrañas y abstraídas de la realidad. En particular los cuadros de Whistler sobre el Támesis estuvieron influenciados de manera notable por las xilografías de Hiroshige.

Con le sue vedute notturne, i Notturni, Whistler raccolse aspre critiche. I suoi contemporanei trovarono le sue composizioni audaci e sfumature di colore troppo strane e avulse dalla realtà. Soprattutto i quadri del Tamigi di Whistler sono fortemente influenzati dalle xilografie di Hiroshige.

Met zijn nocturnes oogst Whistler veel kritiek. Zijn tijdgenoten vinden de gedurfde composities en kleurstellingen veel te buitenissig en abstract. Het zijn vooral Whistler's schilderijen van de rivier de Theems die sterk door de houtsneden van Hiroshige zijn beïnvloed.

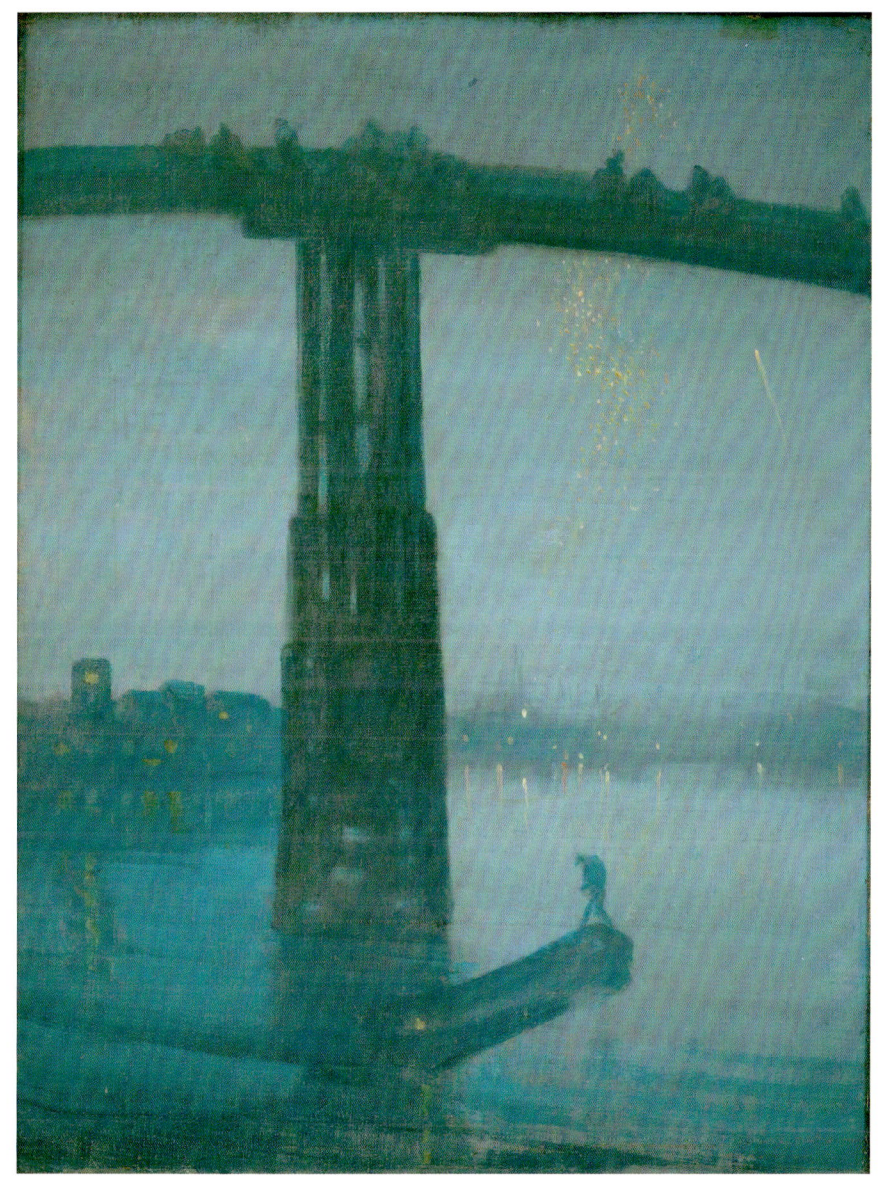

Recommended Literature
Literaturempfehlungen

Bicknell, Julian: *Hiroshige in Tokyo. The floating world of Edo.*
    Rohnert Park, Calif., 1994.
Forrer, Matthi: *Hiroshige. Prints and Drawings.*
    Ausstellungskatalog Royal Academy of Arts, London.
    München, New York 1997.
Schlombs, Adele: *Hiroshige 1797–1858.* Köln 2007.
Monet, Gauguin, van Gogh … Inspiration Japan.
    Ausstellungskatalog Museum Folkwang Essen.
    Göttingen 2014.